TRADE AND DEVELOPMENT

Achieving Industrialization in
East Asia

TRADE AND DEVELOPMENT

A series of books on international economic relations and
economic issues in development

Edited from the National Centre for Development Studies,
Australian National University, by Helen Hughes

Advisory editors

Juergen Donges, *Kiel Institute of World Economics*
Peter Lloyd, *Department of Economics, University of Melbourne*
Gustav Ranis, *Department of Economics, Yale University*
David Wall, *Department of Economics, University of Sussex*

ACHIEVING
INDUSTRIALIZATION
IN EAST ASIA

EDITED BY
HELEN HUGHES

National Centre for Development Studies
Australian National University

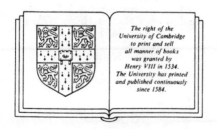

The right of the
University of Cambridge
to print and sell
all manner of books
was granted by
Henry VIII in 1534.
The University has printed
and published continuously
since 1584.

CAMBRIDGE UNIVERSITY PRESS
CAMBRIDGE
NEW YORK PORT CHESTER MELBOURNE SYDNEY

Published by the Press Syndicate of the University of Cambridge
The Pitt Building, Trumpington Street, Cambridge CB2 1RP
40 West 20th Street, New York, NY 10011, USA
10 Stamford Road, Oakleigh, Melbourne 3166, Australia

First published 1988
Reprinted 1989

Printed in Great Britain by
Antony Rowe Ltd, Chippenham, Wiltshire

British Library cataloguing in publication data

Achieving industrialisation in East Asia. –
(Trade and development).
1. East Asia. Industrialisation development
I. Hughes, Helen
338.0951

Library of Congress cataloguing in publication data

Achieving industrialisation in East Asia/edited by Helen Hughes.
p.   cm. – (Trade and development)
ISBN 0–521–35129–4
1. Industry and state – East Asia   2. East Asia – Industries.
3. East Asia – Economic policy.   I. Hughes, Helen, 1928–
II. Series.
HD3616.E184A24   1988
338.95–dc 19   88–15607

National Library of Australia cataloguing in publication data

Achieving industrialization in East Asia.
Bibliography.
Includes index
ISBN 0 521 35129 4.
1. East Asia – Economic policy. 2. East Asia –
Industries. I. Hughes, Helen, 1928–
338.95

ISBN 0 521 35129 4

CONTENTS

	page
List of figures	*vii*
List of tables	*viii*
Contributors to this volume	*xi*
Preface	*xv*
Abbreviations	*xvii*
Symbols	*xviii*

1. Economic Development in East Asia: Doing What Comes Naturally?
   JAMES RIEDEL 1
2. Industrialization and Growth: Alternative Views of East Asia
   HOLLIS CHENERY 39
3. The Role of Trade Policies in the Industrialization of Rapidly Growing Asian Developing Countries
   SEIJI NAYA 64
4. The Role of Foreign Capital in East Asian Industrialization, Growth and Development
   THOMAS G. PARRY 95
5. The Role of Government in Overcoming Market Failure: Taiwan, Republic of Korea and Japan
   ROBERT WADE 129
6. Growth, Industrialization and Economic Structure: Latin America and East Asia Compared
   ARNOLD C. HARBERGER 164
7. Ideology and Industrialization in India and East Asia
   DEEPAK LAL 195
8. Japan: Model for East Asian Industrialization?
   RYOKICHI HIRONO 241

                                                         page
9. The Politics of Industrialization in the Republic of
    Korea and Taiwan
    STEPHAN HAGGARD   260
10. Economic Growth in the ASEAN Region: the
    Political Underpinnings
    J. A. C. MACKIE   283
11. Culture and Industrialization
    WILLIAM J. O'MALLEY   327

Bibliography   344
Index   370

FIGURES

page

6.1 Trajectory of non-tradable goods prices:
simulation of response to debt crisis   193

6.2 Trajectory of real output:
simulation of responses to debt crisis   193

TABLES

		page
1.1	Average annual GDP and GNP per capita growth: 1950–83	5
1.2	The distribution of GDP and employment by sector	8
1.3	Export volume growth rates: 1960–82	9
1.4	The commodity structure of exports	10
1.5	Rates of domestic and foreign savings	12
1.6	Indicators of financial development	14
1.7	Indicators of labour market conditions	17
1.8	Income distribution and growth of the East Asian countries relative to a sample of thirty-four developing countries	20
1.9	Changes in longevity and secondary school enrolment	22
1.10	Classification of export incentives	31
1.11	Rates of nominal and effective protection	32
2.1	Indices of industrialization and growth, 1960–80	42
2.2	Sources of growth: selected economies	46
2.3	Sources of growth for sample economies	52
2.4	Sources of growth: cross-country model	54
2.5	Effects of alternative trade patterns on sources of growth	55
2.6	Simulated effects of trade and borrowing policies	60
3.1	Estimated rate of real economic growth of selected Asian countries	65
3.2	Exports and imports of goods and services of Asian developing countries, United States and Japan as per cent of GNP, 1970–71 and 1982–83	66

3.3	Annual growth rate of total and manufactured exports of Asian developing countries in the 1970s and early 1980s	69
3.4	Exports of NICs by principal commodity groups, 1970 and 1981	70
3.5	Exports of NICs by principal commodity group and destination, 1970 and 1981	74
3.6	Direction of exports of Asian NICs and ASEAN countries, 1970, 1979, 1981 and 1983	75
3.7	Exports of ASEAN countries by principal commodity groups, 1970 and 1981	77
3.8	Exports of ASEAN countries by principal commodity group and destination, 1970 and 1981	80
3.9	Intra-ASEAN trade as a percentage of total trade, 1974–83	82
3.10	Structure of production and labour, 1970 and 1983	85
4.1	Net private direct foreign investment flows	96
4.2	Indicators of capital inflow into East Asia, 1969–83	99
4.3	Capital inflows share of gross domestic investment, 1970–80	107
4.4	Percentage distribution by home countries in the reported stock of foreign direct investment in selected Asian countries, various countries, various years in the 1970s	120
4.5	External bank claims, debt and debt indicators	125
6.1	Shares of GDP in industry and manufacturing	167
6.2	Economic growth, GDP and industrial sector	168
6.3	The role of exports	170
6.4	Investment and inflation	172
6.5	Policy indicators	174
6.6	Distributions of policy variables	178
6.7	Range of real exchange rate variation	182
6.8	Simulation of response to debt crisis: 'Republic of Korea'	191
6.9	Simulation of response to debt crisis: 'Chile'	192
7.1	Some summary statistics: India, Republic of Korea and Taiwan	196
7.2	Index of manufacturing production, 1938	201
7.3a	Parameters of Gompertz curve fitted to trends in various industrial sector variables	202

7.3b	Capital–labour ratios in Indian manufacturing at 1970–71 prices	202
7.4	Total factor productivity growth estimates, 1959–69 to 1969–80	203
7.5	Average social rates of return in Indian manufacturing, Annual Survey of India, 1958–68	204
7.6	Comparative labour efficiency in Japan, India and Britain for low count cotton manufacture in 1932	206
7.7	Industrial disputes in India, 1921–80	207
7.8	Characteristics of sample firms in large and small-scale industries in India	209
7.9	Pre-war and post-war trends in public investment in India	212
7.10	Estimates of poverty in rural and urban India, Gini coefficients of distribution of per capita expenditure, and linear time trends in distributional variables	216
7.11	Trends in real manufacturing wages per worker, India, 1939–76	218
7.12	Some price ratios, India, 1951–79	220
7.13	Foreign investment in the manufacturing sector, 1969–73	221
7.14a	Share of public sector output in basic industries, India, 1983–84	223
7.14b	Relative profitability of public sector, India, 1974–75	223
7.15	Structure and growth of exports for India and all developing countries, 1960–78	226
7.16	Estimates of various indices for ten Industrial Credit and Investment Corporations	227
7.17	Employment in the public sector in India	235
7.18	Percentage changes in real value of emoluments to Indian central government employees since 1 January 1973	236
8.1	Shares of East Asian country manufactured exports in major country markets, 1970 and 1980	254
8.2	International trade, investment and balance of payments for Japan and East Asian countries, 1960–82	256
10.1	Gross domestic product growth in ASEAN and NICs	286
10.2	Governmental autonomy in ASEAN	295

CONTRIBUTORS TO THIS VOLUME

HELEN HUGHES is Professor of Economics and Executive Director of the National Centre for Development Studies at the Australian National University. She is a member of the United Nations Development Planning Committee. Formerly she was Director of the Economic Analysis and Projections Department at the World Bank. She publishes on international trade and economic development and recently gave the Australian Broadcasting Commission Boyer lectures on *Australia in a Developing World*.

JAMES RIEDEL is Professor of International Economics in the School of Advanced International Studies at the Johns Hopkins University in Baltimore and also acts as consultant to the World Bank. He writes on international trade, finance and economic development. He has recently published *Myths and Reality of External Constraints on Development*.

HOLLIS CHENERY is now the Thomas B. Cabot Professor of Economics at Harvard University, after a distinguished career at the United States Agency for International Development and the World Bank. He has published extensively on development with a special interest in industrialization and structural change. He has recently co-authored *Industrialization and Growth: a Comparative Study* with M. Syrquin and S. Robinson.

SEIJI NAYA's academic career has been mainly concerned with trade and industrial development in East Asia. He was the Chief Economist of the Asian Development Bank in the late 1970s and has published widely on East Asia. He is now the Director of the Resource Systems Institute at the East–West Center.

THOMAS G. PARRY is Associate Professor of Economics in the School of Economics at the University of New South Wales. His primary research interests are in industry economics and policy and in international economics as related to development issues, international investment and technology transfer. *The Multinational Enterprise: International Investment and Host-Country Impacts* is his most recent book.

ROBERT WADE is a Fellow of the Institute of Development Studies at the University of Sussex but has recently spent an extended period with the World Bank. He has a background in economics and anthropology and has done research on agricultural development and state institutions in India, Italy and the Republic of Korea.

ARNOLD C. HARBERGER is Professor of Economics at the Department of Economics at the University of Chicago. He has worked in many areas of development during his distinguished career with an important component of his research focused on the economic development of Latin American countries.

DEEPAK LAL is Professor of Economics at University College, London. Until recently he was Research Adviser with the World Bank. His interest in economic development is reflected in his publications which cover many development issues and countries. In 1986 he published *The Hindu Equilibrium*.

RYOKICHI HIRONO is Professor of Economics at the Seikei University. He has presently taken leave to take up the position of Assistant Administrator of the United Nations Development Programme. He has published on development with a principal interest in the economy of Japan and the countries of East Asia.

STEPHAN HAGGARD is Professor of Government at Harvard University. He has written widely on political issues of concern in economic growth with particular attention to the Republic of Korea.

J. A. C. MACKIE is Professor of Political and Social Change at the Australian National University. His major interests are in the politics of developing countries. He specializes in Indonesia and is author of *Konfrontasi: the Indonesian Dispute*.

WILLIAM J. O'MALLEY is an economic, political and social historian of modern Indonesia. He has had extensive periods of fieldwork in Southeast Asia and was until recently a Research Fellow in the Department of Political and Social Change at the Australian National University. He has recently edited *Essays in Indonesian History*.

PREFACE

This book was conceived in response to widespread interest in the economic success of the East Asian market-oriented economies. Whether growth and development are judged in purely economic terms or by a combination of economic and welfare criteria, this group of East Asian countries has established a clear lead over other developing countries. Despite the world-wide recession of the early 1980s, two East Asian economies – Hong Kong and Singapore – are catching up with the high income industrial countries and several other East Asian market economies are poised to do so. The economic performance of the Republic of Korea and Thailand has been particularly striking for they were both among the very low income countries of the world in the 1950s. Even the Philippines, a poor performer among this group of countries, has a better than average record among developing countries.

The East Asian countries range in population size from city states to middle-sized countries and have widely divergent resource endowments and economic histories, but they have faced the same international environment as other countries. Why is their economic performance so successful?

The principal objective of this book is to identify the policies that have been critical to economic success. The conclusion is that 'unshackling exports' (that most of the East Asian countries had themselves at first shackled) has been the key to success. However, it is also clear that successful performance needs several policy strands. Political stability and the rule of law are essential. Economic policies apparently distorted prices less than was the case in most other developing countries; macroeconomic management was relatively successful, all economic sectors, particularly agriculture, were developed, and public investment in social and physical infrastructural facilities was productive. Where these economic conditions did not prevail, as in the Philippines, the economy faltered. Governments thus provided the environment for growth; but private enterprise, despite risk and uncertainty, made the investments necessary and through exposure to international competition became efficient and profitable. There seems little doubt that if other developing countries had followed similar economic policies they would also have grown more rapidly and would thus have been able to alleviate the poverty of their low income groups as well as avoiding high national indebtedness.

Given the importance of economic policies, a second purpose of the book is to analyse the strands of the varied political backgrounds and cultural heritages which have enabled such a disparate group of countries to choose policies that led to rapid growth. It was hoped that some insights into the reasons why other countries did not adopt similar policies would emerge. Here the evidence was much less clear than in the economic analysis. Hypotheses that draw on political and social factors are often put forward to explain the successful development of the East Asian market economies, but these were found wanting. East Asian economic prototypes disintegrated under close examination. Regional influences, however, were as important as they have been in Latin America, Africa and the Middle East. Neighbourhoods appear to matter.

Drafts of the papers in this volume were presented at a workshop held in Canberra in September 1985. The workshop was part of a major research focus in industrialization in East Asia being undertaken by the Research School of Pacific Studies at the Australian National University and work on the trade aspects of industrialization is continuing at the National Centre for Development Studies.

Discussants at the workshop helped to shape the papers. We wish to acknowledge the contribution of Kym Anderson, Heinz Arndt, Romy Bautista, Max Corden, Harold Crouch, Peter Drysdale, Fabio Erber, Clive Hamilton, Hal Hill, Wontack Hong, Anne Krueger, David Lim, Peter McCawley, David Morawetz, Oscar Munoz, Guillermo Perry, Claudia Schatan, Richard Snape, Yun Wing Sung, Rod Tyers, Peter Warr and Lim Chong Yah. We particularly wish to thank the Ford Foundation for funding the participants from Latin America.

Helen Hughes

ABBREVIATIONS

ADB	Asian Development Bank
ASEAN	Association of Southeast Asian Nations
cif	cost, insurance, freight
East Asia	includes Hong Kong, Republic of Korea, Indonesia, Malaysia, Philippines, Singapore, Taiwan and Thailand
ECE	Economic Commission for Europe
EC	European Community
ESCAP	Economic and Social Commission for Asia and the Pacific
fob	free on board
GDP	Gross domestic product
GNP	Gross national product
IMF	International Monetary Fund
ILO	International Labour Organisation
NICs	Newly industrialized countries
OECD	Organisation for Economic Cooperation and Development
OPEC	Organisation of Petroleum Exporting Countries
SITC	Standard International Trade Classification
UNCTAD	United Nations Conference on Trade and Development
UNCTC	United Nations Centre on Transnational Corporations
World Bank	International Bank for Reconstruction and Development

SYMBOLS

n.a.	not applicable
..	not available
–	zero or insignificant
US$	United States dollar; all data in dollars are quoted in US$

JAMES RIEDEL*

1

ECONOMIC DEVELOPMENT IN
EAST ASIA:
DOING WHAT COMES NATURALLY?

> Little else is requisite to carry a state to the highest degree of opu-
> lence from the lowest barbarism, but peace, easy taxes, and toler-
> able administration of justice; all the rest being brought about by the
> natural course of things. (Adam Smith, *An Inquiry into the Nature
> and Causes of the Wealth of Nations*, 1776)

The market-oriented East Asian developing economies, especially
the most successful among them – the Republic of Korea, Taiwan,
Hong Kong and Singapore – have had a profound influence on development economics. Their superlative economic performance,
combined with the relatively poor record of other countries which
adhered more closely to the inward-looking policies universally
prescribed in the 1950s and 1960s, nurtured a 'new orthodoxy' in
development economics.[1] The new orthodoxy was in essence main-
stream, neo-classical economics, dismissed by the old orthodoxy as
inapplicable to developing countries.[2] The experience of this

---

* The paper was written while the author was a Visiting Fellow at the National
Centre for Development Studies. I am indebted to Heinz Arndt, Romeo Bautista,
Max Corden, Isaiah Frank and Helen Hughes for helpful comments and dis-
cussion. Thanks are also due to the late Juliet Jeffcott, Maree Tait and Megan
Werner for excellent research assistance. The usual caveat applies.

[1] The 'new orthodoxy' emerged in the late 1960s and early 1970s from a host of case
studies of industrialization in developing countries done under the auspices of the
Organisation for Economic Cooperation and Development (OECD), National
Bureau of Economic Research (NBER), Kiel Institut für Weltwirtschaft and the
World Bank, and summarized in Little, Scitovsky and Scott (1970), Bhagwati
(1978), Krueger (1978), Donges and Riedel (1977), and Balassa and Associates
(1971).
[2] As Hirschman (1981:3) explains, the traditional view of development economics is
that 'underdeveloped countries as a group are set apart, through a number of

rapidly growing 'Gang of Four' was interpreted initially as proof positive that competitive markets, operating broadly on neo-classical principles, could, even in developing countries, generate high levels of economic efficiency and rapid, self-sustained growth.

That interpretation has, however, come under increasing attack on two fronts. One challenge questions the basic proposition that the East Asian countries have in fact been more successful than other countries when account is taken of dimensions of development other than GNP growth. Sen (1983:753), for example, lays the charge obliquely noting simply that:

South Korea, with its magnificent and much-eulogised growth record, has not yet overtaken [the People's Republic of] China or Sri Lanka in the field of longevity, despite being now more than five times richer in terms of per capita GNP.

The other line of attack on the traditional interpretation of the East Asian experience accepts that it is one of unparalleled success, but attributes the phenomenon to factors other than the efficient working of the market. Some explain the East Asian 'miracle' in terms of unique advantages or pre-conditions for growth that were not shared by other developing countries. To others, the hand of government is more visible than that of the market as the force behind the region's unique success. Political scientists also, naturally, put much stock in the role of government, but emphasize the importance of the type of government (authoritarian versus democratic) rather than the kind of policies which governments pursued. And finally, for those who are baffled by the plethora of conflicting explanations and contradictory evidence, there is refuge in the cultural factor.

A great deal has been written about the East Asian market-oriented developing countries both individually and as a group, yet there is no clear consensus on how to characterize their experience, much less how to explain it and thence draw lessons for other countries. Perhaps consensus has eluded economists and other social scientists because they usually insist on finding the 'key' to things like growth and development, when in fact history suggests that human progress works more like a giant combination lock for

specific economic characteristics common to them, from the advanced industrial countries and that traditional economic analysis, which has concentrated on industrial countries, must therefore be recast in significant respects when dealing with underdeveloped countries'.

which there is no key.[3] A number of tumblers must fall into place to unlock economic growth, but not always the same number nor always in the same combination. As Jones (1981:238) sums up his brilliant, long-run history of European economic growth:

The parts fit together well enough to work, but perhaps not even in a unique combination: it is difficult to gauge retrospectively what the tolerances of the system may have been.

If there is no one key, but instead many factors (important among them unique environmental, cultural and political advantages) which contribute to the East Asian countries' success, can there be any clear, definitive economic policy lessons for other countries? Many have answered no, arguing that the East Asian experience cannot be replicated elsewhere. But surely replication is not a necessary condition for one country to learn from the experience of another, for if it were there would be little point to history or social science. So, what are the lessons that derive from the East Asian experience?

My terms of reference here are to provide an overview, so before overstepping them by drawing conclusions about lessons and the burning issues in development economics, I must confine myself to the task I have been assigned. The next section presents the broad facts about the character of East Asian development, and the following one reviews the various explanations of the East Asian success. The final section offers some tentative conclusions about what it all means.

Since the aim is to give an overview of the experience of eight countries extending over a period of more than thirty years, it will not be possible to discuss all the caveats of the data or to inject into it many interesting details or illuminating anecdotes about any one country. To avoid the tedium of elevator economics, I will let the tables speak for themselves. In reviewing the explanations of East Asian success, I have found it impossible to do justice to the enormous literature on each country and the region as a whole. It is also difficult to give equal attention to the experience of all eight countries. More has been written and is known about some countries than about others; and the experience of some countries is more pertinent to the issues addressed here.

[3] Jones (1981) uses this metaphor to describe European economic growth over the very long run.

I see little merit in trying to justify the sample of countries to be examined. It includes all of the market-oriented countries of East and Southeast Asia that are commonly designated 'developing'. Four – Hong Kong, Taiwan, the Republic of Korea and Singapore – are commonly referred to as newly industrialized countries (NICs) and the other four – Thailand, Malaysia, Indonesia and the Philippines – have recently earned the epithet 'near-NICs'. That, and the fact that they are all Asian, may be reason enough to ignore convention and examine the two groups as one. Throughout what follows, as a matter of convenience, I refer to the eight as the 'East Asian countries', though I am aware that some are in Southeast Asia and that some not insignificant East Asian countries are excluded.

MEASURES OF SUCCESS

Everyone is aware that there are dimensions to development in addition to growth and industrialization. Employment, income distribution and various aspects of social change also deserve attention. In this brief overview of the East Asian record a range of indicators is examined. It is recognized that, in the end, no universally acceptable, value-free indicator of overall performance is attainable. As Little (1982:4) explains, 'An index of development certainly has welfare implications because "development" is a word that undoubtedly carries value overtones'. I suspect, none the less, that some overall assessment of how the East Asian countries stack up individually and as a group can be reached without recourse to values that are too extreme or unconventional.

Growth

The superlative growth record of the East Asian NICs is well known. The numbers for both the NICs and near-NICs are presented in Table 1.1, and require little comment. All, with the exception of the Philippines (a phrase I regret will have to be used repeatedly), have considerably out-performed the average of developing or industrial countries since 1965. In terms of 1983 GNP per capita all eight countries fall into the category defined by the World Bank as 'middle income', with two at the top, three in the middle and three at the bottom of the middle income range.

Table 1.1 *Average annual GDP and GNP per capita growth: 1950–83* (percentage)

	GDP growth		Per capita GNP growth		Per capita GNP
	1950–65	1965–83	1950–65	1965–83	(US$ 1983)
Singapore	5.5[a]	10.3	5.5[a]	7.4	6620
Hong Kong	10.1	8.7	5.5	6.2	6000
Taiwan	5.7[b]	8.9	4.9[b]	6.7	2677
Korea, Republic of	5.7	8.6	3.3	6.7	2010
Malaysia	4.7	7.1	1.7	4.5	1860
Thailand	6.3	7.4	3.3	4.3	820
Philippines	6.1	5.4	2.9	2.9	760
Indonesia	3.2	7.5	1.1	5.0	560
Low-income developing countries	4.0	5.3	2.0	2.7	260
Middle-income developing countries	5.0	5.8	2.4	3.4	1310
Industrial countries	4.6	3.4	3.4	2.5	11060

[a] 1960–65.
[b] 1952–65.
Sources: World Development Report, 1984, 1985 (World Bank, various years); World Bank (1984); Council for Economic Planning and Development (1984).

The three groups of countries appear to be separated from each other by about two decades of growth, as Hong Kong and Singapore's per capita income in 1965 (expressed in 1983 US dollars) is just about equal to the 1983 average for Taiwan, Republic of Korea and Malaysia, while the 1965 average for the latter group is about equal to the 1983 average for Thailand, the Philippines and Indonesia. This configuration of relative income levels is the consequence of differences both in the initial level of income after the Second World War and the starting date of rapid growth. Hong Kong and Taiwan began to grow rapidly in the 1950s, the Republic of Korea and Singapore (the latter from a high base) in the mid-1960s and Thailand, Malaysia and Indonesia only in the 1970s. The Philippines has never achieved spectacular growth, but from the mid-1950s until its recent economic and political misfortunes, it advanced at a respectable rate.

Hong Kong and Singapore, with growth rates three times higher than the average of industrial countries and a per capita income base already half as great, are steadily narrowing the absolute income gap between themselves and the richest of the industrial countries, and are as far as I know the only contemporary developing countries to have done so.[4] Even fast-growing Taiwan and Republic of Korea have some time to wait before their per capita income base is sufficiently high for their rapid growth to narrow the absolute gap. If they continue as they have done, however, it will not be more than a dozen years until they accomplish this, and then they will likely be the third and fourth in the record book behind Hong Kong and Singapore.

Industrialization

Industrialization is essential for economic growth in most countries. Only a few countries, with small populations and great oil or other natural wealth, like Kuwait or Libya, can expect to achieve high levels of per capita income without industrializing. The fact is that no agriculture-based economy has ever achieved per capita income above US$500 for any lengthy period (Kahn 1979:118). Industrialization is not the end of the road, but it is one path that most countries must travel to reach high per capita income.

In terms of the share of income derived from industry, in particular manufacturing, the four East Asian NICs appear to have nearly completed the journey, and the Southeast Asian near-NICs, apart from Indonesia, seem not to be far behind (see Table 1.2). The process of industrialization, however, is more than the shifting of the centre of gravity away from agriculture; it also involves shifts over time in the structure of industry, following comparative advantage from low-technology, labour-intensive activities towards progressively more capital- and technology-intensive branches. However, no developing country, apart from Hong Kong, followed comparative advantage at the outset of industrialization. Import substitution in consumer durables and capital goods industries was the main objective of the 1950s and 1960s. Thus, the common pattern, followed by Taiwan, Republic of Korea, Malaysia, Thailand and the Philippines, was an initial expansion of capital-intensive

---

[4] The absolute per capita income gap declines only when the ratio of per capita income levels is equal to or greater than the reciprocal of the ratio of relative growth rates.

industry, followed by a reorientation towards more labour-intensive sectors and, subsequently, once real wages begin to rise (as in the East Asian NICs), a natural progression into capital- and skill-intensive manufacturing branches. It is in this final phase that the East Asian NICs find themselves, but with some distance still to go.

It is useful for future reference to draw attention also to the changing sectoral distribution of employment in the East Asian countries. Taiwan and the Republic of Korea, which reoriented industrial incentives to favour labour-intensive production in the late 1950s and early 1960s, respectively, have reduced the share of agricultural employment by half or more. The near-NICs, which followed their lead in the 1970s, have also made progress, but need a decade or so of labour-intensive industrial growth to catch up.

Export expansion and diversification

Expansion of manufactured exports has proved to be an essential part of successful industrialization in developing countries, and nowhere more so than in East Asia. There are two main reasons. First, domestic markets, even in the largest of developing countries, are generally not large enough to support an efficient scale of industrial production. Second, to produce industrial products efficiently at world prices requires access to least cost supplies of capital and intermediate goods, which in turn implies a demand for foreign exchange which is generally beyond what can be provided from traditional, primary exports.[5]

As a consequence, in the most successful East Asian countries industrial expansion has been accompanied by equally rapid growth of relatively labour-intensive manufactured exports (see Table 1.3). In the near NICs, growth of manufactured exports since 1970 has also been high, but from relatively low bases. The importance of primary goods exports, though diminishing, is still great in the Southeast Asian countries (see Table 1.4).

---

[5] Both of the above points are as valid for most industrial countries as they are for developing countries. After account is taken of size (measured for example by population), there is no significant difference in the degree of openness of developed and developing countries. Nor is there any significant difference in the composition of their imports. On average, capital and intermediate goods account for about 80 per cent of total imports in industrial and developing countries alike (Riedel 1984a).

Table 1.2 *The distribution of GDP and employment by sector* (percentage)

	Share in GDP								Share in employment					
	Agriculture		Other industry		Manufac- turing		Services		Agriculture		Industry		Services	
	1960	1983	1960	1983	1960	1983	1960	1983	1960	1981	1960	1981	1960	1981
Singapore	4	1	6	13	12	24	79	62	8	2	23	39	69	58
Hong Kong	4	1	13	8	26	22	57	69	8	3	52	57	40	40
Taiwan	33	9	8	10	17	34	42	47	51	19	21	41	29	41
Korea, Republic of	37	14	6	12	14	27	43	47	66	34	9	29	25	37
Malaysia	36	21	9	16	9	19	46	44	63	50	12	16	25	43
Thailand	40	23	6	8	13	19	41	50	84	76	4	9	12	15
Philippines	26	22	8	11	20	25	46	42	61	46	15	17	24	37
Indonesia	54	26	6	26	8	13	32	35	75	58	8	12	17	30
Low-income developing countries	50	37	6	20	11	14	33	29	77	73	9	13	14	15
Middle-income developing countries	22	15	9	15	22	21	21	49	59	44	17	22	24	35
Industrial countries	6	3	10	11	30	24	54	62	17	6	38	38	45	56

Sources: World Development Report, 1979, 1985 (World Bank, various years); Council for Economic Planning and Development (1984).

8

Table 1.3 *Export volume growth rates: 1960–82* (percentage)

	Total exports	Manufactured exports
Singapore	7.3	12.1
Hong Kong	9.8	11.7
Taiwan	17.5	24.4
Korea, Republic of	26.4	38.3
Malaysia	4.4	11.2
Thailand	7.0	21.6
Philippines	3.9	17.1
Indonesia	8.6	28.5

Sources: World Bank (1984); *World Development Report*, 1985 (World Bank, various years); UNCTAD, *Handbook . . .*, 1984 (UNCTAD, various years).

Domestic saving

Growth and industrialization require investment, though that alone is not enough. Some countries, like India, manage high rates of investment, but with relatively little to show for it. There appear to be no instances of countries achieving rapid growth and industrialization without relatively high rates of investment. Even that which growth accountants attribute separately to 'technical change' can be meaningfully regarded as due to investment (Scott 1976, 1981). The allocation of investment largely determines the efficiency of investment, and hence is just as important as the level. At this point, however, our concern is with the level of investment, and that generally boils down to the availability of savings. Ever since the Keynesian revolution, analysis of the determinants of the level of investment has been largely divorced from efficiency and the return to savings and investment. That is another tradition which the East Asian experience calls into question.

Savings and investment, like supply and demand, are necessarily equal, *ex post*. Unlike supply and demand, only one side of the investment-savings identity is generally treated as endogenously determined. Savings are usually assumed to be exogenously set by the (pre-determined) level of disposable income, government fiscal policy and externally-determined levels of foreign savings inflows. Thus, in the 1950s, the prevailing view was that developing countries, with low income levels and poor tax bases, were in-

Table 1.4 *The commodity structure of exports* (percentage shares)

	Fuels, minerals and metals			Other primary commodities			Textiles and clothing			Machinery and transport			Other manufactures		
	1955	1965	1982	1955	1965	1982	1955	1965	1982	1955	1965	1982	1955	1965	1982
Singapore	..	21	30	..	44	13	..	6	4	..	10	26	..	18	28
Hong Kong	4	2	2	23	11	6	50	43	34	—	6	19	23	37	39
Taiwan	2	5	—	87	56	6	6	15	30	—	4	31	4	20	33
Korea, Republic of	31	15	1	50	25	7	15	27	21	1	3	28	2	29	43
Malaysia	23	35	39	72	59	42	—	—	3	—	2	15	1	4	5
Thailand	15	11	7	83	84	64	—	1	10	—	—	6	1	4	13
Philippines	10	11	12	80	84	38	8	1	7	—	—	3	2	5	39
Indonesia	36	43	85	63	53	11	1	—	1	—	3	1	—	1	2
Low-income developing countries	13	11	20	70	85	80	12	16	18	—	1	5	5	7	28
Middle-income developing countries	25	36	37	61	48	21	4	4	8	2	3	11	8	10	23
Industrial countries	11	9	12	23	21	14	7	7	4	30	31	37	29	32	32

Sources: World Development Report, 1980, 1985 (World Bank, various years); United Nations (1956, 1958, 1962); Council for Economic Planning and Development (1984).

capable of raising the rate of investment to a satisfactory level because they were caught in a vicious circle of poverty: unable to save because they were poor, and poor because they were unable to save (Leibenstein 1954; Nelson 1956). Foreign savings, mainly aid, were given the starring role: aid could provide the resources for investment that developing countries were unable to set aside on their own and, by stimulating growth, could hold the key to breaking the vicious circle (Rosenstein-Rodan 1961). The importance of foreign savings was further underscored in the 1960s when it was argued that the inability to import irreplaceable capital goods (because external demand limited export expansion) could render domestic savings redundant (Chenery and Bruno 1962; McKinnon 1964). Foreign savings thus held the key to either one or both of two potential limits to investment: savings and foreign exchange.

The relative importance of foreign and domestic savings in financing investment in the East Asian countries is shown in Table 1.5. No common pattern emerges. In the 1950s, foreign savings, mainly United States aid, financed directly or indirectly a high proportion of investment in Taiwan and the Republic of Korea alone. Both countries were weaned from United States aid in the 1960s, but the Republic of Korea continued to rely on foreign savings, albeit in much smaller proportions than in the 1950s, by shifting to official multilateral and private commercial sources of funds. Taiwan, on the other hand, eliminated its reliance on foreign savings altogether, and indeed became a net international investor at the astounding rate of 12 per cent of GNP by 1984. All eight countries achieved domestic savings rates of 20 per cent or higher in the 1970s, but rates of foreign savings inflow vary. Singapore, for example, combines an exceptionally high domestic savings rate with an equally exceptionally high rate of foreign savings inflow (almost 12 per cent of GDP in the 1970s), relying mainly on direct foreign investment.[6] Thailand, the Philippines and to a much lesser extent Malaysia, like the Republic of Korea, took advantage of improved access to private international financial markets in the 1970s. But with rising real interest rates and poor market conditions in the 1980s, all except the Philippines withdrew to a large extent from international financial markets and thereby avoided

[6] The figures for Singapore are especially suspect because of the large amount of unrecorded trade with Indonesia.

Table 1.5 *Rates of domestic and foreign savings (percentage)*

	Gross national savings rate						Rate of net foreign savings inflow					
	1950–60	1960–70	1970–81	1982	1983	1984	1950–60	1960–70	1970–81	1982	1983	1984
Singapore	..	14.9	29.1	40.0	41.9	..	12.2	8.4	11.6	5.1	3.2	..
Hong Kong	9.2	20.6	28.3	28.2	25.1	29.0	−0.1	—	−1.6	3.5	1.9	−4.7
Taiwan	9.8	19.8	32.3	30.4	31.6	33.8	6.5	2.1	−1.7	−5.8	−8.8	−12.5
Korea, Republic of	3.3	13.7	22.6	24.1	26.4	..	8.2	9.5	6.8	2.3	0.8	..
Malaysia	23.2	20.6	25.6	27.0	29.2	30.9	−11.0	−2.4	0.5	8.3	4.8	0.2
Thailand	15.3	19.9	20.6	20.9	17.9	20.9	0.2	2.6	5.5	0.1	5.1	2.2
Philippines	14.3	18.2	23.8	21.6	20.6	17.4	1.0	1.9	4.9	6.8	6.6	0.5
Indonesia	..	4.9	20.1	18.7	19.9	..	..	6.2	0.1	3.9	4.2	..
Low-income developing countries	..	13.9	14.9	—	..	..	..	2.3	3.7	..	..	..
Middle-income developing countries	..	17.3	20.1	—	21.0	..	−0.5	0.9	2.0	..	1.0	..
Industrial countries	20.9	21.6	22.2	—	20.0	..	..	−0.5	−0.4	..	—	..

Note: A negative sign indicates a net outflow of domestic savings.
Sources: World Bank (1984); Asian Development Bank (1985); Council for Economic Planning and Development (1984).

the debt crisis that afflicted so many countries in Latin America and Africa. Perhaps the most remarkable experience is that of Indonesia which in one decade following a major change in policy raised the domestic savings rate four-fold, though it was no doubt helped by the oil boom (see Arndt 1984:61–71 on the oil boom in Indonesia).

The East Asian countries have an enviable record of domestic savings. There is no evidence of a vicious circle, nor do they appear to have been particularly hampered in transforming domestic savings into foreign exchange by expanding exports. Now that the East Asian countries rely mainly on *private* sources of foreign savings, it is also questionable whether flows of foreign savings are strictly exogenous. Rates of private foreign savings flows (i.e. in proportion to GDP) are positively correlated with rates of investment not only in East Asia but also over a broad sample of countries (Riedel 1984a).

Financial development

The amount and diversity of financial intermediation is another measure of development. A positive relation between real economic growth and financial development is empirically well established, though the direction of cause and effect is more obscure. Certainly as countries grow and accumulate wealth the demand for financial assets and the services of financial intermediaries increases. However, there is also a strong theoretical case for the reverse causation. Financial intermediation can play an important role in mobilizing savings and allocating investment efficiently. The lack of financial institutions or their 'repression' by government regulation of interest rates and/or rapid, erratic inflation can, it has been argued, significantly inhibit economic growth (McKinnon 1973; Shaw 1973).

The ratio of 'broad' money (M2) to GDP is the most commonly used indicator of financial development, and serves well enough as long as the banking system dominates the capital market. That condition holds more or less in all of the East Asian countries, with the exception of Hong Kong and Singapore which alone have ratios of securities (stocks and bonds) to GDP that exceed their M2–GDP ratios. The relatively low ratios of securities to GDP, shown in Table 1.6, for the other East Asian countries are not exceptional given their level of development.

Table 1.6 *Indicators of financial development* (percentage)

	1955	1965	1973	1983	Securities/GDP 1980	Inflation rate 1965–73	1973–83
Singapore	n.a.	56	66	72	130	3.1	4.5
Hong Kong	n.a.	55	78	110	192	6.4	9.9
Taiwan	12	29	51	77	17	4.3	7.9
Korea, Republic of	9	12	40	38	14	15.5	19.0
Malaysia	..	27	42	61	..	1.2	6.5
Thailand	20	25	34	39	16	2.5	8.7
Philippines	18	20	20	25	18	8.8	11.7
Indonesia	n.a.	11	15	21	—	63.0	18.0
United States	47	46	49	64	130	4.7	7.5
Japan	63	79	88	93	99	6.3	7.7

Note: The M2/GDP columns span 1955, 1965, 1973, 1983.

Sources: International Financial Statistics 1955–85 (IMF, various years); Council for Economic Planning and Development (1984); Cole and Patrick (1984); Drake (1984); Liang (1984).

The ratios of M2 to GDP for Singapore and Hong Kong are comparable to, if not higher than, those of the most industrial countries, befitting their status as leading international financial centres. All of the East Asian countries are shown to have experienced some degree of financial development, with the exception of the Philippines which it will be recalled had the lowest growth rate. In the middle income group, the Republic of Korea stands out as the least financially developed despite its superlative growth performance. In part this is illusory since the vigorous growth of an informal credit market is not reflected in these numbers. However, relatively high inflation in the Republic of Korea, which McKinnon (1984:19) blames on loss of monetary control due to excessive foreign capital inflow, may also have inhibited financial development. Relatively low M2–GDP ratios for the Philippines and Indonesia have also been attributed to past episodes of inflation and associated crises in domestic financial markets, combined with relatively free financial access to Hong Kong and Singapore (Cole and Patrick 1984).

The East Asian countries seem to illustrate rather well two basic propositions: (1) that financial development is related and probably also contributes to economic growth; and (2) that inflation is a serious retardant of financial development and potentially of long-run, self-sustained growth. Monetary stability is therefore an important part of successful market-oriented development. In this respect, the experience of the East Asian countries, though not uniformly good, is exemplary by developing-country standards. Moreover, the financially least developed East Asian countries, Republic of Korea, Indonesia and the Philippines, have in response to inflationary pressures stemming from the second oil crisis initiated ambitious programs of financial liberalization, though it remains to be seen how successfully they will be carried out (Cole and Patrick 1984). The model for financial liberalization seems to be Taiwan, which avoided being overwhelmed by excessively expansionary fiscal policy (as in Sri Lanka) or by severe exchange rate overvaluation (as in Chile).

Employment and wages

The measures of development discussed above relate more to the 'quantity' of growth than to its 'quality', by which is meant the extent to which the benefits of growth are shared equitably. The term 'equitable' raises intractable problems, there being no universal agreement about what equitable is. None the less, few would dispute that the quality of growth is higher the more it contributes to full employment, rising wages, reduced poverty, more equal income distribution, higher standards of living and greater opportunity for personal fulfilment generally. The extent to which growth in the East Asian countries has accomplished or at least accompanied the fulfilment of some of these objectives is now examined, beginning with the gains to workers in terms of employment and wages.

Employment and wage data are among the more difficult to come by, and their quality is always open to question. Nevertheless, what is available from a variety of sources on rates of manufacturing employment growth, unemployment and increases in manufacturing real wages is presented in Table 1.7. Increasing opportunities for employment in industry is important not only for the rate of growth (because labour productivity is higher and increases more rapidly in industry), but also for the quality of growth. Because industrial wages tend to be higher and perhaps also because life in urban centres seems more appealing, people in developing countries have flocked to the cities seeking employment. When it is not available the consequences can be disastrous, as anyone who has visited cities in South Asia, Africa and Latin America can attest. In the East Asian countries, the problem is less severe. Rates of growth of manufacturing employment have been exceptionally high since the early 1960s in some of the countries, notably Republic of Korea, Taiwan, Hong Kong and Singapore. The other four achieved comparable rates of growth of manufacturing employment only in the 1970s, but avoided some of the worst aspects of overcrowding by virtue of having less distorted and segmented labour markets than many other developing countries.[7] Consequently, unemployment appears (on the basis of casual observation and, perhaps less convincingly, on the numbers in Table 1.7) to be less of a problem in East Asia than in other parts of the developing world.

The unemployment problem in East Asian countries is greater, of course, than the numbers in Table 1.7 suggest. First, disguised unemployment and underemployment are not taken into account. In the Philippines, for example, Lal (1983) finds that on top of 5 per cent open unemployment in 1976 there was an additional 2.3 per cent (full-time equivalent) visibly underemployed (i.e. involuntarily working less than 40 hours per week). That still leaves the Philippines well below the level of open unemployment in many other countries. Another problem is that unemployment tends not to be spread evenly across a country, but rather to concentrate in urban centres. Thus, for example, while average 1965 unemployment in the Republic of Korea was 7.4 per cent, in non-farm households it was 14.4 per cent, and by comparison only 3.5 per cent on the farm (Hong 1981:354). Aggregation also obscures some of the gains made in reducing unemployment. In the Republic of Korea, for example, unemployment overall fell from 7.4 to 4.1 per cent be-

---

[7] Lal (1983:10) reports that in the Philippines labour markets have functioned efficiently, with little effective interference from trade unions or government, and with considerable intra- and inter-sectoral mobility. Thus, wages in industry and agriculture tend to move together. Likewise, Pitt (1981:194) characterizes Indonesian labour markets as undistorted, and shows that 'Real wage data for some non-manufacturing sectors demonstrate a pattern similar to that of manufacturing'. In Thailand, the data are scanty and experts find 'it is difficult to draw any firm conclusions about the nature of the labour market without further evidence' (Akrasanee 1981:406). Krueger (1983:28–9) includes Thailand in the group of countries she identifies as having less severe urban unemployment.

Table 1.7 *Indicators of labour market conditions* (percentage)

	Growth of real wage		Open employment		Growth of manufacturing employment	
	Period	Rate	Period	Rate	Period	Rate
Singapore	1965–73	0.6	1967–73	6.0	..	..
	1973–83	5.4	1973–83	3.7	1973–83	5.5
Hong Kong	1960–70	4.7	1960–70	4.2	1961–71	4.7
	1970–80	4.2	1970–80	4.5	1971–84	4.3
Taiwan	1960–73	7.7	1960–73	1.6	1960–73	8.1
	1973–83	6.5	1973–83	1.0	1973–83	4.8
Korea, Republic of	1963–73	5.4	1965–73	5.3	1963–73	11.2
	1973–83	9.5	1973–83	4.2	1973–83	6.3
Malaysia	1962–73	—	1967–72	7.2	..	..
	1973–81	5.0	1973–83	5.7	1973–83	8.1
Thailand	1961–73	—	..	..	..	..
	1975–79	2.0	1973–82	0.8	1973–83	10.0
Philippines	1965–73	−1.6	1960–73	6.5	1960–73	2.6
	1973–81	—	1973–83	4.4	1973–83	4.0
Indonesia[a]	1955–67	−3.4	1961–71	5.5	1961–71	3.3
	1971–80	5.1	1976–82	2.5	1976–82	1.2

[a] The Indonesian data are particularly suspect due to changes in definition of organized manufacturing sector over time and other anomalies.
Sources: Ariff and Hill (1985a); Pitt (1981); Hong (1981); Akrasanee (1981); Lal (1983); Kirkpatrick (1985); Sung (1984); Riedel (1974); Council for Economic Planning and Development (1984); Asian Development Bank (1977, 1985).

tween 1965 and 1983, but in urban areas declined from 14.4 to less than 5 per cent in 1983 (Hong 1981:354).

In labour markets that are efficient, which is how analysts typically characterize the East Asian countries, real wages are determined by relative supply and demand. Demand for labour in manufacturing (at least since 1970) appears to have outstripped supply. This has been so everywhere except in the Philippines, Thailand and, despite what real wage data indicate, Indonesia. Thailand and Indonesia are of course latecomers to industrialization. The failure of real wages to rise in the Philippines is more problematic, since the Philippines was one of the first to start industrializing and currently has a larger manufacturing sector in relation to GDP than that of any other East Asian country apart from Taiwan. The Philippine experience seems to suggest that the character (i.e. factor intensity and trade orientation) as well as the rate of industrialization influence real wage trends (Lal 1983; Fields 1984).

Finally, one cannot but draw attention to the truly outstanding performance of real wages in Hong Kong, Taiwan and the Republic of Korea. Singapore is a bit of an anomaly in that real wages began to rise significantly only after 1978. As a consequence of a rather liberal policy towards unskilled as well as skilled guest workers, wages in Singapore were kept down. Since 1979, as part of a comprehensive economic restructuring program, the policy has been to reduce the inflow of unskilled guest workers and to promote higher real wages through the National Wages Council (Lim 1984; Kirkpatrick 1985). It is worth noting that this shift in policy coincided with a rapid increase in real wages in Malaysia, which previously had been Singapore's main source of unskilled guest workers.

Income distribution

After Kuznets discovered an historical tendency for income inequality to increase in the early stages of growth, it became fashionable to recommend that income redistribution measures accompany policies aimed at promoting growth in developing countries. 'Trickle-down' was in disrepute, and the inevitable trade-off between growth and equity had to be faced squarely. In the meantime, the East Asian countries were quietly working away to discredit most of the conventional wisdom about the relation between growth and income distribution.

Rapid growth in Taiwan and Hong Kong was found to be accompanied by a fall rather than a rise in inequality (Fei, Ranis and Kuo 1979; Chow and Papanek 1981; Fields 1984). In the Republic of Korea, income distribution appears to have remained fairly constant despite very rapid growth (Adelman and Robinson 1978; Choo 1980; Fields 1980, 1984). Furthermore, although there is great debate as to whether growth in these countries was due to the market or to government intervention, there is broad agreement that the distributional outcome was mainly the result of market forces. I stress 'mainly' because, even in Hong Kong, the world's most *laissez-faire* country, government expenditures are quite progressive (Lin 1985). Another important qualification is that both Taiwan and the Republic of Korea had successful land reforms prior to rapid growth, supporting Morawetz's (1977:41) hypothesis that 'the initial distribution of assets and incomes may be a crucial determinant of the trend in inequality'.

Because of the great attention that is given to the issue of relative income inequality, it is worthwhile examining how well the East Asian countries compare to other developing countries in this regard. The *World Development Report* (World Bank, various years) provides data on successive quintile shares of total disposable household income for seven of the East Asian countries and for twenty-six other developing countries. Comparable data for Singapore, the one East Asian country for which World Bank data are unavailable, were obtained, yielding a sample total of thirty-four countries.

There are various summary measures of income equality that can be used to order countries, the Gini coefficient being the most popular. The method adopted here, however, is Borda's rule of rank ordering, which has the advantage of allowing a complete ordering on the basis of multiple criteria all taken together.[8] A 'Borda score' is obtained simply by giving a country points equal to its rank with respect to each criterion. Countries are ordered according to the lowness of the sum of ranks (Borda scores). The ordering according to equality of income distribution is obtained by ranking countries according to the household income shares of successive *cumulative* quintile aggregates (i.e. the share of the bottom 20 per cent, bottom 40 per cent, bottom 60 per cent and bottom 80 per cent of households, respectively).

The place of each East Asian country in the ordering of the thirty-four countries in the sample is shown in Table 1.8. Six occupy the top half of the sample, and four fall in the top third. Malaysia is found to have the worst income distribution among the East Asian countries, and perhaps not surprisingly it is there that political sensitivity to distributional issues is most acute. Government also intervenes more directly to redistribute income in Malaysia than elsewhere in East Asia.[9] The Philippines, the slowest growing East Asian country, exhibits the second worst income dis-

---

[8] Sen (1973, 1981) explains the merits of Borda's method and applies it to the same data set.

[9] Snodgrass (1980:57) dismisses, however, the equity measures initiated since the 1969 riots as 'a blend of racial rhetoric and bold promises for the long-range future, on the one hand, and only moderately increasing expenditure levels and general continuity with past policies on the other'.

Table 1.8 *Income distribution and growth of the East Asian countries relative to a sample of thirty-four developing countries*

	Rank out of sample of 34 countries		
	Income distribution	Income and GDP growth	Income distribution and per capita growth
Taiwan	1	1	1
Singapore	5	2	2
Korea, Republic of	8	4	3
Hong Kong	11	5	4
Indonesia	15	8	8
Thailand	16	10	9
Malaysia	26	16	14
Philippines	22	17	17

Source: World Development Report, 1985 (World Bank, various years). See source for a description of the sample.

tribution, and Taiwan, the fastest growing country, the best, not only in East Asia but in the developing world.

The East Asian data seem to indicate a positive relation between growth and equality, but that is not borne out in the broader sample of countries. Income is distributed more evenly in Sri Lanka, for example, than in any East Asian country, save Taiwan. That has led Sen (1981:309) to suggest that 'there is an important similarity between the two strategies [Sri Lanka's, on the one hand, and Taiwan–Korea's, on the other]'. It is only a matter of means: 'While one relies on the successfully fostered growth and dynamism of the encouraged labour market, the other gives the government a more direct role as a provider of provisions'. Of course, there is no similarity at all if the concept of absolute poverty rather than relative poverty is considered, since growth reduces absolute poverty independently of whatever effect it might have on relative poverty. A country growing at the rate of the four East Asian NICs doubles its real per capita income within a decade; hence for real income of the poorest not to rise, their share in the nation's income would have to fall by half in one decade. Of course when growth is slow, even a small slip in the income share of the poorest can be devastating.

The relative performance of the East Asian countries in terms of growth and income distribution combined is shown in Table 1.8. All eight rank in the top half of the sample, six are in the top third, and the four NICs take all the first-place ribbons.

Quality of life

While poverty has not diminished everywhere, there is evidence that the indicators of 'quality of life' have improved in most developing countries (Morawetz 1977; Morris 1979). Table 1.9 presents data for two common indicators, longevity and school enrolment. Secondary rather than primary enrolment is examined because primary enrolment in all eight countries currently exceeds 90 per cent of primary school-age children. Measuring change in these indicators involves complications because it is unclear whether one should consider absolute changes or relative changes, and if the latter whether the benchmark should be the initial level or the maximum attainable (say, 80 years for longevity and 100 per cent for enrolment). The percentage reduction in the shortfall from the maximum attainable levels seems to be the best approach (so argues Sen 1981:272).

Table 1.9 suggests that quality of life in the East Asian countries has improved significantly in the past two decades and, except in Thailand and Indonesia, proportionally more than in other developing countries on average. Life expectancy is particularly low in Indonesia, and while primary enrolment is high in Indonesia and Thailand, their achievements in secondary education have not matched their growth record. The four East Asian NICs, on the other hand, seem to excel in every respect.

EXPLAINING EAST ASIAN SUCCESS

The foregoing review of various indicators of development leaves little doubt about East Asia's economic success. The four East Asian NICs deserve to be considered the most successful of developing countries; the economic performance since 1970 of three of the four near-NICs was also outstanding, and even the Philippines' record, before its current political and economic troubles, was more than respectable by standards everywhere apart from its neighbours. This leads us then to the question of what explains the

Table 1.9 *Changes in longevity and secondary school enrolment*

	Female life expectancy (years)		Decline in longevity shortfall[a] (%)	Secondary school enrolment (%)		Decline in enrolment shortfall[b] (%)
	1965	1983	1983	1965	1982	1982
Singapore	68	75	58.3	45	66	38.2
Hong Kong	71	78	77.8	29	67	53.5
Taiwan	70	75	50.0	53	98	95.7
Korea, Republic of	58	71	59.1	35	89	83.1
Malaysia	59	69	47.6	28	49	29.2
Thailand	58	65	31.8	14	29	17.4
Philippines	58	66	36.4	41	64	39.0
Indonesia	45	55	28.6	12	33	23.9
Low-income developing countries	51	60	31.0	20	32	15.0
Middle-income developing countries	55	63	32.0	20	42	27.5
Industrial countries	74	79	83.3	71	87	55.2

[a] Shortfall from the maximum attainable which is assumed to be 80 years.
[b] Shortfall from 100 per cent enrolment.
Source: *World Development Report*, 1985 (World Bank, various years).

region's unique success, and what lessons it holds for other countries. As this is an overview, the aim is not to offer new evidence or interpretations, but rather to summarize (and criticize) some of those that have already been put forward.

Two different kinds of explanation present themselves: those related to exogenous circumstances and those related to government and economic policy. One can presumably extract lessons from the latter, but not the former. It is questionable how much of the explanation can be yielded to exogenous circumstances without relinquishing the right to generalize about policy lessons. To illustrate, Little (1981:43), in what is widely regarded as the most thorough and persuasive explanation of success in the four NICs, concludes that 'everything can be attributed to good policies and the people'. But, are these really two separate explanations, or did these countries manage good policies only because they have the kind of

people they have?[10] Before examining economic policy it is therefore useful to review briefly the various exogenous circumstances
which might account for East Asian success, and inquire to what
extent their contribution to the overall explanation detracts from
whatever policy lessons emerge.

Exogenous factors

When it is argued that the East Asian countries succeeded because
of exogenous circumstances, what is usually implied is either that
they got a headstart on industrialization, and/or that they were
lucky to possess certain critical, non-reproducible assets or resources in greater proportion than other countries. There are two
key issues: first, whether these resources were indeed more abundant in East Asia; and, second, whether their abundance is in fact
given exogenously.

(i) *Natural resources*
There was a time when being well-endowed with natural resources
was considered a distinct advantage. That was before the mineral-
poor, land-scarce East Asian NICs outperformed everyone, including the oil-exporting countries. Conventional wisdom was then
turned on its head – lucky is the country that has no mining sector
and few farmers. The exceptional performance of the extremely
well-endowed countries of Southeast Asia might be expected to
change once again the fashion of thinking on this point.

There are, however, some reasons why a lack of natural resources, in particular land, might be interpreted as an advantage
(Little 1979a:450). First, it might be thought that having a relatively small mining or agricultural sector would ease the potential
for political resistance to industrialization. However, the problem
of recalcitrant miners and farmers is far greater in the industrial
countries, and with far less justification, than in the developing
countries. Second, productivity growth in agriculture tends to be
lower than in other sectors, so that the smaller the agricultural
sector the easier it is presumably to achieve high growth rates.

[10] Hicks and Redding (1984a:27) make this point. But, to be fair, it is clear that
Little yielded more in the above quote from the conclusion of his paper than he intended. Earlier he states quite unambiguously that 'cultural factors cannot be
more than contributory factors, which may play their part, but only when other
conditions are favourable' (Little 1981:463).

However, while that logic might seem adequate to deal with the record of Hong Kong and Singapore, it fails altogether for any of the other East Asian countries. All (except possibly the Philippines, but including Taiwan and the Republic of Korea) derived a larger share of their income from agriculture in 1960 than currently do the poorest developing countries on average. Finally, there is the problem of dislocations that arise when the primary sector is booming, rather than lagging. This syndrome, known as 'Dutch Disease', has afflicted industrial and developing countries alike, but its severity appears to depend more on the nature of accompanying macroeconomic policy than on the size of the booming primary sector (Corden 1984).

(ii) *External resources*

Our concern here is with exogenous factors, and certainly not all external resource flows to developing countries are determined exogenously. The ability to attract private direct investment and to borrow in international financial markets and (to a lesser extent) from official multilateral lending agencies depends to some degree on growth and export prospects. Foreign aid is a different matter. It tends to be allocated to countries more on the basis of humanitarian, political and strategic considerations. That fact by itself casts doubt on whether foreign aid should necessarily be considered a positive exogenous factor for economic growth.

Much attention has been given to the fact that two of the most successful East Asian countries, the Republic of Korea and Taiwan, received disproportionate amounts of foreign aid prior to rapid growth. There is, however, little doubt that aid flows to both countries were motivated more by political and strategic considerations than by foresight on the part of the United States AID officials about the future prospects of these countries. Indeed, in 1961, after more than US$2 billion of economic assistance and US$1 billion of military assistance, it is reported that 'USAID officials were wondering audibly whether South Korea was to remain indefinitely a pensioner of the United States' (Mason *et al.* 1980: 181). The purpose of United States aid to Taiwan and the Republic of Korea was mainly to help absorb the burden of their confrontation with neighbouring communist states. It did, none the less, allow investment, mainly in infrastructure, that would not otherwise have been possible given their extraordinary defence obligations (Krueger 1979; Kuo 1983). Had the Republic of Korea and Taiwan not faced such a severe external threat, they would likely have received far less aid. However, can it be argued that their prospects for growth, in that case, would have been any less bright? The main contribution of aid in Taiwan and the Republic of Korea seems to have been political and economic stability rather than growth *per se*.[11]

That aid is not a necessary condition for growth is underscored by the experience of some of the other East Asian countries. Hong Kong did not receive much aid, but did get undisclosed amounts of mainland and overseas Chinese capital in the 1950s; Singapore borrowed heavily in the early 1960s from the World Bank and the Asian Development Bank, but on relatively hard terms. In both cases it was presumably their ability to make good use of the resources that counted more than anything else.[12] Indeed, that some rather unsuccessful countries have over the past twenty-five years obtained far more (real dollar) aid per capita in proportion to GNP than did Taiwan and the Republic of Korea in the 1950s, and without the concomitant defence burden, suggests that aid is also not a sufficient condition for growth.

(iii) *Human resources*
Human resources must be measured in terms of both quantity and quality. All of the East Asian countries, apart from Malaysia and the outer islands of Indonesia, are densely populated. At the outset of industrialization, all had or were soon to have more labour than they could employ. In this regard, they were no different from many other developing countries today. What many argue distinguishes the East Asian countries, in particular the NICs, is the

---

[11] Scott writes (1979:371) on aid to Taiwan: 'My own view, for what it is worth, is that aid played a very important role in helping control inflation in the early 1950s, and that this may have been essential for political stability... Nonetheless, it was far from being both a necessary and sufficient explanation of Taiwan's success'. In the Republic of Korea, Mason *et al.* (1980:203) conclude that, 'The massive inflow of foreign assistance before and during the Korean war was essential to the survival of South Korea as an independent country'. However, they suggest that, because of continued massive inflows, 'the government emphasized reconstruction and price stabilization more than growth during the post-war 1950s'.

[12] Chen (1985) suggests that as much as one-third of early Hong Kong investment may have come from mainland and overseas Chinese. Not insignificant amounts of overseas Chinese capital have been invested in other Southeast Asian countries as well (Wu and Wu 1980).

quality of their labour force. Diligence, loyalty, hard work and a strong appreciation of education are virtues which appear to be more abundant in East Asian NICs than elsewhere. Since these countries have common historical roots, the explanation has been found in culture, a factor relegated to the dustbin of development economics for more than three decades. Currently, however, the most popular explanation of Asian dynamism, with an appeal broad enough to embrace the likes of futurologist Herman Kahn (1979) and mathematical economist Michio Morishima (1982), is the teachings of a Chinese philosopher who lived more than twenty-five centuries ago.

Fortunately, the assessment of the role of culture does not come within my terms of reference. I will confine myself simply to raising a couple of questions which seem left open in the literature. Why were the advantages of a Confucian heritage discovered only within the past five to ten years? The most renowned work in this area is Needham's (1954) study of science and civilization in China, which traced the relative *decline* of China as a result of cultural factors. Moreover, despite more than thirty-five years of communism, including a major cultural revolution, some argue still that science and technology in China are severely fettered by 'atavistic cultural traits that have survived the passing of China's traditional Confucian order' (Baum 1982:1167). In the early 1950s, economic stagnation in the Republic of Korea and Japan was routinely attributed to their Confucian heritage (Han 1984:104). Furthermore, if it is Confucianism that explains the success of the East Asian NICs, what explains similar, if not quite as spectacular, economic performances in other developing countries which do not share the same cultural heritage? Innumerable case studies demonstrate that economic behaviour responds to incentives, both positive and negative, in every part of the world. Thriving black markets in South Asia and Africa are testament to that.

One could also question whether the attributes of diligence, hard work and educational attainment are primarily exogenous. Surely attitudes toward work depend as much as anything on the availability of jobs and the reward given for effort, both of which are generally greater in East Asia than in most other developing countries. Even deeply ingrained social attitudes can be changed by concerted action, as is reported to be occurring among Malays regarding attitudes toward female education and employment

(Pang 1982). Finally, educational attainment, the East Asian virtue most frequently referred to, is presumably as much supply as demand determined. Once education is accounted for, there is usually very little variation across racial or ethnic boundaries in economic achievement. In Malaysia, for example, it has been found that 'ethnic inequality is basically due to an inheritance of poverty, or of rural agrarian origin, rather than any strong effect of ethnicity alone' (Hirschman 1975:79).

(iv) Pre-conditions

Some have suggested that part of the explanation of the East Asian countries' relative success is that they simply got a headstart. The facts, however, do not bear this out. All, with the exception of Thailand, were under colonial rule until the end of the Second World War. The Republic of Korea alone experienced some indus-trialization during the colonial period, but that was mostly in what was to become North Korea. Both Taiwan and the Republic of Korea are sometimes regarded as having had a more favourable colonial experience, in terms of economic progress, than other countries, though Singapore and Malaysia were undoubtedly the richest at the end of the war. Whatever advantages Taiwan and the Republic of Korea might have had were largely destroyed by war. In Taiwan, by 1945, agricultural output had dropped to 45 per cent of pre-war levels, and industrial output was less than one-third what it had been before the war (Hsing 1971:1949). The Republic of Korea came out of the Second World War relatively unscathed, but was devastated by the Korean war.[13] Indeed, all the East Asian countries began the 1950s still suffering the effects of war. In this respect, their circumstances were less advantageous than those of many other developing countries.

Of course some advantages are intangible and survive even the ravages of war. Entrepreneurship and commercial expertise were no doubt greater in Hong Kong and Singapore as a consequence of their entrepôt past. It is, however, difficult to know how much weight this deserves. In Singapore, foreign investors took the lead in expanding investment, while in Hong Kong the bulk of manufac-turing investment came from indigenous Cantonese entrepreneurs with no historical link to entrepôt trade (Hughes and Seng 1969;

[13] According to Little (1979a:455): 'About 1.3 million Koreans were killed, and physical damage was of the order of one and a half to two years' GNP'.

Riedel 1974). The main point, however, is that whatever headstart toward industrialization the East Asian countries had in 1950, it should by 1985 have been more than matched in most developing countries. (Indeed in the 1950s the Latin American countries had a considerable lead on the East Asian countries.)

The role of government

(i) *The minimal role*

It was noted at the beginning of this paper that the interpretation of East Asian success as a validation of neo-classical principles at work in developing countries has been called into question. The discovery that governments are deeply involved directly and indirectly in economic affairs, even in the most successful countries, is reason enough for some to reject the neo-classical interpretation, for all too often neo-classical doctrine is equated with *laissez-faire*. That is of course unfounded. Keynes (1926:20) has noted that 'the phrase laissez-faire is not to be found in the works of Adam Smith, of Ricardo, or of Malthus. Even the idea is not present in a dogmatic form in any of these authors' (Lal 1984).[14]

No better exposition of the minimal role of government is there than that set out in Adam Smith's *Inquiry into the Nature and Causes of the Wealth of Nations* (1776):

According to the system of natural liberty, the sovereign has only three duties to attend to; three duties of great importance, indeed, but plain and intelligible to common understandings: first, the duty of protecting the society from the violence and invasion of other independent societies; secondly, the duty of protecting, as far as possible, every member of the society from the injustice or oppression of every other member of it, or the duty of establishing an exact administration of justice; and thirdly, the duty of erecting and maintaining certain public works and certain public institutions, which it can never be for the interest of any individual, or small number of individuals, to erect and maintain; because the profit could never repay the expense to any individual or small number of individuals, though it may frequently do much more than repay it to a great society.

In short, government has the duty of supplying public goods. Unfortunately, the line between public and private goods is often

---

[14] Furthermore, the moral legitimacy of minimal government is consistent with even the strongest formulation of individual rights (Nozick 1974).

unclear; hence it is not always easy to know when government is fulfilling its minimal role and when it is encroaching on what neo-classical economists would consider the legitimate domain of private markets.

These ambiguities notwithstanding, it appears that the East Asian countries have generally fulfilled the minimal functions of government reasonably well. Most of the countries have been at peace during the greater part of the past three decades, though there have been on-going clashes with internal and external insurgent forces in the Southeast Asian countries. In spite of the authoritarian nature of government in the East Asian countries, the administration of justice has also been reasonably good, with the notable exceptions of Indonesia under Sukarno and the Philippines in recent years. In both of these instances the failure of government to fulfil its minimal duty was accompanied by economic decline. Finally, the East Asian countries have generally provided the infrastructure necessary for growth. Nowhere in East Asia are transport, utilities and communications the bottle-necks they are in India, for example. However, aside from Hong Kong, the East Asian countries have claimed a role in economic affairs far beyond that allotted to them by Adam Smith.

(ii) *Industrial incentives*
In developing countries everywhere, apart from Hong Kong, industrialization is a matter of strategy and tactics. In Hong Kong, policy is guided more by a philosophy which the Chief Secretary has labelled 'positive non-interventionism':

When faced with an interventionist proposal, the Hong Kong Government does *not* simply respond that such a proposal *must* by definition, be incorrect. It is true that, more often than not, we come to the conclusion that the balance of advantage lies in not intervening. Yet, in all cases, decisions are made positively, and not by default, and only after the immediate benefits and costs, to the extent that they can confidently be predicted, are weighted against the medium and longer term implications of the interventionist acts proposed (including the inevitable difficulties of unwinding them).[15]

---

[15] This quote is from a speech to the Overseas Bankers Club at the Guildhall, London on 1 February 1982, and is cited in an unpublished government document of the Department of Industry and Trade entitled 'Statement on Government Assistance to Industry', p. 1.

The statement goes on: 'the Government's principal role is to ensure the provision of an adequate infrastructure to enable industry to function efficiently and profitably with minimum interference'. As the economy has grown and diversified, the scope of infrastructural support has broadened to include, for example, the establishment of testing, standards and calibration laboratories and financial support for various high-technology research and development projects. None of these measures, however, directly discriminates between competing industries or firms.

In the 1950s, Singapore was also a free port, but with independence in 1958 tariffs and quotas were imposed to foster industrialization. The rationale for import substitution, the prospect of a common market with Malaysia, was dashed in 1965 when Singapore was expelled from the Federation. Since then the policy has been free trade. However, the Singapore Government intervenes in other ways to promote industrialization and export expansion, including most importantly various tax concessions to exporters and foreign investors (Bautista 1983:20 gives a brief description of the various measures). Furthermore, since the mid-1970s, government has attempted to restructure industry away from labour-intensive activities by encouraging wage increases and giving promotional priorities to more capital- and skill-intensive manufacturing (Lim 1984). It is an open question whether the hard times on which Singapore has recently fallen are in part a consequence of this shift in policy.

Taiwan, like Singapore, realized fairly early that its future was not in import substitution. Already in the late 1950s policy was changing: the exchange rate was unified, the currency devalued and various incentives to exports were introduced or intensified (see Table 1.10). Import liberalization did not get under way until the mid-1960s, but by 1975 more than 96 per cent of 15,366 different import commodities were free from quantitative restriction (Scott 1979:331). Furthermore, as shown in Table 1.11, average levels of nominal and effective protection were reduced to relatively low levels, though in some branches, such as transport equipment, they remain high. The essence of the policy was to create free trade conditions for exporters, but not for everyone throughout the economy.

The pattern of trade policy in Singapore and Taiwan, an initial rise and subsequent steady decline in the level of protection, was

Table 1.10 Classification of export incentives

	Singapore	Hong Kong	Taiwan	Rep. of Korea	Malaysia	Thailand	Philippines	Indonesia
Financial incentives								
a. Loans/interest reductions	x	—	x	x	x	x	x	x
b. Guarantees	x	x	x	x	x	—	x	x
Fiscal incentives								
a. Tax exemption and relief	x	—	x	x	x	x	x	x
b. Depreciation of allowances	x	—	x	x	x	—	x	x
c. Exemption of customs duties	—	—	x	x	x	x	x	x
Factor incentives								
a. Training	x	—	—	—	—	—	—	—
b. Research and development	x	x	x	—	—	—	—	—
c. Sites, buildings, facilities	x	x	x	x	x	x	x	x

Source: Lutkenhorst (1984:58).

Table 1.11 *Rates of nominal (N) and effective (E) protection*
(percentage)

	Consumer durables		Machinery		Transport equipment		Overall	
	N	E	N	E	N	E	N	E
Singapore (1967)	7	10	5	6	1	−1	3	6
Taiwan (1969)	14	29	9	1	27	55	12	15
Korea, Republic of (1968)	31	51	28	43	54	164	11	1
Korea, Republic of (1978)	40	131	18	47	31	135	18	31
Malaysia (1978)	55	173	22	39	—	−5	22	39
Thailand (1978)	57	495	21	58	80	417	27	70
Philippines (1965)	70	86	16	34	..	75	51	51
Philippines (1980)	..	115	..	24	..	..	..	70
Indonesia (1975)	..	224	..	15	..	715	20	30

Sources: Tan and Hock (1982); Lee and Liang (1982); Westphal and Kim (1982); Lutkenhorst (1984); Ariff and Hill (1985a); Power and Sicat (1971); Lutkenhorst (1984); Ariff and Hill (1985a), respectively.

never quite matched in any of the other East Asian countries. Import restrictions have come and gone, but the import regimes established under the import substitution strategy have remained more or less in place. The Republic of Korea, like many other developing countries, stagnated during the early phase of import substitution. This led to a military coup in 1961, and the establishment of a new government and a new policy. The main aim of the Park Chung Hee government was to remove the biases against exports contained in the import substitution policy. This was done primarily by exempting exporters from duties on imported intermediate and capital goods, and by providing them with subsidized credit (see Table 1.10). All in all, the net subsidy to exports in the late 1960s and early 1970s has been estimated at about 8.4 per cent of export value (Westphal and Kim 1982), more than enough to offset the discrimination inherent in the import substitution regime (Hong 1981; Young 1984).

The level of protection in the Republic of Korea, apart from that faced by exporters, has remained high, especially in agriculture, transport equipment and other capital-intensive industrial sectors. In the 1970s, the level of protection was in fact increased to encourage development of 'heavy and chemical industries'. In addition to more protection, these sectors were treated to a generous supply of credit at subsidized interest rates and given tax rebates (described in Young 1984). Whether as a result of the re-intensification of import substitution policy, or for unrelated reasons, growth began to falter in the late 1970s. Following the assassination of President Park and ensuing civil disorder, a new government came to power in 1980, and, like the one which preceded it, began by dedicating itself to import liberalization and promising itself a smaller role in the economy.

Malaysia and Thailand were essentially free trade economies until 1960 when both began industrialization under the import substitution strategy. As shown in Table 1.11, by the mid-1970s both had put in place moderately high levels of protection, but in the early 1970s both encountered the limits to import substitution, and, encouraged no doubt by the success of the four NICs, began to promote exports of manufactures in the usual ways (see Table 1.10). However, it seems apparent that neither country managed, as Taiwan and the Republic of Korea did, to offset fully the anti-export bias of their import regimes.

Indonesia, unlike Malaysia and Thailand, did not begin with a clean slate, but instead inherited from the Dutch a legacy of government controls affecting virtually every aspect of economic life. Gillis (1984:236) suggests that 'this *Weltanschauung* strongly conditioned the policy responses of a whole generation of Indonesian leaders after independence'. The culmination of Indonesian *dirigisme* was Sukarno's 1958 proclamation of the policy of 'Guided Democracy' and 'Guided Economy', which was meant to put all decision-making authority in the hands of Sukarno (Gillis 1984:242). The economic decline which ensued led to political upheaval and a new government in 1966 dedicated to a 'New Order'. The reforms which followed, at least until 1983, were mainly macroeconomic: the imposition of fiscal discipline and the freeing of the foreign exchange market. The incentive system remained more or less unchanged, though tariffs were reduced after 1968. However, while the average level of protection in Indonesia is not exceptionally high by world standards, there are wide differences among industries in nominal and effective protection rates.[16]

[16] According to an unpublished World Bank report, effective protection rates vary from as high as 4315 per cent to as low as −35 per cent in manufacturing.

The first East Asian country to embark on industrialization as a conscious policy decision was the Philippines, though its relative per capita income would seem to belie that fact. Of all the East Asian countries, the Philippines was, and remains, most strongly dedicated to import substitution. Effective protection rates were generally higher, and reliance on quantitative restrictions greater, than elsewhere in East Asia. The Philippines did, however, join the export promotion bandwagon in the 1970s (see Table 1.10) and with some success (see Table 1.3). Nevertheless, the weight of the import substitution regime was simply too great for export expansion to have the same growth effects that it had elsewhere.

(iii) *Other involvement*

Labour markets in East Asia, it was noted above, are generally freer than in many other developing countries. To some degree this is the consequence of a policy of regulating and restricting labour union activity. To the extent that this policy prevents labour unions from restrictive market practices, it might be considered a legitimate part of the minimal role of government. No doubt restrictions on organized labour exceed this in some of the countries. It is interesting that in Hong Kong, for example, where unions are free to organize and strike, they receive little support from workers.[17] In part this may be due to Hong Kong's special political status. It may also be that with real wages rising faster than anywhere else in the world, workers are reluctant to change a system that has served them reasonably well.

One area in which government involvement clearly violates neoclassical tenets is public ownership of the means of production. Until its recent takeover of two failing banks, Hong Kong was the only East Asian country to confine its ownership to utilities and the like. In the other countries, public ownership is common in banking and various capital-intensive intermediate goods industries, including steel, petroleum, petrochemicals, fertilizers and heavy chemicals.

Finally, governments everywhere, except possibly in Hong Kong which alone has no central bank, have claimed responsibility for macroeconomic management. Fiscal, monetary and exchange rate

---

[17] Turner (1981) was chagrined to discover from a large number of interviews that Hong Kong workers were not at all enthusiastic about the prospect of having a system of adversarial labour relations similar to that in Britain.

policies determine the overall economic environment, and hence are often as important for industrial growth and export expansion as is the structure of relative incentives. This proposition seems to be particularly well illustrated in the case of Indonesia, which, according to Gillis (1984:244), 'might be cited as an example of how fairly consistent application of sensible macro policies can counterbalance the ill effects of dirigiste micro policies'. There are also notable examples of the same proposition in reverse – that is, where sensible restructuring of relative incentives has been overwhelmed by excessive fiscal expansion and exchange rate overvaluation.

(iv) *The net effect of government*
There is no escaping the fact that governments have been deeply involved in the economies of all of the East Asian countries. In Hong Kong, at least until recently, government has confined itself largely to minimal functions. Elsewhere involvement has been far more extensive. In addition to serving minimal functions, including the provision of necessary infrastructure, governments have intervened in three broad areas: (1) they have been actively engaged in managing the system of industrial incentives; (2) they have claimed exclusive responsibility for maintaining macroeconomic stability; and (3) they have established some public enterprises apart from utilities to produce what are essentially private goods. The key question is, to what effect?

This is obviously not an easy question to answer. It seems evident, however, that not much of the success of the East Asian countries can be attributed to the third area of government involvement, the direct contribution to GDP of public enterprises. Their share in these economies is relatively small, and their growth has been relatively low, except for the oil sector in Indonesia. Whether the net contribution of public enterprises was positive or negative, as measured against the outcome had the resources they command been employed elsewhere, I am in no position to answer. Clearly, however, the dynamism of the East Asian countries rests in the private sector, in particular that part devoted to manufacturing labour-intensive products for export.

This does not rule out an important role for government. Without the macroeconomic stability that the East Asian countries enjoyed (in varying degrees), it is unlikely that their success, not only in achieving rapid growth and export expansion, but also in improving income distribution and other measures of 'quality of life', would have been anywhere near as great. Granting this, it is important not to give more credit than is due. Certainly it does not make sense to credit government with *not* having created macroeconomic chaos, though it *is* within their power, as is known only too well.

The area of government involvement most difficult to evaluate is the management of the system of incentives which guide private economic activity. It is certain that government manipulation of incentives can be extremely effective. Every major shift in industrial policy in the East Asian countries was followed by a significant change in economic performance. Particularly impressive have been the responses of manufacturers to the removal of impediments to exporting. There is nothing unique about this. Similar responses to shifts in trade policy have been observed in other developing countries.[18] Indeed, looking back over the past 100 years of development experiences, Reynolds (1983:963) has found: 'First, the turning point [in economic growth] is almost always associated with some significant political event... Second, the turning point is usually associated with a marked rise in exports'.

There remains the question, however, whether governments' main contribution to economic success in the East Asian countries was not principally in removing the obstacles to growth which they themselves put there in the first place. Taking everything at face value, this would seem to be largely the case. Under import substitution they generally stagnated; removing the obstacles to exporting, they generally flourished. Backsliding towards protectionism, as in the Republic of Korea in the 1970s, led to decline.

Probably the majority of specialists on the economies of developing countries would not accept the evidence at face value. Even those who strongly advocate export-oriented development judge the early phase of import substitution to be important in laying foundations for future export-led growth (e.g. Balassa 1982a). The fact that Hong Kong did not go through an early phase of import substitution is not very persuasive, given its entrepôt past and the post-war influx of Shanghai industrialists.[19] The view that early

[18] See the case studies cited in footnote 1.
[19] For what it is worth, I have always thought too much was made of both points. Hong Kong's dynamism is largely with local Cantonese businessmen.

import substitution provides the necessary breathing space to develop industrial entrepreneurship and acquire production and marketing skills seems eminently reasonable. Yet hard evidence is
scanty (e.g. Westphal 1982). There is, however, overwhelming evidence that entrepreneurship, in one form or another, abounds
almost everywhere, but that in vast parts of the developing world it
is misdirected in large part by the government.

CONCLUSIONS

Doing what comes naturally?

The quote from Adam Smith at the head of this paper seems an
apposite description of how things worked in Hong Kong, but not
elsewhere. In addition to providing 'peace, easy taxes and a toler-
able administration of justice', governments in the East Asian
countries are found pushing and pulling (in varying degrees) all the
levers of industrial policy at their disposal, but to what effect? That
is undoubtedly the most important question raised by their success.
Removing obstacles clearly works, but whether erecting those
same obstacles in the first instance contributed positively, directly
or indirectly, is an open question.

Governments did play a crucial role in determining economic
performance. Aside from everything else, fulfilling the minimal
duties of government, including the provision of infrastructure and
the maintenance of macroeconomic stability, is undoubtedly a
necessary condition for success. This is no mean feat in itself, but
when compounded by the complex task of having to anticipate and
offset the market distortions that result from *dirigiste* strategies of
industrialization, the burden on government is all that much
greater. Little wonder then that, after sifting through the accumulated historical evidence on 100 years of development in forty-two
contemporary developing countries, Reynolds (1983:976) concluded that 'My hypothesis is that the single most important explanatory variable [in economic development] is political
organization and the administrative competence of government'.

Neo-classical economics vindicated?

After reviewing the post-war development experiences of the eight

East Asian countries, admittedly rather superficially, I am persuaded that Reynolds's hypothesis is right. But I see this in no way a contradiction to the proposition that neo-classical economic principles are alive and well, and working particularly effectively in the East Asian countries. Once public goods are provided for and the most obvious distortions corrected, markets seem to do the job of allocating resources reasonably well, and certainly better than centralized decision-making. That is evident in East Asia, and in most other parts of the developing and industrial world, and is after all the main tenet of neo-classical economics.

Are the East Asian countries more successful than other countries because they give *relatively* more scope to the market, or because they have a superior culture, or alternatively because their governments are more authoritarian and more dedicated to growth? The answer is probably 'yes'; all these were the tumblers in the combination lock that would bring about unparalleled rates of growth. Trying to decipher the relative contribution of each is an interesting exercise, but it is perhaps mainly academic. Even if the latter two hypotheses were dominant, the policy lessons of the East Asian experience would be as valid. As Timmer (1973:76) has aptly quipped, ' "Getting relative prices" right is not the end of economic development. But "getting prices wrong" frequently is.' That is as true for democratic as it is for authoritarian countries, and as true for countries without as for those with a Confucian heritage. The policy lessons that derive from the experiences of the East Asian countries are simple and clear-cut, and for that reason are all too readily ignored or dismissed.

2

INDUSTRIALIZATION AND GROWTH:
ALTERNATIVE VIEWS OF EAST ASIA

East Asia encompasses a variety of post-war development experiences. It is best known for its four super-exporters – Hong Kong, Republic of Korea, Singapore and Taiwan – which have developed an effective pattern of outward-oriented industrialization. It also includes countries such as Malaysia, Thailand and Indonesia, which have been quite successful with more traditional strategies of resource-based development, as well as China, until recently an example of autarkic growth. In all these cases, comparisons with countries outside the region can help to separate the common features of economies at a similar stage in development from the effects of particular policies.

To learn from this diverse experience, we need a common theoretical framework if not a fully articulated model of each country. Here I will start from the suggestion of Little (1982:26) that development theories can be regarded as a spectrum ranging from neo-classical to structuralist, with many analyses and policy prescriptions having elements of both. Since no single framework seems to fit the range of East Asian experience and available data, I will draw on models from different points in the spectrum. This approach can be described as the method of model-based comparisons. Perhaps the best-known example is the series of country studies stemming from Solow's (1957) neo-classical growth equation, which is taken up first.

The drawback to adopting a single analytical framework is that it limits the range of questions and initial conditions that can be explored. For example, the pure neo-classical model tells us little about the kinds of structural disequilibria that prevailed in most

39

developing countries in the 1950s, since it is based on assumptions that ensure the maintenance of equilibrium in factor and product markets. Simple structuralist models based on input–output relations have the corresponding limitation of ignoring substitution possibilities and not being able to analyse the effects of price changes.

My proposed solution to this dilemma is to use three models to organize the experience of East Asian countries and to compare them to other industrializing countries.[1] The first two models are close to the neo-classical and structuralist ends of Little's spectrum and therefore tend to focus on different aspects of development. Each is applied to a range of semi-industrial countries. The third model incorporates a mixture of neo-classical and structural specifications in order to simulate the effects of alternative policies in a given country.

STRUCTURAL TRANSFORMATION

East Asian countries can be regarded as successes as much for the efficient ways in which they have transformed their economic structures as for the rapid rate of growth that was maintained during the process. Following Kuznets (1966), I define structural transformation as a set of changes in the composition of demand, trade, production and factor use that is needed to sustain economic growth (Chenery 1979: chapter 1). This paper focuses on the ways in which an efficient transformation can lead to accelerated growth from different initial conditions. The central feature is the approach taken to industrialization.

In a general equilibrium system, the nature and timing of industrialization are affected by changes in domestic demand, shifts in comparative advantage, sectoral productivity growth, and the accumulation of capital. It will be shown that the largest variations in the transformation can be traced to differences in industrialization and trade policy. In an efficient transformation, industrialization may be deferred because of the availability of resource-based exports – as in Thailand and Indonesia – or accelerated by the need

---

[1] This paper is based largely on results of a World Bank research project on 'Sources of Industrial Growth'. A summary volume, *Industrialization and Growth: A Comparative Study*, by H. Chenery, S. Robinson and M. Syrquin is now in press. The three models are described in chapters 2, 3 and 11 of that volume.

to shift to other sources of foreign exchange – as in the Republic of Korea and Taiwan.

Although its timing varies considerably, a period of industrialization constitutes a logical stage in the transformation of virtually all developing countries. It is manifested historically by rising shares of manufactures in consumer demand, production, exports and employment. By way of illustration, Table 2.1 gives measures of these structural characteristics in 1960 for ten East Asian countries and fifteen other semi-industrial countries. The East Asian group ranges from Japan, which joined the ranks of the industrial countries some time in the fifties, to Indonesia, which has recently moved into a period of accelerated industrialization.

The factors affecting the relations between growth and structural change are outlined later in the paper. Transformation is most rapid when shifts in internal demand towards manufactures are augmented by similar changes in the composition of trade as in the Republic of Korea, Taiwan, Brazil and Turkey. It is retarded – and occasionally reversed – when comparative advantage does not work in this direction, as in Indonesia, Venezuela and other mineral producers. A slow-down of the transformation and subsequent decline in the share of manufactures in production and employment marks the end of the industrialization stage, at least as it is reflected in the post-war experience of the OECD countries.

Neo-classical growth theory has little to say about structural transformation. As long as factors receive equal remuneration in different markets, the required shifts of resources from one sector and location to another will have little effect on total output. Growth is determined almost entirely by factors on the supply side – capital accumulation, human resource development, and productivity growth – and the economic structure is assumed to adjust smoothly to shifts in internal and external demand.

Structural analysis differs in that it investigates the working of mechanisms of accumulation and allocation in specific cases rather than taking them as given by assumption. The form of comparative analysis initiated by Clark (1940) and Kuznets (1957) has led to the identification of a number of common structural features – now called 'stylized facts' – that suggest the underlying constraints that affect the success of the transformation. Their explanation requires the disaggregation of commodities and sectors according to differences in demand, tradability and factor use.

Table 2.1 Indices of industrialization and growth, 1960–80

Country	Population 1980 (million)	GNP growth 1960–80 (%)	Structural change (1960)									
			Production				Exports		Employment			
			Primary S_p	$\triangle S_p$	Manufacturing S_m	$\triangle S_m$	Manufacturing E_m	$\triangle E_m$	Agriculture L_a	$\triangle L_a$	Manufacturing L_m	$\triangle L_m$
East Asia												
Japan	117	8.0	13	−10	34	−4	79	17	33	−21	30	9
Singapore	2	8.6	4	−2	12	17	26	25	8	−6	23	16
Hong Kong	5	9.4	4	−3	27	—	80	17	8	−5	52	5
Taiwan	18	9.6	31	−22	22	20	10	39	56	−37	11	32
Malaysia	14	7.2	41	−9	9	14	6	12	63	−13	12	4
Korea, Republic of	38	9.1	39	−22	14	14	14	75	66	−32	9	20
Philippines	49	5.7	27	−1	20	5	4	30	61	−15	15	2
Thailand	47	7.8	41	−13	13	7	2	23	84	−8	4	5
Indonesia	147	6.2	56	−1	8	1	—	3	75	−17	8	4
China	977	5.5	47	−9	31	15	..	..	..	..	..	..
Latin America												
Venezuela	15	5.5	27	3	16	—	—	1	35	−17	22	5
Argentina	28	3.2	17	−3	32	1	4	20	20	−7	36	−8
Chile	11	3.4	21	−5	28	−7	4	16	30	−11	20	−1
Mexico	70	6.2	21	−5	19	5	12	27	55	−19	20	6
Brazil	119	6.9	17	−4	26	13	3	36	52	−22	15	9
Colombia	27	5.5	38	−8	17	5	2	20	51	−25	19	2
Peru	17	4.0	24	−1	24	13	1	10	52	−12	20	−9

Other

Spain	37	5400	5.6	23	-16	27	1	22	51	42	-27	31	9
Israel	4	4500	6.1	11	-6	23	3	61	19	14	-7	35	1
Greece	10	4380	5.9	24	-5	16	3	10	36	56	-19	20	8
Yugoslavia	22	2620	5.8	24	-13	36	-7	37	35	63	-34	18	17
Portugal	10	2370	5.4	25	-12	29	7	55	21	44	-20	29	7
Turkey	45	1470	6.0	43	-18	13	9	3	25	78	-24	11	2
Ivory Coast	8	1150	7.4	45	-18	7	4	1	7	89	-10	2	2
Egypt	40	580	5.8	29	-7	20	8	12	8	58	-8	12	18

S_p = Share of primary sectors (agriculture and mining) in value added.
S_m = Share of manufacturing in value added.
E_m = Share of manufacturers in merchandise exports.
L_a = Share of agriculture in total labour force.
L_m = Share of industry in total labour force.
$\triangle$ = Change in share (1960–80).
Sources: World Development Report, 1982 (World Bank, various years); Chenery, Robinson and Syrquin (in press: chapter 4).

The following sections illustrate the comparative insights that are attainable by applying different models to some of the twenty-five industrializing countries shown in Table 2.1. When neo-classical and structural approaches are applied to the same historical experience, they must be consistent even though they may stress different interpretations. Conflict between the two approaches may arise when they are used as a basis for judging future policy. The general neo-classical position is that, if policy is focused on achieving well-functioning markets, equilibrium will be maintained and the corollaries of neo-classical theory will provide sufficient guides for resource allocation. There is thus no need to analyse the structural transformation in any detail because it does not affect the general direction of policy. Little's spectrum of intermediate cases can be derived from this extreme position by introducing specific assumptions about the nature of demand, trade or factor mobility and determining their effects, starting from the existing structure of a given economy.[2]

EQUILIBRIUM GROWTH

The aggregate neo-classical model of a closed economy has been the main vehicle for studying the sources of growth for the past thirty years. A central feature of this model is that supply and demand adjust continuously to market forces so as to maintain equilibrium in product and factor markets. As a result, increases in output can be attributed entirely to increases in factor inputs and to their rising productivity. Industrialization will only modify this result if it is associated with higher or lower productivity growth or if the transformation involves a departure from the equilibrium assumptions.

Solow's (1957) version of the neo-classical model has provided the basis for estimates of the sources of growth in more than forty countries. While these studies concentrated initially on the industrial countries, they have now been extended to cover some twenty developing countries as well. These results provide a preliminary set of hypotheses as to the differences in growth processes between industrial and developing countries, including a number in East Asia. They also provide a point of departure for testing the

[2] The neo-classical analysis of 'Dutch Disease' illustrates the benefits of introducing structural assumptions applying to a group of countries (Corden and Neary 1982).

significance of industrialization and other structural features omitted from the closed neo-classical model.

Solow's equation for neo-classical (or equilibrium) growth takes the following form (Solow 1957):

(1) $$G_v = G_a + \eta_k\, G_k + \eta_L\, G_L$$

where G_v, G_k and G_I are the growth rates of value added, capital and labour respectively. The growth of total factor productivity, G_a, is measured by the difference between G_v and the weighted sum of input growth. Each coefficient η_i is defined as the elasticity of output with respect to input η_i, a formulation that can be extended to any number of inputs. Under equilibrium conditions the coefficient η_i is equal to the share of input i in the total product. Since output elasticities are rarely estimated directly, product shares are normally used in empirical estimates of the growth equation. Improvements in the neo-classical approach to growth accounting have allowed for differences in quality and productivity of different types of labour and capital.

A set of fifty-seven estimates of this equation covering thirty-nine countries is used in Chenery, Robinson and Syrquin (in press: chapter 2) to compare the growth processes of developing countries to those of industrial economies. Estimates for the six East Asian countries in this set are shown in Table 2.2 along with those of semi-industrial countries in other regions. If we accept the neo-classical assumptions, these results will provide a basis for comparing the East Asian experience with that of other countries.

Developing versus industrial countries

The average values for the principal elements in equation (1) are shown in Table 2.2 for twelve industrial and twenty semi-industrial countries.[3] Overall growth was somewhat higher in the sample of semi-industrial countries (6.3 per cent versus 5.4 per cent), which is consistent with the full samples of both groups in the period 1953–73. The average growth of capital is about the same for both groups

[3] The original studies covered periods of ten to fifteen years between 1950 and 1975. Whenever possible, two periods per country are included in the averages, giving nineteen observations for twelve industrial countries and thirty observations for twenty developing countries. Except for East Asia only the most recent observations are shown in Table 2.2.

Table 2.2 Sources of growth: selected economies

Country	Observed period	GNP growth (%) (1953–73)	GNP growth (%) Observed period	Capital $\eta_k G_k$	Capital %	Labour $\eta_L G_L$	Labour %	Productivity G_a	Productivity %	Factor inputs	External policy
East Asia											
1 Japan	1960–73	(9.0)	10.9	4.8	(44)	1.6	(15)	4.5	(41)	6.4 (59)	N
2 Singapore	1972–80	(9.3)	8.0	5.8	(72)	2.1	(27)	—		8.0 (100)	M
Hong Kong	1955–60		8.3					2.4	(29)	5.9 (71)	M
3 Hong Kong	1960–70	(8.8)	9.1	3.0	(33)	1.8	(20)	4.3	(47)	4.8 (53)	M
4 Taiwan	1955–60	(8.2)	5.2	1.1	(21)	1.0	(20)	3.1	(60)	2.1 (40)	M
6 Korea, Republic of	1955–60		4.2					2.0	(47)	2.2 (53)	I
6 Korea, Republic of	1960–73	(7.5)	9.7	2.4	(25)	3.2	(33)	4.1	(42)	5.6 (58)	M
7 Philippines	1947–65	(5.6)	5.8					2.5	(44)	3.3 (56)	I
Latin America											
11 Venezuela	1960–74	(6.3)	5.1	4.1	(82)	0.3	(5)	0.6	(12)	4.4 (88)	P
12 Argentina	1960–74	(3.6)	4.1	2.7	(68)	0.6	(15)	0.7	(17)	3.3 (83)	I
13 Chile	1960–74	(4.0)	4.4	2.4	(55)	0.8	(18)	1.2	(27)	3.2 (73)	I
14 Mexico	1960–74	(6.4)	5.6	2.5	(45)	1.0	(18)	2.1	(38)	3.5 (63)	I
15 Brazil	1960–74	(6.8)	7.3	4.3	(59)	1.6	(21)	1.6	(21)	5.7 (80)	I
16 Colombia	1960–74	(4.9)	5.6	2.5	(44)	1.0	(19)	2.1	(38)	3.5 (62)	N
17 Peru	1960–70	(5.7)	5.3	3.1	(58)	1.8	(15)	1.5	(28)	3.8 (73)	I
Other											
18 Spain	1959–65	(6.5)	11.2	3.5	(31)	2.6	(23)	5.0	(45)	6.2 (55)	N
19 Israel	1952–65	(8.8)	10.4	3.7	(36)	2.9	(28)	3.6	(35)	6.7 (65)	N
20 Greece	1951–65	(7.0)	6.9	3.3	(48)	1.2	(17)	2.4	(35)	4.5 (65)	N
23 Turkey	1963–75	(5.9)	6.4	3.8	(59)	0.5	(7)	2.2	(35)	4.2 (65)	I
20 semi-industrial countries (Number of observations = 30)			6.3	2.5	(40)	1.8	(29)	2.0	(31)		
12 industrial countries (Number of observations = 19)			5.4	2.0	(37)	0.7	(12)	2.7	(49)		

Notes: Policies: N = Neutral, P = Primary-oriented, M = Manufacturing-oriented, I = Inward.

Sources: Chenery, Robinson and Syrquin (in press: chapter 2: Table 2); Christensen, Cummins and Jorgensen (1980); Elias (1978).

(5.5 per cent), but labour growth is much higher in the developing countries, even with allowance for quality improvements.

Using the results of Christensen, Cummings and Jorgensen (1980), which make full allowance for the improved quality of labour,[4] the most striking difference in growth processes between the two groups is the relatively large contribution of total factor productivity in industrial countries. Even with these adjustments, half of the growth of industrial countries is attributable to total productivity growth in contrast to 30 per cent in the developing countries.

The case of Japan is particularly interesting, since in 1960 it still had some of the characteristics of a semi-industrial country. In comparison to the other industrial countries, Japan's growth rate was twice as fast as the average for the period 1960–73. The increment of 5.5 percentage points over the average was due in fairly equal proportions to all three elements in the Solow equation, with half of it coming from the more rapid increase in capital.

It is often suggested that the Republic of Korea is following a development strategy similar to that of Japan, but this does not show up in the sources of growth data of Table 2.2. The Republic of Korea's increase of 3.4 percentage points over the average of all semi-industrial countries (SICs) is due primarily to higher productivity growth (4.1 per cent versus 2.0 per cent) and not at all to higher investment.[5]

Effects of policy

Although the neo-classical model does not make explicit allowance for policy differences, we can classify countries by external (or other) policies to see whether they are associated with differences in growth or productivity. For this purpose a trade-based classification into manufacturing (M) outward-oriented, primary-oriented (P), inward (I), and neutral (N) is shown in the last column of Table 2.2.[6]

[4] For the advanced countries, the addition of quality improvement terms to equation (1) adds 25 per cent to the growth of the capital stock and offsets the decline in the average hours worked. For the developing countries of Latin America, Elias (1978) attributes a smaller proportion of input growth to quality improvements.

[5] This comparison cannot be made for Taiwan, since the available study covers only 1955–60.

[6] A more complete analysis is given in Chenery and Syrquin (in press: chapter 4).

We first examine the characteristics of the notably efficient SICs: those with total factor productivity growth (TFPG) more than 50 per cent above the average of 2.0 per cent. There are six of these, falling into two groups:

(1) Outward-oriented manufacturing: Hong Kong, Taiwan and Republic of Korea; and
(2) Neutral: Israel, Japan and Spain.

These results are consistent with several hypotheses, including the advantages of outward-oriented policies and the effects of shifting resources out of agriculture to higher productivity sectors. One exception to these findings is Singapore, which apparently achieved high growth in the seventies entirely through increasing capital and labour. Tsao (1982) offers several possible explanations for these results.

To pursue this analysis further, it is necessary to go beyond the simple aggregate neo-classical model and test the effects of including structural elements such as increasing openness or shifts from agriculture to manufacturing. These topics are taken up in the next section.

DETERMINANTS OF INDUSTRIALIZATION

The structuralist view of successful development gives as much weight to the country's ability to reallocate resources effectively as it does to resource mobilization. The extent to which past resource allocation has been inefficient is reflected in the variation in returns to factors in different uses and in periodic shortages of imports and other essential commodities. Such evidences of disequilibrium were widespread in the 1950s, but they also presented opportunities to accelerate growth by more efficient allocation. One of the stylized facts to be explained is the acceleration of growth that took place in the sixties in East Asia and other SICs.

Although the neo-classical assumptions simplify the task of modelling, the identification of departures from them makes it more difficult. The present section is therefore limited to elucidating the demand side of structural transformation, which is usually omitted from empirical applications of neo-classical models. The approach is analogous to the supply-side growth accounting of the previous section in that it provides a uniform basis for country comparisons.

A model of industrialization

To simplify the problem of modelling structural transformation, the task can be divided into two parts: an explanation of the rate of growth (treated in aggregate terms in the preceding section); and an explanation of changes in the economic structure. In this context, the purpose of a model of industrialization is to explain the changing composition of production as the level of income rises. For historical analysis, this produces a form of demand-side growth accounting in which the growth of each sector depends on demand functions, changes in trade patterns, and technological change, each related to the level of per capita income.

As was shown above, growth accounting becomes more useful if it also identifies the sources of uniformities in the development process. Of the three factors explaining industrialization, the domestic demand and input–output relations show considerable uniformity, while trade patterns are the main source of diversity. The accounting system can be converted into a model by specifying these relations as functions of income and other variables.

The system of growth accounting from the demand side is based on the following accounting identity for each sector of production:

(2) $\quad X_i = D_i + (E_i - M_i) + \Sigma_j X_{ij}$

where

$\quad X_i$ = gross output of sector i

$\quad D_i$ = domestic final demand (consumption plus investment)

$\quad (E_i - M_i)$ = net trade (exports minus competitive imports)

$\quad \Sigma_j X_{ij} = \Sigma_j \, a_{ij} \, X_j$ = intermediate use of commodity i by sector j

$\quad (a_{ij}$ is assumed to vary with the level of per capita income)

$\quad a_{ij}$ = input–output coefficients.

The properties of the input–output system make it possible to eliminate intermediate demand as a separate source of growth by attributing it to the elements of final demand (Chenery 1979: chapter 3; Chenery, Robinson and Syrquin in press: chapter 5). In this way the increase in production of sector i is equated to the sum of four factors:

(i) the *expansion of domestic demand* (DD), which includes the direct demand for commodity i plus the indirect effects on sector i of the expansion of domestic demand in other sectors;

(ii) *export expansion* (EE), or the total effect on output from
      sector i of increasing exports;
(iii) *import substitution* (IS), or the total effect on output from
      sector i of increasing the proportion of demand in each sector
      that is supplied from domestic production;
(iv) *technological change* (IO), or the total effect on sector i of
      changing input–output coefficients throughout the economy
      as wages and income levels rise.

Of these four factors, the one with the strongest basis in theory is
(i) domestic demand, for which generalized systems of Engel functions have been estimated in many countries (see Lluch, Powell
and Williams 1977).

The usefulness of this form of growth accounting depends largely
on the way the economy is disaggregated. In order to concentrate
on differences in external policy, we have stressed the more tradable commodities, which constitute seventeen of twenty-four sectors in our uniform accounting system. In Table 2.3 countries are
compared in terms of three tradable sectors (primary products,
light industry and heavy industry) and one aggregate of non-
tradables (services). Since the latter group typically has an income
elasticity close to unity, it must expand in proportion to GNP but
cannot constitute a leading sector over a long period.

To allow for differences in time periods and growth rates, the historical analysis of sources of growth from the demand side is shown
in Table 2.3 as a percentage of the total increase in output in each
country. The row totals show the contribution of a given sector to
aggregate growth, while the column totals show the contribution of
each of the four components. In the Republic of Korea (1955–73),
for example, exports of light manufactures contributed 15 per cent
of the increase in aggregate output; light manufactures as a whole
contributed 33 per cent; and exports as a whole contributed 35 per
cent.[7]

Country comparisons

The summary comparisons of nine countries in Table 2.3 are designed to demonstrate the differences between internal factors

---

[7] The results are expressed here as shares of aggregate gross output to correspond
with equation (2); an analysis in terms of value added is needed to reconcile the
demand-side and supply-side accounts (see Chenery, Robinson and Syrquin, in
press: chapter 3).

(domestic demand and changes in input–output coefficients) and external factors (export expansion and import substitution) in determining the allocation of resources among sectors. At one extreme are two large countries that have been following inward-oriented policies – Mexico and Turkey. Here internal factors constitute 90 per cent of the total demand and the results are not significantly changed by the inclusion of the external factors. At the other extreme are the outward-oriented economies of Israel, Taiwan and Republic of Korea, where exports account for 35–40 per cent of the increase in total demand. Pre-war Japan followed a similar pattern but with much less rapid growth over the period studied (1914–35).

The second basis for comparison is the pattern of balance of payments adjustment revealed by the composition of the export and import substitution vectors. From previous studies we have identified three typical patterns: a *large country* (L) pattern, usually inward-oriented; a *primary-oriented* (P) pattern based on natural resource exports; and a *manufacturing-oriented, outward-looking* (M) pattern (see Chenery and Syrquin (1975) and Chenery, Robinson and Syrquin (in press: chapter 4)). The M pattern specializes in light manufactures, as in pre-war Japan, Israel, Taiwan and the Republic of Korea; most of the large countries tend to give relatively more emphasis to heavy manufactures, as in Yugoslavia, Turkey and post-war Japan.

Since the demand-side decomposition of the sources of growth is only available for some ten countries, we have sought to supplement it with a model of a representative economy based on cross-country estimates of the separate relations involved. The parameters that determine the internal structure, consisting of the variation in domestic demand (D_i) and input–output coefficients (a_{ij}) with the level of income, are assumed to be independent of the external structure. For the latter, we have made separate estimates of the level and composition of imports and exports, based on samples of twenty countries or more for each of the three typical patterns.

The solutions to these three specifications of the cross-country model given in Table 2.4 constitute 'representative' or 'standard' patterns to which the experience of individual countries can be compared. Although the representative patterns are derived from a rather simple model, they incorporate the experience of a large

Table 2.3 *Sources of growth for sample economies* (per cent)

Country	Sector	Growth rate	DD	EE	IS	IO	Sum
Colombia	Primary	4.5	12.7	9.1	0.5	0.1	22.4
(1953–70)	Light	6.8	15.3	1.5	1.5	3.0	21.3
	Heavy	11.1	9.0	0.8	4.5	1.7	16.0
	Services	5.5	36.7	2.6	0.3	0.7	40.3
	Total	5.9	73.7	14.0	6.8	5.5	100.0
Mexico	Primary	4.8	12.8	0.7	−0.3	−0.5	12.7
(1950–75)	Light	6.0	17.7	0.4	0.5	0.7	19.3
	Heavy	10.8	16.7	1.8	2.9	1.3	22.7
	Services	6.4	43.7	0.7	0.4	0.5	45.3
	Total	6.5	90.9	3.6	3.5	2.0	100.0
Turkey	Primary	2.5	14.9	1.2	0.2	−4.5	11.8
(1953–73)	Light	6.7	15.3	2.1	0.4	1.7	19.5
	Heavy	9.6	18.8	0.9	1.6	3.4	24.7
	Services	6.7	38.3	2.8	0.2	2.7	44.0
	Total	5.9	87.3	7.0	2.4	3.3	100.0
Yugoslavia	Primary	2.6	10.1	3.9	−3.2	−4.6	6.2
(1962–72)	Light	11.0	17.7	6.2	−2.6	1.3	22.6
	Heavy	13.6	23.6	12.2	−6.1	4.4	34.1
	Services	8.8	33.0	5.2	−1.3	0.2	37.1
	Total	8.7	84.4	27.5	−13.2	1.3	100.0
Japan (1)	Primary	1.9	7.6	2.8	−2.3	2.3	10.4
(1914–35)	Light	4.6	15.8	10.5	0.2	−0.4	26.1
	Heavy	8.1	15.2	4.4	1.9	−3.3	18.2
	Services	4.2	35.2	9.0	−0.2	1.3	45.3
	Total	4.1	73.8	26.7	−0.4	−0.1	100.0
Japan (2)	Primary	2.2	4.4	0.5	−1.5	−1.9	1.5
(1955–72)	Light	8.6	14.4	2.0	−0.7	1.1	16.8
	Heavy	18.0	30.9	8.4	−0.1	3.3	42.5
	Services	11.4	35.7	3.0	−0.8	1.3	39.2
	Total	11.5	85.4	13.9	−3.1	3.8	100.0
Korea, Rep. of	Primary	5.7	12.0	3.0	−1.7	−2.5	10.8
(1955–73)	Light	13.6	19.7	15.1	—	−1.9	32.9
	Heavy	22.1	11.1	10.7	1.4	1.9	25.1
	Services	10.3	25.6	6.2	0.2	−0.8	31.2
	Total	11.2	68.4	35.0	−0.1	−3.3	100.0
Taiwan	Primary	7.1	8.8	5.3	−2.0	−1.8	10.3
(1956–71)	Light	13.6	12.7	17.5	0.6	2.0	32.8
	Heavy	22.5	10.2	13.5	2.4	1.0	27.1
	Services	9.7	23.6	7.1	0.1	−1.0	29.8
	Total	12.0	55.3	43.4	1.1	0.2	100.0

Israel	Primary	6.4	2.6	3.6	−0.3	−0.4	5.5
(1958–72)	Light	11.2	11.3	12.0	−2.0	1.2	22.5
	Heavy	14.3	18.7	6.3	−6.6	2.6	21.0
	Services	8.9	39.3	13.9	−1.6	−0.6	51.0
	Total	9.9	71.9	35.8	−10.5	2.8	100.0
Norway	Primary	2.5	3.8	2.4	−1.7	0.3	4.8
(1953–69)	Light	3.7	14.0	6.2	−5.7	3.0	17.5
	Heavy	7.2	10.7	15.6	−2.2	2.2	26.3
	Services	4.8	31.9	21.5	−2.7	0.7	51.4
	Total	4.7	60.4	45.7	−12.3	6.2	100.0

DD = expansion of domestic demand
EE = export expansion
IS = import substitution
IO = technological change
Source: Chenery, Robinson and Syrquin (in press: Table 6–4).

number of developing countries and simulate the whole range of the transformation (from income levels of US$140 to US$2100 in 1970 prices). A comparison of Tables 2.3 and 2.4 leads to the identification of similarities between each prototype and the countries that are closest to it. Pre-war Japan, the Republic of Korea and Taiwan can all be compared to the early stages of the outward-oriented manufacturing pattern (SM). The export contribution to growth (27 per cent) is almost the same in Japan (1) and the (SM) model and somewhat higher in the Republic of Korea (35 per cent) and Taiwan (43 per cent). All show the specialization in light manufactures that is characteristic of this group. The contribution of domestic demand (DD), the other large component, varies inversely with exports in cases of trade liberalization (negative import substitution) – in Israel, Norway and Yugoslavia.

A comparison of the rows in the two tables provides measures of the different patterns of industrialization. Each row total is equal to the growth rate of the sector weighted by its average share in aggregate output. In all the country examples, primary production grows less rapidly and manufacturing more rapidly than GNP, as it does in all of the standard patterns. In the primary-oriented pattern (illustrated by Colombia) primary exports reduce this trend and defer industrialization.

Effects of specialization

The net effect of the difference in specialization among the three

Table 2.4 Sources of growth: cross-country model (per cent)

Income range (US$)	Sector	Large (L)					Small manufacturing (SM)					Small primary (SP)				
		DD	EE	IS	IO	Sum	DD	EE	IS	IO	Sum	DD	EE	IS	IO	Sum
140–280	Primary	11.0	2.4	—	-0.8	12.6	9.4	5.7	-1.9	-0.5	12.7	10.0	12.9	—	-0.5	22.4
	Light	19.8	2.7	1.1	1.7	25.3	18.2	8.5	1.1	1.5	29.3	18.4	1.8	1.8	1.7	23.7
	Heavy	9.5	1.5	3.0	1.3	15.3	2.5	1.2	-0.6	0.2	3.3	4.0	0.8	2.6	0.8	8.2
	Services	42.9	2.6	0.5	0.8	46.8	44.0	10.1	-0.7	1.3	54.7	40.9	3.2	0.5	1.1	45.7
	Total	83.2	9.2	4.6	3.0	100.0	74.1	25.5	-2.1	2.5	100.0	73.3	18.7	4.9	3.1	100.0
280–560	Primary	8.8	1.5	-0.6	-0.7	9.0	6.3	4.5	-2.0	-0.9	7.9	7.7	11.4	-0.4	-0.5	18.2
	Light	20.3	3.3	0.6	1.4	25.6	18.2	9.8	1.2	1.1	30.3	18.9	2.5	1.3	1.4	24.1
	Heavy	12.7	2.8	2.0	1.6	19.1	3.6	2.9	2.8	0.5	9.8	6.9	1.3	3.1	1.1	12.4
	Services	42.8	2.9	0.2	0.4	46.3	41.9	10.3	-0.3	0.1	52.0	40.7	3.3	0.4	0.9	45.3
	Total	84.6	10.5	2.2	2.7	100.0	70.0	27.5	1.7	0.8	100.0	74.2	18.5	4.4	2.9	100.0
560–1120	Primary	7.3	1.0	-1.1	-0.8	6.4	4.3	3.1	-2.1	-0.7	4.6	6.3	9.0	-0.7	-0.7	13.9
	Light	20.5	4.0	0.2	0.9	25.6	17.5	10.6	1.3	0.9	30.3	18.8	3.4	0.9	1.1	24.2
	Heavy	15.3	4.3	1.4	1.8	22.8	6.5	5.5	4.3	0.9	17.2	10.9	1.6	3.3	1.6	17.4
	Services	42.0	3.3	-0.1	—	45.2	39.4	9.2	-0.1	-0.6	47.9	40.8	3.0	0.3	0.4	44.5
	Total	85.1	12.6	0.4	1.9	100.0	67.7	28.4	3.4	0.5	100.0	76.8	17.0	3.8	2.4	100.0
1120–2100	Primary	6.2	0.8	-1.2	-0.6	5.2	3.2	1.8	-1.7	-0.5	2.8	5.5	5.9	-0.6	-0.7	10.1
	Light	20.2	5.1	-0.1	0.6	25.8	16.4	10.6	1.4	0.9	29.3	18.1	4.5	0.7	1.0	24.3
	Heavy	17.4	5.6	1.0	2.1	26.1	10.2	8.7	5.4	1.4	25.7	15.7	1.5	3.3	2.4	22.9
	Services	40.2	3.6	-0.3	-0.6	42.9	36.1	7.0	0.2	-1.1	42.2	40.4	2.4	0.2	-0.3	42.7
	Total	84.0	15.1	-0.6	1.5	100.0	65.9	28.1	5.3	0.7	100.0	79.7	14.3	3.6	2.4	100.0

Note: Aggregate growth of GDP is assumed to be the same for each pattern in a given period.
Source: Chenery, Robinson and Syrquin (in press: Table 6-3).

54

Table 2.5 *Effects of alternative trade patterns on sources of growth* (income level of $560)

Sector	Standard pattern		L pattern		SM pattern		SP pattern	
	ρ_i	ρ_iG_i/G	ρ_i	ρ_iG_i/G	ρ_i	ρ_iG_i/G	ρ_i	ρ_iG_i/G
Primary	21	14	16	11	15	9	26	20
			(−5)	(−3)	(−6)	(−5)	(+5)	(+6)
Light manufacture	16	18	17	18	19	21	15	16
			(+1)	(−)	(+3)	(+3)	(−1)	(−2)
Heavy manufacture	9	12	13	16	6	10	8	11
			(+4)	(+4)	(−3)	(−2)	(−1)	(−1)
Non-traded	55	56	54	55	60	60	51	53
			(−1)	(−1)	(+5)	(+4)	(−3)	(−3)

L   = large
SM = small manufacturing
SP = small primary
Note: Changes from the standard pattern are shown in parentheses.
Source: Chenery, Robinson and Syrquin (in press: Table 3–7).

prototype patterns can be measured by the differences in the sectoral sources of growth (ρ_iG_i) or by the output shares (ρ_i) at a given level of income. For example, the SP export pattern in Table 2.4 has a level of primary exports 50 per cent above the average, but this represents a shift of value added of only 5 per cent from other sectors.

Table 2.5 shows the extent of variation in the structure of production that is associated with the three typical trade patterns of Table 2.4 at a point midway in the structural transformation. The first column gives the share of value added in each sector and compares it to the standard production pattern. The second column shows the contribution that each sector makes to aggregate growth. These figures indicate the extent to which resource allocation throughout the economy is affected by intercountry differences in trade patterns.

The input–output model that generates these results constitutes a first step towards a structuralist model of development. It assumes that all components of domestic demand can be described by Engel functions of per capita income and that these demands, plus the indirect inputs needed to produce them, must be supplied from either domestic production or imports. The effects of resource endowments and external policies on imports and exports are analysed separately and introduced into the solution as exogenous variables or parameters.

What have we learned from this type of analysis? The initial motivation for the present study was to create a simulation model based largely on pre-war Japanese experience that could help to evaluate alternative development strategies. In addition to its demand constraints, the effects of differences in resources and trade policies can be introduced into the model as supply limitations or as a reflection of different policies (protection versus export promotion).

The country studies summarized in Table 2.3 permit us to compare the experience of two of the East Asian super-exporters, Republic of Korea and Taiwan, to pre-war Japan and to the cross-country simulation of typical outward-oriented policies (SM in Table 2.4). In most respects, Israel (1958–72) shows the effects of similar policies. This common strategy can be described as developing a comparative advantage in light manufacturing to offset limited agricultural and mineral resources. Assuming primary production to be the main factor limiting their growth in the long run, this strategy has enabled the three East Asian countries to achieve a growth rate about double the growth of primary production over the observed period of 15–20 years.

The total effects of export expansion on the economic structures of the four countries (including Israel) have been quite similar. Concentration on light manufactured exports has the net effect on resource allocation already noted in the SM pattern of Table 2.5. It is modified in the case of Israel by high capital inflows that permitted import liberalization over this period.

While the input–output model shows the magnitude of structural change in each country, it does not provide direct evidence of its efficiency nor of the effects of different policies. For this purpose it is necessary to turn to a more complete model of general equilibrium.

SUCCESSFUL INDUSTRIALIZATION

Successful industrialization is one aspect of effective development. In comparing countries with different productive structures, some features of successful policies may turn out to be quite similar while others are sensitive to the initial conditions. The empirical techniques used up to now have identified some of the common features of effective development, but they cannot determine the effects of individual policies.

In East Asia there are two groups of relatively successful, industrializing countries: the resource-poor exporters of manufactured products that I have called the SM type (Hong Kong, Taiwan, Singapore and Republic of Korea), and the primary-oriented or P type (Malaysia, Thailand and Indonesia).[8] The following section summarizes some aspects of successful performance in the two groups. I will then simulate the effects of different policies in the SM case, using a computable general equilibrium model based on the structure of the economy of the Republic of Korea in the early 1960s. These simulations try to quantify the effects of several policies thought to have been important to successful industrial performance in the Republic of Korea and Taiwan, such as the shift from inward- to outward-oriented policies and the inflow of foreign capital. My purpose is to suggest plausible orders of magnitude for these effects and to show how they vary with different specifications of the underlying model.

Successful performance

For resource-poor countries, success requires the creation of a base for non-primary (manufacturing or service) exports and their subsequent expansion to pay for increased imports. Since, in this pattern of development, the change in the composition of external trade augments the changes in internal demand, successful M countries in Table 2.1 have all had high rates of industrialization (although much of it may have taken place before 1960, as in Hong Kong and Israel). At an early stage, growth of manufacturing becomes more important than growth of primary production, and the performance of the economy is increasingly dominated by success in expanding manufactured exports. Tables 2.3 and 2.4 suggest that this phenomenon is twice as important in SM countries as in the other two groups.

The availability of resource-based exports leads to quite a different P pattern of structural change, as shown in Table 2.5. The in-

[8] The same distinction is made in Seiji Naya's paper in this volume which compares the trade performance of these two groups.

itial comparative advantage in primary exports makes it more efficient to defer industrialization until it becomes profitable at anticipated world prices and exchange rates. However, it is hard to find countries that have followed this type of policy: the predominant tendency has been to try to accelerate the shift to manufacturing by protection and subsidized import substitution. The only notable successes with the P strategy are Malaysia, Thailand and the Ivory Coast, each of which has had a sustained growth rate above 7 per cent for the past twenty years (Table 2.1) and has made a good start on producing and exporting manufactures.

Turning to the measures of efficiency in Table 2.2, I have already noted that the six countries with high productivity growth have all had neutral or outward policies. Several others – Greece, Turkey, the Philippines and Colombia – made less successful attempts to liberalize trade, which are reflected in intermediate levels of productivity growth (2.0–2.5 per cent).[9] In this respect, the Philippines resembles Latin America more than East Asia.

One general hypothesis that emerges from this survey of economic performance is the presumption that success has resulted from choosing a set of policies to match the country's initial structure and development potential, rather than from a standard prescription for all countries. This is particularly true of the choice of external policies, in which East Asia exhibits considerable variety. In other regions there are as many countries in a position to learn from the experience of Malaysia and Thailand – in diversifying their primary exports and developing manufacturing as the domestic market expands – as there are countries in a position to adopt the more radical structural changes implied by the experiences of the Republic of Korea and Taiwan.

The effects of policy

Although most economists (including the author) are convinced that outward-oriented policies improve performance in a variety of ways,[10] the main analytical support for this view comes from the

---

[9] There are two main exceptions to this observed association of increased productivity with rapid growth: Singapore and Brazil. Both achieved high income growth almost entirely from rapid increases in capital and labour, a pattern that is more common in centrally planned economies.

[10] For a sceptical view, see Jung and Marshall (1985).

theory of comparative advantage. In this section, I will report some results of a series of simulations designed to ascertain how much of the improved performance of economies like the Republic of Korea and Taiwan might be attributed to the direct effects of shifting to outward policies and to suggest plausible magnitudes for other factors involved.

Computable general equilibrium model

To answer these questions, a long-term computable general equilibrium (CGE) model of the effects of shifting away from a protected economy has been designed. The model is based on the structure of the Republic of Korea in 1963 and its subsequent performance.[11] While the policy choices to be simulated focus on the external sector, we also include alternative specifications of the flexibility of the economy (determined by the elasticity of substitution between capital and labour and between imports and domestic products).

The behaviour of the CGE model can be made more or less neoclassical depending on the values assumed for these two sets of elasticities and other constraints on resource allocation. The 'neoclassical specification' in Table 2.6 assumes elasticities averaging about 1.0 for substitution both between capital and labour and between imported goods and comparable domestic products. More structuralist behaviour results from reducing these elasticities, so that larger – and perhaps not feasible – price movements are required to clear markets.

The CGE model simulates the working of a market economy. It includes equilibrium conditions for the supply–demand balances in commodity, labour, foreign exchange and capital markets.[12] Since the demand functions assumed are similar to the preceding input–output model, the main result of endogenizing prices is to determine the effects of different trade and borrowing policies on resource allocation and growth.

[11] See Chenery, Robinson and Syrquin (in press: chapter 11). The interindustry analysis of this country's economy that provided the starting point for the CGE model is described in Kim and Roemer (1979).

[12] The effects of particular assumptions will be noted where they affect the argument.

Table 2.6 Simulated effects of trade and borrowing policies

Strategy	Growth of		Terminal structure				
	GDP	Exports	Import ratio[a]	Savings ratio[b]	Borrowing ratio[c]	Debt export[d]	ER[e] tariff[f]
Initial conditions		0.141	0.086	0.084	—	1.0	
A. Neo-classical specifications							
			Constant borrowing				
1A Inward	5.2	7	0.09	0.23	0.029	3.9	1.70[f]
2A Balanced	5.9	10	0.18	0.24	0.027	1.7	1.2
3A Export promotion	6.3	14	0.19	0.25	0.026	1.1	1.1
			Maximum borrowing				
4A Inward	5.2	7	0.09	0.23	0.029	3.9	1.70[f]
5A Balanced	6.2	10	0.18	0.25	0.044	3.3	1.2
6A Export promotion	6.7	14	0.24	0.26	0.063	3.4	0.9
B. Structuralist specification							
			Maximum borrowing				
1B Inward	4.5	7	0.09	0.22	0.031	4.4	2.80[f]
5B Balanced	6.0	11	0.19	0.23	0.045	3.1	1.25
6B Export promotion	6.7	14	0.24	0.26	0.063	3.4	0.9

[a] Terminal import ratio to GDP (M/Y).
[b] Terminal savings ratio (S/Y).
[c] Average borrowing ratio ($\Sigma F / \Sigma Y$).
[d] Terminal debt ÷ exports.
[e] Average exchange rate.
[f] Average tariff rate.
Source: Chenery, Robinson and Syrquin (in press: chapter 11).

Outward versus inward policies

Although the theoretical effects of shifting from protection to a neutral or outward-oriented policy have been amply described in the literature (e.g. Balassa 1981b), there are several benefits from translating them into quantitative terms. The first is to explore the interactions and relative importance of the several factors involved in 'getting the prices right'. A second, more speculative possibility is to simulate the evolution of the economy over a period of fifteen or twenty years, in a series of *ceteris paribus* experiments. Examples of both types are given below.

Some of the initial conditions for this series of experiments are indicated in the first row of Table 2.6. The pattern of external trade and capital flows is comparable to the Republic of Korea in 1963 with external resources financing a trade deficit equal to 8.4 per cent of GNP. The investment rate of 14 per cent of GNP is sufficient to support an initial growth rate of about 5 per cent. Borrowing constraints are assumed to require a substantial reduction in the trade deficit under existing policies.

From this common starting point, the inward-oriented policy is assumed to maintain external balance by increasing a uniform tariff (or import premium) to make import substitution more profitable. By raising the cost of imported inputs, this policy also makes exports less profitable. To maintain this policy the import premium rises continuously and the bias against exports increases. In determining the rate of growth, we assume that a total factor productivity growth of 1.7 per cent – about average for the import-substituting countries in Table 2.2 – is maintained. The rise in domestic savings and investment offsets the inefficiency of import substitution and a growth rate of 5.2 per cent is maintained.

Taking this simulation of an import-substitution strategy as a point of departure (cases 1A and 4A), it is desirable to measure the effects of two different aspects of outward-orientation; first removing the bias against exports and then taking greater advantage of external borrowing. The two are interrelated in the sense that a country's ability to service external debt depends on its export earnings. Simulation 1A assumes external borrowing averaging about 3.0 per cent of GNP, with debt accumulating to nearly four times annual exports in twenty years. This debt/export ratio is taken as the maximum feasible level.

The other simulations in Table 2.6 are designed to illustrate the effects of alternative policies, assuming first a neo-classical specification of the model. Panel A shows the effect of shifting to more outward-oriented policies in two steps: removing the bias against exports (case 2A) and then raising the growth of exports and increasing specialization (case 3A). To isolate these trade effects the total capital inflow over a twenty-year period is kept constant in cases 2 and 3. It is allowed to increase in proportion to the level of exports (maximum borrowing) in cases 5 and 6.

With constant total borrowing, this shift to outward orientation increases the average growth rate from 5.2 to 6.3 per cent. Much of this improvement comes from the 'balanced' policy of eliminating the anti-export bias, which increases export growth and involves a devaluation of the exchange rate of 20 per cent. Use of the additional borrowing power generated by increasing exports in case 6A raises the growth rate to 6.7 per cent.

If the flexibility of the economy is reduced, we can expect that in case 1B higher tariffs will be needed to hold down imports, which will in turn cause greater distortions and lower growth. In consequence the shift to outward-oriented policies will have a larger effect on growth. To indicate the magnitudes involved, we have simulated in the 'structuralist specification' of panel B the effect of lowering the elasticity of substitution between labour and capital and between imports and domestic products by 50 per cent in all sectors. This assumption reduces the growth rate in case 1 from 5.2 to 4.5 per cent, with a corresponding increase in the benefits from opening the economy. Further reduction in these elasticities has even greater effects on growth as the economy approaches the trade limit assumed in two-gap models.

The simulations underlying Table 2.6 also help to explain the acceleration of growth that was characteristic of East Asia and other countries which opened up their economies in the sixties. Reducing trade barriers reallocates investment, lowers the price of capital goods and thus brings down the incremental capital–output ratio (ICOR). In the longer term the main factor affecting growth is the rising rate of savings, which is partly offset (in the present model) by a decline in the capital inflow and some rise in ICORs. In the export promotion strategy, the growth-accelerating factors predominate, producing a rise from 6 per cent growth in the early years to 8 per cent growth at the end of twenty years. By contrast, in the structuralist specification of import substitution (case 1B), there is no acceleration because rising ICORs completely offset the substantial increase in domestic savings and investment. This phenomenon has been widely observed, notably in India and China until recently.

The experiments just described have tried to generalize the East Asian experience by comparing a stylized version of their shifts to outward-orientation (case 3) to a counter-factual simulation of the effects of continuing with a policy of protection (case 1). Under a moderately structuralist specification we can account for an increase in growth from less than 4.5 per cent to 6.7 per cent in this way, of which three-quarters is attributable to more efficient trade and the rest to the increased borrowing that is made possible. Higher growth is concentrated in manufacturing where the increase is from 5 per cent in case 1B to 11 per cent in case 6B.

There are several factors affecting growth that are not reflected in this analysis. Both the Republic of Korea and Taiwan went from a condition of substantial surplus labour to one of full employment since 1960, implying the possibility of increasing output from re-allocating labour from lower to higher productivity uses. This is in-adequately represented in our model, which assumes neo-classical labour markets. Second, the rapid growth of light manufactures implied by the SM pattern of industrialization described above offers more opportunity for productivity growth from economies of scale and learning by doing than does the more diversified and inef-ficient pattern implied by continued import-substitution. It is thus quite plausible to associate the additional one or two points of growth that are observed in the most successful East Asian cases with these indirect effects of outward-orientation.

SEIJI NAYA*

3

THE ROLE OF TRADE POLICIES IN THE INDUSTRIALIZATION OF RAPIDLY GROWING ASIAN DEVELOPING COUNTRIES

The performance of the East Asian NICs and Southeast Asian developing countries has been impressive: over the past decade they have attained higher rates of real output growth and export expansion with lower rates of inflation than any other group of developing nations. In Table 3.1, real rates of economic growth are compared across countries and regions. The rapid development of the Asian countries may be largely attributed to the outward-looking and market-oriented nature of their economic policies. International trade is an integral part of the economies of the East Asian NICs and Southeast Asian countries. In general, these countries have been very open to international trade and have become increasingly integrated into the world financial markets.

Export–income ratios are very high in these countries (Table 3.2). For comparison, the average ratio of exports to GNP in the NICs and Southeast Asian countries in 1982–83 was over 50 per cent, while the ratios of the United States and Japan were 8 and 16 per cent, respectively.

Generally, it is expected that the trade–income ratio would be inversely related to the size of an economy, though no fixed relationship exists between size and importance of trade. It is remarkable that exports continued to rise in relation to income in the East Asian NICs and (except for the Philippines) in the Southeast Asian countries throughout the turbulent 1970s.

* The paper is based on research conducted by the Resource Systems Institute's Development Policy Program concerned with Comparative Study of Economic Development in Asia. The author acknowledges the assistance of William James and Chung Lee, Research Associates, and Pearl Imada and Udom Kerdpibule, Research Fellows, in preparing the manuscript.

Table 3.1 *Estimated rate of real economic growth of selected Asian countries*

Country	Average annual rate of growth of GDP 1970–87	Rate of real growth GDP (%)			Per capita GNP[a] 1983 US$	Average annual growth rate of GNP 1965–83
	(1)	1982 (2)	1983 (3)	1984 (4)	(5)	(6)
NICs						
Hong Kong	9.9	2.1	5.1	9.6	6000	6.2
Singapore	8.5	6.3	7.9	9.1	6620	7.8
Republic of Korea	8.3	5.5	9.5	7.9	2010	6.7
Taiwan	8.8	3.4	7.3	10.6	2670	..
ASEAN						
Indonesia	7.7	2.2	4.2	5.0	560	5.0
Malaysia	7.7	5.6	5.9	7.3	1870	4.5
Philippines	6.0	2.9	1.1	−4.0	760	2.0
Thailand	7.1	4.1	5.8	6.0	820	4.3
South Asia						
Bangladesh	4.1	0.8	3.3	3.9	130	0.5
Burma	5.0	6.0	5.5	6.3	180	2.2
India	3.6	2.8	7.7	4.5	260	1.5
Nepal	2.7	3.8	−1.4	7.4	170	0.1
Pakistan	5.0	4.4	6.5	5.3	390	2.5
Sri Lanka	4.5	5.2	4.8	5.0	330	2.9
China, People's Republic of	5.6	7.4	5.1	12.0	300	4.4
World	3.0	0.3	2.0	..		
Industrialized	2.7	−0.2	2.5	4.4	11,060	
United States	3.1	−2.0	3.8	7.1	14,020	
Japan	4.6	3.3	3.4	5.3	10,120	
Non-oil developing	5.1	1.6	0.8	..	..	
Africa	3.7	−0.4	−0.7	1.6	..	
Europe	5.3	2.3	2.2	..	..	
Middle East	6.5	4.3	..	..	..	
Western hemisphere	5.4	−1.5	−2.1	3.4	..	

[a] *World Bank Atlas* methodology, 1981–83 base period, rounded to the nearest ten.
Sources: *World Development Report*, 1984, 1985 (World Bank, various years); Asian Development Bank (1983, 1984, 1985); IMF (1985c).

Table 3.2 *Exports and imports of goods and services of Asian developing countries, United States and Japan as per cent of GNP, 1970–71 and 1982–83*

Country/Group	Exports		Imports	
	1970–71	1982–83	1970–71	1982–83
NICs				
Hong Kong	68.9[a]	76.1[a]	80.5[a]	84.1[a]
Singapore	79.9	138.3	127.8	182.7
Republic of Korea	15.0	42.0	25.3	45.8
Taiwan	32.6	48.9	31.3	40.5
ASEAN				
Indonesia	13.9	34.5	16.5	26.4
Malaysia	41.7	49.8	35.7	48.8
Philippines	19.0	18.2	19.5	24.9
Thailand	17.0	17.8	21.0	25.2
South Asia				
Bangladesh	4.9[b]	4.7	8.2[b]	12.7
Burma	5.9	6.8	8.4	13.0
India	4.3	6.8[c]	4.8	10.4[c]
Nepal	..	..	..	..
Pakistan	7.6	9.8	10.4	20.3
Sri Lanka	20.9	30.4[d]	22.9	48.4[d]
United States	5.3	8.1	5.6	9.4
Japan	11.8	16.3	10.0	14.9

[a] Per cent of GDP.
[b] 1973–74.
[c] 1980–81.
[d] 1981–82.
Sources: Asian Development Bank (1983, 1984); IMF (1984c, 1985b).

Trade policies used by countries of the region to spur high growth rates of income and industrialization have become increasingly export-oriented. The export-oriented Asian NICs have chalked up great success in labour absorption, income growth and equity, and flexibility in response to external shocks. The Southeast Asian countries had less success in labour absorption in manufacturing than the NICs, despite rapid growth of exports. With the possible exception of the Philippines, the Southeast Asian countries have still done better than other groups of countries at a similar stage of development. Why export promotion has coincided with successful development is a question of no small importance. From the outset, I acknowledge that export promotion is highly dependent on conditions in foreign markets, and although at present conditions appear rather bleak, this does not change my view. I will argue that exports are not an end in themselves, but the positive efficiency and growth effects of exports comprise the ultimately desired results. Of course, the question we need to answer is how exports bring about these desired effects.

The following two sections of the paper describe the export performance and the changing size, composition, and direction respectively of exports from the NICs and the resource-rich ASEAN countries. Trade policies and changes are discussed in the fourth section with attention to how these have influenced the export performance and patterns. The paper is summed up in the concluding section. I argue that there is a link between more open, outward-looking policies, export performance, and economic development. Stress is placed on the strong interactions between domestic economic policies, trade regimes, and the ability of labour-abundant Asian countries to take full advantage of their resource endowment to achieve growth with equity. The differences in economic development observed between NICs and resource-rich Southeast Asian countries can perhaps be explained by differences in policies and the differing patterns of export expansion. For my purposes, it is convenient to distinguish between the NICs (Hong Kong, Singapore, Republic of Korea and Taiwan) and the Southeast Asian countries – confined to the four resource-rich ASEAN members (Indonesia, Malaysia, the Philippines and Thailand).[1] The classification is natural since the NICs had largely made the transition to export-led growth based on labour-intensive manufactured goods by the late 1960s, and in the 1970s and 1980s had very high trade–income ratios (Table 3.2). The resource-rich Southeast Asian countries only began a rapid increase of their non-traditional, labour-intensive manufactured export share in the 1970s, and,

---

[1] The usefulness of the classification scheme is somewhat complicated by Singapore, which is included as one of the NICs despite its geographical location in Southeast Asia. Structurally, Singapore is very similar to the other NICs with its small agricultural sector, its openness to trade, its high per capita product, and its vibrant industrial sector.

although trade–income ratios are high, they are lower in general than those of the NICs.[2]

The 1970s saw rapid expansion of trade in the region: the Asian NICs as a group were the most dynamic exporters among all developing countries, including other NICs.[3] Total exports grew an average of more than 25 per cent annually between 1970 and 1979. Exports of manufactured goods grew particularly rapidly. They accounted for 70 per cent of the total exports of the Asian NICs in 1970, and maintained an annual average rate of growth of nearly 30 per cent between 1970 and 1979 (Tables 3.3 and 3.4). The Asian NICs' share in total manufactured exports of all NICs increased from 51 to 61 per cent from 1970 to 1979.

Although the growth rate slowed in the 1980s, actually becoming negative in 1982 as a result of the severe recession, by 1984 exports had regained high rates of growth. The vigorous economic expansion in the United States, that began late in 1982 and continued through 1984, had a favourable impact on the growth of manufactured exports of the Asian NICs.

The imports of the NICs also rose rapidly. High rates of economic growth spurred import demand for manufactures and intermediate goods during the 1970s. The share of manufactured imports, however, declined, largely because of the rise in the share of petroleum imports. Petroleum increased from less than 7 per cent of total imports in 1970 to almost 25 per cent in 1981, though it has again declined owing to falling crude oil prices.

The export performance of the Southeast Asian countries is also impressive. In 1970, exports from the ASEAN four consisted almost entirely of primary commodities (ranging from 94 per cent in Malaysia and the Philippines to 99 per cent in Indonesia). Agri-

---

[2] An element of double-counting is involved in measuring exports in relation to income, as exports are in gross value terms, while income is value added. Furthermore, in comparing export-income ratios across countries, differences in the degree of double-counting may magnify perceived differences. For example, Indonesian exports, which consist mainly of primary goods, are likely to involve less 'double-counting' than those exports with lower domestic content such as the manufactured exports of the Republic of Korea.

[3] Other NICs as defined by the OECD: Argentina, Brazil, Greece, Israel, Portugal, Spain and Yugoslavia (OECD 1979).

Table 3.3 *Annual growth rate of total and manufactured exports of Asian developing countries in the 1970s and early 1980s* (per cent)

Country	Total					Manufactures[a]	
	1970–79	1979–81	1982	1983	1984[b]	1970–79	1979–81
NICs	28.5	19.2	−1.1	8.2	20.1	29.7	19.8
Hong Kong	22.1	19.9	−3.7	4.6	29.0	22.0	19.5
Singapore	28.0	19.3	−0.9	5.0	10.2	33.0	20.8
Republic of Korea	37.9	18.9	2.6	9.1	19.6	39.2	18.6
Taiwan	30.8	18.7	−2.3	13.6	21.3	34.2	20.7
ASEAN[c]	26.2	15.0	−4.1	0.1	9.4	39.4	15.5
Indonesia	34.9	23.6	−6.2	−5.3	3.4	47.4	28.1
Malaysia	23.3	3.1	2.3	17.4	15.3	38.0	9.0
Philippines	17.6	11.5	−12.3	−1.8	9.1	33.8	17.0
Thailand	25.2	15.1	−1.2	−11.3	16.1	47.1	20.0
South Asia	15.7	7.4	1.5	8.2	..	17.2	..
Other NICs[d]	20.1	13.2	−5.5	3.7	..	24.1	23.7
Other developing countries	23.7	16.0	−16.2	−13.1	..	23.5	14.8
World	20.6	10.0	−7.2	−2.4	..	19.7	17.4

[a] SITC categories 5+6−67−68+7+8.
[b] Preliminary figures.
[c] Excluding Singapore.
[d] Defined as in OECD (1979): Argentina, Brazil, Greece, India, Israel, Portugal, Spain, Yugoslavia.
Sources: Asian Development Bank (1985); United Nations (1970–81); China, Republic of (1982); IMF (1984b).

cultural export growth in most of the countries was very high, but despite slower growth of world trade and external disturbances such as the first oil shock, the share of manufactures in total exports in 1981 rose to about 20 per cent in Malaysia, the Philippines and Thailand. The least industrialized Southeast Asian country, Indonesia, achieved a similarly high rate of growth in manufactured exports. However, because of the rise in oil export earnings following the oil price rises, the share of manufactures in the total exports of OPEC-member Indonesia was still low (3 per cent) at the end of the decade.

After the second oil shock of 1979, export growth slowed until 1983. Although manufactured exports increased with the growth in demand from the United States, they still comprised a relatively small share of total Southeast Asian exports. The largest trading

Table 3.4 Exports of NICs by principal commodity groups, 1970 and 1981 (as a percentage of total exports)[a]

	Hong Kong 1970	Hong Kong 1981	Korea, Rep. of 1970	Korea, Rep. of 1981	Singapore 1970	Singapore 1981	Taiwan 1970	Taiwan 1981	Total NICs 1970	Total NICs 1981
Primary commodities	7.5	7.9	24.9	18.2	69.0	51.5	27.4	13.1	30.0	22.0
Raw materials	3.6	4.5	15.3	11.3	52.8	44.5	8.8	5.9	19.0	15.8
Ag. & food products	3.9	3.4	9.6	6.9	16.2	7.0	18.6	7.2	11.0	6.2
Manufactured exports[b]	92.2 (100.0)	91.4 (100.0)	75.1 (100.0)	81.3 (100.0)	28.0 (100.0)	41.1 (100.0)	72.3 (100.0)	86.7 (100.0)	69.4 (100.0)	75.8 (100.0)
Resource-based manufactures	5.8 (6.3)	3.7 (4.0)	12.5 (16.7)	8.1 (10.0)	3.5 (11.3)	2.7 (6.6)	9.5 (13.2)	7.2 (8.3)	6.9 (9.9)	5.4 (7.2)
Misc. manufactures	24.6 (26.7)	14.8 (16.1)	13.9 (18.6)	5.5 (6.6)	2.1 (7.5)	2.0 (6.6)	19.6 (27.1)	14.9 (14.9)	14.5 (9.9)	9.5 (9.5)
Textiles	10.9 (11.9)	10.1 (11.0)	10.2 (13.5)	11.6 (14.2)	3.6 (12.9)	1.4 (3.4)	13.8 (19.1)	9.0 (10.4)	9.6 (13.9)	8.1 (10.7)
Clothing	27.8 (30.2)	24.9 (27.3)	25.6 (34.1)	18.2 (22.4)	1.9 (6.9)	2.1 (5.1)	14.9 (20.6)	12.6 (14.5)	18.3 (26.3)	14.6 (19.2)
Transport equipment	0.7 (0.7)	2.1 (2.3)	1.1 (1.5)	9.7 (11.9)	3.4 (12.0)	4.2 (4.2)	0.9 (1.2)	3.6 (4.2)	1.3 (1.9)	4.9 (6.5)
Chemicals	4.0 (4.3)	3.5 (3.9)	1.4 (1.8)	3.0 (3.7)	2.8 (10.3)	3.6 (3.6)	2.3 (3.3)	2.5 (2.8)	3.0 (4.3)	3.1 (4.1)
Electrical machinery	9.2 (9.9)	13.6 (14.9)	5.2 (7.0)	10.8 (13.2)	4.0 (14.2)	14.6 (8.7)	12.4 (17.1)	16.2 (18.7)	8.1 (11.7)	14.0 (18.4)
Non-electrical machinery	1.5 (1.6)	5.1 (5.6)	1.0 (1.3)	2.3 (2.9)	4.4 (14.6)	7.0 (17.0)	3.4 (4.7)	5.7 (6.5)	2.5 (3.6)	5.0 (6.7)
Precision instruments	2.7 (3.1)	9.7 (10.6)	0.4 (0.5)	1.8 (2.2)	9.7 (15.7)	1.6 (1.6)	9.4 (6.5)? 0.4 (0.6)	2.3 (2.6)	1.4 (2.0)	3.9 (5.1)
Total exports	(100.0)	(100.0)	(100.0)	(100.0)	(100.0)	(100.0)	(100.0)	(100.0)	(100.0)	(100.0)

[a] Numbers in brackets represent percentage of manufactured exports.

[b] Does not include SITC category 9 (commodities and transactions not classified elsewhere). Note also that the categories of manufactured exports do not add up to total manufactured exports since not all categories are listed.

Source: United Nations (1970–81).

partner of these countries is Japan, which was slower to recover from the recession. Thus, total exports grew less than 1 per cent in 1983, but, in 1984, export growth rates improved as more countries emerged from the recession.

Despite high export growth rates, import growth outstripped export expansion in all four Southeast Asian countries, causing serious balance of payments problems in the first half of the 1980s, which led to varying degrees of import compression. Indonesia was particularly hurt by oil price declines and had to reduce import growth sharply after 1982. Malaysia was also adversely affected, but its lower dependence on oil revenues made the situation less serious than in Indonesia. Thailand did not adopt import curbs in 1983 and a huge current account deficit resulted. The economic crisis in the Philippines led to negative import growth in 1983 and 1984 as the overall economy contracted.

Manufactured exports have been an important source of growth for the NICs and Southeast Asian countries since the 1960s. For these eight countries, manufactured exports increased at an average rate of over 30 per cent per annum in the 1970s. This growing importance of manufactured exports was accompanied by significant changes in the product composition and destination of exports and imports, though the ASEAN countries are still overwhelmingly exporters of primary products. Tables 3.4, 3.5, 3.7 and 3.8 list the major products (or product groups) that accounted for the bulk of total exports and imports in 1970 and 1981. The next section will examine changes in the composition and direction of trade of the developing countries of Asia.

THE CHANGING PATTERN OF TRADE

Newly industrialized countries

The NICs diversified exports in the 1970s, thus reducing their vulnerability to price and demand fluctuations in individual products. This is reflected in declining export shares of clothing, raw materials (particularly iron ore and wood), and miscellaneous manufactures,[4] although these have continued to be the most important

---

[4] This group combines the SITC categories 812, 831 and 89. It comprises plumbing, heating and lighting equipment; travel goods and handbags; printed matter; articles of plastic; toys and sporting goods; office supplies; jewellery; musical instruments; and a small number of minor items.

individual export products (see Table 3.4). There was also a relative decline of non-manufactured exports (raw materials and agricultural and food products) in the 1970s despite an increase in the export of these products from the NICs to other countries in the Pacific region. Primary commodities still, however, accounted for more than one-fifth of the NICs' total exports.

Simultaneously, more skill- and capital-intensive products have gained ground in the NICs. The export of electrical machinery increased dramatically with a more than 50 per cent increase in the share of this product category in manufactured exports. Furthermore, non-electrical machinery had become exceedingly important in 1981, indicating the increasing competitiveness of the NICs in more sophisticated products.

It should be noted, however, that traditional, mostly labour-intensive exports still accounted for more than half of the exports of the NICs. The 'classical trio' of clothing, textiles and miscellaneous manufactures still comprised 42 per cent of manufactured exports in 1981. Resource-based manufactures (such as leather, rubber, wood and cork products, paper and paperboard, and non-metal minerals) comprised only about 7 per cent of manufactured exports in 1981.

The pattern described above, of course, does not account for variations in the export patterns of the four NICs (see Table 3.4). For example, although the NICs generally concentrated their export efforts on light industrial products (e.g. textiles and electrical machinery), the Republic of Korea, more than the other NICs, has emphasized heavy industries such as transport equipment (e.g. ships), iron and steel. Korean exports of iron and steel in 1981 accounted for 8.6 per cent of total exports as compared to 1.6 per cent in 1970.

The general reliance on exports of labour-intensive consumer goods allowed the NICs to absorb labour rapidly and reach full employment in the 1970s. The NICs have had to compete with countries possessing sufficiently skilled yet inexpensive labour. The NICs' labour-intensive activities are also susceptible to protectionist measures in the markets of both industrial countries and other developing countries where domestic production of such goods is regarded as an important source of jobs. In this respect, the decline of the United States' share in manufactured exports between 1970 and 1981 was especially dramatic; but in spite of the slowdown in its growth, the United States was still the NICs' largest customer for manufactures (Table 3.5). Non-electrical machinery was the only product group in which the NICs were able substantially to increase their sales growth to the United States, but the increase was not sufficient to offset the slow export growth of other manufactures.

The NICs were able to find new markets for their traditional products in the EC, Japan, and in other developing countries outside the Pacific region (mainly the Middle East).[5] None the less, the competitiveness of the NICs in these products was declining; such exports grew much more slowly in the 1970s than other exports, resulting in declining export shares for the traditional products. Other developing countries and the EC have also become important purchasers of both electrical and non-electrical machinery exports, but the NICs were not able to make any inroads into Japanese markets with their more sophisticated export products; in fact, Japan decreased its already small share of NICs' manufactured exports over the period 1970 to 1981 (Table 3.5). About one-half of Japan's imports from the NICs consisted of raw materials while the other half consisted almost entirely of traditional labour-intensive or resource-based products.

The larger share of the NICs' exports going to the United States compared to Japan reflects the wider access NICs have to the United States market and the difficulty of penetrating Japan's market for manufactured consumer goods, especially durables. This trend is likely to continue.

Improved trade relations with the oil-producing countries explain the growing importance of South–South trade, which accounted for over one-third of the NICs' total exports in 1983 (Table 3.6). The NICs were able to increase exports of both traditional and modern manufactured products, and have thus shown that there is scope for intensified trade among developing countries provided that trade is not impeded by protection of national markets. The share of exports to the Middle East increased from 1.5 to 6.2 per cent of total exports between 1970 and 1983, while the share

---

[5] Exceptions are the EC in the case of textile yarn and Japan in the case of resource-based products.

Table 3.5 Exports of NICs by principal commodity group and destination,[a] 1970 and 1981 (percentages of total exports of NICs in each commodity group)

Destination	Raw materials (2−22+3) +67+68		Clothing (84)		Electrical machinery (76+77)		Miscellaneous manufactures (812+831+89)		Textile yarn, fabrics (65)		Agricultural & food products (0+1+22+4)		Resource-based manufactures (61+62+63 +64+66)		Non-electrical machinery (71+72+73 +74+75)		Manufactured exports (5+6−67 −68+7+8)	
	1970	1981	1970	1981	1970	1981	1970	1981	1970	1981	1970	1981	1970	1981	1970	1981	1970	1981
NICs	8.4	16.5	0.7	0.9	9.1	11.1	3.8	4.6	20.5	23.4	7.3	9.6	5.0	9.0	8.6	6.8	7.5	8.6
ASEAN	11.6	22.5	1.1	0.2	3.9	7.4	3.4	3.1	12.7	8.2	15.9	10.9	7.6	6.2	45.6	23.1	8.9	7.5
(Singapore)		(15.1)		(0.1)		(6.0)		(1.9)		(1.8)		(9.3)		(4.6)		(18.8)		(4.7)
South Asia	1.0	6.8b	..	0.03b	0.04	0.8b	0.2	1.1b	1.8	3.9	1.0	6.2b	0.4	4.1b	0.7b	3.8b	0.6	1.8b
Other developing countries	17.3	12.2	67.7	14.5	6.9	11.0	5.6	7.2	17.4	18.3	14.1	15.2	9.2	20.6	12.6	12.7	9.6	15.3
Japan	22.2	18.7	7.0	8.3	5.3	5.1	3.7	5.8	5.6	10.2	23.5	31.0	15.9	8.8	5.2	5.8	7.1	6.9
United States	7.9	8.3	48.5	39.5	61.9	39.0	58.2	40.9	12.4	7.7	14.2	11.5	40.2	22.4	20.7	29.8	41.2	31.9
EC[c]	14.4	4.7	22.0	26.3	10.3	16.0	15.2	23.9	16.2	7.5	18.4	7.4	7.9	13.8	4.0	7.6	14.3	15.8
Other industrial countries	8.5	7.1	12.9	9.1	3.4	6.0	9.9	12.3	13.0	8.4	5.0	4.4	12.8	7.4	2.2	6.0	10.3	8.4
Total Pacific[d]	50.2	66.1	57.3	48.9	79.6	62.6	69.1	54.4	51.2	49.5	61.1	59.2	68.7	46.4	80.1	65.5	64.7	54.7
Total developing countries	38.3	58.0	9.5	15.6	19.9	30.3	13.0	16.0	52.4	53.8	38.3	41.9	22.2	39.9	67.5	46.4	26.9	33.2
Total industrial countries[e]	53.0	38.8	90.4	83.2	80.0	66.0	87.0	82.9	47.2	33.8	60.7	54.3	76.8	52.4	32.1	49.2	72.9	62.6
World	(100.0)	(100.0)	(100.0)	(100.0)	(100.0)	(100.0)	(100.0)	(100.0)	(100.0)	(100.0)	(100.0)	(100.0)	(100.0)	(100.0)	(100.0)	(100.0)	(100.0)	(100.0)

a Definitions of commodity and country groups as in United Nations, *Commodity Trade Statistics*.
b Excluding Taiwan.
c Including England in 1970 and 1981, and Greece in 1981.
d Total Pacific trade includes exports to NICs, ASEAN countries, Japan and the United States.
e Excludes centrally planned economies.
Source: United Nations (1970–81).

74

Table 3.6 *Direction of exports of Asian NICs and ASEAN countries, 1970, 1979, 1981 and 1983*

Destination[a]	Asian NICs				ASEAN countries[b]			
	1970	1979	1981	1983	1970	1979	1981	1983
NICs	7.8	8.7	9.9	7.9	18.9	17.8	17.8	21.0
ASEAN[b]	10.2	9.4	10.3	12.2	5.2	3.1	3.6	3.9
South Asia	0.8[c]	2.5[c]	3.0[c]	3.1	0.6	1.3	1.6	1.7
Middle East	1.5	5.7	5.9	6.2	1.2	1.6	2.3	2.0
Other developing countries	10.0	7.6	9.8	9.6	1.8	3.3	5.9	4.8
Japan	11.7	13.1	10.4	9.1	28.4	33.1	32.7	30.3
United States	31.8	26.5	25.9	31.5	19.6	19.3	17.7	18.7
Australia	2.3	2.5	2.7	2.2	1.8	1.4	1.8	1.2
EC[d,e]	15.0	16.2	13.1	10.9	15.4	14.5	11.3	11.0
Other industrial countries	7.0	6.0	4.9	4.7	3.1	2.3	2.2	2.4
Total Pacific[g]	63.8	62.7	59.2	62.9	73.9	76.0	73.7	75.1
Total developing countries	30.3	33.9	38.9	39.0	27.7	27.1	31.2	33.4
Total industrial countries	67.8	64.3	57.0	58.4	68.4	70.6	65.7	63.7

[a] Definition of country groups as in United Nations, *Commodity Trade Statistics*.
[b] Excluding Singapore.
[c] Excludes exports from Taiwan.
[d] Including United Kingdom.
[e] Including Greece from 1981.
[f] Excluding centrally planned economies.
[g] Pacific trade includes trade with NICs, ASEAN, Japan, United States and Australia.
Sources: See Table 3.3.

of exports to developing countries in the Pacific region remained virtually unchanged.

There were several significant shifts in the product composition of NICs' exports to the developing countries of the region. Exports of raw materials continued to account for about one-quarter of the trade among NICs, and also a significant portion of NICs' exports to Southeast Asian countries. The semi-processed items such as textile yarns and fabrics also continued to be intensively traded among NICs. It is not surprising that exports of traditional products from NICs to Southeast Asian countries have declined in relative terms, as these countries have themselves started to become competitive exporters of such products. Exports of electrical machinery to other NICs and to Southeast Asian countries have expanded while the share of exports of non-electrical machinery to Southeast Asian countries was halved in the 1970s. One may speculate that the NICs used the Southeast Asian countries as test markets for more sophisticated products such as non-electrical machinery until they were able to compete successfully in the markets of the industrial countries.

Southeast Asian countries

Exports of primary commodities, especially non-food products, continue to account for the bulk of total exports from the Southeast Asian countries, ranging from 97 per cent of total exports in Indonesia to 56 per cent in the Philippines (Table 3.7). These consisted largely of natural rubber, wood, tin, copper, and, for Malaysia and Indonesia, oil. The share of raw material exports is especially high in Indonesia, reflecting the large volume and relatively high unit price of petroleum exports for Indonesia in the 1970s. This was less evident in Malaysia which only became an oil exporter in 1975.

In general, the overwhelming importance of primary commodities in Southeast Asian trade decreased somewhat while manufactured exports rose from 4.9 per cent of total exports in 1970 to 12.8 per cent in 1981, thus signalling the emergence of these countries as competitive suppliers of manufactured goods. This increase in manufactured exports, however, may slightly overstate the importance of these exports in the Philippines and Thailand because of transitory declines in world market prices of some primary commodities. Such effects have, however, been more than balanced by price increases for oil and natural gas in Indonesia and Malaysia.[6] Moreover, the annual rates of growth of manufactured exports show that these exports have indeed been expanding rapidly in Southeast Asian countries as a whole. The growth rate, an average of nearly 40 per cent, was higher than that of any other group of countries in the 1970–79 period, leading Havrylyshyn and Aiikhani

---

[6] Using the terms of trade as an indicator of changes in relative prices of commodities and manufactures (1975=100), we find that this index has declined in the Philippines and Thailand from 135 and 114 in 1970, to 93 and 91 respectively in 1979. In Malaysia and Indonesia, the terms of trade increased from 135 and 50 (1971) to 160 and 110 (1979), respectively (Asian Development Bank, *Key Indicators of Developing Member Countries*, various years).

Table 3.7 *Exports of ASEAN countries by principal commodity groups, 1970 and 1981* (as a percentage of total exports)[a]

	Indonesia 1970	Indonesia 1981	Malaysia 1970	Malaysia 1981	Philippines 1970	Philippines 1981	Thailand 1970	Thailand 1981	Total ASEAN 1970	Total ASEAN 1981
Primary commodities	98.6	96.8	92.8	80.0	89.5	55.4	89.5	71.6	91.6	83.8
Raw materials	79.0	91.7	80.2	63.1	49.5	21.2	39.0	17.6	66.2	64.8
Ag. & food products	19.6	5.1	12.6	16.9	40.0	34.2	50.5	54.0	25.4	19.0
Manufactured exports[b]	1.2 (100.0)	2.9 (100.0)	6.3 (100.0)	19.5 (100.0)	6.4 (100.0)	22.8 (100.0)	5.2 (100.0)	24.8 (100.0)	4.9 (100.0)	12.8 (100.0)
Resource-based manufactures	..	1.1 (37.0)	2.6 (40.5)	2.3 (11.8)	4.4 (68.8)	4.3 (18.9)	2.1 (40.4)	5.1 (20.0)	2.3 (46.9)	2.4 (18.8)
Misc. manufactures	..	0.1 (3.4)	0.3 (4.8)	0.5 (2.6)	0.6 (9.3)	2.9 (12.7)	0.4 (7.7)	1.7 (6.9)	0.3 (6.1)	0.8 (6.2)
Textiles	0.2 (16.7)	0.2 (6.9)	0.4 (6.3)	1.2 (6.1)	0.5 (7.8)	1.2 (5.2)	1.2 (23.1)	4.9 (19.8)	0.5 (10.2)	1.3 (10.2)
Clothing	..	0.4 (13.8)	0.3 (4.7)	1.4 (1.4)	..	6.1 (26.8)	0.1 (1.9)	4.9 (19.8)	0.1 (2.0)	2.0 (15.6)
Transport equipment	..	0.3 (10.3)	0.6 (9.5)	0.3 (1.5)	..	0.7 (3.1)	0.3 (5.8)	0.2 (0.8)	0.3 (1.2)	0.3 (2.3)
Chemicals	0.5 (41.7)	0.3 (10.3)	0.7 (11.1)	0.7 (3.6)	0.5 (7.8)	1.8 (7.9)	0.4 (7.7)	0.8 (3.2)	0.6 (12.2)	0.7 (5.5)
Electrical machinery	..	0.3 (10.3)	0.3 (4.7)	10.9 (55.9)	..	1.9 (8.3)	0.1 (1.9)	4.5 (18.1)	0.1 (2.0)	3.8 (29.7)
Non-electrical machinery	0.3 (25.0)	0.1 (3.4)	0.7 (11.1)	1.0 (5.1)	0.1 (1.6)	0.2 (0.9)	0.2 (3.8)	0.4 (1.6)	0.4 (1.6)	0.4 (3.1)
Precision instruments	..	..	0.1 (1.6)	0.3 (1.5)	..	0.5 (2.2)	0.2 (3.8)	0.5 (2.0)	..	0.2 (1.6)
Total exports	100.0	100.0	100.0	100.0	100.0	100.0	100.0	100.0	100.0	100.0

[a] Numbers in brackets represent percentage of manufactured exports.
[b] Does not include SITC category 9 (commodities and transactions not classified elsewhere). Note also that the categories of manufactured exports do not add up to total manufactured exports since not all categories are listed.
Source: United Nations (1970–81).

to coin the term 'Newly Exporting Countries'. They found that the manufactured export growth of these countries was well above that of all NICs before the first oil price shock in 1973, during the subsequent recession in developed countries (1973–75), and during the later period of recovery (1975–79) (Havrylyshyn and Aiikhani 1982).

Diversification of manufactured exports also characterized the export performance of the four Southeast Asian countries, but this process was far less marked than in the NICs. In 1970, when the industrial base was still very small in these countries (with the exception of Indonesia), almost one-half of manufactured exports consisted of resource-based manufactures. In Indonesia, the export of resource-based manufactures was non-existent in 1970 but increased to nearly 40 per cent of total manufactured exports in 1981. In part this reflects the narrow development of Indonesia's industrial exports. The production of resource-based manufactured goods is based on locally available material such as leather, rubber, wood and cork. However, much of what is produced is of low quality and is aimed at domestic rather than international markets. In the four Southeast Asian countries, the share of resource-based products in total manufactured exports declined from 47 per cent to 19 per cent between 1970 and 1981 (Table 3.7). The declining trend may be reversed, however, as in the 1980s the Southeast Asian countries have begun to emphasize downstream industrialization and exports of these processed materials. Examples are canned fish and fruit juices in Thailand and plywood in Indonesia.

As the industrial base of the Southeast Asian countries widened in the 1970s, new products become prominent in the export basket. Some important examples are the 'classical trio' of textiles, miscellaneous manufactures, and especially clothing. The share of clothing increased from 2 per cent to more than 15 per cent of manufactured exports in the 1970s. With respect to these products, Southeast Asian countries were most successful in the markets of the EC. They also competed successfully in the markets of other developing countries in clothing and textiles. They managed to expand textile exports to Japan as well. The United States became the largest single importer of miscellaneous manufactures from the Southeast Asian countries. However, the United States share of clothing exports dropped from 66 per cent in 1970 to less than 30 per cent in 1981. This was due to a large decline in the share of clothing exports from the Philippines, which more than offset substantial increases in the United States share of clothing exports from Indonesia and Malaysia.

Electrical machinery exports from Southeast Asian countries emerged as a new export item in the 1970s. The phenomenal growth of exports of electronic components in the decade was almost entirely derived from sales to the United States. This evidence gives some support to the notion that Southeast Asian electronic components are largely manufactured by subsidiaries of foreign firms. Export growth of these items may therefore be directly related to the business prospects facing the parent companies in the United States.

A comparison of Tables 3.5 and 3.8 reveals that in 1981 the pattern of market destinations of manufactured exports was similar for NICs and Southeast Asian countries. The major difference is the large share of Southeast Asian exports that go to Singapore. Other developing countries, the United States, and the EC emerge as the main markets for manufactured exports of both country groups while Japan does not play an important role. Japan was, however, the main customer for Southeast Asian primary commodities as well as total exports (Tables 3.6 and 3.8). In 1981, exports to Japan accounted for one-third of total Southeast Asian exports. This is not surprising since the natural resource wealth of the Southeast Asian countries is complementary to Japan's relative scarcity of natural resources. Japan even increased its shares in raw materials, agricultural and food exports, which were already significant in 1970. Trade relations between the Southeast Asian countries and Japan, therefore, have maintained the typical 'North–South' pattern with Japan importing energy and raw material and exporting manufactures.

The exports of Southeast Asian countries to developing countries comprised about one-third of total exports in 1983, a slight increase since 1970 (Table 3.9). These were largely exports to Singapore, but the share of the Middle East and other non-Asian developing countries, particularly in primary commodities, and clothing and textiles has increased. As mentioned at the beginning of this paper, the inclusion of the ASEAN-member Singapore in the NICs introduces complications in accounting for trade patterns between Asian developing countries. The result of the inclusion of Singapore among the NICs is to overstate trade between the NICs

Table 3.8 Exports of ASEAN countries[a] by principal commodity group and destination,[b] 1970 and 1981 (percentage of total exports of ASEAN countries in each commodity group)

Destination	Raw materials (2−22+3 +67+68) 1970	1981	Agricultural & food products (0+1+22+4) 1970	1981	Electrical machinery (76+77) 1970	1981	Resource-based manufactures (61+62+63 +64+66) 1970	1981	Clothing (84) 1970	1981	Textile yarn, fabrics (65) 1970	1981	Miscellaneous manufactures (812+831 +89) 1970	1981	Chemicals (5) 1970	1981	Manufactured exports (5+6−67 −68+7+8) 1970	1981
NICs	18.7		17.8	15.1	30.3	33.9	13.1	27.9	6.0	5.1	31.1	25.0	41.2	17.1	38.6	34.1	27.2	25.7
(Singapore)	(16.9)	(11.9)		(9.0)		(24.0)		(13.5)		(3.1)		(9.4)		(9.6)		(14.9)		(15.6)
ASEAN	5.5	2.7	3.8	6.3	13.4	0.2	3.3	4.4	7.9	0.4	11.0	5.2	13.2	2.3	13.3	9.0	8.0	3.9
South Asia	0.3	0.4	0.7	5.6	:	:	0.5	3.6	:	0.02	:	3.6	:	0.6	0.4	4.2	0.7	1.6
Other developing countries	2.3	7.2	2.5	13.6	51.3	0.9	11.5	8.3	3.7	15.3	6.5	11.6	4.5	3.6	10.5	6.0	11.4	8.2
Japan	36.4	44.9	11.7	11.8	:	3.9	8.6	8.4	:	2.3	10.3	10.7	8.1	5.9	7.9	28.4	6.7	6.9
United States	13.5	16.2	34.5	12.3	:	44.8	46.4	18.7	66.0	29.2	17.8	11.8	15.9	33.4	6.3	8.0	28.6	27.9
EC[c]	13.0	6.5	21.5	22.6	:	11.4	12.4	19.3	:	36.4	12.7	18.7	11.1	24.5	18.5	5.4	10.8	18.6
Other industrial countries	5.5	3.3	4.2	3.5	3.5	1.1	4.8	9.1	13.6	10.6	10.4	10.7	4.0	12.3	3.4	4.4	6.1	7.5
Total Pacific[d]	74.1	80.7	67.8	45.6	43.7	86.2	71.4	59.3	79.9	37.0	70.2	52.7	78.4	58.7	65.1	79.5	70.5	64.3
Total developing countries	26.8	27.2	25.2	40.7	94.9	38.6	28.4	44.2	17.5	20.8	48.6	45.4	58.9	23.6	62.8	53.3	47.3	38.6
Total industrial countries[e]	68.4	70.9	71.9	50.2	3.5	61.2	72.2	55.5	79.6	78.5	51.2	51.9	39.0	76.1	35.1	46.2	52.2	60.9
World	100.0	100.0	100.0	100.0	100.0	100.0	100.0	100.0	100.0	100.0	100.0	100.0	100.0	100.0	100.0	100.0	100.0	100.0
Percentage share in total exports	66.2	64.8	25.4	19.0	0.1	3.8	2.3	2.4	−0.1	2.0	0.5	1.3	0.3	0.8	0.6	0.7	4.9	12.8
Percentage share in manuf. exports	:	:	:	:	2.4	29.7	47.4	18.8	3.0	15.8	9.9	10.0	6.5	6.2	11.3	5.1	100.0	100.0

[a] Excluding Singapore.
[b] Definition of commodity and country groups as in United Nations, *Commodity Trade Statistics*.
[c] Including Greece in 1981.
[d] Total Pacific trade includes exports to NICs, ASEAN countries, Japan and the United States.
[e] Excluding centrally planned economies.
Source: United Nations (1970–81).

80

and ASEAN while understating intra-ASEAN trade, since a large part of intra-ASEAN trade revolves around Singapore. According to Table 3.4,. exports among the four ASEAN countries (i.e. excluding Singapore) dropped from 5 per cent in 1970 to less than 4 per cent of total exports in the 1980s. Approximately 13 per cent of total ASEAN exports went to Singapore in 1981, making exports to the three East Asian countries less than 5 per cent of the total. This is due to Singapore's role in entrepôt trade and also to the complementary relationship between Singapore and other ASEAN countries, that is the exchange of Singaporean manufactures for primary products of ASEAN trading partners.

The changes in the trade pattern of the NICs and Southeast Asian countries have been substantial. Both groups have increased exports of manufactured products. The NICs have begun to move into sophisticated industrial products while Southeast Asian countries have begun to concentrate on more labour-intensive manufactured goods. However, Southeast Asia's exports continue to be predominantly resource-based. The next section will discuss the trade policies of these countries in relation to the changing trade patterns noted above.

TRADE POLICIES AND INDUSTRIALIZATION OF ASIAN DEVELOPING COUNTRIES

The Asian developing countries have been expanding the manufacturing sector of their economies. For the Southeast Asian countries as well as for the Republic of Korea and Taiwan this has meant transforming basically agrarian economies into more industrialized ones. The policies and timing selected to implement this task vary by country but similarities can be found within the two sub-groups.

The newly industrialized countries

During much of the 1960s and 1970s, the prominent features of government intervention in industrial development in the NICs was the encouragement of sectors that export a substantial share of production. Hong Kong was from the outset a virtually free-trade economy, while Singapore became one after a brief period of import substitution in the first half of the 1960s. Taiwan and the Republic of Korea made more gradual transitions to trade liberalization.

Table 3.9 *Intra-ASEAN trade as a percentage of total trade, 1974–83 (including Singapore)*

Year	Intra-ASEAN trade as % of ASEAN total trade	ASEAN Exports	ASEAN Imports	Indonesia Exports	Indonesia Imports	Malaysia Exports	Malaysia Imports	Philippines Exports	Philippines Imports	Singapore Exports	Singapore Imports	Thailand Exports	Thailand Imports
1974	14.1	15.3	13.0	8.7	9.4	23.9	14.4	1.3	2.3	22.8	21.8	17.8	2.1
1975	14.7	16.9	12.8	10.3	8.7	24.2	15.2	2.7	4.8	26.0	20.9	17.2	2.7
1976	15.4	16.0	14.8	8.9	14.0	21.5	14.3	3.1	6.5	24.6	23.1	17.2	3.4
1977	15.6	15.7	15.6	10.6	14.3	18.9	14.6	3.9	6.4	22.9	24.6	18.0	4.3
1978	15.6	16.3	14.9	12.7	9.6	18.5	14.3	6.2	5.6	22.3	24.1	15.4	5.9
1979	17.0	17.3	16.7	14.2	11.8	20.1	14.5	4.1	5.8	22.8	26.4	16.7	7.5
1980	17.3	17.7	16.9	12.6	12.4	22.4	16.4	6.5	6.2	24.0	24.8	16.2	9.6
1981	17.3	18.4	16.2	11.9	12.8	26.6	17.9	7.2	6.6	25.1	21.8	14.6	10.1
1982	21.1	22.8	19.6	8.9	8.4	30.0	19.9	7.1	6.5	31.4	25.0	15.4	12.0
1983	22.5	23.9	21.2	9.2	10.4	28.8	19.7	7.1	8.6	33.3	26.0	14.3	14.2

Notes:
(1) Singapore trade with Indonesia derived from Indonesian trade data using conversion factor cif/fob of 1 to 12.
(2) 1981 Indonesian trade with Singapore estimated using Indonesian data for 10 months.
(3) Singapore total trade includes (1).
Source: IMF (1977b, 1984b).

During the 1950s, both the Republic of Korea and Taiwan implemented policies designed to protect the domestic market through the use of multiple exchange rates and import controls. However, both countries quickly recognized that, because of their narrow domestic market, import substitution was a self-limiting process. Once domestic markets of consumer goods are exhausted, industrial growth will slow down and adjust to the expansion of domestic demand unless the expansion can be carried over to foreign markets.

After the completion of the first phase of import substitution in the 1950s, a major policy change provided relatively equal opportunities for expansion of all economic activities. Tariffs were reduced and exchange controls were abolished as both countries moved towards export-oriented growth.

The negative protection on exports resulting from import barriers was counterbalanced by a subsidy scheme (mainly tax and credit preferences) so that exports remained as profitable as domestic sales; this also prevented home country exporters from being disadvantaged *vis-à-vis* foreign competitors. In addition, protection and other development policies did not result in discrimination against agriculture in Taiwan and the Republic of Korea, though agricultural development occurred later in the latter country. The stable price ratio among sectors, especially in Taiwan, encouraged agricultural investment and technological improvements in agricultural production which in turn led to an increasing supply of agricultural inputs into industrial and food production and prevented excessive migration of labour away from rural areas (Ranis 1980:7 ff).

On average, manufacturing output in 1970 accounted for more than 25 per cent of GDP in the NICs and its share of employment was 22 per cent. In the 1980s, manufacturing activities made up more than 30 per cent of GDP and employment (Table 3.10). Labour absorption by the rapidly growing manufacturing industry was exceptional. By the early 1970s, full employment had been reached and many farm households derived the greater part of their income from industrial or other non-farm employment. The rapid growth of the manufacturing sector in terms of both output and labour force resulted from the early emphasis on labour-intensive exports. The increased demand for labour and the subsequent rise in wage rates helped spread the benefits of growth widely and encouraged directly productive activities and attitudes. These attitudes arising from export-orientation contrast strongly with so-called rent-seeking behaviour associated with excessive import substitution.

The incentive system applied in the NICs was, of course, not entirely free of bias. Some industries, particularly intermediate and engineering goods industries, enjoyed heavily protected domestic markets at the expense of traditional consumer goods industries. The latter had to pay artificially increased prices for protected inputs without being compensated for these additional costs.

In the mid-1970s, the NICs again readjusted their industrialization strategy. The slow growth of world trade and increasing protectionism combined with the decreasing competitiveness due to rising wages in these countries, compelled the governments to implement policies aimed at diversifying industrial exports.

These policies were based on the assumption that the negative effects of the new protectionism in developed countries and a loss of competitiveness due to increasing domestic wages could best be avoided by shifting the emphasis of industrial production towards heavy and technology-intensive industrial activities. The new strategy also reflected the concern of these countries about their own balance of payments situation which had deteriorated because of the increasing oil bill. It was thought that some raw materials and machinery hitherto imported should be produced domestically in order to save foreign exchange. The impact of this strategy is clearly reflected in the changing composition of industrial output in these countries. In the Republic of Korea and Taiwan, incremental output shifted to machinery, basic metal industries and chemicals, while light consumer-goods industries maintained an important share in the growing total output.

Some differences in the strategies pursued by the NICs should be noted. The Republic of Korea had embarked on an industrialization policy emphasizing the development of heavy industry by providing credit at artificially low interest rates, strengthening direct government intervention through state-owned companies, and by introducing import controls in addition to tariff protection for selected goods. Such policies, while encouraging private investment to reach an unprecedented level in 1979, unfortunately also accelerated domestic inflation during a period in which output

Table 3.10 Structure of production and labour, 1970 and 1983 (percentage of GDP and employment)[a]

Countries	Agriculture 1970	Agriculture 1983	Industry 1970	Industry 1983	Manufacturing 1970	Manufacturing 1983	Services 1970	Services 1983
NICs								
Hong Kong	2 (2)[b]	1 (1)	37 (35)[b]	30 (36)	30 (35)[b]	22 (38)	61 (63)[b]	69 (63)
Singapore	2 (3)	1 (1)	30 (22)	32 (29)	21 (22)	20 (28)	68 (74)	67 (70)
Korea, Republic of	31 (50)	16 (30)	26 (13)	41 (24)	18 (13)	28 (23)	43 (36)	43 (47)
Taiwan	18 (35)	7 (18)	41 (22)	52 (33)	33 (20)	43 (35)	41 (43)	41 (49)
Southeast Asia								
Indonesia	47 (75)[c]	30 (55)[d]	22 (14)[c]	30 (11)	9 (..)	15 (10)	31 (17)[c]	40 (34)
Malaysia	29 (53)[b]	22 (36)	27 (12)	30 (16)	14 (9)[b]	18 (15)	44 (36)	48 (47)
Philippines	29 (54)	25 (50)	29 (12)	36 (16)	23 (12)	25 (..)	25 (34)	39 (42)
Thailand	32 (72)[f]	24 (68)[d]	24 (8)[f]	30 (8)[d]	16 (8)[f]	21 (11)	44 (20)[f]	47 (24)
South Asia								
Bangladesh	58 (75)[e]	49 (68)	6[e] (7)[d]	15 (8)	6[e] (7)[e]	10[g] (8)	36[e] (19)[e]	36 (25)
Burma	38 (67)	38 (66)	15 (7)	16 (8)	11 (7)	11 (8)	47 (26)	46 (26)
India	47 (74)[c]	33 (71)[d]	22 (11)[c]	26[d] (13)[d]	14 (..)	16 (..)	31 (15)[c]	41[d] (16)[d]
Pakistan	39 (57)	29 (53)	23 (15)	27 (13)	16 (15)	18 (13)	38 (28)	45 (34)
Sri Lanka	35 (50)	27 (45)	18 (10)[b]	24 (11)[h]	10 (9)[b]	17 (11)[h]	47 (40)[b]	49 (44)[h]

[a] Numbers in parentheses represent percentage of employed.
[b] 1971.
[c] 1965 percentage of labour force.
[d] 1982 percentage of labour force.
[e] 1973.
[f] 1972.
[g] Including mining.
[h] 1981.

Source: Asian Development Bank (1984: country tables; 1985); *World Development Report*, 1980, 1984, 1985 (World Bank, various years).

growth slowed down and even turned negative. The latter unfortunately also occurred during 1980, a year burdened with social and political unrest compounded by a poor harvest and rising prices of food and other necessities. The crisis led the new government in the Republic of Korea to undertake a critical reassessment of the heavy-industry strategy.

Meanwhile, Taiwan and Singapore opted for a different structural-adjustment path, aimed at sustaining export-led growth through expanded production of standardized products involving fairly high levels of skill and technology inputs (calculators, watches, colour televisions, video recorders), and further expansion in selected heavy engineering goods (ships, machinery, oil rigs). Instead of direct intervention in capital markets and foreign trade, Taiwan focused on facilitating the inflow of advanced technology and on supporting its implementation by establishing a science-based industrial park. The Singapore government opted to intervene in the labour market. After an early announcement, administered wages were raised in several successive increments by a total of about 80 per cent over the 1979–81 period, and at the same time measures were taken to upgrade the skills of the labour force. The wage increases were meant to induce a shift from unskilled to skilled labour-intensive activities, in which higher labour productivity would allow higher wages without granting specific advantages to physical capital-intensive industries. Singapore's slow-down of growth in the mid-1980s is causing the government to take a hard look at its strategies and policies in the science-based, skill-intensive sectors.

Southeast Asia

The Southeast Asian countries, like most developing countries, adopted import-substituting strategies in an effort to push ahead with their industrialization efforts. They have relied primarily on policies that provide selective protection of domestic producers against foreign competition by raising domestic output prices over world market prices. Tariffs and import quantity ceilings and surcharges were frequently used to achieve this.

Because protection allows domestic industries to produce goods with a higher value added and higher profits than under free trade, productive resources are induced to move into the protected industries. These policies, therefore, often simultaneously discourage export-oriented industrial production and even non-industrial activities via reduced availability of productive factors, that is, higher factor costs and higher prices of inputs. Simultaneously, overvalued domestic currency sustained by import protection has the effect of further discouraging exports.

Though the pattern of government intervention was similar among the four Southeast Asian countries and did not change significantly during the 1960s and early 1970s, some important distinctions must be made. Indonesia, the largest country in terms of population and geography, could be characterized as having the most inward-looking industrial orientation. Indonesia has a history of large-scale government intervention, ownership, and regulation of the economy. The present government partially dismantled the import licensing and exchange controls erected under the Sukarno regime, but continued in the 1970s to make extensive use of non-tariff trade barriers and price controls. Indonesia's trade policy in the 1970s consisted primarily of exporting oil and importing manufactures.

Malaysia also followed the usual pattern of import-substitution in the 1960s and early 1970s but did not discriminate seriously against other traded goods nor overvalue their domestic currency. It had few non-tariff trade restrictions, and though tariff rates diverged widely, the overall simple average tariff rate on manufactures was quite low. Thailand, like Malaysia, did not favour widespread import substitution, although its tariffs were higher than those of Malaysia. The Philippines, on the other hand, began its import substitution process early (in the 1950s) and provided substantial protection to its domestic producers of consumer goods.

Since these import substitution measures were typically introduced on an *ad hoc* basis and their structure changed frequently, it is difficult to assess their impact. Nevertheless, it is generally agreed that the effect of most protection policy packages has resulted in a 'cascading' structure of protection; that is, the highest levels of protection are granted to finished goods and the lowest to raw materials and primary products.

This cascading protection structure has a three-fold effect. First, it discriminates against the domestic production of raw materials and primary products by shifting the internal terms of trade in favour of manufacturing. Second, producers of finished goods enjoy higher effective protection than would otherwise be the case, since their gains from protection in terms of additional value added are much larger than their costs of protection through increased input prices. Finally, these same producers are often allowed drawbacks on duties paid on imported inputs. If the exporter is denied these same drawbacks, then the magnitude of the discrimination is even larger.

In addition to import protection, strong incentives in these countries favoured the use of physical capital. Indeed, the use of capital was subsidized to a great degree while the use of labour was somewhat discouraged, giving rise to an obviously distorted set of incentives in labour-abundant economies. This was reflected in the poor labour absorption in manufacturing. In Southeast Asia, the share of manufactures in GDP rose, on average, from 16 per cent in 1970 to 20 per cent in 1984. Manufacturing employment, however, increased from 9 per cent to about 10 per cent of the labour force (Table 3.10). The striking disparity between labour absorption in the NICs and the Southeast Asian countries would appear even greater if underemployment could be taken into account. The failure of rapid manufacturing output and export growth to absorb labour in Southeast Asia during the 1970s is the result of severe distortion in factor prices and other incentives for capital-intensive development.

This is not to deny the existence of special so-called export promotion policies in the Southeast Asian countries. Some producers of exportables have enjoyed a variety of preferences, ranging from partial or total drawbacks on import taxes on certain inputs such as machinery or raw materials, to tax holidays and preferential access to credit. However, these measures were not sufficient to offset the incentives granted to producers of import substitutes. Even these subsidized exporters were still at a net disadvantage compared to producers of import-competing goods.

Replacing imports with domestically-produced output has never led to a reduction in total imports. (This point is stressed by Little, Scitovsky and Scott 1970.) On the contrary, the more inward-looking industrialization is, the greater the requirement for imported capital and technology. The increased import dependence that accompanies import-substituting industrialization caused severe balance of payments problems for the oil importers during the 1970s, when their import bills were additionally burdened by increasing oil prices. Until then, their rich natural resource endowments allowed them to keep their trade deficits within reasonable limits by using agricultural and raw materials export earnings to finance imports of capital and technology necessary for continued import-substituting industrialization. Since the ability and willingness of international institutions and private lenders to finance ever-increasing balance of payments deficits is constrained by evaluation of a country's debt servicing capability, governments in Southeast Asia predictably tended to resort to foreign exchange controls and import rationing. Such measures have a destabilizing effect on the investment climate in general and especially on industries depending on imported inputs. The Philippines experience has provided repeated examples of both of these effects at various times, most recently in the mid-1980s.

In the second half of the 1970s, however, in an effort to adjust to the increases in the oil-import bill, the governments of Thailand and the Philippines attempted to increase manufactured exports. Export controls were relaxed and export taxes abolished. Governments granted duty-free importation allowances for necessary inputs to exporters, introduced special rebates on income and turnover taxes, and opened new (mostly short-term) export credit facilities.

Some countries (such as the Philippines and Indonesia) even made cautious attempts to reduce the overvaluation of their currencies, but because their domestic inflation rates remained above those of their major trading partners, real exchange rates soon returned to their former levels.[7] Indonesia's 1978 rupiah devaluation was designed to prevent the erosion of incomes in the non-oil sectors of the economy, particularly for smallholders in agriculture. It had a surprisingly strong positive impact on manufacturing exports which surged until the inflation differential and a boom in the domestic economy took a toll on manufactured export growth. The second oil price bonanza of 1979 and 1980 put any worries regarding foreign exchange earnings out of the way until oil prices fell. In addition, current account deficits mounted in 1981, 1982 and 1983. It then became apparent that Indonesia would have to make a major effort to expand non-oil exports if it were to attain

---

[7] Bautista, Power and Associates (1979:29–30, 79ff). Rana (1983) also found that real effective exchange rates appreciated in the Philippines, Thailand and Indonesia between 1967 and 1979, including a loss of competitiveness in export markets.

acceptable economic growth without unacceptable foreign debt into the 1990s. As a result, a second major devaluation occurred in March 1984. The devaluation was coupled with reforms in customs and ports, taxation, and pricing policies.

Thailand, a country that studiously avoided devaluation in the 1970s, took a bold step in devaluing the baht substantially in 1984. In conjunction with World Bank 'structural adjustment loan' (SAL) programs, Thailand and the Philippines have sought to provide more balance to the incentive systems in order to promote a more efficient and resilient industrial growth pattern. Indonesia and Malaysia have undertaken similar reviews of their trade and industrial policies in the mid-1980s with a view towards promoting more vigorous manufacturing export growth.

Although it is premature to make a final judgment on the long-term effects of these policy changes (because changing from an inward to an outward industrialization orientation is a lengthy process), the nature of the policies adopted allows some general conclusions concerning their likely effects.

The new policies favouring manufactured exports were adopted without simultaneously reducing protection and other preferences promoting production for domestic markets. As a result, the average effective rate of protection seems to have risen and then declined for some industrial sectors, the export incentives thus having little impact on the sectoral pattern of incentives. This means that discrimination against exports was only partly mitigated by the new measures, and that the incentive structure favouring capital- and energy-using industrial activities remained basically unchallenged.

A major shortcoming of Southeast Asian development patterns has been the weak labour absorption in manufacturing. The growth in manufacturing exports and GDP shares has not been matched by growth in manufacturing employment.

Despite various programs and measures to promote manufacturing employment, exports and efficiency, the main thrust of government industrial planning in Southeast Asia continues to favour import substitution and investment in capital-intensive heavy industries. The inability of import substitution industry to provide sufficient employment opportunities has been amply proven. Unless the pattern is changed, serious social problems will result, as labour-force growth is extremely high.

CONCLUDING REMARKS

The importance of world trade expansion and trade policies of industrial nations for export and economic growth in Asia has been alluded to already. However, the point requires some further elaboration. Commercial policies of advanced industrial countries have substantial impact on the ability of developing nations to expand exports of manufactured goods. Whether or not trade restrictions or liberalizations are aimed at developing nations is less important than the direction in which policy is headed. Unquestionably, trade policy is becoming more protectionist in the majority of industrial nations.

In the case of commercial policies aimed at developing nations, we can cite the tightening of quotas under the Multi-fibre Agreements. The institution of strict graduation clauses in the Generalized System of Preferences by the United States is aimed at excluding the NICs from the lower tariffs granted previously. Other measures to restrict imports of specific goods like footware from developing Asian countries are being contemplated along with more generally restrictive measures.

Even more dangerous for Asian developing countries than direct legislation in rich countries to restrict their exports could be the indirect fallout from trade frictions between industrial nations. The handling of the United States–Japan trade conflict has serious implications for the NICs and Southeast Asia. Failure to achieve market-opening by Japan, coupled with impossibly large United States trade deficits, could lead to wide-ranging United States restrictions. Measures such as a large (20 per cent) surcharge on imports by the United States could have serious direct and indirect adverse effects on Asia. The cost of a protectionist approach to settling trade imbalances between the United States, the EC and Japan is substantially higher to developing Asia than the market-opening approach that has so far been favoured by the rhetoric of American and Japanese political leaders.

With exports looming so large in the economic performance of the Asian developing countries, it is important to ascertain whether export growth can continue to outstrip income growth. Can the relative importance of exports be expected to rise substantially in -future, given the somewhat restrictive trade policy environment in many advanced countries? Developing Asian countries will have to seek to promote greater trade within the region. Countries such as Taiwan and the Republic of Korea will have to boost domestic market growth as well. Cultivating markets in developing countries is difficult, but will be extremely important for future trade.

The entry of China into the international economy as well as the liberalization measures gaining ground in South Asia introduce new elements into the regional picture. While the rapid expansion of trade with China (and to a lesser degree with South Asia) offers new scope for growth of exports from the NICs and Southeast Asia, there is formidable competition for Chinese and South Asian markets. It is also the case that China, India and other South Asian countries will pose a new competitive threat to the NICs and Southeast Asia in labour-intensive manufactured exports (textiles, clothing, processed food and electronics). The broadening of trade relations between the developing countries should be sought through trade policy reforms and encouragement of direct investment and joint ventures. The openness of markets in major countries such as the United States and Japan will continue to be vital to the economic prospects of the NICs and Southeast Asian countries.

Market-opening and trade liberalization appear to be gaining momentum in large parts of Asia (India and China as well as Indonesia, to cite major countries). I hope that the 'mature' economies continue to resist protectionism and do everything they can to nurture the liberalization trend. The announcement of new market-opening measures in Japan must be followed by action. Japan has the capacity to absorb a far greater amount of manufactured goods exported from the NICs and Southeast Asia than it had previously. The United States and the EC also bear considerable responsibility to provide developing countries with reasonable access to their markets. In turn, trade policies in Asia should be responsive to provide consumers and firms opportunities to purchase competitive products from the industrial countries.

The preceding discussion of export performance and patterns in the NICs and ASEAN countries argues that there is a link between outward-looking, market-oriented policies and rapid economic development. The link is complex, involving both static and dynamic effects. Part of the answer may be because outward-looking policies help bring about more efficient allocation of resources. However, as Anne Krueger emphasizes, the ability to capture the dynamic gains associated with an export-oriented strategy are possibly even more important (Krueger 1984). What these dynamic gains are and why an export-oriented strategy leads to their capture remains to be fully assessed.

Flexibility in resource deployment; competitive abilities that arise from production for contestable markets abroad; learning of technological and managerial skills; fostering of good work habits and attitudes rather than 'rent-seeking' behaviour; all tend to be more associated with export-oriented, outward-looking development strategies. In turn, these dynamic gains are reinforced by domestic economic policies that allow both market forces to work and improve the infrastructural and institutional framework of the economy.

The better performance of the NICs with respect to economic growth, employment and income distribution compared to the resource-rich ASEAN countries can, to a large extent, be related to a combination of more thorough and timely adoption of outward-looking, market-oriented policies and rapid improvements in human resource and institutional development. The NICs, to some extent, were forced by circumstances to adopt the policies they did. They lacked natural resource wealth and had little beyond abundant labour with which to begin their impressive modernization drive.

It is ironic that, to some degree, wealth in natural resources in labour-abundant countries, such as those in Southeast Asia, makes it more difficult to adopt policies that promote growth with equity through labour absorption in an outward-looking manufacturing sector. Resource wealth (outside of agricultural crops) tends to have concentrated ownership as well as a requirement for capital-intensive technologies for development. The effect of natural resource booms on non-resource sectors capable of producing exports is often negative because of 'Dutch Disease' effects. Often the sectors that are adversely affected are labour-intensive. Government control of natural resources (such as oil and minerals) has not usually led to very equitable distribution of benefits, and as recent experience with oil and other commodities has shown, government control does not prevent occurrence of severe fluctuations in export earnings from resource-based products. Natural resource wealth may also encourage adoption of policies that lessen incentives to produce while providing subsidies to domestic consumers.

For all these reasons, ASEAN countries may have found it more difficult to achieve a pattern of industrial growth that made use of the abundant labour resources. Further study is needed to compare the experiences and policies of these countries in this context. However, there is no inherent reason why ASEAN or other natural resource-rich countries could not improve the policy framework in order to make better use of the resources they possess.

4

THE ROLE OF FOREIGN CAPITAL IN EAST ASIAN INDUSTRIALIZATION, GROWTH AND DEVELOPMENT

There is no dearth of literature on foreign capital inflows into East Asia. Direct foreign investment has attracted a vast amount of attention, but aid flows were an important area of analysis in the 1950s and 1960s, and during the last decade attention has shifted to bank flows and the ensuing debt issues. The large volume of writing has not, however, led to clear hypotheses about the role of foreign capital inflows in East Asia's industrialization or growth. Typically of capital flow information, the data base is conceptually and statistically weak (Table 4.1) so that attempts at quantitative empirical analysis have usually foundered or led to conflicting results. Much of the empirical literature is accordingly devoted to the microeconomic costs and benefits of capital inflows, but these are not linked to the key host and home country policies that determine their incidence and magnitudes.

Although the East Asian countries represent a growing economic entity in the world economy, notably with respect to trade, in relation to global capital flows they have been to date a 'small country'.[1] As international capital markets developed after the Second World War, the supply of capital for international flows was largely determined by the industrial countries. 'Low absorption' petroleum exporters added to supply from the mid-1970s, and other developing countries including some in East Asia began to contribute to as well as borrow from international capital markets.

[1] To avoid 'fallacy of composition' comments, it should be noted that even the total demand of developing countries for external capital from private sources must be regarded as a 'small country' demand, at least to the mid-1980s. Total annual capital inflows into developing countries still account for less than 10 per cent of the total (national and international) capital flows originating in industrial country and other major money centre banks.

Table 4.1 Net private direct foreign investment flows (US$ million)

		1969	1970	1971	1972	1973	1974	1975	1976	1977	1978	1979	1980	1981	1982	1983
Hong Kong	OECD	23	26	31	58	143	81	215	154	145	252	342	374	1088	652	609
	IMF	:	:	:	:	:	:	:	:	:	:	:	:	:	:	:
Indonesia	OECD	48	49	117	90	348	182	1289	747	-67	418	-383	300	2584	537	300
	IMF	32	83	139	207	15	-49	476	344	235	279	226	183	133	225	292
Korea, Republic of	OECD	5	14	32	67	261	81	51	83	28	184	1	-207	261	107	-62
	IMF	-3	38	56	63	93	105	53	75	73	61	16	-7	60	-76	-57
Malaysia	OECD	6	37	32	65	139	123	73	133	134	-5	77	242	252	-429	234
	IMF	80	94	100	114	172	571	349	381	406	500	573	934	1265	1397	1371
Philippines	OECD	70	-3	17	14	60	140	117	154	116	144	330	128	115	126	-168
	IMF	6	-29	-6	-21	54	4	97	126	210	164	73	40	292	16	104
Singapore	OECD	9	16	22	46	105	92	70	67	86	147	355	650	980	280	416
	IMF	38	93	110	191	389	596	611	651	335	739	941	1669	1917	1803	1389
Taiwan	OECD	:	:	:	:	:	:	:	19	19	28	67	163	119	57	120
	IMF	51	61	52	27	62	83	35	64	42	110	123	67			
Thailand	OECD	17	14	8	21	20	44	19	18	42	38	38	218	219	128	202
	IMF	51	43	39	68	77	189	86	79	106	50	51	187	288	189	348

Sources: 1. OECD figures, 1969–75: Billerbeck and Yasugi (1979); after 1975: OECD (1980, 1981 and 1984).
2. IMF figures: International Financial Statistics (IMF, various years).

But the East Asian countries have mainly been capital importers and price takers in the international market for capital. Their demand for foreign capital, determined by their domestic policies, has largely determined the volume of capital they have attracted (Hughes 1985). The supply of foreign capital is segmented: concessional official flows (aid), short-term (of one year's duration or less) trade credit, medium-term suppliers' credits, direct foreign investment, portfolio investment, medium- to long-term bank flows and (to a very limited extent) bonds are the principal forms of international capital flows, each with its own complementary and competitive demand and supply characteristics and with specific costs and benefits. The form of early capital flows to the East Asian countries, typical for developing countries, largely took the form of aid and short-term trade credit. As their economies strengthened in the 1950s, the East Asian countries became more creditworthy for commercial capital flows, attracting suppliers' credits and direct investment. By the end of the 1960s they were economically strong enough to be able to use bank flows and, to a small degree, portfolio investment. Bond flows failed to develop on a significant scale.

All capital flows, of course, have private and social costs as well as benefits. The ratio of benefits to costs is largely determined by a country's domestic policies, although home country policies also play a role. For example, home countries' non-tariff import barriers stimulated direct investment flows from Hong Kong and Taiwan to Singapore, Malaysia, Thailand, the Philippines and Indonesia. Home countries' subsidies to suppliers' credits for capital goods exports required similar mercantilist measures in the Republic of Korea, increasing the demand for external borrowing. However, the principal influences on the ratio of capital inflow costs to benefits were the host countries' own policies: trade policies through the allocation and utilization of factors of production; monetary, financial and fiscal policies through their impact on key prices, notably exchange and interest rates and the overall rate of inflation; manpower and social and physical infrastructure policies through their effect on capital output; and capital–labour ratios and productivity more generally. Sectoral and industry-specific policies and barriers and incentives to foreign investment were of secondary importance overall, although they sometimes have important effects on particular firms at particular times.

It is not surprising that empirical studies of the quantitative impact of foreign capital inflows on such components of the economy as domestic savings, investment, and the share of manufacturing and exports in GNP generate a wide range of results. Foreign capital inflows, moreover, have indirect and qualitative as well as direct and quantitative effects. The association of technology transfer with direct foreign investment is widely accepted and frequently discussed, but other capital flows also have qualitative impacts. Thus even apart from the questionable value of the data, the share of foreign capital in gross capital formation and shares of capital inflows to GNP (Table 4.2) are of limited value as indicators of the impact of foreign capital inflow on an economy.

Assessing the role of foreign capital in East Asia's industrialization (as well as in its growth and development) also involves an evaluation of the effect of host and home country policies on the volumes, prices and qualitative impacts of the principal components of foreign capital flows, that is, of aid, direct foreign investment and bank flows including suppliers' credits.

AID FLOWS

Aid flows to East Asia, including all official concessional flows in the form of grants, concessional loans, technical assistance and so forth from bilateral and multilateral sources, have been limited since the early 1970s with three economies – Hong Kong, Singapore and Taiwan – effectively having 'graduated' from aid flows. However, at the beginning of the region's development effort, aid flows were very considerable. The United States made substantial military and other 'aid' contributions to Taiwan from 1950 to 1965. In the early 1950s United States civilian aid of some $90 million a year financed about 40 per cent of Taiwan's goods and services imports (Galenson 1979). United States aid to the Republic of Korea began before the Korean war and rose from about $60 million in 1950 to nearly $200 million in 1953 and stabilized at that level until 1962 and 1963 when it peaked at about $250 million. Total United States flows continued to fluctuate about this level but with concessional loans beginning to replace grants (Krueger 1979). United States aid flows and military expenditures also contributed to the Philippines economy. As the war in Vietnam developed, Thailand became a civilian and military aid recipient. The

Table 4.2 Indicators of capital inflow into East Asia, 1969–83

	1969	1970	1971	1972	1973	1974	1975	1976	1977	1978	1979	1980	1981	1982	1983
Indonesia															
(US$ million unless indicated otherwise)															
Use of fund credit (SDR[a] million)	112	138	125	107	19	—	—	—	—	—	—	—	—	—	425
Private unrequited transfers	47	66	46	51	55	49	27	15	24	14	30	55	250	134	104
Official unrequited transfers	32	83	139	207	15	−49	476	344	235	279	226	183	133	225	292
Direct investment										103	60	46	47	315	368
Portfolio investment															
Other long-term capital	235	207	238	293	505	541	567	1638	1256	1214	1034	1927	1971	4556	4663
Other short-term capital	6	3	60	154	217	−87	−1889	−268	−391	121	−454	−820	−290	526	731
Capital inflows as a share of GNP[b] (per cent)	4.2[c]	4.0[c]	5.3	6.6	5.1	1.9	−2.8	4.8	2.5	3.5	1.8	2.0	2.7	6.6	8.2
Share of GNP capital inflows as a share of gross fixed capital formation[b] (per cent)	32.9[c]	28.6[c]	32.6	34.1	27.2	10.5	−13.2	22.4	12.2	16.4	8.3	9.2	11.5	28.3	32.6
Korea, Republic of															
(US$ million unless indicated otherwise)															
Use of fund credit (SDR million)	—	—	—	—	—	110	217	302	280	202	104	535	1071	1142	1293
Private unrequited transfers	142	95	105	119	155	154	158	193	170	434	399	399	422	447	566
Official unrequited transfers	102	83	63	50	36	67	67	153	53	37	40	50	79	52	26
Direct investment	−3	38	56	63	93	105	53	75	73	61	16	−7	60	−76	−57
Portfolio investment								74	70	42	8	40	60	15	188
Other long-term capital	578	425	559	447	507	939	1291	1183	1257	2008	3047	1954	3517	1858	1660
Other short-term capital	142	224	287	−16	3	697	1123	534	−10	18	2282	3983	1090	2159	524
Capital inflows as a share of GNP (per cent)	9.8[c]	8.7[c]	9.9	5.2	4.7	9.8	12.2	7.0	3.9	4.3	8.4	9.8	7.1	5.7	3.1
Capital inflows as a share of gross fixed capital formation (per cent)	46.2[c]	38.1[c]	46.1	25.7	20.2	38.5	47.7	29.2	14.5	14.0	25.5	30.8	24.8	18.7	9.8

Table 4.2 (*cont.*)

	1969	1970	1971	1972	1973	1974	1975	1976	1977	1978	1979	1980	1981	1982	1983
Malaysia															
(US$ million unless indicated otherwise)															
Use of fund credit (SDR million)	—	—	—	—	—	—	—	93	—	—	—	—	190	248	315
Private unrequited transfers	-68	-65	-62	-62	-76	-52	-48	-48	-46	-68	-36	-43	-55	-53	-35
Official unrequited transfers	9	6	17	7	14	9	15	8	14	23	28	23	21	21	26
Direct investment	80	94	100	114	172	571	349	381	406	500	573	934	1265	1397	1318
Portfolio investment	..	..	87	67	-11	11	266	50	65	79	194	-11	1131	1804	1409
Other long-term capital	57	2	45	139	72	85	105	174	184	111	158	98	178	404	1278
Other short-term capital	-41	-6	21	-4	105	152	-66	-95	-399	-63	-724	414	42	140	-255
Capital inflows as a share of GNP (per cent)	2.9c	2.5c	6.5	6.6	4.8	9.1	7.4	4.9	2.1	4.2	1.2	6.4	11.2	15.0	13.6
Capital inflows as a share of gross fixed capital formation (per cent)	18.9c	11.9c	30.5	30.0	19.4	29.4	28.1	20.6	8.6	14.8	4.1	21.4	32.4	39.7	37.2
Philippines															
(US$ million unless indicated otherwise)															
Use of fund credit (SDR million)	55	69	90	95	76	68	165	348	418	441	507	669	823	755	899
Private unrequited transfers	44	29	34	80	94	123	165	148	148	197	229	229	325	322	237
Official unrequited transfers	111	90	100	107	136	154	153	120	111	122	126	148	182	164	235
Direct investment	6	-29	-6	-21	54	4	97	126	210	101	7	-106	172	16	105
Portfolio investment	..	..	—	-1	11	-43	27	16	7	-1	13	4	3	1	7
Other long-term capital	152	159	-3	137	68	267	393	995	648	831	1090	980	1131	1548	1044
Other short-term capital	141	112	251	168	80	625	577	60	123	857	453	1806	712	1281	-1550
Capital inflows as a share of GNP (per cent)	5.0c	4.7c	4.4	4.7	3.3	6.8	7.9	7.4	5.3	7.9	5.6	8.0	5.7	7.7	-0.5
Capital inflows as a share of gross fixed capital formation (per cent)	27.9c	29.3c	27.0	29.5	21.3	36.7	32.5	29.9	21.8	32.8	21.7	31.3	21.9	29.9	-1.9

Singapore
(US$ million)

Use of fund credit	—	—	—	—	—	—	—	—	—	—	—	—	—	—	—
Private unrequited transfers	-16	-21	-23	-2	-14	-41	-38	-46	-41	-36	-31	-46	-50	-101	-170
Official unrequited transfers	3	13	11	5	10	2	—	-3	-4	-3	-4	-5	-12	-13	-14
Direct investment	38	93	116	191	389	596	611	651	335	739	941	1669	1917	1803	1445
Portfolio investment	:	—	—	—	—	76	—	36	121	-6	-12	-13	-12	-20	-89
Other long-term capital	35	47	42	51	25	92	58	79	64	-14	253	-106	-93	97	16
Other short-term capital	-58	33	129	129	242	-172	-89	83	86	294	-183	136	471	335	1337
Capital inflows as a share of GNP (per cent)	1.0[c]	9.7[c]	13.3	13.9	18.1	10.0	10.3	12.2	9.3	13.0	10.6	15.4	17.3	15.2	16.5
Capital inflows as a share of gross fixed capital formation (per cent)	4.2[c]	30.1[c]	36.8	36.9	50.1	26.1	29.3	40.1	27.8	37.7	30.2	37.6	40.0	31.9	34.3

Taiwan
(US$ million)

Use of fund credit[d]	—	—	—	—	—	—	—	—	—	—	—	—	—	—	—
Private unrequited transfers[d]	13	20	13	15	5	13	11	22	7	-19	-221	-92	-84	-125	-42
Official unrequited transfers[d]	-5	-6	-2	2	-5	-2	-5	-1	-2	-7	-1	-3	-8	-10	-1
Direct investment[d]	51	61	52	27	62	83	35	64	42	110	123	45	85	145	41
Portfolio investment[d]	:	:	—	—	—	—	—	—	—	—	—	—	—	—	—
Other long-term capital[d]	-116	14	-93	-10	218	386	332	488	284	177	434	913	1149	1626	-906
Other short-term capital[d]	14	98	-69	-20	-703	631	217	-223	-1360	-1817	-573	1134	3473	-2179	-1797
Capital inflows as a share of GNP (per cent)	-1.2[c]	3.0[c]	-1.7	—	-4.2	8.0	4.0	1.9	-5.3	-6.4	-0.1[e]	6.4	11.5	-8.7	-1.2
Capital inflows as a share of gross fixed capital formation (per cent)	-5.2[c]	13.5[c]	-7.5	-0.1	16.1	27.6	13.1	6.8	-19.6	-25.1	-0.2[e]	22.4	37.1	-30.1	-7.2

Table 4.2 (cont.)

	1969	1970	1971	1972	1973	1974	1975	1976	1977	1978	1979	1980	1981	1982	1983
Thailand															
(US$ million unless indicated otherwise)															
Use of fund credit (SDR million)	—	—	—	—	—	—	—	67	67	136	182	143	606	636	867
Private unrequited transfers	4	3	7	30	117	215	74	29	66	110	210	451	526	693	999
Official unrequited transfers	53	46	37	29	27	26	24	18	18	34	37	142	119	108	124
Direct investment	51	43	39	68	77	189	86	79	106	50	51	187	288	188	348
Portfolio investment	::	::	—	—	13	12	1	−1	—	76	180	96	44	68	108
Other long-term capital	78	67	41	88	−11	188	169	240	322	520	1246	1824	1553	1128	1008
Other short-term capital	39	54	16	38	240	137	215	221	617	715	499	−63	594	58	662
Capital inflows as a share of GNP (per cent)	3.6c	3.2c	1.9	2.8	3.3	4.1	3.4	3.4	5.6	6.1	7.5	6.7	7.4	4.4	5.8
Capital inflows as a share of gross fixed capital formation (per cent)	14.9c	13.4c	8.4	13.4	16.1	19.0	15.3	15.5	22.0	24.3	28.5	25.3	30.0	19.8	25.1

a Special drawing rights.
b Excluding use of fund credit and private unrequited transfers.
c Assuming that there is no portfolio investment.
d 1969–79: IMF, *International Financial Statistics*; 1980–83: China, Central Bank, *Financial Statistics* (various years).
e 1979 GNP and gross fixed capital formation as in China, Central Bank, *Financial Statistics* (various years).
Sources:*International Financial Statistics* (IMF, various years); China, Central Bank, *Financial Statistics* (various years).

United Kingdom contributed to Malaysia and Singapore before their independence in 1959 through infrastructural development, civil grants and a military presence. The Malaysian 'emergency' had capital inflow spillovers. Hong Kong's administration was subsidized by the United Kingdom until the 1960s. Hong Kong, Singapore, Republic of Korea and Taiwan were also able to take advantage of the United States military presence in Southeast Asia in broader economic terms. Indonesia attracted aid from Eastern Europe as well as from the market-economy industrial countries after its independence, and received substantial contributions from the United States and other industrial country donors and multilateral development sources after the replacement of the Sukarno government by that of Suharto in 1965. Japan paid reparations to most of the East Asian countries and began to assist developing countries in East Asia through concessional lending. With such notable exceptions as Anne Krueger's analysis of aid in the Republic of Korea (Krueger 1979) the role of aid flows to East Asia remains to be analysed, but the main features may be summarized.

The initial form of aid to the developing countries of East Asia in the late 1940s and early to mid-1950s took the form of grants for budget support, at first to colonial administrations, and then to the newly independent governments. The United States and the United Kingdom were the principal aid contributors. Thailand, because it had never been a colonial country and Indonesia, because it had to fight for its independence from the Netherlands, largely missed out on this stage of aid flows. Aid accounted for the bulk of foreign inflows because capital from private sources was in the main confined to short-term trade credit in this period.

The late 1940s were years of post-war reconstruction. Budget aid kept governments going. Malaysia, Singapore and Hong Kong were able to move towards a growth path by restoring and improving their social and physical infrastructures, but growth rates largely reflected world primary commodity prices for Malaysia and entrepôt opportunities for Singapore and Hong Kong. Aid enabled the Republic of Korea, Taiwan and the Philippines to expand their social and physical infrastructures, but also to pursue subsidized import substituting pro-urban industrialization policies at the cost of agricultural development, and, hence, the mass of the population. Corrupt governments were entrenched in several countries and the vested interests that are still an obstacle to liberalization in several countries in the region were established.

Despite large volumes of budget support, the donor countries had little impact on domestic policies in the newly independent countries. Home country governments were anxious to avoid being accused of colonial intervention, and the aid establishment in home countries had as little development experience as the developing countries. The Joint Commission for Rural Reconstruction, composed of United States and Taiwanese staff, which offset the pro-industry, pro-urban biases that hampered Taiwan's farmers, was an exception. By the end of the 1950s Taiwan's agricultural output was at least back to 1939 production levels. Otherwise aid flow costs were considerable. Aid flows exacerbated the problems of import-substituting industrialization by overvaluing local currencies that in any case tended to move in that direction because of inflationary monetary and fiscal policies that accompanied the conventional development policies of the day. Budget aid support reduced the pressure for monetary, financial and fiscal reform. Aid as a 'rent' had other distorting effects. Resources and factors of production were drawn to the 'rent' – in this case the government – sector. The tendency for public sector intervention in non-public goods areas of the economy was encouraged: aid-supported developing countries could afford more public investment than they would have otherwise, particularly in 'basic' industries. Large numbers of public servants could be employed in administration, emphasizing a trend already inherent in the newly emerging ideology of development and resulting from new sources of political patronage.

A second stage in aid flows came in the late 1950s. In the United States critical public perceptions of the inefficiency of aid were supported by technical analyses of the economic performance of aid beneficiaries. To obtain annual aid appropriations through the parliamentary system, aid agencies in home countries moved from budget support to program and project aid, building in attempts at conditionality. As USAID in Washington initiated country aid programming policy, debates about development began to influence Taipei and Seoul as well as other aid donors and the principal international agencies, notably the IMF and the World Bank, which were beginning to emerge as important actors in the aid arena. AID staff helped to persuade first Taiwan and then the Republic of Korea to stabilize prices, move to realistic exchange rates and overcome chronic balance of payments difficulties by adapting export-oriented strategies that United States aid workers had effectively introduced in Puerto Rico to take advantage of that country's access to United States markets. The Joint Commission for Rural Reconstruction had laid the foundations for food processing, but the monetary exchange rate and trade policy reforms were essential to making the exports of canned food, wigs, artificial flowers, clothing and other labour-intensive goods possible. The debate between AID and Taiwanese officials was an important component of the process. As a market for literate workers developed, and as the need for goods, roads and power grew, the earlier support for infrastructure began to pay dividends.

The supply of aid was expanded as European countries and Japan, fully recovered from the Second World War, began to join the former East Asian colonial powers as aid donors. Aid programming and concern with broader aid policy issues spread to bilateral donors and to the IMF and the World Bank which were emerging as a strong influence in development because their rhetoric was backed by capital flows. The World Bank's Consultative Group system increased the diversity of donors, raised aid flows and managed a development debate of increasing sophistication. Policy advice *per se* from bilateral and multilateral donors was not necessarily wise. For example, the World Bank-sponsored 1963 Rueff Report strongly encouraged the Federation of Malaysia to focus on import substitution for the domestic market, contributing to the break up of Malaysia and Singapore and serious structural problems in Malaysia. However, the policy debates to which such policy advice led, raised host country understanding of development issues and encouraged the employment of technically trained staff in the public services of developing countries. Home country reviews of aid programs drew attention to the host country policies which determined the effectiveness of aid. Aid flows to East Asian countries reached a plateau in the 1960s so that aid to GDP ratios fell and aid became less concessional. However, host country policies which determined the effectiveness of aid improved, and therefore increasing absorptive capacity improved, 'rent' effects became less important as the weight of aid in the economy declined, and aid became more effective.

Aid flows entered a third stage in the 1970s. The development debates associated with conditionality led to a shift from bilateral to multilateral aid by most bilateral donors; the Asian Development Bank (ADB), the International Fund for Agricultural Development (IFAD), OPEC and Arab funds were added to World Bank funding which also grew rapidly in the 1970s in real terms. The IMF considerably expanded its facilities for developing countries. East Asian countries moved ahead in using multilateral concessional sources of funds ahead of other developing countries. They were prepared to pay the 'price' of conditionality from the development banks and funds because host country technocrats largely agreed with the analytical perceptions that lay behind the conditions of the multilateral lenders. Moreover, interest differences between private and multilateral loans diminished the repayment terms of the IMF and development banks facilitated debt management. Thus East Asian countries used IMF facilities more intensively than, for example, did Latin American countries.

By the end of the 1970s the IMF's and the World Bank's pressure to lend in order to maintain their position in international capital flows was often leading to competition between them and thus leaving 'conditionality' behind. The World Bank's project loan disbursements were, moreover, lagging so far behind commitments that 'adjustment assistance' loans, reminiscent of the budget support aid of the 1950s, were evolved to ensure rapid disbursement. The debt difficulties of many countries also led to a revival of conditionality considerations. The Philippines, borrowing excessively from private sources, was typically one of the first borrowers from the new facility. A few other East Asian countries also used 'adjustment assistance' loans, but more carefully, not because they disagreed with the 'conditions' but because they feared the 'rent' effects of such borrowing. The disastrous effects of aid without a policy debate had become so evident in countries such as the Philippines by the time of the 1981–82 recession (when the availability of non-concessional funds declined and the procyclical lending of the development banks found these short of lending capacity), that the 1980s saw a return to 'conditionality' policy dialogues between donors and recipients. In East Asia, however, neither bilateral nor multilateral donors are any longer in a position to lead the development debate. Concessional flows are declining, and, more importantly, the capacity of policy analysis of several host countries has outpaced that of the donor country.

Table 4.3 *Capital inflows^a share of gross domestic investment, 1970–80* (per cent)

Country group	1970	1977	1978	1979	1980
Low income countries	4	7	6	10	8
Asia	3	4	4	7	5
China	—	—	1	5	1
India	7	5	4	4	7
Africa, south of Sahara	29	40	43	52	59
Middle income countries	15	18	18	17	15
East Asia and Pacific	19	16	14	14	15
Middle East and North Africa	17	21	16	14	10
Africa, south of Sahara^b	16	13	20	22	17
Southern Europe	12	17	19	22	22
Latin America and Caribbean	13	18	21	21	17
Middle income oil importers	15	17	19	20	18
Middle income oil exporters	13	18	16	15	11
All low and middle income developing countries	11	15	15	16	13

^a Official transfers, net foreign direct investment, and net medium- and long-term borrowing.
^b Excludes South Africa although it is included in all sub-totals and totals.
Source: Hughes (1985).

FOREIGN DIRECT INVESTMENT

Capital inflows in total, comprising official transfers, net foreign direct investment and medium- and long-term borrowing, have made a modest contribution to the financing of gross domestic investment for developing countries as a whole during the 1970s (Table 4.3). Even allowing for the unreliability of the statistics, the role of the different forms of foreign capital in investment among the nations in which we are interested appears to have varied considerably. As a proportion of gross fixed capital formation, foreign direct investment has assumed relative importance over the period 1970–83 in Singapore, Malaysia, the Philippines, Indonesia and Thailand. Foreign direct investment has assumed far less importance as a proportion of capital formation in the Republic of Korea and Taiwan.

The size of capital inflows in general as well as the structure of those inflows assumes importance in terms of the more traditional interpretation of foreign capital in development. In terms of explaining 'success' in growth and industrialization, the traditional view of foreign direct investment looks at its role in supplementing both domestic investment and foreign exchange inflows (Riedel 1984a). In this context, foreign direct investment as a form of capital inflow has important characteristics. Foreign direct investment does not necessarily involve either a significant supplement to domestic saving or a significant net inflow of foreign exchange.

In the first place, a proportion of *de novo* foreign direct investment is financed by local borrowing, in which case that part of foreign direct investment involves neither direct foreign savings nor a direct foreign exchange inflow. In addition, the financing of a proportion of the expansion of established foreign direct investment involves both retained earnings and some local borrowings, rather than a new inflow of foreign saving and foreign exchange. The evidence suggests that a large proportion of foreign direct investment is in fact funded by local borrowing (Riedel 1979) which does not *directly* entail either foreign saving or foreign exchange (though these flows may be affected indirectly). Specifically, some 60 per cent of total United States outward foreign direct investment over the period 1975–82 was funded by retained earnings, with local borrowings also playing a significant role: foreign-financed equity capital accounted for only a small percentage of total foreign direct investment (IMF 1985b). Recent estimates for the Bataan export processing zone in the Philippines, for example, show that 91 per cent of the total foreign direct investment in that zone over the period to 1977 was raised domestically, of which 95 per cent was *domestic* borrowing (Warr 1986).

The financing of foreign direct investment raises a number of issues. The first obvious point relates to the perceived external-sector (balance of payments) implications of foreign direct investment compared with other forms of foreign capital inflow. The point has been made that the cost of servicing foreign direct investment has different impacts compared with the cost of servicing other private foreign capital *inflows*. In particular, other private foreign capital inflow generates a servicing debt burden regardless of what income it generates and regardless of the economic conditions. By contrast, foreign direct investment usually has a servicing commitment which varies directly with the income that it generates which is itself dependent on economic conditions in the domestic or export markets to which the investment is oriented. In addition, foreign direct investment entails risk-sharing and is cyclically compensatory in the balance of payments (see Hughes and Dorrance 1984:20 for a discussion).

The pattern of financing of foreign direct investment places these arguments in a somewhat different context. To the extent that foreign direct investment is financed by domestic borrowings rather than directly by foreign savings, the context for the debt-servicing comparison of foreign direct investment with other forms of private capital inflow changes: a significant part of foreign direct investment debt-servicing may not be related to any net foreign savings or foreign exchange inflow. The risk argument also changes. Subject to any guarantees provided by the overseas firm, the risk assumed in the case of foreign direct investment falls on local lenders and local governments which act as guarantors as well as the foreign investor. For many large multinational enterprises, 'letters of comfort' are often used rather than legally-binding guarantees in their local borrowings, and host-country governments often guarantee the local borrowings of the local subsidiary operation. The point is that, because of the financing pattern of foreign direct investment, the comparison between it and other forms of private capital inflow may not be as sharp as assumed in some of the risk and debt-servicing arguments.

The development contribution of foreign direct investment and its role in East Asian industrialization is not normally seen as exclusively financial. In the context of industrialization and development, the issue in question is the net effect of foreign direct investment compared with other forms of private (and official) capital inflow on productive activity and on the level and growth of GNP and its distribution. In view of the financing pattern of a large proportion of foreign direct investment, its direct contribution in terms of the two-gap model (savings and foreign exchange) is even less certain. Rather, the (potential) development contribution of foreign direct investment is bound up with the familiar 'package' of product, technology (and, more broadly, know-how), market -access and capital.

Before turning to the development contribution of foreign direct investment in the East Asian context, however, we need to consider another issue involving foreign direct investment in relation to foreign capital flows more generally. One of the earlier concerns with foreign capital flows was their potential 'crowding out' effect in the host country: foreign saving may displace rather than fully complement domestic saving – leading to an increase in domestic consumption, and foreign-financed investment may displace domestic investment via a crowding-out effect in a market where limited investment opportunities exist (see, for example, the discussion in Riedel 1979).

Relatively large foreign capital inflow may have a crowding-out effect, of course, where limited investment opportunities exist, although foreign direct investment and other capital inflows which are directed towards productive uses such as infrastructure are more likely than not to lead to additional investment opportunities in which domestic firms may participate: the 'virtuous circle' effect of foreign direct investment. Of course, the potential for indigenous firms to participate in domestic investment opportunities depends on the structure of the economy and the nature of government policies as much as the availability of specific investment opportunities. Foreign direct investment may 'compete' with other forms of foreign capital inflow in the context of a given monetary or exchange-rate policy. Foreign direct investment may also compete with other capital inflows as well as with domestic investment for scarce domestic resources of various types. It is important, therefore, for developing countries to identify the most appropriate mix not only between foreign saving and domestic saving but also between forms of foreign capital 'inflow'. It is in this context that the role of foreign direct investment and its associated resource 'package' assumes considerable importance.

Even though the relationship between either foreign capital inflow in general or foreign direct investment in particular and economic growth is rarely established statistically (IMF 1985a; Riedel 1984a), there is a general belief that they are important as a part of – though not a prerequisite for – development (Hughes and Dorrance 1984; Parry 1980). Foreign direct investment is seen as both a complement and a stimulus to domestic investment, and technology transfer embodied in (though increasingly available separately from) foreign direct investment is perceived to be critical to development (Balasubramanyam 1980). Foreign direct investment in particular has an important role in growth and development, in overcoming significant bottle-necks which hamper the development process. The role is evident in the East Asian economies in different ways, with bottle-necks in 'know-how' and market access at least as important as the financial bottle-necks implied by the two-gap model for the East Asian countries with which we are concerned.

The financial side of capital flows is still important – for example, the capital requirements of the still important natural resource sector of the ASEAN countries of East Asia are considerable. This has required a significant amount of external support: the extraction, refining and processing needs of the natural resource sectors of these countries are both capital- and technology-intensive and extend to both foreign capital and foreign know-how (Naya 1985). It is not only the resource sector where foreign direct investment is still important. Foreign direct investment and external know-how continue to be important in other sectors and for a variety of specific activities. The specific form of 'external support' clearly varies between the developing countries of East Asia (and elsewhere), and itself changes over time. The experiences of the Republic of Korea and Singapore with regard to the role of foreign direct investment and foreign capital stand in sharp contrast, even though some similarities have emerged in more recent times for some of the more technologically-advanced manufacturing activities.

Foreign direct investment and
developing country exports

There are several areas where the potential impact of foreign direct investment has been identified as important for the developing Asian economies (Ozawa 1980). In view of the increasing emphasis on export-based industrialization, an important area involves the links between foreign direct investment and trade. The growth in East Asian exports, particularly manufactured exports, and its significance in the development process are well recognized. The role of foreign direct investment has been of considerable importance, though that role varies for different types of exports as well as in different markets. The importance of multinational enterprises in the trade of developing nations should not be surprising in view of the intra-firm trade activities associated with multinational enterprises and foreign direct investment generally, particularly United States-based multinational enterprises. Indeed, intra-firm trade has been identified as growing rapidly in the Asia–Pacific region, though much of this growth has been in areas other than manufacturing (Hill and Johns 1985).

The share of direct multinational enterprise exports in the total manufactured exports of several developing countries has been estimated by Nayyar (1978) as:

Hong Kong	10 per cent
Taiwan	20 per cent
Republic of Korea	15 per cent
India	5 per cent
Pakistan	10–15 per cent
Singapore	70 per cent

The proportion of exports which are indirectly related to multinational enterprise activities has not been quantified, but is believed to be significant (UNCTAD 1978; Keesing 1979).

There are broadly three areas of multinational enterprise involvement in the exports of developing countries. First, multinational enterprises still play some role in exports of the primary sector including resource trade, though the form of their overall involvement has changed. Even with the increased importance of indigenous ownership including state enterprises, in the resource sector generally, multinational enterprises still play a role in several aspects of trade. Multinational enterprises are still important as direct purchasers and users of a variety of mineral and primary products, even if they have no equity in the extraction stages. An involvement in the marketing, distribution and purchasing of primary commodities by multinational enterprises can play an important part in the export performance of primary-product developing countries. This role is common in the region and extends to a range of commodities such as bauxite, copper, lead, iron ore, bananas, fish, timber, tobacco, tea, and others, where multinational enterprises still exercise a significant influence in export markets both directly as buyers and via their dominance in marketing and trading channels (UNCTAD 1978; Helleiner 1973).

Second, multinational enterprises have some involvement in 'traditional' manufactured export trade including, for example, clothing, textiles and footwear, leather goods and processed foodstuffs. In these traditional products, the role of multinational enterprises is primarily in the buying, marketing and distribution of goods in industrial-country markets rather than in production within the exporting country. Even though direct equity involvement may be small – which it is in several of the East Asian economies where traditional manufactured exports are still important – the role of the foreign firm can be critical in the transport, distribution and, especially, the marketing channels on which these traditional exports depend.

For these traditional manufactured goods, where product differentiation advantages which are embodied in the product's characteristics are less relevant, successful market access does depend on marketing skills and market links. Some of the East Asian economies have these marketing skills and connections which do not depend on the involvement of foreign firms; it is suggested that indigenous Hong Kong firms perform as well as foreign firms in this function (Chen 1983). Other countries' indigenous firms have not developed the necessary international marketing skills and links, and have relied more on foreign firms in this regard. The question of causation with respect to this latter observation necessarily arises. Perhaps more generally important has been the role of multinational enterprises in maintaining access to the industrial-country markets for traditional manufactured exports in the presence of increasing pressure to extend the trade barriers around these markets in North America and Europe (a role identified by Helleiner 1973). This has played some role in the continued exports of countries such as Singapore, Malaysia and the Republic of Korea (in textiles and electronics), through the late 1970s to the present time.

Finally, multinational enterprises play a more direct role in the exports of other manufactured products, especially those products with a greater proportion of product differentiation and/or 'technology content'. The role of multinational enterprises in the production and exports of differentiated manufactured products – both finished products and components – by developing countries is clearly recognized (UNCTAD 1978; ECE/UNCTC 1983). Multinational enterprises have located manufacturing facilities orien-ted to export markets in the East Asian region, notably Hong Kong, Singapore, Taiwan and Republic of Korea, with increasing activity in other Southeast Asian developing nations such as Malaysia, Thailand and the Philippines. The production of differentiated manufactured goods for export markets includes finished products (mainly consumer products) as well as components and other intermediate inputs such as electronic, engineering and chemical products. Some of this production has been located in free-trade, export processing zones in the region. The role of foreign firms in the manufacture of 'differentiated' exports is more widespread than in the case of 'traditional' manufactures and primary products. In 'differentiated' manufactured exports, multinational enterprises play a greater role in production proper as well as in trade and marketing activities, though this role varies with the home-country of the foreign firm as well as the host country within which the multinational enterprise operates. Where marketing links are important, the role of foreign direct investment has been critical in export performance in these commodities.

The home-country influence is one feature which has received some attention – particularly the so-called Kojima thesis about 'trade creating' Japanese foreign direct investment compared with 'trade destroying' United States foreign direct investment (Kojima 1979). The nature of the foreign direct investment activity is heavily influenced by the technology associated with the product and process in question. At one extreme, the production of primary exports and 'traditional' manufactured goods, where technology is standardized, is likely to be largely in the hands of indigenous firms. The multinational enterprise's role in the export of these products is primarily confined to marketing activities such as transport, packaging, distribution, inventory control, warehousing and the like. For products with a greater 'technology intensity', that is, the differentiated components and final products, where inputs of know-how are far more important in the production phase, the direct role of multinational enterprises in production as well as marketing and, hence, exporting is more important.

The importance of foreign direct investment in the export of manufactured products varies between the different countries of the region. Thus, in Hong Kong, while foreign firms are active in exporting manufactured products such as textiles, clothing, plastic products, electronics and toys, it has been suggested that there is no obvious marketing advantage enjoyed by foreign firms over indigenous firms in the marketing of these consumer products

(Chen 1983). In Singapore, on the other hand, foreign firms, both Japanese- and United States-based multinational enterprises in particular, are dominant in exporting manufactured products, including those 'traditional' products that are still being manufactured. In the case of Malaysia, one of the key contributions of foreign direct investment has been associated with the growth of exports generally, including manufactured exports, in which the marketing role of multinational enterprises has been particularly noted (Hoffmann and Tan 1980).

In the case of the Republic of Korea, the role of foreign firms in exporting is important in certain sectors. Foreign firms, usually operating via joint ventures, have been identified as playing an important role in the exports of the petrochemicals, electric and electronic machinery and textiles industries (Westphal *et al.* 1981; Bohn-Young Koo 1982). Japanese-based firms have been dominant in foreign investment in these industries and the role of foreign direct investment in exporting appears to be proportionately more important than its role in the economy overall: the proportion of total commodity exports directly accounted for by foreign firms increased from 6.2 per cent in 1971 to 17.6 per cent in 1975 (Westphal *et al.* 1981) and to over 20 per cent in 1978 (Bohn-Young Koo 1982). The role of foreign firms in exporting from the Republic of Korea has been most important in textiles and electrical-electronic products. In the cases of electrical and electronic products, the role of multinational enterprises has extended to the provision of 'production know-how and critical inputs' (Westphal *et al.* 1981:55). In textiles, where Japanese firms have dominated foreign direct investment, marketing links have been far more important. Indeed, it may be the provision of *market know-how* which becomes an increasingly important function of multinational enterprises as production technology becomes more widely available from other sources.

Changes in the international market for technology, notably increased competition among suppliers of production technology, has meant the increased potential availability of that technology via non-foreign direct investment channels. Developments in technology markets have been more rapid than changes in marketing and market know-how proper. It may be that, for economies such as the Republic of Korea, where access to production know-how via licensing and other formal channels, as well as its own industrial research and development, becomes 'easier' and less costly, the main problem area will be developing marketing contacts and know-how in the absence of formal foreign direct investment links which provide such contacts and know-how.

Foreign direct investment and the transfer of know-how

A major potential contribution of foreign direct investment to development is the provision of technology and know-how. These know-how links are not confined to production technology proper, reflecting the results of industrial research and development. Equally as important is the formation of skills associated with the employment and training activities of foreign firms. Indeed, it is in the area of human capital or formation of skills that there seems to be greatest agreement about the development contribution of foreign direct investment. This has also been one of the major contributions of foreign direct investment to industrialization in the East Asian region.

The creation of employment opportunities simply in terms of jobs associated with foreign direct investment is less clear cut. A number of studies suggest that there has been little direct employment creation associated with foreign direct investment, partly reflecting the capital-intensity of the industries in which multinational enterprises operate in production within the developing country. Specific studies of foreign firm operations have concluded that there has been weak aggregate employment growth associated with the activities of foreign firms in Malaysia (Hoffmann and Tan 1980), and foreign firms have had little to do with the employment growth associated with Hong Kong's manufactured export success (Chen 1983).

The contribution of foreign direct investment appears to have been much greater in formation of skills than in net aggregate employment growth *per se*, and it is in this area that there has been a significant development contribution in the region. Whereas foreign direct investment has not been seen as accounting for employment growth in Hong Kong, it has been identified as playing an important role in the training of indigenous personnel. Management training has also been identified as a significant benefit arising from the activities of multinational enterprises in an otherwise critical survey of foreign direct investment in the Philippines (Lindsey 1981; Hill 1985). In export processing zones, where benefits to the host country are generally very limited, an important contribution of foreign direct investment comes from management training and technical quality control (Warr 1986).

Indeed, the development of management and technical skills has been identified as one of the most important benefits arising from multinational enterprise activities in developing countries generally (Reuber *et al.* 1973). The benefits of this human capital formation are not fully captured by the foreign firm, but there are important spill-over effects by way of direct links with suppliers and customers as well as indirect leaks to competitors and other firms (and the government) in the host nation. The opportunities for these spill-over benefits to flow to the host economy are important. The spill-overs take the form of training supplier and customer personnel by foreign firms, as well as via the movement of trained personnel from foreign firms to indigenous competitors in the industry and other local firms. The direct flow-on benefits are less evident in the case of export processing zones where links with suppliers and customers lie primarily outside the developing country. These spill-overs and direct links have played an important part in the industrialization process of East Asia.

Foreign direct investment, as a particular form of foreign capital flow involving the multinational enterprises, plays an important role in the provision of market and marketing know-how as well as in the transfer of know-how in the form of human capital – the formation of skills effect. Multinational enterprises also play an important role in the provision of 'hard' production technology, though their role and the nature of alternatives is different in this area of know-how. Technology transfer and the provision of know-how to developing countries is recognized as a major function of foreign direct investment (IMF 1985a; Naya 1985). There are, however, important alternative means of access to production technology.

The cases of Singapore and the Republic of Korea again provide a stark contrast. Nearly all technology transfer to Singapore takes place via foreign direct investment (Pang 1983), while in the case of the Republic of Korea, around 75 per cent of all overseas licensing agreements over the period 1973–80 were negotiated by locally-owned firms (IMF 1985a). Indeed, in various industries in the Republic of Korea, especially the machinery sector, licensing agreements entered into by local firms have been far more important than foreign direct investment as the means of gaining access to technological know-how (Bohn-Young 1982). In other East Asian countries, there has been a mix in the channels of access to production technology, with both foreign direct investment (including joint ventures) and licensing agreements separate from foreign direct investment playing some role. Among the East Asian NICs, the Republic of Korea stands out with respect to its use of contractual technology agreements separate from foreign direct investment.

The international market for production technology has changed dramatically over the last ten to fifteen years. With the exception of the 'frontier' high-technology areas such as aerospace and bio-genetic engineering, for example, there has been a significant increase in the number of suppliers of technology in the international market. There has also been an increase in the activities of 'independent' consulting engineering firms involved as middlemen in the technology market. More suppliers from a number of different countries, greater competition among suppliers as well as improved information on the part of buyers, largely reflecting the activities of middlemen, have led to greater competition in many parts of the market for production technology. This has meant changes in the costs of, and terms and conditions associated with technology (Parry 1984).

Change in the market for production technology has coincided with the increased importance of *formal* channels of technology transfer for countries such as the Republic of Korea as well as for other countries where licensing unrelated to foreign direct investment is becoming more important. As the costs of formal technology fall (including the costs associated with the terms and conditions imposed on the use of the technology), 'informal' access to production technology becomes less attractive. Informal access by way of copying, for example, does not often represent a complete technology transfer and may not be an efficient form of transfer. As long as the price (and costs) of formal technology transfer via licensing is regarded as 'excessive', then informal channels will be used where available.

When a country reaches a different stage of development and becomes involved in technically more advanced production activities, especially for export markets ('moving up the technology ladder'), informal channels of access to technology become less satisfactory. If formal technology transfer also becomes less expensive – both in terms of price as well as conditions of use – then countries will increasingly rely on these formal channels for technology transfer. This has taken place in the East Asian NICs and ASEAN countries in the form of technology transfer embodied in foreign direct investment as well as formal licensing agreements with unaffiliated foreign firms. Informal technology transfer may become very much less important during the second half of the 1980s than it was during the 1960s and 1970s.

While the conditions surrounding access to production technology have changed, the situation in other areas of 'know-how' may be somewhat different. In particular, unlike production technology, marketing know-how and market links are more likely to continue to be dominated by multinational enterprises. To the extent that the market for production technology differs from the market for other 'know-how' in this respect, then foreign direct investment will continue to have an important role to play in development. This is not to say that foreign direct investment is unimportant in the provision of production technology. Rather, for some developing countries, with the Republic of Korea being one of the main examples, access to *production technology* has successfully taken place without foreign direct investment.

Alternative channels of access to market links and marketing know-how, whether informal or formal, that do not involve foreign direct investment, however, do not yet appear to be as well developed.

Intra-regional direct investment

An important source of foreign direct investment in some of the East Asian developing nations has been intra-regional direct investment. As shown in Table 4.4, Malaysia, Thailand and Indonesia had a significant proportion of the stock of foreign direct investment attributed to intra-regional investment sources. Hong Kong is perhaps the largest source country of foreign direct investment in the region (and perhaps among developing countries generally), with an estimated stock of outward direct investment of US$1800 million (Chen 1984). The main host countries for Hong

Table 4.4 *Percentage distribution by home countries in the reported stock of foreign direct investment in selected Asian countries, various countries, various years in the 1970s*

Home countries	Host countries													
	Indonesia		Malaysia		Hong Kong		Singapore		Rep. of Korea		Philippines		Thailand	
	1972	1978	1971	1977	1971	1978	1972	1977	1971	1978	1972	1978	1972	1978
Japan	23	36	12	24	22	19	16	15	43	58	1	25	38	37
United States	16	6	15	19	54	47	33	33	39	19	58	34	14	13
Western Europe	14	9	23	18	16	20	39	32	9	3	6	17	12	14
Australia	4	3	2	3	4	4	—	—	—	—	—	4	—	—
Total of industrial countries listed	57	54	52	64	96	90	78	80	91	90	65	80	64	64
Southeast Asia as home economies	25	20	39	34	3	7	9	9	1	1	7	12	22	23
Western hemisphere, Middle East and others	4	1	9	1	—	3	—	—	7	7	2	2	—	3
Unspecified	14	25	—	1	1	—	13	11	1	2	26	6	16	10
Total of all home countries	100	100	100	100	100	100	100	100	100	100	100	100	100	100

Source: Ozawa (1980).

Kong-based foreign direct investment are Indonesia, Taiwan and Malaysia (and China). There is also significant foreign direct investment from Malaysia in Indonesia and Thailand; from the Philippines in Indonesia; from Singapore in Malaysia, Indonesia and Hong Kong; and from Thailand in Hong Kong (UNCTC 1978). Taiwan has also been active in outward foreign direct investment in the Philippines, Indonesia, Singapore, Thailand and Malaysia (Amsden 1984b).

Associated with this intra-regional foreign direct investment there have been effects on both commodity trade and technology trade. Some of the foreign direct investment within the region has been associated with relocating trade-oriented activities to take advantage of changing comparative advantage, particularly that arising from real labour costs of production. In addition, relocating trade-oriented production within the region via foreign direct investment has been one means of by-passing various trade restrictions imposed in the industrial-country markets on various manufactured exports, such as clothing, textiles and other consumer products. Apart from the intra-regional foreign direct investment related to exporting to industrial-country markets, some of this investment may also have been the result of attempts to protect the market share within the region.

Intra-regional foreign direct investment has also been associated with significant flows of production technology and know-how more generally. Not all these technology flows have been embodied in foreign direct investment, however, and licensing arrangements have also played an important part in intra-regional technology transfer. This intra-regional technology transfer has been particularly important in the case of Hong Kong, Taiwan and the Republic of Korea. Hong Kong has tended to export know-how embodied in foreign direct investment, with an emphasis on production design and management and marketing know-how (Chen 1984). Taiwan's main technology exports have been embodied in equipment exports rather than foreign direct investment or turn-key operations as such, particularly small-scale metal processing plants, while her foreign direct investment has been oriented to securing raw materials and maintaining market share (Amsden 1984b). The Republic of Korea's technology exports have been embodied in her outward foreign direct investment as well as in overseas construction, technology licensing and exports of machinery and equipment independent of foreign direct investment (West-phal *et al.* 1984).

Intra-regional foreign direct investment and technology transfer are complements to more traditional sources of these flows. Their potential contribution to development within the region extends not only to the recipient nations but also to the exporting nation. For the technology and capital exporter within the region, intra-regional foreign direct investment and technology transfer provide a base on which to develop and exploit areas of know-how advantage. The ability to exploit production technology, management skills and market access by the developing-country know-how exporter can only be enhanced by intra-regional foreign direct investment and technology transfer. Whether this takes place via foreign direct investment, exports of machinery and equipment, construction operations or technology licensing may not much matter to the know-how exporter; what matters is the opportunity to extend the base on which such know-how can be developed and exploited. For the recipient nations within the region, intra-regional foreign direct investment and technology transfer bring with it capital and know-how which, if put to productive uses, will contribute to development.

Some other issues

There are other ways in which foreign direct investment (and technology transfer) have contributed to development and industrialization in East Asia. This is not the place to develop all the arguments about foreign direct investment (see, for example, Hughes and Dorrance 1984; Parry 1980). On the positive side, foreign direct investment has a potentially important contribution to development which goes beyond its effects on productive capacity, exports and know-how development. Significant tax revenues can be generated by foreign direct investment operations that would not otherwise result either because domestic investment would not have taken place or because foreign direct investment is more productive than the domestic investment that would have taken place. This revenue effect has been identified as especially important in the case of foreign direct investment in Malaysia, for example (Hoffmann and Tan 1980).

On the negative side, there are a range of problems that have been linked with foreign direct investment and technology transfer. A high import propensity, inappropriate and over-priced technology, the erosion of domestic firms and industries by 'unfair' competition and an excessive reliance on imported inputs, and the abuse of monopoly power including the use of transfer pricing, are all problems which have been associated with foreign direct investment, particularly via the multinational enterprise. There is no doubt that these problems do arise and that they detract from the net gains accruing to the host country, whether developing or industrial. This is the result both of a reduced aggregate increase in the gains from foreign direct investment and of a change in the distribution of gains between the foreign investor or technology supplier and the host country.

In most instances, the erosion of benefits arises as a direct result of responses to inappropriate government policies – specific industry policies as well as general macroeconomic policies – rather than as a result of an inherent unsuitability of foreign direct investment (Hughes and Dorrance 1984; Parry 1980). If this view is correct, the lesson is simple: governments must formulate policies which maximize the development contributions of foreign direct investment. This becomes especially important as the nature of that investment changes and as the international markets within which foreign direct investment and technology transfer take place change.

MEDIUM- AND LONG-TERM CAPITAL FLOWS

Industrial countries began to assist developing countries to become eligible for private suppliers' credits in the 1950s by making export credits available from official sources and by insuring private export credits. Mercantile policies also led to credit subsidies which were often justified on the grounds of aid. Governments and private entrepreneurs in the East Asian countries were often first eligible for suppliers' credits in the 1950s in association with aid flows or foreign direct investment. Unlike many other developing countries, however, by the 1960s their overall policy framework with its strong export orientation was able to avoid debt problems arising out of suppliers' credits at a time when countries with distorted economic policies contributed to widespread 'debt crises'. By the mid-1960s the East Asian countries also began to make use of bank loans and syndications directly as their economies strengthened further and as the supply of capital increased with the growth of the Euro and other off-shore markets. The large firms in the Republic of Korea were particularly anxious to avoid foreign direct investment, especially from Japan, and the government therefore facilitated the use of bank funds for private investors and used them for public investment. Private enterprises borrowed for business purposes, sometimes with their host government guarantees, sometimes with guarantees from parent corporations in home countries. Packages of foreign direct investment, suppliers' credits and bank loans became increasingly common. Governments also borrowed through suppliers' credits for public utilities, and towards the end of the 1960s began to use syndicated bank loans. Packages of official aid, suppliers credits and syndicated loans were also widely used, with high elasticities of substitution among the various capital flows. In the short but sharp recession of 1975 some East Asian governments began to borrow more broadly for budgetary purposes to offset declining exports and the fall in income that followed the rise in petroleum prices.

Low real interest rates encouraged shifts from foreign direct investment to bank borrowing and increased overall borrowing. The Pertamina episode of excessive borrowing in Indonesia in 1975, Korean borrowing and particularly Philippine borrowing all increased rapidly. Repressed financial systems and the tendency to overvalue exchange rates discouraged domestic savings despite high private profits, particularly in protected domestically-oriented industries. Entrepreneurs smuggled out funds by falsifying transfer prices. The same entrepreneurs then borrowed abroad at low real interest rates to invest at home at considerable further private profit, but where investment was in protected industries it did not create the export capacity to service the debt created. Government banks guaranteed such loans. Where public investment was inefficient, corruptly managed, and in infrastructural facilities that had low financial and social rates of return, a large volume of debt was created for little return. The East Asian countries form a continuum from those with appropriate policies for industrialization and growth where foreign funds were utilized efficiently, to the Philippines where a relatively low level of borrowing has led to major debt problems (Table 4.5).

Short-, medium- and long-term capital outflows began to emerge

Table 4.5 *External bank claims, debt and debt indicators*

	External bank claims December 1984 (US$ billion)	Medium- and long-term public debt outstanding December 1983 (US$ billion)	Medium- and long-term non-guaranteed debt outstanding December 1983 (US$ billion)	Percentage, to debt (2) (2) + (3) GNP	Percentage total debt of exports	Debt service ratio	Reserve to debt ratio
	(1)	(2)	(3)	(4)	(5)	(6)	(7)
Hong Kong	6.1	0.2	n.a.	1[a]	n.a.	n.a.	n.a.
Indonesia	14.5	21.8	n.a.	29[a]	109[a]	13[a]	23[a]
Malaysia	11.4	10.7	n.a.	39[a]	64[a]	6[a]	44[a]
Philippines	14.0	10.4	3.3	40	168	22	7
Singapore	2.3	1.2	n.a.	8[a]	4[a]	1[a]	45[a]
Korea, Republic of	31.2	21.5	1.6	31	76	4	11
Taiwan	6.1	n.a.	n.a.	n.a.	n.a.	n.a.	n.a.
Thailand	7.5	7.1	2.7	25	116	21	26

Notes and sources: (1) OECD and Bank for International Settlements (1985). (2)–(7) World Bank (1985). These figures include debt owed to official sources, but exclude short-term debt, and debt not guaranteed by host governments. Figures marked ([a]) exclude non-guaranteed debt.

within the region in the 1960s. Hong Kong was one of the first developing countries to become an international capital market location. The openness of its financial systems and institutions, the stability of its currency and its location in a time zone some twelve hours from the principal European and North American financial markets, all contributed to this. Singapore followed in the mid-1970s, the growth of its financial intermediation role stimulated by political uncertainty in Hong Kong and growing savings and investment operations in the region. The Republic of Korea and Taiwan have also become international lenders. They had to establish subsidized suppliers' credit facilities to match industrial countries' terms for capital goods sales. As they continued to be net borrowers they had to borrow additionally in world capital markets to provide suppliers' credit facilities that would not exert strong inflationary trends on their domestic economies. Taiwan has taken advantage of high interest rates in the United States.

With the exception of the Republic of Korea, East Asian countries have traditionally been fairly modest borrowers among developing countries. The shift from borrowing largely from official sources (at fixed interest rates) to borrowing from private sources (at variable interest rates) is reflected in the composition of debt (Lee 1983).

Debt data do not include equity or other foreign direct investment obligations. Debt service estimates and ratios similarly exclude foreign direct investment dividends, licence fees and other obligations. It is frequently argued that service on foreign direct investment is less onerous than interest obligations because it only has to be paid when a firm is profitable. A firm, however, may be privately profitable though with socially costly investments, and it may be making profits though the economy has balance of payments difficulties. Moreover the 'foreign' equity may have been built up through borrowing in the host country and through retained profits so that profit remittances may bear no relation to foreign capital inflows. Foreign direct investment considerations are obviously important in Singapore where the bulk of foreign capital inflows have taken the form of foreign direct investment, but they must also be taken into account in the other East Asian countries.

With this caveat, Table 4.5 suggests that the debt obligations of the East Asian countries are relatively modest, particularly in relation to heavy borrowers in Latin American countries. The data clearly indicate that debt problems do not arise from the ratio of debt to GNP but to exports, where the Philippines obligation is much higher than that of other East Asian countries though it is not as high as it is in Latin American countries. The Philippines were thus caught in the late 1970s–early 1980s 'scissors' of a sudden large increase in real interest rates combined with a decline in commodity prices and the world fall in the demand for all exports in 1981–82. The Republic of Korea was able to manage despite its much higher indebtedness because of its strong export performance.

CONCLUSIONS

Foreign capital flows to East Asia during the past thirty years have varied considerably in composition and in total among countries and periods and by type of flow.

The relationship between capital inflows and growth is at best tenuous. The countries which grew more rapidly used foreign capital relatively less intensively than those that grew less rapidly, a finding confirmed by the econometric analyses of larger samples of countries. But this negative relationship is not the result of a negative impact of foreign capital on domestic savings. Domestic savings were highest in the Republic of Korea which has had large inflows of foreign capital in the form of aid and banking flows.

The demand for foreign capital (even from such 'aid' sources as the IMF) is determined by a country's domestic policies, and these also determine its impact. A country can have a low demand for foreign capital and it can be used ineffectually, but a country can also have a high demand for foreign capital that it can use effectively. Many different types of capital inflow can be combined. Any combination of outcomes is possible depending on domestic policies, and these will also determine the impact of foreign capital flows on domestic savings, entrepreneurship, the rate of industrialization, the share of exports, and so on. These will determine the further demand for capital.

The qualitative impact of capital inflows, chiefly associated with aid and foreign direct investment, is important and particularly subject to domestic policy influence. Multinational corporations, in particular, are profit-maximizing organizations which are highly responsive to the economic rules of the game. Their impact on industrialization arises particularly through the technology and market links to industrial-country markets. The extent and way in which this impact benefits the host country is heavily influenced by policies adopted in those countries. Host country policies largely determine the volume of foreign direct investment they wish to obtain and its effects on the economy, not by special foreign investment 'incentives', but by their basic economic 'rules of the game'.

ROBERT WADE*

5

THE ROLE OF GOVERNMENT IN
OVERCOMING MARKET FAILURE:
TAIWAN, REPUBLIC OF KOREA AND JAPAN

Governments ought not to give more incentives to some industries than to others, except to overcome inherent market failure. Inherent market failure is uncommon, even in developing countries. Most apparent market failures are policy induced; they arise from government action or inaction – action to restrict market access, or failure to establish a capital market, for example. The appropriate role of government is therefore to help create and sustain an economic environment in which price signals drive industrial change. This it can do by adopting a neutral policy regime, the core of which is a free trade (or almost free trade) regime and a small public sector, unable to impose 'political' prices.

Powerful empirical evidence for the validity of this proposition comes from the contrast between the East Asian developing countries and Japan, on the one hand, and most of the rest of the developing world, on the other. The superior economic perform-ance of the East Asian capitalist countries has gone with a rela-tively neutral policy regime; the inferior economic performance elsewhere went with varying degrees of distortions. The causality is from distortions, or lack of them, to results.

That, I believe, is a fair summary of the central interpretation of the East Asian experience by *neo-classical* development econ-

* This paper is based on parts of a book-length manuscript, called *Sweet and Sour Capitalism: Industrial Policy Taiwan-style*. The views expressed are my own and are not to be mistaken for the views of the World Bank. Taiwan is referred to as a 'country' purely for expositional convenience. I acknowledge with gratitude the comments of Fred Bienefeld, Colin Bradford, Ron Dore and Paul Streeten; and am grateful for discussions with Stephan Haggard, Chalmers Johnson, Larry Westphal and Frank Veneroso.

omics. While it is correct in some respects, it is also, I argue, wrong in others. In particular, Japan, Taiwan and the Republic of Korea have not maintained a close approximation to a neutral policy regime over the post-war period. They have all actively fostered the development of many new industries, and successfully so, in the sense that many of those industries have become internationally competitive. If this argument is accepted, the implication is that a neutral policy regime is not a *necessary* condition for rapid (or 'best attainable in the circumstances') growth.[1]

A basic weakness of neo-classical development economics is its inattention to the idea that governments differ in their *capacities* to guide the market. The argument against selective government fostering is made in universalistic terms; and it has recently been strengthened by an equally universalistic theory of *non-market* failure (Wolf 1979). The latter makes the eminently sensible point that while market failure may establish a *motive* for government intervention, the benefits of the proposed intervention have to be assessed against the likelihood that the benefits will actually be realized (that the intervention will be implemented as intended), and against the additional costs generated by that intervention. Wolf provides a whole series of reasons why one would expect extensive non-market or governmental failure. The thrust of the argument pushes us back to the prescription of 'getting the prices right' and letting market signals drive resource allocation.

My argument is that the governments of Taiwan, Republic of Korea and Japan have an unusually well developed capacity for selective intervention; and that this capacity rests upon (a) a powerful set of policy instruments, and (b) a certain kind of organization of the state, and of its links with other major economic institutions in the society. The East Asian three show striking similarities with respect to both instruments and institutions.[2] They also, of course, show striking similarities with respect to (c) superior economic performance – notably with respect to rapid restructuring of the econ-

---

[1] This is the weakest implication. The strongest is that a non-neutral policy regime – systematic intervention in search of dynamic gains in comparative advantage – is a necessary (but not sufficient) condition for rapid growth and restructuring.

[2] Whether one emphasizes similarity or difference depends on the question and the person comparing. Pye and Pye (1985) emphasize differences between Japan, Republic of Korea and Taiwan in terms of concepts of power and hence political structure. My emphasis on similarity follows Johnson (1981, 1983). Note that my references to Japan are primarily to Japan of the 1950s and 1960s.

omy towards higher technology production. The question is: what are the causal connections between (a), (b) and (c)?

The short answer is that we do not know. There is a dramatic paucity of empirical evidence on this question, and especially for the country with the best economic performance of all, Taiwan. This is only partly because of the practical difficulties of collecting relevant data; it is also because the perspective of neo-classical development economics tends to exclude these questions from serious consideration. In this paper I can give only a few components of my own tentative answer. I shall first establish that the governments do have powerful instruments of selective industrial promotion at their disposal. I then discuss the argument that the use of these instruments has in fact contributed to superior industrial performance. Finally I ask about the conditions which have allowed these potential net benefits to be realized in the East Asian cases, though they may well not be realized in other conditions.

INSTRUMENTS

For a government to lead industrial restructuring, it must be able to wield instruments capable of discriminating between industrial sectors, and it must be able to check the influence of foreign-owned firms in the domestic economy. Can the governments of Taiwan, Republic of Korea and Japan do this? We begin with financial instruments, then consider those of trade and foreign investment.

Financial instruments

Let us start from Zysman's (1983) distinction between capital market-based and credit-based financial systems. The two types of systems have very different implications for the potential influence of governments and/or banks over business. In a capital market system, securities (stocks and bonds) are the main source of long-term business finance. There is a wide range of capital and money-market instruments, and a large number of specialized financial institutions competing strongly in terms of price and service. Prices are determined in large part through the interplay of supply and demand. Financial institutions have arm's length relations with particular firms. The United States and British financial systems are clear examples of the type.

In a credit-based system the capital market is weak, and firms depend heavily on credit for raising finance beyond retained earnings. A cut-off in credit raises the prospect of immediate liquidation. Firms are therefore heavily dependent on whoever controls credit – on banks, to the extent that banks are the main suppliers. The banks may be relatively autonomous of the government, as in Germany, or they may themselves be dependent on the government. In this latter case, the government sets financial prices, and both through prices and the government's ability to influence the allocation of bank lending more directly, the government can exercise a powerful influence over the economy's investment pattern.

The East Asian three all have credit-based financial systems, with government-administered prices. Firms' dependence on credit is seen in the high debt-to-equity ratios typical of the corporate sector; using official figures (not inflation-adjusted), corporate debt/equity ratios were in the 300–400 per cent range in Japan over the 1950s and up to the 1970s, much the same in the Republic of Korea over the 1970s, and 160–200 per cent in Taiwan over the 1970s. United States and United Kingdom debt/equity ratios have been around 50–100 per cent.

Securities markets are weak in virtually all developing countries (van Agtmael 1984), so a simple distinction between capital market-based and credit-based financial systems does not differentiate those of the Republic of Korea and Taiwan from those of other developing countries. Direct comparison of corporate debt/equity ratios might be one criterion. By this standard many other industrializing countries have much lower ratios than the Republic of Korea and Taiwan; Brazil and Mexico, for example, had a ratio of 100–120 per cent over the 1970s.[3] But such comparisons are hazardous, especially because of differences in accounting for inflation. Another criterion might be the percentage of total credit subject to government credit controls on sectoral allocation. This too is problematic, because when the government has much influence over the banks and the banks are the major source of credit, the government may exert influence over credit allocation by informal control, in ways impossible to quantify.[4] Having stated

[3] I thank Peter Wall, of the International Finance Corporation, for the above debt/equity figures. The numerator includes short-term debt. The samples on which the figures are based are not fully consistent either across time or across countries, and must be taken as rough orders of magnitude only.

[4] A third criterion is the variation in bank interest rates and collateral requirements

some of the difficulties in comparing the financial systems of the East Asian three with those elsewhere, I shall bypass them by using a first approximation argument in what follows, recognizing that it should be made explicitly comparative.

In all three countries firms depend heavily on credit for financing, and the banks are by far the most important source of credit.[5] All three governments have been wary of allowing a rapid growth of non-bank financial institutions, which might pose a challenge to the dominance of the banks. In Taiwan, virtually the entire banking system is government owned. In the Republic of Korea the same was true until 1980–83, and the government still reaches far down into the now officially denationalized banks in terms of personnel policies, appointment of senior managers, range of services, and the like. In Japan the banks are mostly privately owned, but depend on the central bank for access to supplementary deposits on which to expand their lending. They borrow enormous amounts from the central bank, not as a right but as a privilege against the obligation to respect the central bank's conditions for the allocation of lending. In all three cases government sets interest rates and limits on collateral requirements.

Thus the three governments seem to have been more than happy to do little to overcome capital market failure, and have even encouraged it. (Firms themselves have tended to resist going public, for fear of losing control.) Are there advantages to the alternative credit-based model, despite its being less market-driven?

The first advantage is that a credit-based system permits faster investment in developing country conditions than would be possible if investment depended on the growth of firms' own profits or on the inevitably slow development of securities markets. Increases in

between industrial sectors. Another is the importance of retained earnings in relation to credit; in some developing countries retained earnings are so important as to warrant calling their financial system 'retained-earnings-based'.

[5] The curb market, an unregulated, semi-legal credit market, supplied some 20 to 30 per cent of total borrowings in Taiwan over the 1970s and very roughly the same in the Republic of Korea (Wade 1985b). Two other important sources of finance are foreign loans and disbursements from the government budget – both controlled by government. In the Republic of Korea, the National Investment Fund has accounted for about 10 per cent of total borrowings in recent years, and is aimed at heavy and chemical industries; another 35 per cent is covered by quotas for commercial bank loans to small and medium enterprises (whose sectoral composition is not clear). Taiwan has a variety of special funds at concessional rates (such as the Sino-American Fund and the Development Fund) and also uses the mechanism of the loan guarantee to encourage more lending to certain sectors.

the deposit rate of interest can effect a faster increase in resources which can be invested than is possible through the growth of equity. Also, the government is able to restrict the use of investible resources for mergers, speculation, paper entrepreneurship, and consumer borrowing; savings have a better chance of being translated into *productive* investment, and productive investment is less affected by speculative stock exchange booms (Matthews 1959:148).

The second advantage is that a credit-based system encourages more rapid sectoral mobility, and permits the government to guide that mobility. Even small changes in the discount rate or in concessional credit rates between sectors can have a dramatic effect on resource allocation, because the effect of such changes on firms' cash flow position is greater than where firms have smaller debt/equity ratios. Thus, where the government is not just trying to promote rapid growth in aggregate, but is doing so by means of selective fostering of 'key' sectors, a credit-based financial system gives it a powerful mechanism for inducing firms to enter sectors they would otherwise not enter.

Third, the credit-based system helps to avoid the bias towards short-term company decision-making inherent in a stock market system. The creditor needs the borrowing company to do well; it is concerned about the company's market share and ability to repay loans over the long term, and these depend on how well the company is developing new products, controlling costs and quality, and so on. These therefore become the criteria which managers are concerned with, rather than stock market quotations (Johnson 1985; Dore 1985).

The fourth advantage is more directly political. Industrial strategy requires a political base. Control over the financial system, and hence over highly leveraged firms, has been used in all three countries to build up the social coalitions needed to support the government's objectives – thus helping *implementation* of the industrial strategy. Firms are dissuaded from opposing the government by knowledge that opponents may find credit difficult to obtain.

These are four major potential advantages of a credit-based, administered-price financial system. However, such a system contains certain inner imperatives for government action which must be met if these advantages are to be realized, and which have profound implications for the government's overall role in the economy (Wade 1985a).

The first is that the government must help to socialize risk. Increases in deposit interest rates can increase the flow of financial savings; but at the new rates the private sector may not be prepared to borrow the savings unless the government intervenes to socialize some of the prospective private losses. Even if in the short run the savings are translated into loans, the higher savings and investment made possible by the higher rates will not be sustainable in the longer run without measures to socialize risk. This is because highly leveraged firms are vulnerable to declines in current earnings to below the levels required by debt repayment, repayments on debt being fixed (whereas payments on equity are a share of profits). With firms vulnerable in this way, so are the banks which carry the 'non-performing' loans; so where debt/equity ratios are high, there is an ever-present danger of financial instability in the economy:[6] bankruptcies, withdrawal of savings, a fall in real investment, and slower growth. To ease such dangers, firms are likely to borrow less, and banks to lend less, than if the government were to socialize some of the risks of private loss – to shift on to government some of the risks to which lenders and high debt/equity producers are exposed. If the government does socialize some of the risk of losses, the supply and demand of loanable funds will be greater, and so investment and hence growth can be higher.

This advantage applies especially in the case of *highly correlated risks*, to which most firms in major sectors are exposed. It therefore applies especially to interest rate changes, or economy-wide recession, or changes in major export markets, or political risks. Thus the impetus for government to shoulder some of the risks of investment and saving in an economy with high debt/equity ratios is especially strong in *trade-dependent* economies, like Taiwan and the Republic of Korea, and in *polities under external or internal threat*, again like Taiwan and the Republic of Korea. The impetus is reinforced where, as in all three of our cases, the economy is investing heavily in *large lump projects*, where entry and exit both take a long time.

[6] The implications of high debt/equity ratios also depend on profitability at the firm level: in an economy where profitability is higher and more secure the danger of economy-wide financial instability is less. The same applies to the implications of high debt/equity ratios for the relationship between banks and business.

This impetus then leads the government to provide a battery of ways to reduce the risks of financial instability; not only lender of last resort facilities and deposit insurance, but also subsidies to banks imperilled by loan losses, product and credit subsidies to firms in financial difficulties, banks' shareholding in companies, government shareholding in banks and in large lump projects, and even government ownership of the banks; plus, of course, government control of interest rates and exchange rates, to dampen firms' exposure to market fluctuations in these two important sources of correlated risk. In short, the logic of high debt/equity ratios forces the government to become involved in corporate financing.

The second imperative is for the supplier of credit to become intimate with company management. The supplier of credit may for this purpose be the government (Republic of Korea), or the banks (Germany), or some of both (Japan). In any case, the reason for involvement with management is that the creditor cannot simply withdraw when a company runs into difficulties by selling the securities in the secondary capital market – for the reason that the secondary capital markets are little developed. Given that the 'exit' strategy of the capital market model is not available, the alternative is 'voice' and 'loyalty', to try to restructure company management so as to make it more competitive, and to take the long-term view.

Nevertheless the government and/or the banks must – as the third imperative – develop an institutional capacity to discriminate between responsible and irresponsible borrowing, and to penalize the latter. That is, firms which borrow without due commercial caution and run into trouble must not expect the government or the banks to continue to bail them out (the moral hazard problem).

Once market signals are blunted by administered pricing and socialized risk, the government must (the fourth imperative) create a central guidance agency capable of supplementing market signals by its own signals as to which sectors will be most profitable.

Finally, the government must maintain a cleavage between the domestic economy and the international economy with respect to financial flows, so as to be able to control these flows in and out. Without such control, with firms free to borrow as they wish on international markets, government's own control over the cost of capital to domestic borrowers is weakened, as is its ability to guide sectoral allocation. At the same time, speculative inflows seeking exchange rate gains can precipitate accelerating movements in exchange rates, with damaging consequences for the real economy. Uncontrolled outflows make it difficult for government to arrange a sharing of the burden of adjustment to external shocks between the owners of capital and others; the others are likely to be made to take the burden, with political unrest, repression and interrupted growth as the likely result.

These five imperatives are reflected in readily identifiable features of the financial systems of all of our countries (Wade 1985a). For example, the central guidance agencies in each country are well known: the Ministry of International Trade and Industry (MITI) in Japan; the Economic Planning Board in the Republic of Korea; the Council for Economic Planning and Development and the Industrial Development Board in Taiwan. Again, banks are only too well aware of the restrictions on their foreign transactions, and in all of the countries foreign banks are only allowed into those pockets of business where the local banks cannot do well. Taiwan's banks must report all foreign transactions weekly to the central bank, its foreign banks must report *all* transactions daily. Central allocation of foreign exchange has been a very powerful instrument of control over firms and sectoral growth in all three countries (because of common dependence on imports of raw materials).

For all the similarities in the structure of the financial system and the financial instruments available to policymakers, there are also important differences between the three countries. It has been said that 'The Japanese banking system is among the most centralized and controllable in the world' (Pempel 1978:152). But Japanese banks are mostly privately owned, and have some autonomy with respect to criteria of lending and response to 'bad' loans. Involvement in company management is shared between bank creditors and government (e.g. MITI). Banks in the Republic of Korea and Taiwan, on the other hand, are state owned (Korea's until 1980–83), and have less autonomy than Japan's.

Banks in the Republic of Korea operate as direct instruments of government policy (at least with respect to big loans); their criteria of lending are set by government, and in cases of bad loans the government directs them to continue lending or not. (The high inflation of the 1970s in the Republic of Korea was related to a government policy of lending many firms out of difficulties.) Hence collateral requirements are not a major requirement (except for small companies), so the banks are not, in that sense, 'pawn-brokers'. However, the banks do not have the capacity to undertake independent analysis of company balance sheets, market prospects and cash flow projections; or at any rate, they are not able to make such analysis a basis for lending decisions. Thus not only are the banks in the Republic of Korea not pawnbrokers, they are not venture capitalists either. Instead of the banks having intimate ties with (big) company management, it is the government itself which has these ties.

As for Taiwan, collateral requirements are higher for private firms than in Japan or the Republic of Korea, and banks are commonly known, pejoratively, as 'pawnshops'; conversely, they have no more of a venture capitalist capability (in the above sense) than the Korean banks. As in the Republic of Korea, it is the government, more than the banks, which is involved with company management. This involvement, however, seems to be less than in the Republic of Korea, as far as the private sector is concerned; government–private business relations are somewhat more arm's length than in either the Republic of Korea or Japan. This may be because: Taiwan has fewer giant companies than the Republic of Korea or Japan:[7] ethnic tensions exist between the mainland-dominated government and the islander-dominated business sector; and also because the *public* enterprise sector in Taiwan is bigger than in the Republic of Korea and much bigger again than in Japan.[8] Therefore, government–business relations which in the Republic of Korea and Japan involve crossing the public sector–private sector boundary are in Taiwan already contained within the public sector, and hence do not *appear* to represent 'government interference' in (private) business management. There are close (which is not to say always friendly) relations within the triangle of central decision-makers, government-owned banks, and public enterprises.

Thus the cases of the Republic of Korea and Taiwan represent

---

[7] Of the 500 largest (by sales) non-financial non-United States companies in 1981, Taiwan had two, the Republic of Korea ten, and Japan 130 (Post and Richman 1982).

[8] Using the percentage share of public enterprises in gross fixed capital formation (the only index for which information on many countries is readily available), Taiwan is in the top quintile of developing countries (in a sample of fifty-one: Short 1983). In the period 1965–80 Taiwan averaged about 31 per cent, Republic of Korea 23 per cent and Japan 11 per cent.

distinct sub-species of the credit-based model. That governments can wield a great deal of influence over (big) firms and over the economy's investment pattern more generally (via their influence over credit and foreign exchange) is common in all three cases. As Zysman (1983:76) puts it, 'Selective credit allocation is the single discretion necessary to all state-led industrial strategies'. Governments in economies with capital market-based financial systems do not have anything like the same degree of steerage capability.

Trade instruments

Trade controls have been important instruments of steerage in all three countries (Japan before the 1970s, if not later). The governments have not allowed the domestic market for tradables to be directly integrated into the international market; they have not allowed the use of foreign exchange, the composition of imports, to be decided by domestic demand in relation to prices set outside the country. They have influenced the volume and composition of imports by a combination of selective controls on trade, both (non-discretionary) tariffs and (discretionary) quantitative controls. I shall concentrate here on Taiwan because less is known about its trade controls, and because the most familiar reason for trade controls – the need to save scarce foreign exchange – has *not* been a reason for maintaining Taiwan's elaborate apparatus of trade management; Taiwan (unlike the Republic of Korea) has run balance of payments surpluses most years since 1970. The reason is more directly to do with building up technological and supply capacity *within* Taiwan.

Taiwan's tariff structure is minutely differentiated by product, with tariffs ranging from zero to well over 100 per cent. It is quite inconsistent with the modified neo-classical prescription for a 10–15 per cent uniform rate of effective protection for all manufacturing other than the infant industries, which should get a uniform rate of no more than double the normal rate (e.g. Balassa 1977). I have no evidence on how closely the structure of tariff protection corresponds with the government's sectoral development priorities.

The situation with respect to quantitative controls is clearer. For the most understandable of reasons the government is anxious not to be seen to be doing anything which might provide a pretext for other countries to put up barriers to its exports, and takes care to keep most of the quantitative controls out of sight. The public classification of imports into 'prohibited', 'controlled', and 'permissible' does not capture the scope of the system, for many items on the 'permissibles' list are in fact not freely imported (Westphal 1978a; Wade 1984a, in press). The 'permissibles' list is covertly divided into two parts, one part containing items which really are freely imported (though they may be subject to restrictions as to origin, and as to what kind of agency can import them), the other part containing items for which special permission must be obtained. When a would-be importer applies to a bank for a licence (all imports and exports must be covered by a licence), the bank checks to see whether the item is on the 'covertly controlled permissibles' list. If so, the request is referred back to the government (normally the Industrial Development Board). Typically the would-be importer will be asked to provide evidence that the domestic supplier(s) cannot meet his terms on price, quality or delivery. He may be asked to furnish a letter from the relevant producers' association to that effect.

This could be called the 'referral' mechanism of import control, or the 'law of similars' (but it is not a *law*). It has almost certainly – I know of no direct evidence – been an important instrument of secondary import substitution. Petrochemicals, chemicals, steel, other basic metals (these sectors, characterized by standardized, basic products with high capital requirements) are covered by the referral mechanism, as are some machinery and components, including some machine tools, forklift trucks, and bearings. (The present tense refers to 1978–83.) At the least, the mechanism serves the useful function of stimulating – in fact forcing – increased contact between purchasers and potential local suppliers (Westphal 1978a); which has to be balanced against the cost of delays, on which I have no information. For machinery, the referral mechanism provides only weak protection in general, because the planners are well aware of the importance of allowing industrialists to use the equipment they think best suited to their particular market. For more standardized capital-intensive products like chemicals, importing can be much tougher once local capacity exists. A manufacturer who needs a higher percentage purity in his caustic soda than the local supplier can match, may become so dissatisfied with delays in his requests to import that he decides to help one or two local producers to upgrade to the point where he can buy his requirements from them. This is just what the Taiwan government wants.

The government can use international prices to discipline the price-setting of protected domestic producers because it is able to control quantities of goods crossing the national boundary. It is very sensitive to the point that there must be good reasons why domestic prices of protected items are significantly higher than international prices, especially in the case of items to be used for export production. (There are some glaring exceptions to this rule, notably in the automobile assembly industry.) Therefore the *threat* of allowing in imports if the prices of domestic substitutes get too far out of line can be sufficient to hold prices to near international levels, without there being a free flow of goods across the national boundary.

When little is known about the referral mechanism today, it is all the more difficult to judge how important it was during the 1960s and 1970s. Little and Scott both claim that progressive trade liberalization occurred through the 1960s 'until in the 1970s Taiwan was virtually free of trade controls' (Little 1979a:474; Scott 1979:327). One hypothesis is that all quantitative controls were indeed lifted by the early 1970s, only to be reimposed just after the time when Little and Scott were writing, in 1976–77. Certainly the referral mechanism was well established by 1978, when Westphal (1978a) described it. The second hypothesis is that the controls were in place through the 1960s and 1970s, as in the 1950s and as in the 1980s. All through the 1950s the planners had justified quantitative controls in the face of economists' criticism, on the grounds of their greater accuracy and flexibility than tariffs for managing trade quantities. But the official system of 'controlled' and 'permissible' items was then, and is now, cumbersome in terms of the procedures needed to get items on and off the lists. What may have happened in the liberalization of trade controls was a switch of items from the formally controlled to the *de facto* controlled list, so as to permit the planners more flexibility to manage trade quantities while appearing to liberalize. This is not to say that the whole of the increase in the share of import items on the 'permissible' list was illusory; only that part of it was, and a fluctuating part depending on the priorities and needs of the moment. If so, the easing of quantitative restrictions during the liberalization of 1958–62, which bears so much of the weight of the neo-classical explanation for Taiwan's subsequent rapid growth, may have been less real than the official figures suggest.[9]

What is the import position of exporters? In the neo-classical story the most important reason for Taiwan's boom in manufactured exports (after the availability of cheap labour) is that exporters faced a virtual free trade regime; they could buy inputs for exports at world market prices, and hence have not had a net incentive to sell on the domestic market rather than on the international market (unlike in the textbook import substituting trade regime).

It is true that exporters pay no tariff duty on intermediates used for export production. However, some very important intermediates are not freely importable, because they are subject to the mechanism of quantitative import control just described. In principle, items can only be put on the list subject to this control if the price of the domestic substitute is equal to the cif price of imports when the imports are to be used for export production, or equal to the cif price plus all tariffs and other charges when the imports are to be used for domestic market production. In practice there is scope for negotiation in favour of the domestic producer.

As for capital goods, exporters *do* have to pay duty – unless they make products which appear on a list of specific items to be encouraged (e.g. high voltage insulation tape with working tolerance of 6.6 kv or more), and unless a domestic substitute for the capital good is not available (again there is room for negotiation on what constitutes a substitute). In addition, a variety of capital goods is subject to quantitative import controls, even if they are to be used for export production. Exporters are, however, exempt from indirect taxes on input purchases. They have also in the past been given an incentive through the specification of side-conditions on the list of items to be given fiscal incentives, which said that the fiscal incentive would only be given if a certain minimum share of the output was exported.

The fact that exporters have to pay duty on many capital goods (often of 20 or more per cent in the late 1970s) and cannot freely import some very important intermediates as well as some capital goods, must qualify the proposition that exports have faced a free trade regime.

Little quantitative evidence is available on the magnitude of pro-

[9] For an excellent account of overt and covert import controls in the Republic of Korea see Luedde-Neurath (in press).

The Role of Government   143

tection. The only comparative study for Taiwan and the Republic of Korea uses data from the late 1960s. It suggests that, while the economy-wide average level of protection was relatively low for both Taiwan and the Republic of Korea by the late 1960s, parts of the manufacturing sector were heavily protected, giving high variance around the average. Hsing (1971:144), using 1966 data for Taiwan, calculates an effective protection for home market consumer goods of 126 per cent. In Balassa's classification, the 'import-competing' manufacturing industries (those in which less than 10 per cent of domestic production is exported, and in which imports account for more than 10 per cent of domestic consumption) received an effective protection rate of 133 per cent in Taiwan in 1969 (Lee and Liang 1982:325), and 64 per cent in the Republic of Korea in 1968 (Westphal and Kim 1982:246). For the same industries net effective subsidy rates strongly favoured domestic market sale over export sale: 61 against 15 per cent for Taiwan, and 100 against 39 per cent for the Republic of Korea (Balassa 1982b:35). To interpret these figures one needs to know how much of the economy's activity is included in the highly protected sectors,[10] as well as the degree of correspondence between the highly protected sectors and the infant industries that the government was trying to promote. One then needs corresponding data from other countries. Lacking this, I conclude with a proposition in need of careful testing, that parts of the manufacturing sector have received relatively high levels of protection in Taiwan and the Republic of Korea (*a fortiori* in Japan), and that the industries which the government has tried to promote are included in these parts.

In all three countries import controls have had the central function of reducing the risk to which investors in new, especially capital-intensive industries, are exposed, thereby encouraging the expansion and deepening of domestic supply capability. They have encouraged domestic manufacturers to invest on a scale sufficient to generate the increasing returns to which manufacturing is subject; and they have then helped to provide strong and reliable domestic demand for the products of the protected industries, so

[10] Even if the amount of value added from these sectors equals only 10 per cent, say, of the total, this does not mean that protection to these sectors can be treated as quantitatively trivial in the overall picture. If there is, roughly speaking, a positive relationship between the government's selectivity with respect to promoted industries and the effectiveness of that promotion, one would expect effective intervention to go with a rather small share of total value added.

that these industries can spread overheads over larger output and thus lower their unit costs. At a more aggregative level, import controls have served the function of retaining within the domestic economy more of the growth in demand from the export market, thus providing domestically based firms with a more expansive economic environment than if more of the additional demand generated by exports leaked abroad in the form of imports. With a more expansive economic environment, domestic firms are more likely to keep their productivity driving forward, and hence increase their international competitiveness at a later stage.

Direct foreign investment controls

If the domestic economy is dominated by multinational companies, the development consequences of the above logic will be different than if the firms are predominantly nationally owned. In much of Latin America and sub-Saharan Africa, multinationals control most firms producing for the upper income levels of the domestic market. In Taiwan, Republic of Korea and Japan, by contrast, multinationals have had a small presence in relation to the economy as a whole. (In Taiwan over the 1970s, foreign investment accounted for about 8 per cent of investment in manufacturing, less in the Republic of Korea and Japan.) More importantly, they have had restricted access to the domestic market. By one means or another the governments have directed them towards exports (though export requirements are less the more the government wants their technology).

This particular interference with the international market has advantages in terms of the development of national production capabilities and income distribution. It means that government efforts to promote the growth and restructuring of domestic production capacity do not have to go through the multinationals, whose objectives may not wholly coincide with the development of *national* production capability. The government is able to use funds that can be invested according to specific priorities designed to integrate the domestic market further, through having more influence over the firms that produce for the domestic market than if those firms were predominantly multinationals. Second, multinationals operating on the domestic market tend to follow marketing strategies that have little to do with average incomes or traditional consumer behaviour; which may tend to accentuate income inequalities. In the East Asian three, the diversification of goods made available to consumers is a gradual and controlled process geared to the population's purchasing power. Thus in the Republic of Korea, the most modern of consumer goods, manufactured chiefly by multinationals, were for a long time restricted for export. Only gradually have some of these products become available for domestic purchasers, as basic needs in food and clothing have been met (Ikonicoff 1985).

Other instruments

Other intruments of industrial steerage are also important in different degrees in the three countries. Japan is known for its 'administrative guidance', a practice of governmental consultation with and persuasion of company management without the backing of law; but the same thing occurs routinely in the Republic of Korea and Taiwan, and is, indeed, a potential instrument in any credit-based financial system where the government has much control over the banks (as we have seen). Japan and the Republic of Korea have made much use of market structure policy, not of the anti-trust kind but of nearly the opposite – to promote the development of large-scale firms and trading companies, able to compete against the United States and European giants. Taiwan has done much less to foster the development of agglomerates (see footnote 7). But it does have a large public enterprise sector, unusually large even when compared to that of the Republic of Korea (see footnote 8), and an array of 'special status', ostensibly private firms linked to the party or the military which, given the centralized nature of the state, are also available as instruments of selective intervention. Taiwan has, in addition, an elaborate scheme of fiscal incentives for the production of tightly specified products. (The specifications change over time, so as to keep the incentives pressing against production frontiers.) Like the Republic of Korea, Taiwan has a forest of research and development organizations under state auspices, though their name translates as 'Research and Service' rather than 'Research and Development' organizations, for they are intended to be an industrial extension force as much as a research staff. In Japan the government has relied more on encouraging groups of private firms to form their own research and development cartels.

However, neither research and development organizations nor technology licensing have been the main sources of new industrial technology in Taiwan and the Republic of Korea. Rather, they have relied on imported capital goods, students sent overseas for higher level education and attracted back by vigorous government efforts, and foreign experts employed to work locally alongside locals (Westphal, Kim and Dahlman 1984). All three flows of 'embodied' technology have been subject to government influence.

Aggressiveness

There is no need to labour the point: all three governments have the means to intervene powerfully in markets, to set constraints on the scope of market decision-makers, with the object of bringing about certain market outcomes. The industrial policies of Japan and the Republic of Korea have been more aggressive than that of Taiwan, in the sense that the government has put more pressure – more incentives, more penalties for non-compliance – behind its attempts to shift the economy in certain directions. The reasons may have to do with the following differences:

(i) *In savings*. Taiwan's domestic savings rate has been much higher than the Republic of Korea's, so the government has been able to favour certain sectors without the tight rationing of other sectors which Korea has had to undertake in order to do the same (even though that country has borrowed heavily abroad to make up some of the difference).

(ii) *In degree of openness of the economy*. Japan's domestic savings are also high, so the first consideration does not serve to explain the difference between Taiwan and Japan. Part of that difference may be due to the fact that Japan's economy is less exposed to the international economy, and so the government can, with the same amount of administrative effort, rig markets more aggressively than in a more open economy.

(iii) *In the public enterprise sector*. Taiwan's large public enterprise sector gives the government an instrument of industrial strategy whose use does not involve crossing the boundary between the public and private sectors, and which is therefore less likely to generate a sense of aggressive interference.

(iv) *In the organization of the private sector*. Japan and the Republic of Korea both have more highly centralized private sectors than Taiwan (the result, in part, of government intention in each case). With the governments of Japan and the Republic of Korea both facing larger private agglomerates, themselves well organized into peak associations, stronger instruments of governmental inducement and penalty are sometimes required to shift firms in desired directions than in Taiwan. Moreover, the ethnic conflict in Taiwan, running close to the public sector–private sector divide, enjoins on the government a more subtle approach in private sector steerage than the governments in Japan and the Republic of Korea need take.

(v) *In foreign economic policy*. Japan and the Republic of Korea have both planned head-on confrontation with other countries (notably the United States) in key industries; their production capacity decisions only make sense on the assumption that they could knock out capacity in other countries. Taiwan has been more circumspect, seeking market niches more complementary than competitive with those of the United States, and the government has had to be correspondingly less active in orchestrating and supporting the activities of firms which would challenge the United States and European giants.

EFFECTS OF INDUSTRIAL STRATEGY

A common response of neo-classical development economists to the proposition that the East Asian three have had a vigorous industrial strategy is to say that the various sectoral policies amount to no more than 'hand-waving'; or even that economic performance would have been still better without them. Little is more careful: he admits that if by planning is meant any promotion of industries that would be unlikely to start in response to price signals, there was a lot of planning in Taiwan in the 1950s, again in the latter part of the 1960s, and all through the 1970s (Little 1979a:489). Yet in an 18,000 word paper on Taiwan he makes no attempt to describe or assess the impact of this planning. Whether the promotion of industries that would be unlikely to start in response to price signals helps development or not is, he says, 'a futile question' because of the absence of a counterfactual. Futile question or not, his own implied answer is that deliberate industrial steerage has been a minor enough element for it to be completely ignored in a long account of Taiwan's success. Ranis (1979), in an equally long account of Taiwan's industrial development, does more or less the same. Hosomi and Okumura (1982:150) allege explicitly that it was Japan's high economic growth that allowed industrial policy and the consensus mechanism to work, not the other way around – with no evidence either way. David Henderson, an economist attached to the United States Council of Economic Advisers, has no doubt that 'The real explanation for the Japanese economic miracle is the country's *laissez-faire* policies on taxes, antitrust, banking, and labour. Japan teaches a lesson ... about the vitality of the free market' (1983, cited in Johnson 1985:3). The idea that Japanese industrial policies actually hindered economic performance is caught in the assertion that 'Without MITI Japan would have grown at 15 per cent per annum', instead of only 10 per cent (unnamed Japanese economist quoted by Little 1979a:491). Saxonhouse (1983) and Trezise (1983) make more serious arguments to the effect that selective industrial steerage has been a very minor element in Japan's success.

There is indeed a colossal identification problem. How can one tell that market liberalization (coupled with general infrastructural and educational investment) was the most important factor by far? What kind of evidence is needed to show that industrial strategy made a difference too important to ignore?

The question is complicated by the need to distinguish two levels of industrial strategy – the generic level, on the one hand, including policies on the exchange rate, finance, taxation, and so on, which together establish the broad thrust of government policy towards industrial growth and competitiveness *vis-à-vis* redistribution and consumption; and the sectoral level, on the other. The effect of sectoral policies can be expected to depend partly on the net effect of generic policy. Separating out the relative impact of policies at these two levels is clearly a major undertaking in itself. Putting that aside, how might one assess impact at the sectoral level?

One might study a set of industries to examine the connection between promotion measures and subsequent growth. In practice, such an exercise would be fraught with difficulty. Complete information on the amount of assistance, even if measured only in terms of financial disbursements or exemptions, would be difficult to find (much information on the use of concessional credit in Taiwan is confidential, for example). Worse, promotional measures cannot be limited to financial disbursements or legal directives. In all three countries, the pilot agencies lack large funds and firm statutory powers; so it is virtually impossible to connect straightforwardly manufacturing successes with financial help or clear directives. Many of the channels of transmission of influence are difficult to detect, let alone quantify. For example, development bank loans may trigger a greater volume of commercial bank credit in the same directions than would otherwise have followed: this 'announcement effect' might be used to explain why the Japan Development Bank, although a relatively small source of loans, has still been important in industrial steerage. There is the further difficulty of holding other things constant for high assistance and low assistance sub-sectors. But beyond all this the question remains of how to interpret the results: if sub-sectors which received a lot of assistance grew more slowly than those which did not, does this indicate the failure of assistance measures, or does it indicate effective interest in industries that need assistance as a condition of subsequent fast growth?

Even if such studies show effectiveness at the industry level, however, they leave open the question of whether the country would not have been better off doing things other than developing those particular industries. 'Local' optimality does not establish 'global' optimality (global in the sense of the national economy). It is tempting to use aggregate production function analysis to estimate the extent of 'global' optimality, with the size of the residuals indicating the maximum possible extent of the government's contribution. The problem is that the size of the residuals depends on how the production function is specified, which is a matter calling for a large element of subjective judgment. The 'global' issue can be got at another way, by comparing countries which in many important respects are similar but where the role of government has been significantly different; Japan and Italy in the post-war period, for example (Boltho 1981). The hazards are obvious.

At best one can make a circumstantial case that industrial strategy has made a positive contribution. For example, we have Yusuf and Peters' (1984) conclusion that, for analysing investment in the Republic of Korea, a model based on government policy objectives and planners' preferences gives better results than a standard neo-classical market-determined model. We have Taizo's (1984) study of the Japanese automobile industry from 1900 to 1960, which shows how each government intervention changed firms' behav-

150   *Achieving Industrialization in East Asia*

iour, and how the changed behaviour in turn gave rise to changes in the nature of the subsequent intervention. We have Magaziner and Hout's (1980) study, which shows for several Japanese industries the connection between government promotion or non-promotion and subsequent performance. We also have Westphal's (1982:264) work on Korean infant industries, which suggests that many of the promoted industries have become internationally competitive, able to compete internationally and domestically without subsidies; 'many' in the sense of a high average, which includes some much publicized failures, especially in the late 1970s and early 1980s. He would be the first to admit that his evidence is not conclusive; but in the context of the other evidence cited it is suggestive. Although I have not seen data for Taiwan on what has happened subsequently to those highly protected import-competing industries of 1969, they could be found.

Several studies examine the issue comparatively. For example, Enos (1984) studies the adoption of the same petrochemical technology supplied by the same United States supplier in the Republic of Korea, Chile and Hong Kong, and finds that Korea's lead on all of several measurable indexes of adoption can be related to specific actions of that country's government. Mody (1985) asks why in the 1980s the Republic of Korea has taken a commanding lead over Taiwan in microelectronics, even though by conventional measures of comparative advantage Taiwan should be well ahead. He finds the reasons are related to the Korean government's determination to build large agglomerates (in part through the aggressive rationing of credit which has come in for much neo-classical criticism), and its closure of the domestic market to direct foreign investment.

Several more studies question the neo-classical argument more directly. Some say that the neo-classicals have some of their crucial facts wrong about individual country cases (e.g. Wade in press; Amsden 1984a; Luedde-Neurath in press; Haggard and Moon 1983; Cumings 1984; Boltho 1984; Park and Westphal 1986). Others argue with evidence that price distortions do not in fact correlate closely with inward or outward oriented trade regimes or with measures of national economic performance (Bradford 1984; Aghazadeh and Evans 1985). This questions the proposition that market liberalization could have been the driving force behind the success of the East Asian three.

All these studies can be challenged, but it is not enough for neo-classicals to query their validity; they must themselves provide counter-evidence. This evidence cannot be limited to economy-wide averages like 'outward' and 'inward' oriented, but must also address the issues of dispersion around the average. Thus in the comparison between Taiwan and the Republic of Korea on the one hand, and India and Latin America on the other, the first important fact about trade regimes is that the East Asian type is more 'liberal' in the sense that the average level of protection is much lower. The second important fact, however, which the neo-classical argument has tended to ignore, is that dispersion around the average is much higher in East Asia, because the selective promotion of some industries requires high protection to a small number. The fact of high variance takes on all the more importance given the low average.

This counter-evidence must also address the question of causality. Even if it is true that liberalization is often followed by superior economic performance, it may be that this happens only where the economy has already been brought by 'non-liberal' means close to the point where important sectors can compete internationally, and where the liberalization can hence be sustained. This can be put in the form of a question: is the import substitution period in the development of Taiwan and the Republic of Korea to be regarded as a mistake or as an essential preparation for the gradual liberalization which followed? In making these arguments, the neo-classicals have to be careful to emphasize not only the flexibility of the unguided market, but also its tendency to generate instability; and to emphasize not only the difficulty facing government officials in 'picking the winners' but also the difficulty facing private businessmen. Otherwise one counterposes the real-world experience of government intervention against an idealized version of the free market.

I can find little empirical support for the proposition that the sectoral industrial strategies of the East Asian three amounted to mere 'hand-waving', or that their overall economic performance would have been superior if they had had a more neutral policy regime. Can it be seriously argued that if the Governor of the Bank of Japan had got his way in the mid-1950s, and prevented a concentration on steel and automobiles on the grounds that Japan's comparative advantage lay in textiles, Japan would now be economically better off (Hofheinz and Calder 1982:130)? The Republic of Korea in the late 1970s may be an exception; but this is because the objective of intervention shifted away from fostering economic competitiveness towards attaining military self-sufficiency. At the least the evidence on industrial strategy supports the proposition that active and selective government intervention in a market economy *can* co-exist with outstanding economic performance.[11] A neo-classical might then reply that the intervention simply 'mimicked' the market, helping to reach results that an 'ideal' market would have produced. Whether this is so or not is beside the point; in reality the unguided market would not have produced the same result. To claim otherwise is to claim extraordinary ability to forecast extraordinary performance.

However, the force of empirical evidence also depends on the adequacy of the underlying theory, and it is true that the theoretical basis for a selective industrial strategy is less well developed than that which supports a non-interventionist approach. This reflects the neo-classical emphasis on trade rather than technological change as the central process of industrialization. When techno-

---

[11] Hong Kong has had similarly good performance without government promotion of selected industries. This suggests that a non-neutral policy regime is not a *necessary* condition for good performance. But how significant is the Hong Kong case? In neo-classical eyes Hong Kong clinches the argument for the ineffectiveness of industrial steerage: if Hong Kong did as well as the other four economies, then the causes of success must be something common to all five, and whatever that may be, it is not industrial policy. In this view, the industrial policy activities in the other four are best seen as the attempt of governments to *associate* themselves with private sector success so as to bolster their legitimacy (Brian Hindley, pers. comm.). Another interpretation is that Hong Kong is a very special case: first, because of small size (which means that it is under less pressure to deepen its industrial structure, because mercantile activity could until recently be at a sufficiently high volume to give high per capita income while not being so high as to trigger protectionist reaction); and, second, because it had the organizational and marketing capacity already in place prior to industrialization, built up over many decades by British-linked trading companies. Taiwan and the Republic of Korea, for example, did not. To extend the argument one would have to look at the East Asian regional economy and see how, given the industrial-policy-influenced industrial structure in the other countries, Hong Kong could be successful without industrial policy. A third interpretation is that Hong Kong is simply a variant of the developmental state, being to the Republic of Korea and Japan what Germany is to France. All five countries have a point of concentration of financial and economic power at which coherent nationally-oriented strategies can be negotiated (unlike the United States and the United Kingdom); but in Hong Kong as in Germany this point of concentration lies outside the state, in an association between banks and major firms kept insulated from non-establishment interest groups by the authoritarian colonial state.

logical change is made the centrepiece, an economic rationale for selective industrial promotion follows from two propositions.

The first is that national comparative advantage is not simply the result of given endowments of capital, labour and natural resources, but is also the result of government promotion; because comparative advantage rests on accumulated capital and skills ('technological mastery', in Westphal's phrase: 1982) which can be enhanced by a long-term national strategy. The second is that some sectors and products are more important to the economy's future growth prospects than others. These sectors have major 'externalities', in the sense that the people affected by a decision about production and price go far beyond the immediate buyer and seller. The externalities argument for public provision of physical infrastructure is well recognized in neo-classical theory. But externalities are treated as aberrations from normal economic behaviour. The governments of the East Asian three have acted as though externalities were very important in some sectors, which have then been treated as part of the *industrial infrastructure*.

The industries so treated are especially those where a large commitment of time or capital is required in production. Any complex economic system encounters a source of instability arising from the uncertainty inherent in the attempt to match supply decisions now with demand decisions at some time in the future. If prices and profits are left to the vagaries of the market (the international market as well as the domestic market), investment in industries which require a large commitment of time or capital may not be made, and a higher than desirable proportion of the economy's investment will go into quick-return projects. Also, individual firms on their own may be more inclined to stick within a narrow range of familiar product lines than branch into new industries and products. An exogenous (non-market) force is needed to favour such shifts, to lead economic agents from shorter- to longer-term investment and marketing strategies, to channel profits from currently profitable activities into investment in those likely to become profitable in the future.

In these same large-lump, long-gestation sectors, production economies of scale are likely to be important. Competitive advantage can be gained by firms if they are encouraged to develop a scale large enough to capture the cost advantages. Learning-curve economies, to do with the acquisition of technological mastery, may also be important; costs per unit of output typically fall sharply as (and if) firms acquire technological mastery over a newly introduced technology (Westphal 1982; Park and Westphal 1986; Fransman 1985).

Where external economies, economies of scale, and learning-curve economies are important, the market structure is unlikely to generate socially desirable outcomes – rapid growth and shifts in economic structure towards higher value added products. In Taiwan, Republic of Korea and Japan, government policy has probably played an important role in stimulating their realization, and hence in improving domestic ability to compete against other countries' suppliers. The object has been to encourage investment on a scale sufficient to capture economies of scale where these are important; to coordinate the development of backwards and forwards links so that external economies from any one activity are captured *within* the national unit; and to encourage domestic producers to upgrade their technological capability by tying some of the incentives to such upgrading. If one accepts that external economies, economies of scale, and learning-curve economies are major sources of technological advance and productivity growth, the efforts of the state to make sure that market conditions do not obstruct their realization within the national unit take on great significance in explaining the superior economic performance of the East Asian three.

THE CONDITIONS OF SUCCESSFUL INTERVENTION

We come now to the question of how and why the governments of Taiwan, Republic of Korea and Japan were apparently able to reap the potential benefits of an industrial policy, when many other governments could not (e.g. Wade 1979, 1982b, 1982c, 1984a). What is it that defeats the sorts of expectations that go under the rubric of 'nonmarket failure'?

Of course the demand side is important. With the opening of the United States market to imports of cheap labour manufactures in the 1960s, Taiwan, Republic of Korea and Japan had a huge range of profitable production possibilities open to them. This, coupled with a responsive production system, pulled the economy powerfully along. The question is, what made the production system highly responsive?

I have focused on one of several components[12] of an answer: the industrial leadership exercised by the three governments. What characteristics of the exercise of leadership have been most important for the success of the governments' interventions? Three stand out: (a) interventions were (generally speaking) aimed at promoting competitive production;[13] (b) they were selective between industries; and (c) they were cumulative in their impact.

(a) The central economic bureaucrats of all three countries seem to have realized that mere protection was not sufficient to generate rapid growth. They have sought to couple *protection* with *competition*, so as to ensure that the lethargy-inducing effect of protection was swamped by the investment-inducing effect. In Japan, with its large domestic market, the policy has been to keep out imports (other than raw materials and high technology) and rely on a partly government-created market structure to induce 'cut-throat oligopoly' (Hadley 1970). The Republic of Korea and Taiwan, with smaller domestic markets, have allowed more monopolistic production in heavy and chemical industries. But the government of the Republic of Korea has strongly encouraged the infants of these industries to start exporting very soon (Westphal 1982), thus exposing them directly to international competitive pressure – even when exports had to be sold at a loss, recouped by the firm from profits on imports tied to export performance. In other words, the Korean definition of competitiveness emphasized *export* success to an unusual degree. The Taiwan Government seems to have put less pressure on the infants to export, and relied more on the threat of allowing in imports if the prices of domestic substitutes moved much above international prices. This may be part of the reason

[12] In a wider treatment I would also emphasize the widely diffused entrepreneurial drive; the sheer will to do better, reinforcing, but independent of, the desire to become richer. That drive is related to the very high levels of education in the population at large. The education system emphasizes engineering and other technical subjects, so much so that of the middle-income countries Taiwan has one of the highest number of engineers per 1000 people employed in manufacturing; in Zymelman's 14 middle-income countries the average is 4.6; Taiwan has 8; only Singapore is higher with 10 (1980, using data from early to middle 1970s). No data are given for the Republic of Korea.

[13] A lot of Japanese intervention *has* been motivated by redistribution objectives, though the overall balance is (in contrast to the United States) clearly on the side of competitive production. There has been, not only in agriculture, a good deal of easing of decline by protection and subsidy. Showing some concern for the losers has had important political effects, reinforcing a sense of fairness which has gained support for the general thrust of growth and restructuring policies.

why, even though they export little, Taiwan's public enterprises are more effective than those in many other countries; they supply to downstream firms which do export, from whom comes pressure to match the costs of overseas competitors.

Just why the central economic bureaucrats saw the need to couple protection with competition, when their counterparts in many other countries did not, is an open question. In any case the outcome was a form of protection quite different from the typical form in Latin America where there was little encouragement either for competition between foreign firms and domestic firms on the domestic market, or for domestic firms to export.

(b) Interventions have been selective. Large parts of the economy are more or less ignored in terms of government promotion. The discriminatory nature of state intervention is taken for granted as much as the opposite is taken for granted in the United States or Britain, where the declaration that an economic policy is discriminatory is an act of condemnation. Park and Westphal (1986) argue that the axis of discrimination is between 'well-established' industries (in the sense of being internationally competitive) and 'infant industries'. The former face a largely neutral policy regime, the latter (or some of them) face positive industry bias, but the governments also seem to be quite interventionist with respect to 'commanding heights' kinds of industries (those that by their links with other sectors can affect the entire economy's growth), even if well established. We certainly need more evidence on the criteria of selection, the degree of selectivity, and on how temporary infant industry protection is. But in any case, given that intervention is selective and that the criteria of selection have something to do with future competitiveness, this serves to differentiate East Asian intervention from much of Latin American, Indian, and New Zealand intervention, where the assumption has tended to be that controls of trade, coupled with unselective support of any domestic market industrial investment, would be sufficient to promote the right kind of industrialization.[14]

---

[14] With respect to Latin America there are two alternative propositions: one, that even the planners made this assumption; two, that the planners (those using the approach of the Economic Commission for Latin America, for example) wanted to exercise selectivity in much the same way as the East Asians, but their principles were not translated into policies.

(c) Interventions have a high degree of coherence, in the sense that their impact is cumulative. The activities that get help through trade controls also get help through preferential investment finance and/ or fiscal incentives too. Taiwan's fiscal incentives, to take a small example, are aimed at three lists of products to be promoted: items on the first and most inclusive list receive the least incentives; those on the second list, a sub-set of the first, receive additional incentives; and those on the third list, a sub-set of the second, receive still more. Again, however, the question of how cumulative the promotional measures are, and the logic of the pattern of cumulation, is in great need of empirical research.

What are the organizational requirements for such a pattern of intervention to be realized? One is a *credit-based financial system* in which government exercises influence over the allocation of significant amounts of credit: it can support more rapid growth than would be possible in developing country conditions through a capital-market system or one based on retained earnings; it also gives the government a powerful lever for promoting particular sectors and influencing the balance between investment and consumption; and it can be a discipline on government intervention, because the other side of firms' dependence on government and the banks is the government's and the banks' need for the firms to do well.

The second organizational characteristic could be described as a *centralized decision-making structure* within the state. There needs to be a point where relative priorities can be decided, where the externalities facing private agents can be internalized, and judgments can be made about how to encourage the transfer of resources from currently profitable activities to those which are promising for the future (the same judgments as the management of a large firm must make, but taking account of externalities, and based on an exercise of foresight which the ordinary businessman could not afford to cultivate). The Republic of Korea's version of this centralized decision-making structure is contained in the links between the Blue House, the Economic Planning Board, the Ministry of Commerce and Industry, and the Ministry of Finance. Taiwan's is built on the links between the Cabinet, the Council for Economic Planning and Development, the Industrial Development Board, and the central bank.

It has been argued by Johnson among others that a third organizational requisite is a *high degree of public-private cooperation* between the managers of the state and the managers of private enterprise. He says:

> This cooperation is achieved through innumerable, continuously operating forums for coordinating views and investment plans, sharing international commercial intelligence, making adjustments to conform to the business cycle, or other changes in the economic environment, deciding on the new industries needed in order to maintain international competitive ability. . . . (Johnson 1981:13)

The implication seems to be that the private sector, like the state, needs to be arranged into peak associations through which representation to these 'continuously operating forums' can be made, so that a centralized state faces a centralized private sector, and negotiation takes place between them. This certainly corresponds to Japan, and it corresponds to what is emerging in the Republic of Korea. It is further away from Taiwan, however, where the private sector remains strikingly decentralized, and where Johnson's continuously operating forums are not much in evidence. This is not to say that all or most government–private sector relations in Taiwan are 'arm's length'. It is to say, however, that these relations do not, in the main, involve representatives of large aggregations of business interests, as they do in Japan and to an increasing degree in the Republic of Korea. On the other hand, Taiwan does have an active business press through which is built up a consensual identification of the problems facing the economy and the direction in which they should be solved; which perhaps matters more than the existence of coordinating organizations.

How then is the use of this concentrated mass of public power kept disciplined? Why is there not extensive non-market failure? Six points are important. First, the central decision-making structure is staffed by the best managerial talent available in the system.[15] Second, the central decision-makers are relatively insulated from all but the strongest of pressure groups. Consequently it makes no sense in these countries, as it does in some others, to see public policy as the vector of particular interests bearing on the

---

[15] This proposition is well established for Japan, less well established for the Republic of Korea, and still less well established for Taiwan, where information on recruitment to such agencies as the Council for Economic Planning and Development, the Industrial Development Board, and the Research and Development Evaluation Commission is almost wholly lacking.

state, or to see government agencies as the fiefdoms of particular private interests.

Third, the insulation of the central decision-makers, in turn, is based on an authoritarian, executive-based political structure, in which the executive jealously guards the feebleness of the legislature. Political and civil rights are much more fully developed in Japan than in the other two; but even in Japan, the most that the legislature can do to influence the direction of policy is to threaten to withhold authority. The weakness of the legislature ensures that, even in Japan, popular participation in elections does not translate into the exercise of real power. This matters especially because any government with a powerful elected legislature will find it difficult to hold the line against unbalanced increases in consumption at the expense of investment. As it is, the state has been left free to justify itself and negotiate with a narrow constituency on particular issues and tactics. However, the authoritarian character of these regimes should not be exaggerated. Compared to other middle-income countries, Taiwan and the Republic of Korea come about half way down a ranking by civil and political rights; so many middle-income countries (and more low-income countries) have a worse state of civil and political rights than these two.[16]

Fourth, none of these countries has a powerful labour, or left-wing movement. In the Republic of Korea and Taiwan such a movement scarcely exists, partly because of government repression. In Japan it exists but is excluded from politics. This may help explain why state-provided economic security schemes are little developed even in Japan. Yet the extraordinarily rapid rises in mass living standards (compared to other countries) suggests that governments which exclude 'labour' do not necessarily follow anti-labour policies. The East Asian capitalist experience suggests that, *if* a rapid reinvestment occurs, the rate of employment can rise so quickly towards full employment that government-imposed constraints on the operation of the market are not needed; welfare guarantees can be provided by firms and families. It is a big 'if', however (see footnote 13).

Fifth, none of the three countries experiences the conflict, chronic in many other countries, between powerful natural re-

---

[16] This is based on data in Gastil (1973, 1984), taking the middle-income countries as those so classified in the *World Development Report* (World Bank, various years).

source owners and manufacturers. In countries with substantial natural resource wealth, the natural resource owners typically want a close approximation to free trade; they want to be able to export and use their export earnings to purchase the best manufactures available on the international market; they do not see why they should have to buy the second-rate products of domestic manufacturers. The domestic manufacturers, on the other hand, want state help for domestic manufacturing. The conflict between these two sets of interests tends to make it difficult in many developing countries to sustain a long-term view of the nation's best economic interests.

These five points relate to the effect of state organization and the structure of politics on the use of public power. There is finally the matter of the goals sought by the central decision-makers, a matter of much greater importance in this kind of state than where power is more dispersed. The central point is that in all three countries the political élite sees a pattern of growth which makes sense in the long run as essential to its own survival. Political legitimacy is to an unusual degree based on economic success (compare, for example, Italy or Egypt: Wade 1979; Mason 1984). Especially in Taiwan and the Republic of Korea, the geo-political situation of the country has made it simply too risky for the élite, in its own perception, to take an umpiring, 'let the market work', view of its responsibilities. The élite has therefore needed success for the perpetuation of its own power, and has been relatively insulated from pressures. Beyond this are factors more cultural than situational. The central decision-makers are the kind of people who identify with the objectives of their organizations and of the state and do have some sense of moral responsibility for achieving objectives other than the use of public power for private enrichment. They have demonstrated an unmitigated confidence in the need for the state to be a leading player in the market (Pye and Pye 1985).

Little is known about how the public service organizations work in these countries: about management control systems, learning from errors, or negotiation and competition between bureaux. It appears that, contrary to orthodox public administration precepts, Taiwan derives great benefit from an overlapping of economic bureaux in the public sector, competition between which serves to keep bureaux on their toes – or else by-passed (Wade 1985a). I suspect that the standard image of East Asian bureaucracies as tightly integrated, from the top down control systems needs major qualification (Michell 1984; Wade 1982a). Yet somehow there does seem to be a closer than normal correspondence in these countries between, on the one hand, the goals that apply to non-market organizations to guide, regulate and evaluate agency personnel and performance (what Wolf (1979:116) calls 'internalities'), and the national goals enunciated by central decision-makers on the other. Explaining how this occurs is a very important topic for research, for it relates directly to how government interventions can be oriented mainly towards growth, competitiveness and restructuring concerns.[17]

Thus we arrive at the great East Asian capitalist synergism, between a public system oriented towards developmental and national security goals, and a private system geared towards long-term profit maximization. The interaction between the two systems affects the decisions made in each. The intent of the public system is to manipulate the inputs into private (or public) enterprise decision-making so as to secure development goals; but the content of the public system's actions is modified by feedback on profit and loss conditions, market prospects, and raw material costs (Johnson 1983; Inkster 1983). The market and private property are not displaced, only modified.

The public system takes the form of a 'competitively-oriented strong state'. 'Competitively-oriented' serves to differentiate it from many other 'strong' states, notably those of a communist variety. A corollary of competitively-oriented is that the state intervenes selectively, paying attention to some industries more than others, and paying more attention to capital and technology markets than goods markets, and more to goods markets than to labour markets. Much is left to private sector initiatives feeding off the base provided by the public system; indeed, the area left to private initiatives tends constantly to expand, without going as far as to erode public control over the vital aspects. 'Planning' in this arrangement does not involve any serious attempt to coordinate the whole economy, except at the level of macro-balance. It

---

[17] A comparative study of forms, scale and causes of corruption in these countries and other developing countries remains to be written. Corruption in parts of the civil service is common in Taiwan (e.g. public works, police and customs). My impression is that it is kept away from matters which are seen as important for national welfare (e.g. within the customs, it is concentrated away from imports of important export inputs) and takes the form of cost inflation for well-built public works, rather than sub-standard construction of properly priced public works (compare Wade 1982a, 1982b).

focuses on a relatively small number of sectors chosen for special emphasis. These countries therefore fit *both* the 'Japan, Inc.' image and the *laissez-faire* image to the extent that they fit either: but in different sectors and different factor markets. The point of interest is not which image fits better, but how their processes interact. Somewhere in this interaction lies the reason why East Asia's abundant 'social coalitions' or 'cartels' do not have the stagnation-inducing effects that Olson's theory (1982) would predict; quite the contrary. That theory is posited on the assumption that a free market works best, and that inferior performance is explained by 'interferences' (by politics and special interest groups) with the free market. It is just this assumption which the East Asian experience questions.

If we have evidence that these governments take growth and competitiveness as primary goals (such evidence can be independent of growth and competitiveness outcomes), and that the governments are organized in such a way as to have the means to intervene in pursuit of these goals, then this feeds back to the earlier argument about the effects of industrial strategy. It adds another piece of circumstantial evidence to the argument that industrial strategy in Taiwan, Republic of Korea and Japan has been effective.

In the future one can expect that forms of selective intervention will change in the Republic of Korea and Taiwan, and perhaps decline overall as has already happened in Japan over the 1970s. It may be argued that after twenty to thirty years of rapid post-war development, markets are less likely to fail now; that the growing economic strength of private agents will be translated into greater political power and thence into greater corruption of the intervention process; and that selective promotion now produces higher cost reactions from trading partners. On the other hand, it can be argued that in the severely competitive international environment now prevailing, with volatile exchange rates, interest rates, and capital flows, long-term decisions focused on a national interest will only be taken in a context of deliberately created stability, and stable political compromises to share adjustment costs will also only be effected in such a context. The art of government intervention is then to create this stability in key sectors without removing competitive pressures, and without incurring the wrath of trading partners. This brings us back to the point of departure –

that governments differ in their capacity to guide the market, that current interventions need to be assessed against their effect in augmenting or eroding future capacity, and that development theory needs to address this as a central issue.

6

GROWTH, INDUSTRIALIZATION AND ECONOMIC STRUCTURE: LATIN AMERICA AND EAST ASIA COMPARED

The purpose of this paper is to explore the similarities and differences between a set of very successful countries on the Pacific rim of East Asia and a group of Latin American countries which, by reputation at least, have not fared so well. As I can claim no expertise at all in the East Asia region, and as my knowledge of Latin America derives not from being a student *of* the area but an economist who has found himself repeatedly *in* the area working on an assorted set of problems, I will draw heavily on my favourite sources of international data, *International Financial Statistics* (IMF, various years) and the *World Development Report* (World Bank, various years). These data provide as much comparability across countries as I can hope for.

The paper begins with a sort of guided tour of what the *International Financial Statistics* and the *World Development Report* can tell us about the differences and similarities among the countries covered. Broadly speaking, the differences are probably smaller than is commonly perceived, but none the less the Latin American countries fall short of their Asian counterparts in a number of respects. They seem to be systematically prone to higher rates of inflation, and in recent years at least they have been outstripped by the capacity of the Pacific rim countries for capital formation. Beyond these relatively crude comparisons there is some slightly more subtle evidence of policy performance: three policy indicators that show quite similar performance most of the time, with deviations from similarity that more often reflect policy weakness in the Latin American cases while tending to show notable resistance to temptations by the Asian countries.

The guided tour of the data concludes by examining real exchange rate volatility in the two sets of countries. This volatility is without doubt much greater for the Latin American set of countries than for the Asian set, leading one to wonder what factors or circumstances might have given rise to such a difference. The simple hypothesis is that the greater volatility is largely due to the low elasticity of supply of tradables in most Latin American countries (at least as compared with some important Pacific rim countries).

The exploration of this hypothesis was motivated by the apparent ability of the Republic of Korea to surmount an important international debt problem with relatively minor costs of adjustment, while Chile, even though she did rather well in avoiding major policy mistakes, none the less underwent a very painful adjustment. The exploratory vehicle is a simple model of tradable and non-tradable goods, which I have found useful in a number of different settings. Parameters similar to those for Chile are inserted into this model to find the sensitivity of the real exchange rate (in this case the price level of tradables relative to that of non-tradables) to a sharp drop in the rate of inflow of capital. A comparative static version of the model is sufficient to reveal that simply altering one's assumptions as to the elasticity of supply of tradables can have a sharp impact in reducing the extent to which a 'debt crisis' affects the real exchange rate.

Richer insights flow from the dynamic version of the model. This version allows for long-run supply elasticities to be greater than short-run ones; it also builds in the process by which economic agents get rid of excess cash balances, or build them up from a perceived shortfall below their 'desired' level. Using the dynamic model, an attempt is made to get closer to the reality of Chile's recent experience by superimposing three disturbances: a drop equal to 10 per cent of GDP in the rate of inflow of capital; a fall in world copper prices causing a reduction in equilibrium real GDP of 6 per cent; and a reduction in the public's desired holdings of cash from an initial equilibrium level of 25 per cent to a new level of 15 per cent of GDP. With this combination of disturbances, the model tracks a very deep recession, including a dramatic depreciation of the real exchange rate. The current plight of the Chilean economy is easily understood, once Chile is seen as probably being somewhere in the middle of the dynamic process depicted.

By way of contrast, when the supply elasticity is raised, so as to turn 'Chile' into a 'Republic of Korea', and when the copper shock and the squeeze on real cash balances are eliminated, the result is an astonishingly quick rebound from the shock of a sharp reduction in the rate of capital inflow. The conclusion is that there may be objective reasons, rooted in differences in their economic structure, that have helped to produce the superior economic performance of some East Asian countries and that have operated as a drag on some of the Latin American economies.

That, in a sense, is the main substantive point of this paper. The elasticity of tradable goods supply is an important but neglected determinant of the outcomes we observe. It has a definite place in the *vade mecum* that we use for diagnosing economic ills and prescribing economic remedies.

SOME BROAD COMPARISONS

The tables which follow trace the data of thirteen countries in Latin America and seven in East Asia. They are chosen with a view to their relevance to the question that is implicit in the title of my paper. Of the ten main Latin countries of South America, only Bolivia is left out.[1] In Central America, Guatemala and Panama were left out because of incomplete data, El Salvador and Nicaragua because of the political turmoil that has plagued them in recent years. In East Asia, political turmoil once again was an important factor in the cases of Vietnam, Laos and Cambodia, while Burma was omitted simply because I perceive its economic policies and stance to isolate it from the countries that were included; Burma does not represent the Southeast Asia pattern that I am trying to juxtapose with that of Latin America. Two countries (Cuba and Taiwan) were omitted because they do not appear in *International Financial Statistics* and *World Development Report*, though Cuba would probably have been omitted even if it had appeared, because, like Burma, it is not representative.

The countries of Latin America are arrayed in three groups: the Southern Cone (Argentina, Brazil, Chile, Paraguay and Uruguay), the Andean Group (Colombia, Ecuador, Peru and Venezuela) and

---

[1] Bolivia is experiencing the most rapid inflation on record in recent times – well over 1000 per cent per year. It also has the distinction of having experienced more changes in government than it has years in its history.

Table 6.1 *Shares of GDP in industry and manufacturing*

	Per cent GDP in industry				Per cent GDP in manufacturing			
	1960	1965	1982	1983	1960	1965	1982	1983
Latin America								
Southern Cone								
Argentina	38	42	..	39	32	33	..	28
Brazil	35	33	..	35	26	26	..	27
Chile	35	40	34	36	21	24	20	20
Paraguay	26	19	31	26	17	16	16	16
Uruguay	28	32	33	28	21	..	26	..
Andean Group								
Colombia	26	25	31	28	17	18	21	17
Ecuador	20	22	40	40	16	18	12	18
Peru	33	30	39	41	24	20	24	26
Venezuela	22	23	42	40	..	..	16	17
Central America and Caribbean								
Costa Rica	20	23	27	27	14	..	20	..
Dominican Republic	23	20	28	19	17	14	16	18
Honduras	19	19	27	26	13	12	17	15
Mexico	29	31	38	40	19	21	21	22
Median	26	24	33.5	35.5	18	19	19	18
East Asia								
Gang of Three								
Hong Kong	39	40	..	30	26	24	..	22
Korea, Republic of	20	25	39	39	14	18	28	27
Singapore	18	24	37	37	12	15	26	24
Rest								
Indonesia	14	12	39	39	8	8	13	13
Malaysia	18	24	30	35	9	10	18	19
Philippines	28	28	36	36	20	20	24	25
Thailand	19	23	28	27	13	14	19	19
Median	20	24	36.5	36	13	15	21.5	22

Sources: World Development Report, 1984, 1985 (World Bank, various years).

Central America and the Caribbean (Costa Rica, the Dominican Republic, Honduras and Mexico). In Southeast Asia, we distinguish the Gang of Three (Hong Kong, Republic of Korea and Singapore) from the rest (Indonesia, Malaysia, the Philippines and Thailand).

Table 6.2 *Economic growth, GDP and industrial sector* (per cent)

	GDP growth		Industry growth		Manufacturing growth	
	1960–70	1970–82	1960–70	1970–82	1960–70	1970–82
Latin America						
Southern Cone						
Argentina	4.3	1.5	5.8	1.0	5.6	−0.2
Brazil	5.4	7.6	..	8.2	..	7.8
Chile	4.4	1.9	4.4	0.6	5.5	−0.4
Paraguay	4.2	8.5	..	10.7	..	7.8
Uruguay	1.2	3.1	1.2	4.2	1.5	3.4
Andean Group						
Colombia	5.1	5.4	6.0	4.4	5.7	5.2
Ecuador	..	..	..	..	..	..
Peru	4.9	3.0	5.0	3.3	5.7	6.0
Venezuela	6.0	4.1	4.6	2.4	6.4	4.8
Central America and Caribbean						
Costa Rica	6.5	4.5	9.4	6.1	10.6	6.0
Dominican Republic	4.5	6.0	6.0	6.9	5.0	5.9
Honduras	5.2	4.2	5.3	5.7	4.5	9.3
Mexico	7.6	6.4	9.4	7.2	10.1	6.8
Median	5.1	4.5	5.5	5.7	5.7	6.0
East Asia						
Gang of Three						
Hong Kong	10.0	9.9	..	..	..	..
Korea, Republic of	8.6	8.6	17.2	13.6	17.6	14.5
Singapore	8.8	8.5	12.5	8.9	13.0	9.3
Rest						
Indonesia	3.9	7.7	5.2	10.7	3.3	13.4
Malaysia	6.5	7.7	..	9.2	..	10.6
Philippines	5.1	6.0	6.0	8.0	6.7	6.6
Thailand	8.4	7.1	11.9	9.3	11.4	9.9
Median	8.4	7.7	11.9	9.3	11.4	10.3

Sources: As for Table 6.1.

Table 6.1 reveals that, on the key question of the extent of industrialization, there is today very little difference between the Latin American and the Southeast Asian groups. The median percentage of GDP in industry, for the two years 1982 and 1983 taken together, is 35.5 per cent and 36 per cent respectively. In manufacturing, as defined by the *World Development Report*, the corresponding percentages are 20 and 22. There may be differences in the kind of industrialization, but not in its extent.

Some differences appear as we follow the relevant percentages over time and over sub-groups of countries. With the exception of Hong Kong and possibly the Philippines, the fractions of GDP in industry and in manufacturing grew significantly in the Asian countries between the early 1960s and the early 1980s. This was true also for many Latin American countries, but not for Argentina, Brazil, Chile, Colombia and Uruguay, all of which in 1960 had reached percentages close to where they were in 1983. These were the first to industrialize, and their wave of import-substitution was pretty well complete by 1960.

The remaining Latin American countries were still in the process of import-substitution during the 1960s and in some cases beyond. In none of the Latin American cases can one say that the growth of the share of industry or of manufacturing was export-led. This is in marked contrast at least to the Gang of Three (with Hong Kong's ratios growing before 1960 – earlier than those of the other two), all of which enjoyed a strong export-led industrialization. I do not know enough about Indonesia, Malaysia, the Philippines and Thailand to say for sure, but nothing in their patterns looks alien to one familiar with the Latin American scene.

Table 6.2 reveals that, even where the ratios of Table 6.1 changed significantly, the bulk of the story is that the growth rates of industry were quite similar to those of GDP. (This is virtually inevitable with orders of magnitude like those here; even if the industry/GDP ratio grew by 20 points between 1960 and the early 1980s, this would only mean that the average annual rate of growth of industry was about one percentage point higher than that of GDP.) The data of Table 6.2 show rough coincidence in growth rates between GDP and industry; they obviously do not reveal the direction of causality. In particular, they are quite compatible with the hypothesis that in some cases export growth stimulated a higher rate of growth of GDP and of industry while in others import substitution policies ended up by constraining both exports (through the elastic but ineluctable bond that links total exports with total imports) and the rate of growth of GDP.

Table 6.3 delves further into the role of exports. The truly dramatic change in the ratio of exports to GDP occurs in the Republic of Korea. Its growth rate of exports also stands alone against the

Table 6.3 *The role of exports* (per cent)

	Exports of goods and non-factor services/GDP				Average annual growth of exports	
	1960	1965	1982	1983	1960–70	1970–82
Latin America						
Southern Cone						
Argentina	10	8	13	13	3.8	8.3
Brazil	5	8	9	8	5.3	8.8
Chile	14	14	22	24	0.7	9.5
Paraguay	18	15	8	8	5.4	5.8
Uruguay	15	19	15	24	2.8	5.9
Andean Group						
Colombia	16	11	11	10	2.6	2.2
Ecuador	16	16	21	25	2.8	−1.3
Peru	20	16	19	21	2.1	4.8
Venezuela	32	31	25	26	1.1	−7.2
Central America and Caribbean						
Costa Rica	21	23	43	35	9.6	4.5
Dominican Republic	24	15	14	15	−2.1	4.0
Honduras	21	27	27	27	10.9	3.4
Mexico	10	9	17	20	3.4	8.6
Median	16	16	16.5	21	3.1	4.8
East Asia						
Gang of Three						
Hong Kong	82	71	100	95	12.7	9.4
Korea, Republic of	3	9	39	37	34.7	20.2
Singapore	163	123	196	176	4.2	..
Rest						
Indonesia	13	5	22	25	3.5	4.4
Malaysia	54	44	51	54	6.1	3.8
Philippines	11	17	16	20	2.3	7.9
Thailand	17	18	25	22	6.2	2.6
Median	17	18	39	37	6.1	6.2

Sources: As for Table 6.1.

rest in both periods, in what is unquestionably a case of tremendously successful export-led growth. When the two regions are compared, the dominant feature is the growth of the export ratio in Southeast Asia, as between the early sixties and the early eighties, compared with its relative constancy in Latin America. The principal cases of growth in the export ratio are Mexico and Ecuador (where the oil booms of the 1970s appear to be the proximate cause) and the Southern Cone countries, where trade liberalization (in degrees which varied greatly from case to case) seems to have been the prime mover.[2]

The dramatically better growth performance of the Southeast Asian countries surely has many explanations. The export-led growth, especially of the Gang of Three, has already been mentioned. In addition, we should note that every one of the Southeast Asian countries significantly raised its investment/GDP ratios between the early 1960s and the 1980s, while with a few scattered exceptions (especially Paraguay and the Dominican Republic) the Latin American countries did not. As neither exports nor investment is a policy variable, it is easy to find cases where a country's policy has through artificial incentives caused too much of one or the other. Yet I have no doubt that it is one of the duties of good economic policy to provide a climate in which healthy investment can occur, and which does not put obstacles in the path of healthy export growth.

From what I know of particular cases in Latin America, I feel confident that ill-advised policies had a role in limiting the growth of exports, and in keeping the investment ratio low when in Southeast Asia it was able to increase strongly. To my mind it is no accident that the Latin American countries whose investment ratios increased most (Paraguay, the Dominican Republic, Ecuador and Colombia) were among the leaders of the region with respect to the growth rates achieved in the 1970–82 period. Nor is it an accident that most of the great growth booms of the period (Brazil 1967–73, Chile 1976–81, Uruguay 1974–80, Paraguay 1976–81) were export-led.

On the other side of the coin one has inflation, an indicator of policy weakness rather than strength. Here (see Table 6.4) the record of the listed Southeast Asian countries is much better than that of the Latin American group, though interestingly and once again the cases of most successful growth (Costa Rica, Dominican Republic, Mexico, Paraguay, Venezuela) tend to be those with low inflation rates; and even among inflationary countries like Brazil,

---

[2] Paraguay is a special case here, having had its own export bonanza in the late 1970s and early 1980s in the sale of labour and other services for the construction of the great hydroelectric complex at Itaipu. These factor services are not included in the data shown in the table.

Table 6.4 *Investment and inflation* (per cent)

	Gross domestic investment/GDP				Average annual inflation	
	1960	1965	1982	1983	1960–70	1970–82
Latin America						
Southern Cone						
Argentina	22	19	19	13	21.4	136.0
Brazil	22	25	19	21	46.1	42.1
Chile	14	15	10	8	33.0	148.3
Paraguay	17	15	26	26	3.1	12.7
Uruguay	18	11	15	10	50.2	59.3
Andean Group						
Colombia	21	16	26	19	11.9	22.7
Ecuador	14	14	25	17	6.1	14.5
Peru	25	21	17	13	10.4	37.0
Venezuela	21	24	26	12	1.3	12.3
Central America and Caribbean						
Costa Rica	18	20	23	21	1.9	18.4
Dominican Republic	12	9	21	22	2.1	8.8
Honduras	14	15	16	17	2.9	8.7
Mexico	20	22	21	17	3.5	20.9
Median	18	16	21	17	6.1	20.9
East Asia						
Gang of Three						
Hong Kong	18	36	29	27	2.4	8.6
Korea, Republic of	11	15	26	27	17.5	19.3
Singapore	11	22	46	45	1.1	5.4
Rest						
Indonesia	8	7	23	24	..	19.9
Malaysia	14	18	34	34	−0.3	7.2
Philippines	16	21	29	27	5.8	12.8
Thailand	16	20	21	25	1.8	9.7
Median	14	20	29	27	2.4	9.7

Sources: As for Table 6.1.

Chile and Uruguay, their major spurts of growth coincide with periods of substantial disinflation.[3]

[3] Brazil's inflation rate fell from an average of 76 per cent per year in 1963–65 to an average of 17 per cent per year in 1971–73, while her growth rate averaged over 10 per cent per year during 1966–73. Chile's inflation rate was 352 per cent in 1973 and did not fall below 300 per cent until 1976, reaching an average of 29 per cent in

I must make it clear that I do not see inflation *per se* as being the mechanical or proximate cause of economic stagnation, nor disinflation as being the mechanical or proximate cause of rapid growth. Rather, inflation, like fever, is a symptom of a general systemic weakness or breakdown. In most Latin American episodes of high and growing inflation, the printing of too much money is mixed up with many other (often egregious) policy mistakes. Periods of successful disinflation, on the other hand, typically entail the correction (or amelioration) of many of these mistakes simultaneously with a slowing of the printing press.

SOME POLICY INDICATORS

For some years now, in a quite different context from that of the present paper, I have calculated and analysed three relatively 'objective' policy indicators for a number of countries and situations. The context of that work was largely inflation (and the related phenomenon of devaluation crises), but, as I have indicated, the record seems to say that inflation is in most cases just one reflection of a deeper policy *malaise*. It is in this spirit that I present data for the relatively recent past for the countries under review.

First, we must define the variables. They are thought of as being policy variables that have in some sense equal (or nearly equal) validity, regardless of what exchange rate regime a country has. Obviously, the public sector can refrain from pumping new credits from the banking system (β) under any exchange rate system. So, too, can it determine (over time at least) whether the accumulated volume of such credits will be large or small as a percentage (γ) of the total volume of outstanding bank credit. Finally, even though the money supply is either totally or largely an endogenous variable under many exchange rate systems (fixed exchange rate, prefixed crawling peg – the *tablita* of the Southern Cone countries, ordinary crawling peg, etc.), the volume of domestic credit is subject to fairly wide policy control, with expansions in credit under the indicated exchange rate regimes being largely bought at the cost of reductions in international reserves. Thus, the rate of

1979–81; her growth rate meanwhile averaged nearly 9 per cent per year from 1976 to 1981. Uruguay averaged 85 per cent inflation in 1973–75 and grew at an unprecedented rate of over 5 per cent per year between 1976 and 1981. (Uruguay's growth rate of per capita income was negative over a quarter of a century prior to a major policy reform starting in 1974.)

Table 6.5 *Policy indicators*

	Median year, 1979–83			Latest year (1983)		
	Δ Govt credit/ GDP β	Govt credit/ Total credit γ	% Change/ bank credit λ	Δ Govt credit/ GDP β	Govt credit/ Total credit γ	% Change/ bank credit λ
Latin America						
Southern Cone						
Argentina	0.017	0.072	209.3	0.027	0.051	400.8
Brazil	0.026	0.164	83.7	0.115	0.450	178.0
Chile	0.019	0.094	47.2	0.019	0.094	10.9
Paraguay	0.005	<0	25.6	0.005	0.011	25.6
Uruguay	0.012	0.034	72.4	0.127	0.252	29.6
Andean Group						
Colombia	0.003	<0	38.3	0.017	0.148	38.3
Ecuador	0.006	<0	37.1	0.015	<0	59.1
Peru	0.028	0.410	16.4	0.104	0.440	164.6
Venezuela	0.011	<0	20.5	0.002	<0	6.2

Central America and Caribbean						
Costa Rica[a]	0.060	0.362	30.2	0.080	0.422	24.3
Dominican Republic	0.031	0.364	18.1	0.031	0.426	16.6
Honduras	0.026	0.262	15.6	0.022	0.320	17.8
Mexico	0.062	0.482	49.5	0.093	0.665	56.0
Median	0.019	0.094	37.1	0.027	0.252	29.6
East Asia						
Korea, Republic of	0.014	0.113	29.4	0.003	0.113	16.0
Singapore	<0	<0	42.5	0.092	<0	42.5
Indonesia	<0	<0	18.7	<0	<0	18.7
Malaysia	0.025	0.081	22.9	<0	0.098	16.1
Philippines	0.012	0.160	24.6	0.026	0.216	30.0
Thailand	0.023	0.264	18.1	0.016	0.264	26.3
Median	0.013	0.097	23.7	0.010	0.105	22.5

[a] Costa Rica's figures are for 1978–80 and 1980.
Source: IMF (various years).

expansion of domestic credit (λ) is subject to a degree of policy control that under many exchange rate regimes is quite a bit greater than the degree of control that the authorities can exercise over the rate of expansion of the money supply.

Explicit definitions of the three variables follow:

β = net increase, during the year, of banking system credit to the public sector, expressed as a percentage of the year's GDP. Thus, if the public sector's borrowings from the banking system stood at 200 at the beginning of the year, and went to 300 by year's end, the net increase would be 100. If GDP of the year were 800, then β would be 0.125 (= 100/800).

γ = fraction of total banking system credit going to the public sector. Thus, if at the beginning of the year total bank credit were 400, and if at the end it were 500, then (using public sector credit figures from above) γ would be 0.50 (= 200/400) at the beginning of the year and 0.60 (= 300/500) at the end. In the tables presented in this paper γ is always measured from end-of-year data. Whenever the public sector is a net lender to the banking system, γ is simply recorded as <0.

λ = percentage increase during the year in total domestic credit of the banking system. This, with the figures just presented, would be 25 per cent [= (500/400) − λ] × 100.

Table 6.5 gives data on these variables for the countries under review (except for Hong Kong, which does not appear in *International Financial Statistics*). The striking thing about Table 6.5 is how little the medians of the two groups of countries appear to differ. Intimations of genuine differences are there, none the less. For example, no East Asian country reveals a median β even approaching the level of 0.06 displayed by Costa Rica and Mexico. Similarly, Argentina and Brazil are far and away the champions when it comes to expanding bank credit.

These hints of difference are sharpened somewhat when, in the same table, we look only at the most recent year available (1983 except for Costa Rica). Here the medians of β and γ pull more sharply apart, and more sharply extreme values are revealed, in the Latin American sub-set, for all three variables. We have three countries (Brazil, Peru and Uruguay) in which the government sucks new credits from the banking system to the tune of 10 per cent or more of GDP. Mexico's value for γ means that the government in 1983 was the recipient of two-thirds of the total amount of outstanding bank credit. And we also have three cases in which bank credit expanded by more than 100 per cent. Looking at the East Asian group, we find no such extreme observations.

Table 6.6 reveals how different has been the policy behaviour of the Latin American countries from that of their East Asian counterparts. It is clear from the table that in the middle classification the percentage of observations are quite similar between the two sets of countries (this, given the relatively substantial proportions of observations located in the middle groups, helps explain why the median observations do not differ greatly). However, there are dramatic differences in the two extreme groups. In each panel, the left hand group contains a substantially higher proportion of East Asian than of Latin American observations. Similarly, for the right hand group the proportion of Latin American observations is much greater. This means that when the East Asian countries deviate from average behaviour, they deviate on the side of prudence; when the Latin American countries do so, their deviations are on the side of risk.

The significance of the differences observed in Table 6.6 can be tested using χ^2. The separate panels yield χ^2 in the probability range of 5 to 10 per cent. The table as a whole is significant at a one per cent level. That is, the probability that panels a, b, and c would be generated by chance alone (given their respective marginal row and column totals), by sampling from a single population, is less than one in a hundred.

All in all, I find this exercise to be a convincing demonstration that economic policy was indeed quite different in the Latin American countries from that in East Asia, that the difference took the form of the East Asians being more prudent, and the Latin Americans being more prone to risky policies. Moreover, as is the case with most aberrant behaviour in this world, risky policies are not an everyday event in Latin America. Policy behaviour there tends to be quite 'normal' most of the time; it only goes awry intermittently, but I believe this occurs at great cost to the people of the countries concerned.

When we speak of policy behaviour, I believe we have to introduce a moral tone into our pronouncements. Most policy mistakes, in my view, reflect a weakness of will, a lack of spine and discipline,

Table 6.6 *Distributions of policy variables* (number of observations in interval)

Group	Interval of β			Total
	Below zero	0 to 0.04	Over 0.04	
a. $\beta = (\triangle$ Bank credit to government)/GDP				
Latin America	12 (19%)	37 (59%)	14 (22%)	63
East Asia	9 (30%)	19 (63%)	2(7%)	30
Total	21	56	16	93
	$\chi^2(2) = 4.16$		$[\chi^2_{0.10}(2) = 4.61]$	

Group	Interval of γ			Total
	Below zero	0 to 0.4	Over 0.4	
b. $\gamma = $ (Bank credit to government)/Total bank credit				
Latin America	17 (27%)	35 (56%)	11 (17%)	63
East Asia	11 (37%)	19 (63%)	0	30
Total	28	54	11	93
	$\chi^2(2) = 6.09$		$[\chi^2_{0.05}(2) = 5.99]$	

Group	Interval of λ			Total
	Below 25%	25% to 50%	Over 50%	
c. $\lambda = $ % Increase in total bank credit				
Latin America	20 (32%)	21 (33%)	22 (35%)	63
East Asia	15 (50%)	12 (40%)	3 (10%)	30
Total	35	33	25	93
	$\chi^2(2) = 6.74$		$[\chi^2_{0.05}(2) = 5.99]$	
	Total $\chi^2(6) = 16.99$		$[\chi^2_{0.01}(6) = 16.81]$	

Source: IMF (various years).

a drift into taking 'the easy way out'. Simple rules, like 'the government should *never* borrow from the banking system' or that 'bank credit should never expand at more than 20 per cent per year' are surely good rules on the whole, but they are hard to implant and maintain. The trouble is, one can point to too many cases where these rules were flouted with apparent impunity. (Even noble Singapore nearly doubled total domestic bank credit in 1981.)

Though simple rules are not a bad idea, what is more urgently needed is a general sense of discipline in economic policy. The consequences should be surveyed before policy actions are taken; precedent-setting moves should be treated with particular caution. Above all, one must never lose sight of the absolute truth that the potential line of claimants on the public purse is endless. Bad policy, by caving in to some dubious claims, quite naturally invites others. It is an integral part of good policy to discourage pressures and claims, and to prevent all but the most meritorious from getting very far.

A vital part of this message is that economic policy is made by people, and that the personal force and strength of character of particular individuals can and do make a difference. Thirty years of observation in Latin America has provided me with a small firmament of heroes of economic policymaking – individuals who provided leadership that enabled their countries to emerge from a profound crisis (Roberto Campos in Brazil), to turn around a situation of stagnation or retrogression (Alejandro Vegh Villegas in Uruguay), or simply to run a well-tuned policy machine for year after year in a most responsible fashion (Rodrigo Gomez and Antonio Ortiz Mena in Mexico, Jose Gil Diaz in Uruguay). There are others in that firmament in Latin America, and they certainly must have counterparts in the East Asian countries. Also, we should recognize that great performances entail not only the right man but also a reasonably receptive environment. Thus for every star that made it into my firmament, there are probably several others who might have been there had they been placed in a somewhat more receptive or favourable setting (which often means, had the crisis been more unbearable when they came on the scene, or had a different president been in office). Obviously history is the result of both individuals and 'forces': I emphasize individuals mainly because that is something that we ourselves, the profession of economists, can do something about.

REAL EXCHANGE RATE VOLATILITY

While the preceding section focused on policy weaknesses, the present one concentrates on what I consider to be somewhat adverse objective circumstances faced by a number of Latin American economies. These circumstances have their symptoms in a high degree of real exchange rate volatility, which we here attempt to document.

The concept of the real exchange rate is a tricky one, to which different authors ascribe different meanings. My thinking about the subject runs as follows. In theoretical expositions, where world prices are taken as given, the real exchange rate is the nominal exchange rate (peso price of the dollar) deflated by a general price index of the (small) country in question. This real exchange rate equilibrates the supply and demand for foreign currency, measured, of course, in foreign currency units (dollars' worth). Movements of this real exchange rate ($E/\bar{p}_d$ can occur through movements of the nominal exchange rate (E) such as would occur under a flexible exchange rate regime, or through movements of the general level of internal prices and costs ($\bar{p}_d$), such as occur under fixed exchange rates. This much is needed to establish the equivalence of real comparative-statics results under alternative exchange rate systems, and is as far as we need to go to obtain a definition of the real exchange rate for theoretical purposes.

For empirical purposes, however, a further step is necessary. World prices do not stay quietly in the pound of *ceteris paribus* as the clock and calendar move on. The dollar's worth of one year is not the same as that of another, and empirical work that traces movements of the real exchange rate through time must recognize this by defining, in a sense, the basket of goods whose price we call a real dollar. There are reasons why this basket should in principle be a basket of tradable goods, and equally good reasons why the deflating index $\bar{p}_d$ should include non-tradable goods. These considerations have led to a modest drift toward a consensus that the real exchange rate should be defined as $\bar{p}^*_d \, E/\bar{p}_d$, where $\bar{p}^*$ is a world index of wholesale prices and $\bar{p}_d$ is a domestic index of general prices (consumer price index (CPI) or GDP deflator).

I have followed this convention here. In every case the nominal exchange rate E is the local-currency (peso) price of the US dollar and the deflating index $\bar{p}_d$ is the local consumer price index. There are two alternative dollar price indexes $\bar{p}_d$. The first is simply the United States wholesale price index (WPI) which in effect defines the United States WPI basket as the one whose relative price is being measured by the real exchange rate. Alternatively, a multi-national WPI is constructed, using the weights that were used to define the special drawing rights (SDR) beginning in January 1981.[4] The weights are applied to each non-dollar WPI, and converted into dollars at the prevailing exchange rate between that currency and the US dollar. The result is an index of the dollar[5] price level of a basket of goods consisting of the WPI baskets of five major nations.

Table 6.7 presents ranges of real exchange rate variations for thirteen Latin American and six East Asian countries. The first two columns take as their basic observations the annual average nominal exchange rates adjusted by annual average price levels. The figures presented are the ratios of the highest real exchange rate to the lowest real exchange rate observed over the span of years 1970–83. The last two columns concentrate on quarterly rather than annual observations, and deal with the period 1980–83. Again, the figures recorded represent, for each country, the ratio of the highest quarterly real exchange rate to the lowest quarterly real exchange rate recorded during this period.

The difference in the range of variation between the two groups of countries is quite clear. In the annual comparisons only Indonesia among the East Asian nations shows a range of more than 1.4, while for the Latin American countries only five out of thirteen have less than this range when the United States WPI is used and only two out of thirteen have less than this range when the SDR WPI is used. In the quarterly data for the most recent period only the United States WPI observation for the Philippines has a range of more than 1.4, while eight (col. 3) or nine (col. 4) of the Latin American countries exhibit a wider range than this.

There are various reasons why real exchange rates might be more volatile in one place than in another, but they can easily be grouped into two broad categories: reasons why the demand and supply of foreign exchange might themselves be more volatile (e.g., world prices of principal export products are more variable for some countries than for others); and reasons why a given percentage shift of the demand or supply of foreign exchange would cause a greater change in the equilibrium real exchange rate. Here

---

[4] These weights are 0.42 for the US dollar, 0.19 for the German mark, and 0.13 each for the French franc, the Japanese yen and the British pound.

[5] It must be a dollar price index because the exchange rate is that between each given currency and the US dollar. This price index would decrease, however, to reflect a depreciation of the nominal exchange rate of, say, the United Kingdom or Germany *vis-à-vis* the dollar.

Table 6.7 *Range of real exchange rate variation* (high observation of period ÷ low observation of period)

	Annual observations, 1970–83		Quarterly observations, 1980–83	
	US WPI.$(E/\bar{p}_d)$	SDR WPI.$(E/\bar{p}_d)$	US WPI.$(E/\bar{p}_d)$	SDR WPI.$(E/\bar{p}_d)$
Latin America				
Southern Cone				
Argentina	2.90	2.68	4.62	3.98
Brazil	1.92	1.70	1.55	1.49
Chile	1.97	1.74	1.79	1.53
Paraguay	1.72	1.81	1.65	1.60
Uruguay	1.86	1.74	2.15	2.01
Andean Group				
Colombia	1.33	1.45	1.20	1.32
Ecuador	1.33	1.34	1.28	1.22
Peru	1.60	1.71	1.29	1.19
Venezuela	1.34	1.51	1.67	1.73
Central America and Caribbean				
Costa Rica	2.81	2.55	2.81	2.53
Dominican Republic	1.21	1.39	1.21	1.39
Honduras	1.21	1.47	1.21	1.47
Mexico	1.55	1.47	1.81	1.72
Median	1.60	1.71	1.65	1.53
East Asia				
Korea, Republic of	1.28	1.35	1.19	1.19
Singapore	1.34	1.27	1.07	1.29
Indonesia	1.78	1.44	1.35	1.31
Malaysia	1.22	1.22	1.13	1.28
Philippines	1.24	1.20	1.46	1.36
Thailand	1.10	1.19	1.14	1.23
Median	1.26	1.25	1.16	1.28

E = nominal exchange rate in local currency units per dollar.
$\bar{p}_d$ = local consumer price index.
Source: IMF (1985b).

I shall focus on the latter, and within it on the elasticity of supply of tradable goods.

To me, one of the biggest dividends that was produced by looking at the equilibrium real exchange rate as equilibrating the demand and supply of tradables rather than (or actually in addition to and simultaneously with) equilibrating the demand for imports and the supply of exports is the light shed by this more aggregative focus on the so-called 'elasticities problem'. The trouble is, the demand for imports is typically an excess demand function; so, likewise, is the supply of exports an excess supply function. Their elasticities are complex multiples of the component elasticities of total domestic demand and supply for importables in the one case and exportables in the other. When excess demand or supply is involved these elasticities will themselves be volatile, depending critically on the proportion of total demand that is met by imports or the proportion of total supply that is exported. Partly for this reason, these trade elasticities have been incredibly difficult to estimate empirically for use in practical work.

In comparison, the elasticities of demand for and supply of tradables are easy to deal with. The demand for tradables is that for a very large composite commodity, whose elasticity virtually has to be low. I think of tradables as being on the whole manufactures plus agricultural products, and of non-tradables as being predominantly public utilities, transport and services. An elasticity of substitution of 0.5 between them is not an excessively low guess. This would imply own-price elasticities of about 0.25 for tradables and for non-tradables, assuming that the two groups have about equal weight in total expenditures.[6] Just as I was always troubled by uncertainty concerning the old-fashioned trade elasticities, so now I am extremely confident that demand elasticities for the broad categories of tradables and non-tradables are quite low. (Whether they are 0.15 or 0.40 hardly makes much difference in most uses to which they are put.) Thus, if these low elasticities of demand for tradables can be put to fruitful use to solve problems whose answers were obscured by the penumbra surrounding the traditional trade elasticities, the profession will have received a great boon. I believe that this is the case.

If the demand elasticity for tradables is low everywhere, this means that the volatility of the real exchange rate in response to given percentage shifts of demand or supply will depend on the elasticity supply of tradables. My hypothesis is that this elasticity is low in countries like Chile, Argentina and Uruguay and high in countries

---

[6] For two mutually exclusive and exhaustive categories of goods, their compensated own-price elasticities of demand, summed together, are equal in absolute value to the elasticity of substitution between them.

like the Republic of Korea, Taiwan, Singapore and Hong Kong. Once again the concept of total supply versus excess supply comes to our rescue. We are not asking about how the supply of exports of Argentine wheat will change in response to a rise in its price. We are asking instead how the total supply of all agricultural goods will respond to a rise in all of their prices relative to non-tradables. Wheat supply can be expanded by constricting the planting of maize and sunflowers, but the total supply of agricultural products from the pampas is not going to be equally responsive. On the whole, we can say that the total output of the agricultural and mining sectors is likely to be quite inelastic and that the elasticity of the overall supply of tradables will depend largely on the relative importance of agriculture and mining.

Countries concentrated in manufacturing have a much greater capacity for rapid expansion of production of tradables in response to real exchange rate changes. True, it is more expensive in most cases for a factory to work multiple shifts than single shifts, but the premium required in order to make it worthwhile to add a second or third shift is typically not huge. Moreover, over a longer range, capital equipment can add almost indefinitely to manufacturing capacity, something that is not true of agriculture and mining.

The following section presents a simple model together with some simulations of how the real exchange rate might behave, in response to certain assumed disturbances, in a country like Chile as compared to one like the Republic of Korea.

A SIMPLE MODEL AND SOME SIMULATIONS

The model presented here is intended to be as spare and simple as possible. In a sense it tries to do for small-country macroeconomics what simple supply and demand models do for ordinary markets. It follows a minimalist criterion, incorporating only what is most essential. I do not believe you can devise a simpler model to handle the types of problem than this model does. We have two classes of goods: home goods (H) and tradables (T). The demand functions for these goods embody the notion that normally all income is spent (implicitly the capital and credit markets are supposed to bring this result about); the supply functions are so designed as to be compatible with movements along a product transformation curve, but not to require that one always stays on such a curve;

excess money (i.e. $M^s > M^d$) is spent in some pattern over time; and foreign borrowing (B) enters as a separate argument in the demand functions for goods.

The comparative static model incorporating these assumptions is set out below. The variables of the model are:

$H^d = H^s$	Demand and supply of home goods.
T^d, T^s	Demand and supply of tradables.
$B = T^d - T^s$	Net foreign borrowing less net interest paid (= deficit in merchandise trade plus that in non-financial services).
$y = H^s + T^s$	Aggregate output.
p_T	World price of tradable, taken as given and therefore equal to the exchange rate.
p_H	Price level of home goods.
w	Wage level (index of factor costs). (Initial prices and wages are all assumed equal to unity, so that dp_T, dp_H, and dw all represent percentage changes. Initial levels of H^s and T^s are each assumed to be equal to $0.5y$).
$M^s = M^d$	Money supply and demand (broad definition).

The equations of the model in its comparative static form are:

(1) $H^d = a_0 - a_1(p_H - p_T) + a_2 y + a_3 B$

(2) $T^d = -a_0 - a_1(p_T - p_H) + (1 - a_2)y + (1 - a_3)B$

(3) $H^s = b_0 + b_1(p_H - w)$

(4) $T^s = c_0 + c_1(p_T - w)$

(5) $y = H^s + T^s$

(6) $B = T^d - T^s$

(7) $M^d = ky[f_1 p_H + (1 - f_1)p_T]$

(8) $w = f_1 p_H + (1 - f_1)p_T$

(8a) $w = w_0 + \beta[f_1(p_H + p_{H0}) + (1 - f_1)(p_T - p_{T0})$ } Alternatives

(8b) $w = w_0$ } to (8)

(9) $H^d = H^s$

One key attribute of this model is its assumption that all income is spent. This is motivated by the fact that, in the countries and in the periods dealt with here, credit markets seem to have worked to channel unspent funds to those able to put them to use. A second attribute is the treatment of net international borrowing (B) as a separate argument in the demand functions for goods. This is because there is no reason why borrowed funds should be spent in the same way as extra income would be spent (i.e. $a_3 \neq a_2$), and indeed in actual fact international borrowings are at different times distributed in very different proportions between tradables and non-tradables.

In the present exercise the assumption is also made that the economy stays on its production frontier. This is assured by setting $dy = dH^s + dT^s = 0$, which yields $b_1 \, dp_H + c_1 \, dp_T = (b_1 + c_1)dw$, thus defining f_1 in (8) as $b_1 / (b_1 + c_1)$.[7]

The model can be used either for fixed or flexible exchange rate cases. With a flexible exchange rate the money supply becomes an exogenous variable; in the fixed exchange rate case money is (as it should be) endogenous. We will work here with the assumption of fixed exchange rates ($p_T \equiv 1$) throughout. This makes no difference for the equilibrium solutions, which in real terms will be the same under either assumption regarding the exchange rate regime.

The equilibrium solution for the change in the real exchange rate consequent upon a change in the flow of capital (dB), with a fixed exchange rate ($dp_T = 0$) and neo-classical supply ($dy = 0$) is $- dp_H = - [a_3/(b_1 + a_1 - f_1 b_1)]dB$. Setting $a_1 = \eta_h H^d$; $b_1 = \varepsilon_h H^s$,[8] and $H^d = H^s = H$, and multiplying and dividing by y and H, we have $- dp_H = - \{a_3(y/H)/[(1 - f_1) \varepsilon_h + \eta_h]\}dB/y$.

Our assumptions about magnitudes are as follows:

$a_3 =$ fraction of borrowings spent in non-tradables = 1. This is close to what happened in Chile, and in a number of other Latin American countries in the capital-inflow booms of the late 1970s and early 1980s. In all cases the real exchange rate fell

---

[7] If the Keynesian alternative (8b) or the semi-Keynesian one (8a) is used, real wages rise, even in long-run equilibrium, as a consequence of a reduction in the rate of capital inflow (the principal disturbance we will be analysing). Since this runs counter to both intuition and observation, I decided to stick to the neoclassical wage equation (8). To the extent that non-tradable supply is more elastic than tradable supply, nominal wages would fall more than a standard value-weighted price index. This is what we appear to observe in the Latin American countries.

[8] These define the demand (η_h) and supply (ε_h) elasticities for home goods, assuming the initial price $p_H{}^o$.

	(appreciated) dramatically, something which would not have occurred had the capital inflows been spent on tradables.
$H_0^s = T_0^s = 0.5y$	Initially, half of total supply comes from tradables, half from non-tradables.
$f_1 = b_1/(b_1 + c_1)$	See above, with equal initial shares in production, f_1 is equal to $\varepsilon_h/\varepsilon_h + \varepsilon_T)$, where the εs are supply elasticities.
$\eta_h = 0.25$	(defined as positive). As indicated in the preceding section the own-price elasticity of demand for non-tradables is almost certainly very low in every country.
$\varepsilon_h = 4$	This builds in the idea that home goods production is on the whole quite readily expandable, at least in the middle to long run.
$\varepsilon_T = 1$	for 'Chile'; 4 for 'Republic of Korea'. This expresses the idea that tradables supply is significantly less elastic for Chile than for the Republic of Korea and some other East Asian countries.
$dB / y = 0.10$	This reflects a stoppage of a capital inflow that was running at the rate of 10 per cent of GDP per year. (Chile's actual inflow in 1981 was 15 per cent of GDP! It fell to about 5 per cent in 1982.)

These numerical assumptions permit us to calculate that dp_H for 'Republic of Korea' will be $- 0.089$, while that for 'Chile' will be $- 0.190$. The simple alteration of our assumption concerning the supply elasticity of tradables brings this about.

Perhaps of greater interest is the dynamic exercise that we are about to present. Here the 'Republic of Korea' case remains essentially the same as that in the comparative static example just completed, but the 'Chile' case is modified to make it more true to recent history in two important respects. First there is superimposed on the reduction in capital inflows a 'copper shock'. From an initial level of 20, copper's contribution to the national income is reduced to 14 through an assumed reduction in its world price. This reduction is accomplished through an autonomous movement over three successive periods, in steps from 20 to 18 to 16 to 14. Thereafter copper's contribution remains constant at 14.

The second modification does not influence the final equilibrium situation for any variable other than real cash balances themselves. This modification is a reduction of k of the Cambridge equation ($M^d = kpy$) from an initial value of 0.25 to an ending value of 0.15 This move takes place in five steps of -0.02 each. This alteration of the initial assumption accords with an observed reduction in the ratio of M_2 to GDP from about 0.25 in 1981 to a bit over 0.15 in 1984.

An additional assumption made in the dynamic version of the model should be noted. For both tradables and non-tradables in 'the Republic of Korea' and for non-tradables in 'Chile' it was assumed that the full supply response to a given price disturbance would be spread evenly over four periods. In the case of tradables for 'Chile' the assumption was that the supply response was spread evenly over ten periods. This assumption reflects the physical difficulty of achieving a quick response in the mineral and agricultural (vineyards, orchards, olive groves) sectors. It also builds in a recognition of what I call the 'hot stove syndrome' in the manufacturing sector. Having been burnt many times before by false price signals, economic agents do not show haste in responding to new signals.

The dynamic version incorporates the following assumptions:

(a) last period's income is spent this period;
(b) this period's foreign borrowings are spent this period;
(c) any excess supply of money coming out of last period is spent, in whole or in part, this period (i.e. specified fractions of $M^s_{j-1} - M^d_{j-1}$ are spent on tradables and non-tradables in period j; these fractions may add up to less, but not more, than one);
(d) any excess of foreign borrowing over the trade deficit is converted into money during the same period (money multiplier $= 1$); and
(e) the supply response of goods to changes in the price/wage relationships is spread out over four periods (except for the case of tradables in 'Chile'). The equations that embody these assumptions are as follows, using j as the time subscript:

(1') $H^d_j = a_0 - a_1 (p_{Hj} - p_{Tj}) + a_2 y_{j-1} + a_3 B_j + a_4 (M^s_{j-1} - M^d_{k-1})$

(2') $T^d_j = -a_0 - a_1(p_{Tj} - p_{Hj}) + (1-a_2)y_{j-1} + (1-a_3)B_j + e_4 (M^s_{j-1} - M^d_{j-1})$

(3') $H^s_j = b_0 + b_1 \overset{3}{\Sigma}/m = 0(.25) (p_{H,j-m} - w_{j-m})$

(4') $T_j^s = c_0 + c_1 \overset{3}{\Sigma}/m = 0 \,(.25)\, (p_{H,j-m} - w_{j-m})$ for 'Republic of Korea'

$T_j^s = c_0 + c_1 \overset{9}{\Sigma}/m = 0 \,(.1)\, (p_{H,j-m} - w_{j-m})$ for 'Chile'

(5') $y_j = H_j^s + T_j^s$

(6') B_j = foreign borrowing during period j

(7') $M_j^d = ky_j[f_1 p_{Hj} + (1-f_1)p_{Tj}]$ = money demand
at end of period j

(8') $w_j = f_1 p_{Hj-1} + (1-f_1)p_{Tj-1}$ (wage equation
used in simulations)

(8a') $w_j = w_0 = \beta \,[f_1(p_{Hj-1} - p_{H0}) + (1-f_1) \,(p_{Tj-1} - p_{T0})]$

(8b') $w_j = w_0$

(9') $H_j^d = H_j^s$

(10') $M_j^s = M_j^s{}_{-1} + \Delta R_j$ (money supply fed by change
in international reserves)

(11') $\Delta R_j = T_j^s - T_j^d + B_j$ (reserves grow when foreign
borrowing exceeds trade deficit).

The numerical values placed on the various parameters are:

$a_0 = 0$

$a_1 = 12.5$ (This builds in a demand elasticity of 0.25 for home goods.)

$a_2 = 0.4$ (This makes for an income elasticity of 0.8 for home goods.)

$a_3 = 1$ (The capital inflow, whose interruption creates the principal disturbance being analysed, was initially being spent fully on non-tradables.)

$a_4 = 0.2$ ('Excess' money balances are worked off at the rate of 40 per cent per period, with half being spent on tradables, half on non-tradables.)

$b_0 = 50$ (These constants represent the initial equilibrium
$c_0 = 50$ quantities H_0^s and T_0^s, when $P_T^0 = P_H^0 = w = 1$.)

$b_1 = 200$ (This builds in an elasticity of supply of 4, around the initial equilibrium quantity $H_0^s = 50$.)

$c_1 = 200$ for 'Republic of Korea' (same as above, but for tradables)

$c_1 = 30$ for 'Chile' (this represents an elasticity of supply of unity on that portion of 'Chile's' tradable supply that does not consist of copper. The reduction in the world price of copper can be thought of as reducing c_0 through time from 50 to 44).[9]

The results of the simulations are summarized in Tables 6.8 and 6.9, but for our purposes Figures 6.1 and 6.2 convey nearly all the necessary information. The important conclusion is that a country like Chile may have to pass through very difficult times in response to external shocks, even if it pursues policies that are quite reasonable. Note that the value of p_H for 'Chile' in Figure 6.1 moves rather quickly close to its new steady state level. There is a very large difference between this trajectory and that for 'The Republic of Korea'. The contrast is even more dramatic when it comes to the time path of real output. Here there is just a brief lapse of output from its equilibrium level of 100 for 'Republic of Korea', but a very large shortfall below both the old equilibrium level of 100 and the new equilibrium level of 94 for 'Chile'.

The picture traced for 'Chile' in Figures 6.1 and 6.2 is quite similar to the actual record. Between 1981 and 1982 real output fell by 14 per cent, followed by nearly another percentage point drop from 1982 and 1983. Only in 1984 did GDP bounce back a bit, with about 6 per cent real growth, but it remains far below its previous peaks and well below its trend level, as 'Chile' is about halfway through the period traced in Figure 6.2. Similarly, Chile's real exchange rate in 1983 (calculated using the SDR WPI) reached a level 50 per cent above its level of the third quarter of 1981; in this respect the trajectory of Figure 6.1 is quite faithful to reality.

By way of contrast, the Republic of Korea passed from a current account surplus in 1977 to a deficit of over \$4 billion in 1979 and 1981, and of over \$5 billion in 1980, before pulling back to a more sustainable deficit level of \$1.6 billion in 1983 (Chile's deficit hit nearly \$5 billion in 1981 and was back to \$1 billion by 1983). But while Chile's travail was great, the Republic of Korea came off with

[9] For a more thorough treatment of how copper is handled here, see Harberger (1983). The paper treats the case of an oil price shock for a country like Indonesia, but the underlying assumptions are identical to those used here for copper in the case of 'Chile'. There are two easy ways to visualize the treatment in question. First one can consider that all output other than copper is valued at initial prices (Laspeyres output index) while physical output of copper (and the corresponding resource use) are taken as given, and the contribution of copper to 'y' is taken to be its world price times the fixed output. Alternatively one can consider 'y' to value all tradable goods (including copper) at their (exogenous) world prices, with non-tradable goods entering as a Laspeyres index using initial prices.

Table 6.8 *Simulation of response to debt crisis: 'Republic of Korea'*

Period (i)	Home goods prices (p_H)	Real output (y)	Home goods demand (H^d)	Trad- ables demand (T^d)	Trad- ables supply (T^s)	Change in reserves ($\triangle R$)	Money supply (M^s)	Money demand (M^d)	Wages (w)	International capital flow (B)
1	1	100	50	50	50	—	25	25	1	10
2	0.840	92.00	42.00	58.00	50.00	−8.00	17.00	21.16	1.000	—
3	0.839	91.97	37.97	52.36	54.00	1.64	18.64	21.15	0.920	—
4	0.909	95.44	37.43	53.54	58.01	4.47	23.11	22.77	0.920	—
5	0.973	99.09	38.58	56.99	60.51	3.52	26.63	24.44	0.950	—
6	0.886	102.65	41.50	58.47	61.15	2.69	29.31	24.20	0.987	—
7	0.899	103.36	43.35	61.35	60.01	−1.34	27.97	24.53	0.943	—
8	0.930	101.45	42.91	61.82	58.54	−3.29	24.69	24.47	0.949	—
9	0.954	98.99	41.20	60.33	57.80	−2.54	22.15	24.18	0.965	—
10	0.869	99.14	40.84	57.35	58.31	0.96	23.10	23.16	0.977	—
11	0.893	99.73	40.99	58.14	58.74	0.60	23.71	23.61	0.934	—
12	0.925	99.69	40.84	58.92	58.84	−0.08	23.63	23.99	0.947	—
13	0.945	99.46	40.49	59.05	58.96	−0.08	23.55	24.18	0.963	—
14	0.878	100.38	41.18	58.02	59.20	1.17	24.72	23.56	0.972	—
15	0.906	100.51	41.56	59.28	58.95	−0.33	24.39	23.94	0.939	—
Steady state	0.911	100.00	41.11	58.89	58.89	—	23.89	23.89	0.956	—

Assumed parameter values: $a_0 = 0$; $a_1 = 12.5$; $a_2 = 0.4$; $a_3 = 1.0$; $a_4 = 0.2$; $e_4 = 0.2$
$b_0 = 50$; $c_0 = 50$; $b_1 = 200$; $c_1 = 200$; $k = 0.25$.

Source: IMF (various years).

191

Table 6.9 Simulation of response to debt crisis: 'Chile'

Period (j)	Home goods prices (p_H)	Real output (y)	Home goods demand (H^d)	Tradables demand (T^d)	Tradables supply (T^s)	Change in reserves ($\triangle R$)	Money supply (M^s)	Money demand (M^d)	Wages (w)	International capital flow (B)
1	1	100	50	60	50	—	25	25	1	10
2	0.840	90.00	42.00	58.00	48.00	-10.00	15.00	17.82	1.000	—
3	0.784	84.56	38.14	50.73	46.42	-4.32	10.69	14.42	0.861	—
4	0.768	80.95	35.97	47.09	44.98	-2.11	8.57	12.29	0.812	—
5	0.770	80.10	34.52	44.95	45.58	0.64	9.21	10.89	0.799	—
6	0.667	82.06	35.87	43.56	46.19	2.63	11.84	8.74	0.800	—
7	0.668	84.65	37.60	45.70	47.06	1.36	13.19	9.03	0.710	—
8	0.687	86.53	38.60	47.71	47.92	0.21	13.40	9.45	0.711	—
9	0.708	87.79	39.05	49.06	48.74	-0.32	13.08	9.82	0.728	—
10	0.638	88.79	40.29	48.80	49.50	0.70	13.79	9.23	0.746	—
11	0.659	91.54	41.09	50.53	50.45	-0.08	13.70	9.66	0.685	—
12	0.691	92.62	41.29	51.87	51.34	-0.53	13.57	10.16	0.704	—
13	0.711	92.99	41.27	52.56	51.72	-0.84	12.34	10.44	0.731	—
14	0.653	93.82	41.91	51.84	51.91	0.07	12.41	9.83	0.749	—
15	0.676	94.31	42.09	52.76	52.22	-0.54	11.87	10.16	0.699	—
Steady state	0.679	94.00	41.61	52.39	52.39	—	10.16	10.16	0.721	—

Assumed parameter values: $a_0 = 0$; $a_1 = 12.5$; $a_2 = 0.4$; $a_3 = 1.0$; $a_4 = 0.2$; $e_4 = 0.2$; $b_0 = 50$; $c_0 = 50, 48, 46, 46, 44, 44 \ldots$; $b_1 = 200$; $c_1 = 30$; $k = 0.25, 0.21, 0.19, 0.17, 0.15 \ldots$

Source: IMF (various years).

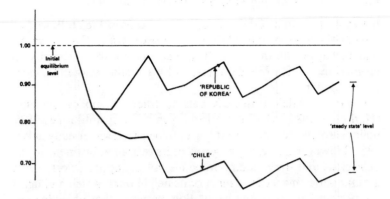

Figure 6.1
Trajectory of non-tradable goods prices: simulation of response to debt crisis (plus
copper shock and monetary adjustment for 'Chile')
Source: Derived from Tables 6.8 and 6.9.

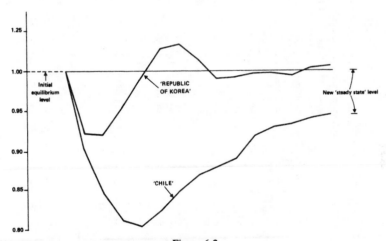

Figure 6.2
Trajectory of real output: simulation of response to debt crisis (plus copper shock
and monetary adjustment for 'Chile')
Source: Derived from Tables 6.8 and 6.9.

hardly a ripple in its GDP – a fall of 3 per cent in 1981 followed by growth of 6.9 per cent in 1982 and 5.5 per cent in 1983 – and with a real exchange rate that actually appreciated by about 10 per cent *vis-à-vis* the SDR while depreciating by a similar amount *vis-à-vis* the US dollar.

Some of Chile's trajectory can be traced to policy mistakes (Harberger 1985:451–62), particularly in delaying until June 1982 a policy response to a crisis that began to be perceived already in late 1981. However, certainly in terms of its overall adjustment to the debt crisis and the contemporaneous fall in copper prices, Chile gets far better marks than most of its neighbours, which highlights the principal point of the simulation exercise, that objective circumstances may cause economies like Chile's to have to pass through painful adjustments that far exceed those required by the objective circumstances of luckier economies like the Republic of Korea's.

DEEPAK LAL*

7

IDEOLOGY AND
INDUSTRIALIZATION IN
INDIA AND EAST ASIA

In 1950 if someone had been asked to predict the Third World country most likely to embark on an industrial revolution and with the best prospects of fostering modern economic growth – in Kuznets' sense – the unanimous choice would probably have been India. It had a potentially large domestic market, a relatively diversified natural resource base, a relatively efficient bureaucracy, a political leadership seemingly committed to development, fairly elastic supplies of skilled and semi-skilled labour, and no shortage of domestic entrepreneurship. Yet, despite these favourable factors, apart from creating a highly diversified industrial base, both the absolute level of industrialization as well as its contribution to per capita growth has been disappointing, and dismal compared with the experience of the so-called 'Gang of Four' of East Asian countries (Singapore, Hong Kong, Taiwan and the Republic of Korea). Table 7.1 provides some summary statistics which give a comparative and historical perspective. India's relative failure to industrialize compared with the comparative ease with which the four East Asian economies have succeeded in transforming their formerly agricultural economies into fully modern industrial ones, is the focus of this paper.

When I write of India I shall be referring not to the political entity which covered the whole sub-continent until 1947, but only the successor state of that name which resulted from the partition which accompanied independence from British rule. I shall be

---

* The views expressed in this paper are those of the author. The findings, interpretations and conclusions are the results of research supported by the World Bank; they do not necessarily represent official policy of the Bank.

Table 7.1 *Some summary statistics*: *India, Republic of Korea and Taiwan*

1. India

Manufacturing growth rates: value added 1868–1979 (constant prices)	per cent per annum
1868–1900	10.36
1900–1913	6.00
1919–1939	4.80
1956–1965	6.90
1966–1979	5.50

Rates of growth of employment in manufacturing, 1902–79	
1902–1913	4.43
1919–1939	2.29
1959–1965	3.60
1966–1979	3.50

Rates of growth of capital stock in manufacturing, 1959–79	
1959–1965	13.60
1966–1979	6.80

2. Level of Asian exports[a] fob 1850–1950 (US$m)

	1850	1913	1937	1950
Ceylon	5	76	124	328
China	24	294	516	(700)
India	89	786	717	1178
Indonesia	24	270	550	800
Japan	1	354	1207	820
Malaya	24	193	522	1312
Philippines	..	48	153	331
Thailand	3	43	76	304

3. The Republic of Korea

(A) Mining and manufacturing growth rate: net value of commodity product (constant price) 1910–76	per cent per annum
1910–40	9.70
1953–60	11.10
1960–76	18.40

[a] Trade figures refer to customs area of the year concerned. In 1850 and 1913 the Indian area included Burma. The comparability of 1937 and 1950 figures is affected by the separation of Pakistan.

(B) Incremental capital output ratio,
   1953–74

1953–60	2.59
1960–74	1.33

(C) Growth rate of employment in
   manufacturing, 1963–76

	12.10

4. Taiwan
Rate of growth of manufacturing output,

1930–75	per cent per annum
1930s	6.00
1953–58	8.90
1958–63	12.60
1963–68	19.70
1968–72	23.10
1972–75	7.10

Compound annual percentage growth
rates of total employment, 1952–76

1952–55	1.20
1955–60	2.10
1960–65	2.30
1965–70	4.30
1970–75	3.80
1975–76	2.50
Total growth rate	2.90

Average marginal capital output ratios

1952–60	1.68
1960–66	1.97
1966–73	2.20
1975–80	3.96

Percentage growth in industrial
   employment

1952–60	69.00
1960–66	41.60
1966–75	116.70

Sources: India: Manufacturing growth rates derived from data in Heston (1983) and Sivasubramanian (1977), and post-Second World War rate of growth from the national accounts; pre-independence rates of growth of employment are taken from Sivasubramanian (1977), post-independence from Ahluwalia (1985: Tables A.5.2 and 3); rates of growth of capital stock are from Ahluwalia (1985).
Level of Asian exports, 1850–1950: Maddison (1971:59, Table III–1).
Republic of Korea: Mason *et al.* (1980: Tables 4, 12 and 18).
Taiwan: Data from Lee and Liang (1982), Council for Economic Planning and Development (1984) and Galenson (1979).

treating the historical experience of Indian industrialization in depth, with only passing references to that of the East Asian economies. This in part reflects my own expertise and partly my desire to tell an analytical story about the sources of the Indian failure. This is the subject of the first section of this paper. The second section examines various explanations for India's continuing industrial stagnation and finds them wanting. In this part, the comparative experience of the East Asian countries is brought into the picture. The third and more speculative section of the paper provides more deep-seated reasons – 'ideological' and 'environmental' – which have in my view led to the very different policies which, I shall argue, have ultimately led to the various outcomes in South and East Asia.

In this context I shall also examine the hoary debate about the influence of ideas relative to vested interests in preventing India from switching its industrial and trade policies when these had apparently become inimical to its development, for apart from Hong Kong, the other members of the Gang of Four also underwent an initial phase of forced industrialization promoted through protectionist trade regimes. Unlike India, however, they switched towards a relatively more neutral trade regime in the early or mid-1960s, which most observers consider to have been an important if not the crucial element in determining their subsequent spectacular industrial and economic growth.[1] Why has India failed to make an equivalent switch, and what are the prospects of its succeeding in its latest attempt at liberalizing the trade and industrial controls which have shackled its industrial growth?

HISTORY OF INDUSTRIALIZATION IN INDIA, WITH SOME REFERENCE TO EAST ASIAN INDUSTRIALIZATION[2]

In setting Indian industrialization in historical perspective, it is important to note that India was one of the pioneers of Third World industrialization. Moreover, it began its industrialization in the 1860s at a time when *laissez-faire* and free trade were the cornerstones of economic policy in Britain and its colonial dependencies.

---

[1] See Mason *et al.* (1980) and Galenson (1979) for the most authoritative available surveys of two of the major members of the Gang of Four.

[2] This and the following sections are based on various parts of Lal (1983, 1986).

The rate of growth of Indian industry (10.4 per cent per annum) during the latter part of the nineteenth century (1868–1900) has not been bettered since (see Table 7.1). Yet the conventional view cites the historical experience of industrialization in India as an example of stunted development during the colonial *laissez-faire* period, in contrast to the post-independence promotion of a large and diversified industrial base through a network of the most *dirigiste* industrial policies outside the communist world. Balogh (1963:11) succinctly expressed this popular view of the effects of nineteenth-century free trade and *laissez-faire* on the development of Indian industry:

The destruction of the large and prosperous Indian cotton industry by Britain without any compensatory long-run advantage to India simply cannot be explained in these terms: it is altogether different from an event, such as the end of the silk industry in Coventry. In the latter case there *was* compensatory expansion. In the former there was not.

Recent research has cast serious doubt on the empirical bases of these historical perceptions fed by influential Marxist and nationalist writings. I shall not go into the details[3] but the following points need to be noted. First, there is little doubt that the introduction of cheap Lancashire textiles (between 1812 and 1830) destroyed the Indian export trade in cotton textiles, which, according to estimates by Maddison (1971:55), had amounted to about 1.5 per cent of national income in seventeenth-century Moghul India. The decline of India's trade in textiles was inevitable in the face of the technological revolution taking place at that time in the West. There was as a consequence some undoubted destruction of industry-specific factors of production in the traditional (handloom) textile industry. However, from the 1850s, with the establishment of modern textile mills using Indian entrepreneurship and capital and imported machinery, manufactured cotton exports from India began to expand. Also, employment in the manufacturing industry (primarily in textiles by the nineteenth century) similarly increased. With the development of a modern textile industry, Indian products increasingly captured both the domestic and foreign markets they had lost to Lancashire in the middle of the

[3] See Kumar (1983) and Lal (1986) for a fuller discussion and references to this literature.

nineteenth century.[4] Thus there was *at most* a relative decline in the employment and output of the handicrafts sector, as is borne out by the fact that handloom production remains a substantial industry in India. It would be incredible if the current size of the handloom industry (supposedly destroyed in the 1820s) were to be explained as the result of government promotion since independence in 1947.

The growth of modern industry was not, moreover, confined to cotton textiles during the second half of the nineteenth century. The first jute mill was set up in 1852, only three years after the first cotton textile mill, and the first steel mill was established by the Tata family in 1911. Other industries, including paper, and engineering goods, were also established during the free trade and *laissez-faire* period. The overall rate of industrial growth was higher in India (4–5 per cent per year between 1880 and 1914) than in most other tropical countries, and also exceeded that of Germany (4 per cent). As Lidman and Domerese (1970:320–1) have observed:

An index of industrial production, based on six large-scale manufacturing industries, more than doubled from 1896 to 1914 ... By 1914 the Indian economy had developed the world's fourth largest cotton textile industry and the second largest jute manufacturing industry.

Nor was India's performance in exporting manufactures insignificant during this first phase of industrialization. By 1913 about 20 per cent of Indian exports were of modern manufactured goods. Total exports amounted to 10.7 per cent of national income – a share not reached either before or since this free trade and *laissez-faire* period. It was India's agricultural export growth rate that was disappointing. While aggregate exports grew by 3 per cent per annum between 1883 and 1913, agricultural exports grew at an annual rate of only 1.4 per cent. Japan's agricultural exports grew at an annual rate of over 4 per cent during the same period.

As Table 7.1 shows, after this initial burst, the growth rate of Indian industry has stagnated in the twentieth century, but, even in the 1913–38 period, Indian industrial growth was above the world average (see Table 7.2). However, unlike the pre-1913 period which was broadly one when free trade and hence 'border prices'

---

[4] Maddison (1971:57) estimates: 'in 1968, Indian mills supplied only 8 per cent of total cloth consumption; in 1913, 20 per cent, in 1936, 62 per cent; and in 1945, 76 per cent. By the latter date there were no imports of piece goods.'

Table 7.2 *Index of manufacturing production, 1938* (base 1913 = 100)

Country	Index	Country	Index
South Africa	1067.1	Norway	169.2
USSR	857.3	Canada	161.8
Japan	552.0	Latvia	158.0
Greece	537.1	Germany	149.3
Finland	300.1	Czechoslovakia	145.5
India	239.7	Hungary	143.3
Sweden	232.2	USA	143.0
New Zealand	227.4	Austria	127.0
Chile	204.2	UK	117.6
Netherlands	204.1	France	114.6
Denmark	202.1	Poland	105.2
Italy	195.2	Belgium	102.1
Australia	192.3	Switzerland	82.4
Romania	177.9	Spain	58.0

Source: Ray (1979:Table 3:16).

ruled, the period after the First World War saw the introduction, largely for reasons of fiscal expediency, of a system of discriminating protection. Whereas the market price based growth rates of industrial output (value added) in the free trade period were likely to have been close to those in terms of shadow prices, for well-known reasons, this was unlikely to have been the case with the growing divergence between 'border' and market prices of tradables as protection was gradually extended in scope and intensity after 1913.

Nevertheless, even if we judge performance by crude and inadequate criteria such as the rate of growth of manufacturing output, employment and investment, the performance during the pre-1913, free trade period was better than in the protectionist 1919–39 period. Of the industries that were growing in the protectionist period, a proper evaluation of the social return to investment is only available for sugar (see Lal 1972). This shows that such investment was socially unprofitable.

Comparing the periods 1900–13 and 1913–39, industrial employment grew twice as fast during the free trade period than it did during the protectionist period (see Table 7.1). Though the investment rate did not rise, the increase in the volume of investment, combined with a slower expansion of industrial employment,

Table 7.3a *Parameters of Gompertz curve fitted to trends in various industrial sector variables* $(Y = k(a)^{bt})$

		k	a	b
Industrial production	1900–45	368.67	1.32	1.04
	1953–79	457.09	0.11	0.95
Industrial employment	1902–46	11511.40	0.058	0.986
	1953–76	2200.10	0.001	0.995
Capital stock in the non-agricultural sector	1948–67	185.13	25.15	1.02

Note: In interpreting these results, note that:
(i) if a <1 and b<1, the Gompertz curve is increasing at a decreasing rate of growth, with an upper asymptote;
(ii) if a >1 and b>1, the curve is increasing at an increasing rate of growth, with a lower asymptote.
Source: Lal (1986: Table 11.11).

Table 7.3b *Capital–labour ratios in Indian manufacturing at 1970–71 prices*

	Registered	Unregistered	Total
1. Fixed capital per worker (Rs)			
1950–51	4662[a]	790	1583
	(6359)		
1960–61	12711	2024	4508
1970–71	20056	2402	7670
2. Annual average growth rate (per cent)			
1950–71 (20 years)	..	5.72	
1950–61 (10 years)	..	9.86	
1960–71 (10 years)	4.67	1.73	

[a] Not comparable as the employment figures include workers in electricity. The figure in brackets is for the capital-labour ratio for registered manufacturing cum electricity.
Source: Datta and Chowdhry (1983: Table 6, Appendices 2 and 3).

meant a rise in the capital intensity of industrial production. Moreover, if the whole period of protection (from 1913 until the late 1970s) is considered then (by fitting Gompertz curves to the relevant time series data)[5] it appears from Table 7.3a that there has

---

[5] See Rudra (1978) for the reasons why this form of curve fitting is desirable, as it enables one to judge whether growth is accelerating, decelerating or constant over the relevant period.

Table 7.4 *Total factor productivity growth estimates, 1959–69 to 1969–80*

Country	Per cent per annum
India	−0.2 to −1.3
Korea, Republic of	5.7
Turkey	2.0
Yugoslavia	0.8
Japan	3.1

Sources: Ahluwalia (1985:132–5). The estimates other than India are Ahluwalia's based on Nishimizu and Robinson's (1983) estimate which is in turn based on a gross production function to a value added production function as for India.

been an accelerating trend in the capital employed in industry and a decelerating trend in labour employed. Since independence, a decelerating trend has also developed in industrial output. Thus there has been a rising capital–labour ratio (see Table 7.3b) in this labour-abundant economy!

Even more telling evidence on the growing absolute relative inefficiency of Indian industry is provided by the estimates of total factor productivity growth in the 1960s and 1970s for India, Republic of Korea, Turkey, Yugoslavia and Japan summarized in Table 7.4. Nor does it appear that there was any break in this rate of decline in total factor productivity growth in India in the mid-1960s, when the Indian industrial sector obviously began to stagnate in terms of output growth. I do not have capital stock data for the earlier periods to ascertain whether the negative rate of factor productivity growth in India is just a post-independence phenomenon or whether it goes back to the start of the protectionist period in 1913. My tentative hypothesis is that the latter is likely. Further support for the declining social profitability of industrial investment in India is provided by estimates of social rates of return on Little–Mirrlees lines that have been made elsewhere (Lal 1980a, summarized in Table 7.5).

How then does one explain this relatively dismal Indian industrial performance, particularly as compared with the performance of the Gang of Four in the last two decades? There are two obvious sets of policies which differentiate the industrial environment in India with those of East Asia.

The first, as I have argued above, is protectionism, which pre-

Table 7.5 *Average social rates of return in Indian manufacturing,*
Annual Survey of India, 1958–68

Year	SWR = W (%)	SWR = 0 (%)	SWR = 0.6W (%)
1958	1.6	36.0	15.4
1960	1.6	39.0	16.6
1961	2.4	37.0	16.2
1962	0.9	29.0	12.1
1963	1.9	29.0	12.7
1964	1.4	26.0	11.2
1968	−6.1	22.6	5.4

SWR = Shadow wage rate
W   = Market wage
Source: Lal (1980a:44).

dates independence. But India was not unique in this respect in the inter-war period or even in the 1950s. The Japanese colonial governments of Taiwan and Korea both introduced tariff protection in the 1920s. In the 1950s these members of the Gang of Four as well as Singapore followed the common Third World practice of attempting to foster primary import substitution behind ever higher tariff walls and quantitative import controls.

Moreover, as argued above, India's industrial performance, though not as good as in the free trade period, was still above average in the protectionist inter-war period. If protection had continued to be offered only through tariffs and at the relatively mild tariff rates (7–30 per cent)[6] of the inter-war years in the post-independence years, it is likely that, despite lowering efficiency and labour absorption, it would still not have led to the large short-falls in actual below-potential social returns as in the post-independence period.

Equally important is the need for some explanation for the success of the three *dirigiste* members of the Gang of Four in switching trade policies in the mid-1960s while India, despite belated and half-hearted attempts since the devaluation of 1966, has failed to liberalize its foreign trade and industrial controls.

---

[6] Thus, Kumar (1983:924) estimates that 'the gross revenue from import duties was 7 per cent of the value of imports in 1920–21, 18 per cent in 1925–26, and 31 per cent in 1931–32'.

The second difference in the economic environment facing industry in India and East Asia is less well known and discussed, but in my judgment is perhaps as important as that due to differences in the trade and industrial control regimes. This concerns the industrial labour market. In marked contrast to the Gang of Four, India has had protective factory legislation since the late nineteenth century, which has raised the cost of industrial labour to employers to an unquantifiable extent.

Some of the troubles of the Indian textile industry in the early part of the twentieth century which led it to seek protection arose from the introduction in 1881 – soon after similar rights had been granted to workers in Britain – of legislation to protect industrial labour from perceived abuses. The first of these factory acts was aptly described as 'the result of agitation (in the United Kingdom) by ignorant English philanthropists and grasping English manufacturers' (Bhattacharya 1979:170). As is usual in such alliances, the selfish English protectionist interest was better served by the legislation than the altruism of the philanthropists. By effectively raising the cost of labour they provided an incentive to producers, to choose relatively capital-intensive techniques in industrial production. As these laws only applied to the large-scale sector, they presented an entry barrier to small-scale producers seeking to expand. Thus began that fragmentation of the industrial sector in India into the industrial caste system that now exists – with special size categories of industries, each with its own specially legislated conditions of employment and controls on outputs and investments, leading to variously and differentially protected segments of the labour force as well as of the population of industrial firms.

The rights granted to Indian labour in 1881 hobbled the Indian textile industry in competing for exports, and later domestic markets, with the industry of Japan. Lower Indian wages reflected lower efficiency (see Table 7.6). Whereas the Japanese textile industry and subsequently the industries in most of the Gang of Four were built on using female labour working two shifts a day, 'the use of female labor on such a scale was inconceivable in Bombay, nor did the labor laws permit such long working hours' (Ray 1979:67). Indian textile producers demanded protection and got it. The large homemarket, which provided an easy life as it was increasingly protected from imports, gave them little incentive to increase efficiency.

Table 7.6 *Comparative labour efficiency in Japan, India and Britain for low count cotton manufacture in 1932*

	Looms per weaver	Average efficiency per loom (%)	Working hours index (Britain = 100)	Wages (Rs per worker per day)
Ordinary looms (Japan)	5.5	..	..	..
Japan average	6.0	95–6	250	2–4
Toyoda looms	50.0	..	..	..
Britain	4.0	85	100	4–8
India	2.0	80	125	2

Source: Derived from Ray (1979:66, Table 17).

By 1950, in marked contrast to the Gang of Four, India

had built up one of the most comprehensive labor codes to be found in any country at India's level of economic development. The standards laid down by the ILO had been accepted and measures were being worked out to attain these standards (Bhattacharya 1979:186).

No quantification of the adverse effects on the relative industrial performance of India with that of the Gang of Four – with their relatively free industrial labour markets – is possible. But some judgments on the effects of the costs of this labour legislation and the attendant growth of trade unionism in India can be formed from Tables 7.7 and 7.8. The former shows the number of industrial disputes and man-days lost since the rise of trade unions in 1921 in India. It can be seen that, as early as 1928, nearly 32 million man-days were lost through stoppages, a figure nearly as high as that of about 44 million man-days in 1974 and 1979.

Table 7.8 is based on the results of a series of interviews I conducted in India in 1980 of about twenty firms covering both large- and small-scale industries, which encompassed the technological spectrum of sophistication (petrochemicals) to simplicity (soap making). Lal (1980a) provides details of the interviews, while Table 7.8 summarizes the responses to some questions concerning the factors which influenced the producers' choices concerning the recruitment and training of labour, as well as the effects of existing labour legislation and trade unionism on their operations. The dominant impression from the interviews was that firms were behaving as cost minimizers, where the major components of

Table 7.7 *Industrial disputes in India, 1921–80*

Year	No. of stoppages	No. of workers involved	Man-days lost
1921	396	600,351	6,984,426
1922	278	435,434	3,972,727
1923	213	301,044	5,051,794
1924	133	312,462	8,730,918
1925	134	270,423	12,578,129
1926	128	186,811	1,097,478
1927	129	131,655	2,019,970
1928	203	506,851	31,647,404
1929	141	531,059	12,165,691
1930	148	196,301	2,261,731
1931	166	203,008	2,408,123
1932	118	128,099	1,922,437
1933	146	164,933	2,160,961
1934	159	220,808	4,775,559
1935	145	114,217	973,437
1936	157	169,029	5,358,062
1937	379	647,801	8,982,257
1938	399	401,075	9,198,708
1939	406	409,075	4,992,795
1940	322	452,539	7,577,281
1941	359	291,054	3,330,503
1942	694	772,653	5,779,965
1943	716	525,083	2,342,287
1944	658	550,015	3,447,306
1945	820	747,530	4,054,499
1946	1629	1,961,943	12,717,762
1947	1811	1,840,784	16,562,666
1948	1259	1,059,120	7,837,173
1949	920	605,457	6,600,395
1950	814	719,883	12,806,704
1951	1071	691,321	3,818,928
1952	963	809,242	3,336,961
1953	772	466,607	3,332,608
1954	840	477,138	3,372,630
1955	1166	527,767	5,697,648
1956	1203	715,130	6,992,040
1957	1630	889,371	6,429,319
1958	1524	928,566	7,797,385
1959	1531	693,616	5,633,148
1960	1583	986,268	6,536,517
1961	1357	511,860	4,918,755
1962	1491	705,059	6,120,576
1963	1471	563,121	3,268,524
1964	2151	1,003,000	7,725,000
1965	1835	991,000	6,470,000
1966	2556	1,410,000	13,846,000
1967	2315	1,490,000	19,148,000
1968	2776	1,669,000	17,014,000

Table 7.7 *(cont.)*

Year	No. of stoppages	No. of workers involved	Man-days lost
1969	2627	1,827,000	19,048,000
1970	..	..	..
1971	2752	1,615,000	16,546,000
1972	3243	1,737,000	20,544,000
1973	3370	2,546,000	20,626,000
1974	2933	2,855,000	40,262,000
1975	1943	1,143,000	21,901,000
1976	1459	737,000	12,746,000
1977	3117	2,193,000	25,326,000
1978	3187	1,916,000	28,340,000
1979	3048	2,874,000	43,854,000
1980	2856	1,900,000	21,925,000

Sources: Karnik (1978:409–10, Appendix 2); India, Government of, Central Statistical Office (various years and 1982).

labour costs were perceived to be those attached to 'trouble-makers' and the resulting impediments to the maintenance of labour discipline resulting from the complex labour legislation granting various legal rights to industrial labour and trade unions. The new neo-classical hierarchical labour market reasons (see Lal 1979b for a review) for promotional ladders and the usefulness of trade unions as a tool for managing labour did, however, seem to be important for the larger and technologically more sophisticated firms. Despite this, it would be fair to say that most industrial producers look upon existing labour laws and the legal rights granted to trade unions as major (though unquantifiable) costs in their employment decisions.

These two elements of the economic environment – the current highly complex and differentiated effective protective rates facing Indian industry, and the equally complex labour laws it confronts in hiring and firing labour – seem to be crucially different in India and the Gang of Four. Taken together with the system of industrial licensing and all the special reservations for industries by sizes and class for different groups of workers, a vast politically determined set of entitlements has been created in independent India, which defies any economic rationale.

By contrast, the undoubted continuing *dirigisme* of three of the members of the Gang of Four seems almost like *laissez-faire* to this Indian – *though of course it is not*! The roots of Indian *dirigisme* as I have been at pains to emphasize lie in the colonial period, and in

Table 7.8 *Characteristics of sample firms in large- and small-scale industries in India*

Firm product	Firm size	Technology	Training provided by the firm		Casual labour type screening of labour	Use of existing workers to hire labour	Promotional ladders	Labour legislation and trade union pressure cited as determinants of wage structure	New neoclassical type cost minimizing reasons given for wage structure	Would they themselves organize a trade union to ease supervisory problems?
			General	Specific						
Shoes	Large	Medium	Yes	Yes	No	No	No	Yes	No	No
Oil mills	Large	High	Yes	Yes	Yes	No	Yes	Yes	Yes	Yes
Soap	Small	Low	Yes	No	No	Yes	.	Yes	No	No
Petro-chemicals	Large	High	Yes	Yes	No	No	Yes	Yes	Yes	Yes
Conglomerate	Large	Medium to high	Yes	Yes	Yes	No	Yes	Yes	Yes	No
Printing	Medium	Medium	No	Yes	Yes	Yes	No	Yes	No	No
Printing	Small	—	No	Yes	Yes	Yes	No	Yes	No	No
Rubber manufacture and plantation	Large	Medium to low	—	—	Yes	Yes	No	Yes	No	No

Source: Lal (1980a).

understanding the continuing hold of the resultant *Weltanschauung* on the Indian mind (particularly of its intellectuals and bureaucrats) it is necessary to explore the reasons why a particular set of ideas associated with their colonial heritage have been found more persuasive by Indians than an earlier set of ideas associated with the same rulers. It is hoped this will also provide some reasons why, unlike policymakers in the Gang of Four who switched policies, Indian policymakers have tenaciously held on to policies which experience has shown are dysfunctional. Before attempting this exploration it is necessary to dispose of some arguments currently used to explain away the relative failure of India to industrialize compared with the Gang of Four.

INDIA'S CONTINUING INDUSTRIAL STAGNATION AND A COMPARISON WITH THE EAST ASIAN COUNTRIES

There is one set of arguments which seeks to dispose of explanations based on the virtually free trade policies of the Gang of Four as a source of their success. These are essentially based on either a misunderstanding of the modern theory of trade and welfare, or else on a *non sequitur*. On this set of arguments, far from the East Asian experience supporting the case for free trade, it merely provides support for what Streeten (1977) has called 'enlightened discrimination' towards trade and industry : that is for the rational *dirigisme* of Platonic Guardians.

The essence of the modern theory of trade and welfare is that the case for free trade does not depend upon that for *laissez-faire*. While, as I have argued, the policy of free trade followed by the British Raj in the nineteenth century did not harm Indian industrial development, its policy of *laissez-faire* can be faulted for reasons that are well known. Manufacturing industry, particularly that producing engineering and capital goods such as steel, was in part hampered by a shortage of a trained labour force, as the example of the Tatas' iron and steel mills showed. They had to establish their own apprentice school in 1927 for training fitters, welders, machinists, blacksmiths, etc. The private provision of such skills can create economies external to the firm but internal to the economy, and a case can be made for the public provision of such industrial training or else some subsidization of the private firms' training costs.

More important, however, is the provision of social overhead capital in the form of power, transport and education. As there are likely to be increasing returns in the production of a large part of this infrastructure – which also has many of the characteristics of public goods – natural monopolies may emerge if they are privately provided. Some government regulation may be necessary, and given the costs of information required for such regulation, public provision may be desirable.

Although the British did begin to provide this infrastructure, hamstrung as they were by a continual fiscal crisis, they did not do as much in this area of state promotion of industry as they could have. Table 7.9 shows the differences in the levels of provision of social overhead capital during the last century of British rule and the first decades after independence. Potentially, an extremely important and desirable change in the economic environment of industry was the increased provision of infrastructure, but this great expansion of social overhead capital has not resulted in a marked change in the economic environment facing Indian industry because of the inefficient utilization of this public infrastructure.[7] In fact it is ironical that the following summary by Morris (1974:552–3) of the reasons why industry did not develop faster during the *laissez-faire* period of the British Raj seems to be as applicable to present-day *dirigiste* India:

Lack of complementary facilities means that the entrepreneur typically had to provide his own power and his own repair and replacement facilities and inventories. Thus he needed not only more fixed capital but more working capital than the same enterprise would require in a developed system. Yet the businessman faced a situation where capital was typically more costly than in developed regions. Because local systems of credit were badly underdeveloped, capital would flow only in fitful fashion. . . . All this suggests that the entrepreneur encountered higher real costs that needed the promise of higher rates of return if a gamble was to be taken. . . . The great areas of uncertainty combined with the obvious objective obstacles to inhibit rapid expansion of modern industry.

The major reason for the inefficiencies in the provision of infrastructural services must again be laid at the door of the labour laws which have prevented the efficient utilization of the large invest-

---

[7] See Ahluwalia (1985: chapter 5) for a demolition of the argument that it is lack of public sector investment on infrastructure rather than its inefficient use which has caused industrial stagnation.

Table 7.9 *Pre-war and post-war trends in public investment in India* (Rs m)

Pre-war years	Gross public investment	Per cent of net national income	Annual change in public investment	Annual change in railway investment	Post-war years	Gross public investment	Per cent of net national income	Per cent of gross national investment	Gross fixed investment in railways
1925–26	644	:	+ 88	+ 58	1948–49	2100	2.3	25	361
1926–27	735	:	+ 91	+ 81	1949–50	2570	2.9	28	374
1927–28	827	:	+ 92	+ 81	1950–51	2620	2.7	28	256
1928–29	750	:	– 77	– 84	1951–52	2860	2.9	25	654
1929–30	814	:	+ 64	+ 69	1952–53	3035	3.1	29	637
1930–31	670		–144	–173	1953–54	3375	3.2	30	701
1931–32	488	3.0	–182	– 96	1954–55	4300	4.5	34	846
1932–33	338	1.5	–150	– 86	1955–56	5700	5.7	38	1271
1933–34	334	1.6	– 4	– 4	1956–57	6900	6.1	39	1505
1934–35	350	1.4	+ 16	+ 30	1957–58	8300	7.3	46	2159
1935–36	436	2.2	+ 86	+ 28	1958–59	8600	6.8	44	2226
1936–37	359	1.8	– 77	– 36	1959–60	7800 (est.)	6.1 (est.)	:	1346
1937–38	358	1.7	– 1	+ 4	1960–61	9600	6.6	:	2590

Sources: Estimates of gross public investment in undivided India: Thavaraj (1960). These figures refer to investment (real asset creation) undertaken by all the public enterprises and state trading organizations belonging to the Central, Provincial, other local governments and other public bodies, except the port trusts.

National income and gross public investment in new India were obtained from India, Government of, Central Statistical Office (1961). These figures cover investment by the central and state governments, port trusts, improvement trusts, municipal corporations, district and local boards and village panchayats. They also include railways, posts and telegraphs, forests, road transport, irrigation and electricity departments of the central and state governments, but certain public corporations (e.g. Indian Airlines) are not included. Estimates of gross national investment are given by S. J. Patel in the *Economic Weekly*, January 1960. Railway investment figures are from India, Government of, Ministry of Railways (various years).

ments independent India has made in developing its infrastructure. This is in marked contrast to the performance of infrastructural public enterprises in East Asia.

Thus if rational government intervention is required but protection is not, we could expect the successful East Asian countries to have much of the former and little of the latter. Yet in a recent article Sen quoted Little's (1979b:42) assessment of the Republic of Korea's development thus:

'The major lesson is that the labour-intensive, export-oriented policies, which *amounted to almost free-trade conditions for exporters*, were the prime cause of an extremely rapid and labour-intensive industrialisation which revolutionised in a decade the lives of more than fifty million people, including the poorest among them.' [Sen then comments:] There is indeed much in the experience of 'the four' to cheer Adam Smith, and *the invisible hand would seem to have done a good deal of visible good*. But is this really the 'major lesson' to draw from the experiences of the four? I would now like to argue that this may not be the case (Sen 1981:297, emphasis added).

He goes on (drawing on Dutta–Chowdhry) to cite instances of government intervention in the Republic of Korea, such as import controls and export incentives, as a supposed counter to Little's proposition. But this is mistakenly to identify the argument for free trade with *laissez-faire*. Little himself made it clear in the published proceedings of the conference at which he made the statements quoted above that he 'had not used the term "free trade" to be synonymous with *laissez-faire*. In fact, he had never said that *laissez-faire* should be adopted' (Little 1979b:12). It is Sen's mistaken identification of Little's 'major lesson' about the desirability of free trade with Adam Smith's invisible hand of *laissez-faire* which leads him into the wholly spurious argument that, since the government of the Republic of Korea is interventionist, Korea's success story provides no empirical validation of the case for free trade policies in the Third World.

Nor does the fact of government intervention imply, as Sen seems to suggest, that intervention is on balance *responsible* for success in the Republic of Korea. Indeed, it could be argued that success has been achieved despite intervention. Thus the change in trade policies in the early 1960s from favouring import substitution to broad neutrality between import substitution and exporting – considered to have been a major reason for the Republic of

Korea's subsequent success – entailed the introduction of interventionist export incentives to counteract the effects of import controls which, though undesirable from their inception, were not (and have not been) entirely removed. If the inefficient import controls were to be maintained, export incentives were desirable on second-best welfare grounds to restore a position amounting to a virtual free trade regime for export production. However, this does not mean that the import controls which made the export incentives necessary were themselves desirable. It would have been best not to have import controls in the first place, that is, no government intervention in foreign trade. To have two sets of intervention, each to neutralize the harm the other would do alone, is hardly a glowing recommendation for government intervention in trade, and certainly not 'the lesson' that can be drawn from the experience of the Republic of Korea and other East Asian countries.

Furthermore, the broad neutrality in the Republic of Korea between production for export and import substitution ended in the mid-1970s, the existing *dirigiste* machine being used to 'guide' domestic production towards more import substitution in heavy industry and a highly subsidized agricultural sector. This about-turn has led to both a slackening in the growth rate of income (in 1980 GNP fell for the first time in nearly twenty years – by about 6 per cent – after having grown in the late 1960s and early 1970s at annual rates of 10 to 15 per cent) and a rise in the rate of inflation (from about 15 per cent a year in the early 1970s to nearly 35 per cent in 1980 (see Kim 1981)). The new government in the Republic of Korea has had to reassess the promotion of heavy industry and seems to be reverting to the former policy of maintaining a rough neutrality between the incentives offered to different branches of industry by restoring the virtual free trade regime of the earlier period. It should enable the Republic of Korea to grow in line with its emerging comparative advantage, which lies increasingly in the production of goods using highly skilled labour though not necessarily much physical capital. Far from confuting the liberal case for free trade, the Republic of Korea provides one example of how periods of virtual free trade have been accompanied by a high rate of income growth which has been lowered whenever that policy has been abandoned.

There is of course no shortage of explanations – based essentially on insufficient *dirigisme* – for Indian industrial stagnation. The broad thesis runs somewhat as follows.[8] Because of the power of the *kulaks* there has been a general tendency for the agricultural terms of trade to turn against industry which has reduced the demand for industrial products. A purported worsening in the income distribution increased the demand for luxury goods; however, as investment in luxury goods production rose even faster, capacity utilization declined. Furthermore, a purported decline in rural and industrial wages meant that the demand for industrial mass consumption goods fell. Meanwhile foreign capital was 'a highly effective mechanism of extracting surplus' from the host country. Finally big private capitalists, instead of expanding their productive capacity through capital accumulation, have been more concerned for their firms to grow by acquiring subsidiaries through mergers and takeovers.

The factual bases of nearly every one of the above claims is false. The best available study on income distribution is by Dutta (1980). He has used the National Sample Survey consumer expenditure data for the years from 1960–61 to 1973–74 to compute two different indices for rural and urban India: (a) the headcount measure of the percentage of people below a fixed poverty line; and (b) Sen's poverty index, which also takes account of the distribution of poverty among the poor and which gives more weight per unit of lower incomes. From the same data source he has also computed Gini coefficients to determine changes in the relative inequality of consumption in both urban and rural India.

The measurement of trends in poverty and income distribution is bedevilled by the problem of the choice of the correct index number of prices to be used to determine 'real' consumption changes (see the debate between Minhas 1970 and Bardham 1970). Ideally, expenditure class-specific price indices are needed. Dutta uses adjusted estimates (made by Murty and Murty 1977) of fractile specific price indices to determine real consumption trends (Dutta 1980: part 2). He makes use of Dandekar and Rath's (1971) estimate of Rs15 per capita per month at 1960–61 prices as the rural poverty line, and Rs20 per capita per month for urban areas. The urban figures were derived by converting the rural into an equivalent urban poverty line by using the estimated rural urban price

---

[8] Desai (1981) provides a bibliography of the writings of what we can label the 'radical' school on industrial development. For a representative sample see Sau (1981), Vaidyanathan (1977) and Mitra (1977).

Table 7.10 *Estimates of poverty in rural and urban India, Gini coefficients of distribution of per capita expenditure, and linear time trends in distributional variables*

(a) Estimates of poverty in rural and urban India

	Rural		Urban	
Year	Pr_H	Pr_S	Pu_H	Pu_S
1960–61	38.03	0.141	40.40	0.156
1961–62	39.30	0.133	39.36	0.155
1963–64	44.50	0.163	42.52	0.161
1965–66	47.41	0.181	46.43	0.180
1967–68	56.20	0.234	48.32	0.188
1968–69	50.40	0.199	45.53	0.176
1969–70	49.20	0.189	44.50	0.168
1970–71	45.40	0.170	41.50	0.158
1973–74	44.30	0.155	38.70	0.130

(b) Gini coefficients of distribution of per capita expenditure

Year	Rural: G^r	Urban: G^u
1960–61	0.323	0.348
1961–62	0.310	0.358
1963–64	0.287	0.351
1965–66	0.297	0.347
1967–68	0.293	0.341
1968–69	0.305	0.329
1969–70	0.293	0.340
1970–71	0.283	0.327
1973–74	0.280	0.301

(c) Linear time trends in distributional variables (terms in parenthesis denote T-ratios)

Dependent variable	Estimated coefficient			
	Constant	Time	R^2	F
Pr_H	41.47	0.9245 (1.3504)	0.270	1.824
Pr_S	0.154	0.0040 (0.9795)	0.121	0.9598
G^r	0.317	−0.004[a] (3.3807)	0.558[a]	8.837
R^r	223.84	−0.2487 (0.2307)	0.01	0.063

Dependent variable	Estimated coefficient			
	Constant	Time	R^2	F
P^u_H	42.72	0.0486 (0.1066)	0.0016	0.0112
P^u_s	0.168	−0.001 (0.2614)	0.036	0.2614
G^u	0.359	−0.005[b] (3.6762)	0.616[a]	11.229
R^u	253.16	0.788 (0.6012)	0.049	0.3611

[a] The coefficient is significantly different from zero at the 5 per cent level of significance.
[b] The coefficient is significantly different from zero at the 1 per cent level of significance.
P^r_H (P^u_H) Rural (urban) poverty (% of population below poverty line).
P^r_S (P^u_S) Rural (urban) poverty, Sen Index.
G^r (G^u) Gini coefficient rural (urban).
R^r (R^u) Richness index rural (urban) given by the ratio of the mean income of the rich to the mean income in the sector.
Source: Dutta (1980).

differential of 20 per cent estimated by Chatterjee and Bhatta-charya (1971), and adjusting upwards slightly to take account of 'certain imposed and induced needs in urban areas' (Dandekar and Rath 1971:126).

Dutta's estimates of the two poverty indices and the Gini coefficients of nominal per capita expenditure in urban and rural India are reported in Table 7.10. Panel (c) of this table also reports the computed linear time trends in these variables. The following conclusions emerge:

(a) There is no evidence to suggest that there is any trend change in poverty in either the rural or urban sector.[9]

(b) There are, however, cyclical fluctuations in the incidence of poverty, with it rising in the 1960s and declining thereafter.

(c) There has been a significant trend decrease in inequality (in terms of the Gini coefficient) in both sectors.

(d) The decline in the Gini coefficient has been caused by an *absolute* fall in the living standards of the top 15 per cent of the population in the two sectors, and not by a transfer of consumption

[9] This is also Ahluwalia's conclusion (1978) for the rural sector to which his analysis is confined.

Table 7.11 *Trends in real manufacturing wages per worker, India, 1939–76*

Year	Payment of wages data		ASI and CMI
	Workers earning less than Rs 200/month (1939 = 100)	Workers earning less than Rs 400/month (1960 = 100)	All workers (1951 = 100)
1939	100	..	..
1940	109	..	..
1941	104	..	..
1942	89	..	..
1943	67	..	..
1944	75	..	..
1945	75	..	..
1946	73	..	..
1947	78	..	..
1948	84	..	..
1949	92	..	..
1950	90	..	..
1951	92	..	100
1952	101	..	106
1953	98	..	104
1954	103	..	106
1955	115	..	125
1956	106	..	116
1957	105	..	111
1958	102	96	116
1959	101	96	119
1960	105	100	127
1961	105	100	132
1962	106	103	138
1963	104	103	142
1964	95	95	133
1965	..	98	135
1966	..	92	135
1967	..	87	130
1968	..	92	137
1969	..	98	147
1970	..	98	151
1971	..	92	158
1972	..	98	..
1973	..	88	155
1974	..	68	137
1975	..	..	146
1976	..	..	160

CMI = Census of Manufacturing in India   ASI = Annual Survey of India
Source: Satyanarayana (1981: Tables 1.4, 1.5, 1.6).

from the rich to the poor. This is evident from Dutta's (1980) separate estimates of the trends in the mean real per capita consumption of the rich and the poor in the two sectors. He finds that, while the mean real per capita consumption of the poor shows no trend increase, that of the rich shows a statistically significant decline of 0.8 per cent per annum in the rural and 0.7 per cent per annum in the urban sector.

(e) Moreover, as Lal (1976) and Ahluwalia (1978) have shown for interstate data on poverty and agricultural growth, the latter aids rather than hinders the redressing of poverty, and is also good for equality.

Thus, although about 40 per cent of the population appears to be poor in both urban and rural areas, there has been no marked impact for better or worse in this ratio over the post-independence decades. If any immiseration has taken place, it is of those in the *top 15 per cent* of the income distribution in both rural and urban areas which has led to a lowering of the concentration ratio, low in any case by historical standards (see Maddison 1971 and Lal 1986).

Real rural and industrial wages have not fallen. The falling industrial wage thesis (for instance propounded by Chakravarty 1977) is based on the use of the unsatisfactory Payment of Wages Act (PWA) data, whose coverage is limited to workers earning less than a cut-off wage (Rs 400/month for the 1951 base series). If the more comprehensive data based on the Census of Manufacturing in India (CMI) and Annual Survey of India (ASI) are used then the real wage trends in industry are as given in Table 7.11 (see also Madan 1977), and show a sustained and continuous rise in real industrial wages between 1951 and 1976/77.

As regards rural real wages, I have surveyed the evidence in Lal (1976, 1984) and do not find any marked decline in rural real wages, which seem to have been determined by the interaction of rural labour demand and supply. As agricultural output has grown at about 2.4 per cent in the post-independence period (to 1980), and rural labour supply has increased by about 2 per cent per annum, not much of an increase in rural real wages can be expected. My best estimate (Lal in press) is that as a result rural real wages rose at the compound rate of about 0.4 per cent per annum between 1950 and 1978. Thus the distribution of income has not worsened and real rural and industrial wages have not fallen. Evidence on the other claims is given below.

Table 7.12 *Some price ratios, India, 1951–79*

Year	Agriculture/ Manufacturing	Rice/Wheat	Cotton/ Agriculture	Jute/ Agriculture
1951	94.6	94.7	109.3	151.4
1952	87.7	94.0	109.0	108.5
1953	87.6	99.0	104.2	86.3
1954	82.1	98.1	117.3	99.2
1955	80.0	97.8	117.1	131.9
1956	82.9	97.1	117.7	116.0
1957	84.8	103.2	109.4	120.7
1958	86.0	100.4	98.4	104.0
1959	86.6	89.4	96.6	97.2
1960	83.4	107.5	101.6	141.4
1961	73.2	105.1	107.7	181.3
1962	82.8	111.2	96.1	94.4
1963	80.3	119.9	99.6	97.0
1964	89.1	101.3	89.8	95.0
1965	94.9	89.2	82.2	116.2
1966	97.0	102.8	75.6	139.4
1967	84.6	95.2	84.7	108.9
1968	97.1	101.3	81.5	107.5
1969	102.4	96.1	84.0	118.3
1970	101.9	97.3	91.8	99.9
1971	92.7	105.6	111.4	94.4
1972	89.2	106.5	84.5	99.1
1973	97.9	121.9	83.8	80.8
1974	101.2	106.6	98.5	59.8
1975	94.4	111.1	84.4	67.9
1976	88.9	102.9	117.9	81.5
1977	96.9	104.9	115.5	83.5
1978	96.9	102.7	100.4	86.8
1979	89.7	110.4	89.9	96.1

Source: Desai (1981).

Table 7.12 shows the terms of trade for agriculture and manufacturing between 1951 and 1979. There has been no continuous improvement in agriculture's terms of trade. The famed power of the *kulaks* has certainly not been sufficient to raise agricultural prices above manufacturing ones. Mitra (1977:131) also asserts that, as a larger proportion of the marketed surplus of wheat is produced on large farms than on smaller ones, the *kulaks* have succeeded in raising the price of wheat relative to rice. No such conclusion is warranted from the data presented in Table 7.12.

Table 7.13 *Foreign investment in the manufacturing sector, 1969–73*
(Rs/crores)

Year	Foreign business investment outstanding	Fixed capital in the census sector	Ratios 1/2 (%)
	(1)	(2)	
1969	1619	7609	21
1970	1641	8324	20
1971	1680	8802	19
1972	1756	10185	..
1973	1816	..	18

Source: *Statistical Abstract of India* 1978: Tables 96:101, 37:95 (India, Government of, Central Statistical Office, various years).

On luxury consumption, Desai (1981:387) notes:

According to figures computed by Mitra [1977:164] from Reserve Bank statistics, the weight of consumer durables in the index of industrial production rose from 2.21 per cent in 1956 to 5.68 per cent in 1960, 7.84 per cent in 1970, and 8.09 per cent in 1972. According to Reserve Bank of India [India, Reserve Bank 1977a], however, their weight was only 2.92 per cent in 1970!

Any comment would be superfluous.

'The state of foreign capital in the Indian economy is quite significant ... The involvement of foreign capital in the manufacturing industries of India is increasing' (Sau 1981:57). Table 7.13 gives the ratios of outstanding foreign business investments in India between 1969 and 1973, and total fixed capital in the manufacturing census sector of the ASI. Private foreign investment has accounted for about 20 per cent of the fixed capital stock (based on book values) in Indian manufacturing and this share is declining. Nor can any 'net drain' from this foreign investment be deduced. There is an obvious fallacy in computing this drain by comparing undiscounted sums of the inflows and outflows on foreign capital account. If the foreign investor is to get a positive rate of return on his investment, the undiscounted sums paid out on account of the repatriation of capital and dividends and interest must exceed the inflows which made the outflow possible (see Lal 1975). Yet the fallacy continues to be perpetuated (as in Sau 1981). What is more, no overall deleterious effects from the foreign investment that has occurred can be deduced from social cost–benefit studies conducted of these investments in India (see Lal 1975, 1978). Where the social returns to India were low or negative, the major reason was the high effective protection provided by the system of import controls set up since the late 1950s (see Lal 1975).

The 'new orthodoxy' fails to note that the most important cause of the concentration of industry is the growth of the public sector, whose share of output in organized manufacturing grew from 8 per cent in 1960/61 to 30 per cent in 1975/76 (India, National Planning Office 1978:184). In basic industries (see Table 7.14a) the public sector has a near monopoly of domestic production. Judged by conventional accounting criteria the performance of the public sector has been abysmal compared with the private sector. The latter's performance in itself is not particularly noteworthy as judged by social profitability, but for three industries in which there are both private and public enterprises, some estimates of social profitability (at world prices) by Jha (1985) and summarized in Table 7.14b show the relatively poor public sector performance. It is the growing dominance of an inefficient public sector which should worry those concerned about the evil effects of the concentration of industry rather than any highly debatable tendency for concentration in private industry. In any case, as the continuing debate in developed countries shows, there is no clear economic reason to expect any increase in concentration of industry through mergers or take-overs to be necessarily detrimental in terms of economic welfare. All these special explanations for Indian industrial stagnation which abstract for the environmental variables – protection and labour legislation – are therefore unconvincing.

Little (1979a) has already disposed of the other special exogenous factors – such as culture, initial conditions, resource base, etc. – which it might be argued enabled the Gang of Four to industrialize faster than India. I need not repeat his arguments, except to add one supplementary point which is relevant both to my discussion in the next section, and in dispelling some popular views about the different cultural values engendered by Confucianism as compared to Hinduism. It is true that all the members of the Gang of Four have either predominantly Chinese populations or those historically influenced by Confucian ethics. It might be thought that, unlike Hinduism, Confucianism is a 'this world' religion which confers a high status on those practising commerce and

Table 7.14a *Share of public sector output in basic industries, India, 1983–84*

	Percentage
Coal	96.97
Lignite	100.00
Crude petroleum	100.00
Saleable steel	74.50
Aluminium	27.90
Copper	100.00
Lead	100.00
Zinc	89.30
Nitrogenous fertilizer	47.70
Phosphatic fertilizer	27.30
Telephones	100.00
Teleprinters	100.00

Source: Jha (1985).

Table 7.14b *Relative profitability of public sector, India, 1974–75*

Industry	Ratio of value added to GCE at market prices		Ratio of value added to GCE at border prices	
	Public	Private	Public	Private
Engineering	11.42	23.12	10.57[a]	18.95[a]
Chemicals	6.26	21.26	4.01[a]	10.07[a]

[a] No attempt has been made to calculate gross capital employed (GCE) at border prices. These figures are valid therefore only for intersectoral comparisons.
Source: Jha (1985: Table 2).

trade, so that the leaders in the Gang of Four have found the promotion of these elements of a market economy culturally congenial. However, as Mason *et al.* note, Confucian culture assigns a low value to business activity, and they find it perplexing that

it has accommodated itself to the rise of so many successful entrepreneurs ... One possibility is that the modernisation process is subtly, or not so subtly, changing the rank order of Confucian values. In South Korea, indeed, there is substantial evidence that business careers, once denigrated, are now regarded as acceptable rivals to those in government officialdom (Mason *et al.* 1980:284–5).

The obvious conclusion holds: different policy choices explain the different industrial outcomes in India and East Asia. What needs still to be explained is why East Asian policymakers who had very similar predilections, culture and a heritage of colonial policies very similar to India's (except in the all-important area of labour legislation), nevertheless succeeded in switching horses, whereas India has, despite some feeble attempts since the mid-1960s, still failed to do so.

<h2 style="text-align:center">IDEOLOGY AND INDUSTRIALIZATION:
DIFFERENT OUTCOMES</h2>

It is here that the interrelationship of ideas and vested interests needs to be brought in. Though Keynes's dictum about the power of ideas is probably true in the long run, in the medium run (measured in decades), policies generated by certain ideas and ideals can create vested interests which make the reversal of these policies almost impossible when the climate of opinion (in the light of experience) changes. That is one of the major differences between India and the Gang of Four.

During the phase when import-substitution and forced industrialization, based on the belief in 'export pessimism', were being promoted in most of the Third World, the Gang of Four never went much beyond primary import-substitution. India, by contrast, with the adoption of Mahalanobis's heavy industry strategy, explicitly aimed to import substitute as far back in the chain of production as possible. In this it was successful even though the social cost was enormous. This has made the switch to an 'export promotion' strategy – or more correctly the movement towards a more neutral trade regime (as between exports and import substitutes) – through the granting of export incentives which offset the biases of trade controls by creating a virtually free trade regime for exporters, extremely difficult in India.

As Krueger has emphasized:

Korea was able to make a smooth transition to an export-oriented policy in the early 1960s because import substitution had not yet progressed to the development of high-cost intermediate and capital goods industries. In other words, if import substitution in the 1960s had already reached the stage where most imports of intermediate and capital goods were replaced by domestic production, pressures from domestic industry might have prevented duty-free imports of low-cost intermediate and capital goods for export production. Under such circumstances, Korean exporters would have encountered great difficulty in producing export goods efficiently enough to be competitive in world markets (Mason *et al.* 1980:164).

The Indian policy of and success in import-substitution in intermediates and capital goods, by contrast, has meant that when attempts have been made to offset the biases against exports the so-called 'indigenous availability' criterion has prevented exporters from freely importing intermediate inputs. Thus, unlike the Republic of Korea, when India undertook the promotion of exports through various export incentive schemes, it created a system as complex and bureaucratic as its system of import allocation. The effect was to create a host of new distortions in the export sector (see Bhagwati and Srinivasan 1978; Lal 1975). Though manufactured exports did increase (see Table 7.15) so that, unlike the 1950s and 1960s, India's export performance (in these crude terms) matched the developing country average, the social efficiency of the form of export subsidization which promoted these exports is dubious. Table 7.16 shows the estimates made elsewhere (Lal 1979a, 1980a) of the social profitability of the exports promoted in a sample of export industries by the export incentive schemes. This shows that the subsidy system has not in general succeeded in raising the implicit exchange rate for goods with higher social export profitability, and that the relative divergences between private and social profitability have been altered by the export incentive system in essentially arbitrary ways, for which no clear economic justification can be provided. One of the major stumbling blocks in the adoption of a rational system has been the opposition from mainly (but not only) public sector intermediate and capital goods producers to the abrogation of the 'indigenous availability' criterion. But the creation of these vested interests in India was not inevitable. It was fostered both by ideas and what I shall loosely label 'environment'.

To take the last first, it is more tempting for planners in countries with large populations, and with a fairly varied natural resource base to attempt the secondary and tertiary phases of import substitution. Thus if domestic iron ore and coal are available, the conspicuous production of domestic steel – that intermediate good loved by planners as it is required for both machinery and weapons

Table 7.15 Structure and growth of exports for India and all developing countries, 1960–78

Export	Composition of exports (per cent)				Growth rates of export volume (per cent a year)					
	Developing countries		India[a]		Developing countries			India[a]		
	1960	1978	1960/61	1978/79	1960 to 1978	1960 to 1969	1970 to 1979	1960/61 to 1978/79	1960/61 to 1969/70	1970/71 to 1978/79
Food[b]	42.4	28.7	32.8	27.6	2.8	2.6	2.1	3.0	0.3[c]	4.4
Raw materials[d]	37.4 (44.7)	18.6 (23.4)	18.7	9.3	2.9 (3.4)	2.8 (5.0)	0.7 (−0.2)	3.3	4.3	1.3[c]
Manufactures[e]	20.2 (12.9)	52.7 (47.8)	48.6	63.1	11.6 (13.6)	9.9 (10.1)	11.6 (14.4)	6.8	4.5	11.2
Total	100.0	100.0	100.0	100.0	5.8	4.5	5.8	5.1	3.4	7.6

[a] The indices for India are those with 1968/69 weights.
[b] SITC 0 plus 1.
[c] The growth rate is not significantly different from zero at the 0.05 per cent confidence level.
[d] SITC 2 plus 4. For developing countries the figures in parentheses show the addition of SITC 68 (refined metals), an insignificant element for India except in a few years when sales from private silver stocks are permitted. For developing countries, however, exports in SITC 68 are important (7.3 per cent of exports in 1960) and fall naturally under raw materials.
[e] SITC 5 to 9 for the composition of exports and SITC 5 to 8 for growth rates. For developing countries the figures in parentheses show the results of the exclusion of SITC 68.

Note: Errors due to rounding. All growth rates are semi-logarithmic least squares trends. Petroleum is excluded throughout.
Sources: Wolf (1981: Table 2.6), and UNCTAD (various years).

Table 7.16 *Estimates of various indices for ten Industrial Credit and Investment Corporations*[a]

Industry in which firm is engaged	e_{di}[b] 1972	e_{di}[b] 1974	e'_{di}[b] 1972	e'_{di}[b] 1974	$r(\%)$[c] 1972	$r(\%)$[c] 1974	$r^P_x(\%)$[d] 1972	$r^P_x(\%)$[d] 1974	$r^P_d(\%)$ 1972	$r^P_d(\%)$ 1974	$r^P_{xe}(\%)$[e] 1972	$r^P_{xe}(\%)$[e] 1974
Light commercial vehicles	0.48	0.33	0.53	0.33	28	20	6	−9	49	41	44	13
Wire ropes	0.33	0.10	0.33	0.16	−27	26	35	6	42	28	−20	22
Textile machinery I	0.24	0.13	0.24	0.13	50	75	12	8	14	11	25	17
Textile machinery II	0.12	0.14	0.14	0.14	17	24	−8	−19	4	−3	−4	−11
Abrasives	0.04	0.13	0.04	0.13	−55	−38	−42	−31	16	15	−30	−26
Electrical equipment	0.08	0.18	0.08	0.18	20	23	−2	−8	3	−2	2	2
Castings and forgings	0.12	0.04	0.12	0.04	−10	34	−14	19	24	21	−9	22
Steel tubes and pipes	0.90	0.35	0.90	0.35	−5	57	−22	14	14	22	−5	55
Textiles	0.05	0.24	0.05	0.24	−3	20	−21	−3	7	9	−19	25
Chemicals	—	—	—	—	108	32	51	−15	37	1	51	−15
Mean	0.24	0.16	0.24	0.17	n.a	n.a.	n.a.	n.a.	n.a.	n.a.	n.a.	n.a.
Standard deviation	0.28	0.11	0.28	0.11	n.a.	n.a.	n.a.	n.a.	n.a.	n.a.	n.a.	n.a.

e_{di} = percentage excess of the implicit over the official exchange rate assuming the full capacity imported inputs *are not* provided to exporters.
e'_{di} = percentage excess of the implicit over the official exchange rate assuming the full capacity imported inputs *are* provided to exporters.
r^s = social rate of profit.
r^P_x = private rate of profit assuming all the output is exported, and there are no incentives.
r^P_d = private rate of profit assuming all the output is sold in the domestic market.
r^P_{xe} = private rate of profit assuming the output is exported and receives the same indirect and direct rate of subsidy as current exports of the firm.

[a] Derived from the ICICI export firm survey data.
[b] Where no premium rates were available as no Import Replacement Licence (REP) was nominated, the two e_d values will be the same.
[c] The social rate of profit has been derived from the data for each firm with the inputs being shadow priced on Little–Mirrlees lines by using the shadow price estimates in Lal (1986). The capital data were from the balance sheets of the firms. The output was priced at free on board prices. The resulting rates of profit are those which would accrue assuming the actual degree of capacity utilization if inputs and outputs were priced at 'border' prices.
[d] This private rate of profit has been obtained by valuing the output at fob prices and the inputs at market prices. The capital figures were taken from the balance sheets.
[e] This rate of profit was obtained by valuing the output at fob prices plus total subsidies on actual exports and inputs at market prices. The capital figures were taken from the balance sheets.
Source: Lal (1979a: Table 3).

– is irresistible. What is more (as for steel in India), the country may in fact have a comparative advantage in producing some of these capital and intermediate goods. By comparing a resource-poor country (say a 'rock' like Hong Kong) it will be less easy for planners to justify even to themselves such an obviously irrational development policy. Thus apart from the incentives for introducing various other policy induced distortions that an abundant and/or balanced natural resource base creates for policymakers, in terms of the economic dynamics of policymaking, these ecological pressures to create dysfunctional vested interests provide another reason for looking upon natural resources, in Hla Myint's evocative phrase, as a 'precious bane'!

There is another important self-serving reason for rulers of relatively resource-poor countries to embrace the culture of commerce and trade despite their ideological predilections. The individuals who at any time constitute the state have at least some interest (even in the most benevolent of states!) in the tax base which provides them with their means of livelihood. It is a well-known fact that external trade is likely to be more important against internal trade for relatively resource-poor countries (see Kuznets 1966). The self-interest of the rulers in expanding the tax base of a naturally resource-poor economy which must inevitably depend upon external trade for much of its livelihood can be expected to induce them to set up the property rights required for a mercantile economy (see North 1981; Hicks 1969).

But these 'environmental' factors cannot by themselves explain the tenacious hold on a particular ideology among a fairly wide spectrum of Indian officials and economists. Despite its factual basis being controverted they still hold to a view of the world which is marked by a suspicion of markets, merchants and the profit motive.

Hicks (1969) has stressed that in the evolution of modern Western economies the rise of the merchant and the market were important preconditions for that phase of modern economic growth 'which began as a European accident, [but] has become an obligatory command for the whole world' (Baechler 1975). At least since the sixth century B.C. (argued elsewhere in Lal 1986), India has had a substantial and prosperous mercantile class. Yet since its ideological vehicle, the republican anti-caste sects of Buddhism and Jainism lost out to caste in the early Christian era, the ideals and values of merchants have never had much appeal to India's rulers. The contempt in which merchants and markets have traditionally been held in Hindu society was given a new garb by the Fabian socialism which so appealed to the newly westernized but traditional literary castes of India.

Not all the politicians who were the inheritors of the Raj showed this 'aristocratic' contempt for business and commerce. Gandhi, a *Vaishya* (*bania*–merchant caste) by birth, certainly did not, but, after designating Nehru as his successor, he withdrew into the spiritual shadows and, within six months of having achieved Indian independence, he was dead at the hands of an assassin.

Nehru was a towering personality and an intellectual, but also a *Brahmin*! He professed to being a socialist, and was much impressed by the *dirigiste* example of the Soviet Union in transforming a backward economy into a world power within the lifetime of a generation. He had imbibed the Fabian radicalism of the inter-war period, and, with so many British intellectuals, was an ardent advocate of planning – which was identified with some variant of the methods of government control instituted in the Soviet Union.

But his was not just a fantasy dreamt up in an intellectual's ivory tower. Many businessmen, who identified their relative success during the last half of the Raj with the gradual erosion of the policies of *laissez-faire* and free trade, also advocated planning as a panacea for India's economic ills. It was nationalist businessmen who produced the early precursors of post-independence Indian plans, in their so-called Bombay Plan. While Nehru certainly, and the nationalist businessmen more doubtfully admired the Soviet model, Nehru balked at the suppression of liberty that the Stalinist model of development entailed. He hoped, instead, as a good Fabian socialist, to combine the 'order' and 'rationality' of central planning with the preservation of individual and democratic rights in India. Moreover, he was, at least in his own mind, a socialist, but it is interesting to see what socialism meant for him. In his autobiography, he wrote:

right through history the old Indian ideal did not glorify political and military triumph, and it looked down upon money and the professional money-making class. Honour and wealth did not go together, and honour was meant to go, at least in theory, to the men who served the community with little in the shape of financial reward. Today [the old culture] is fighting silently and desperately against a new and all-powerful opponent – the *bania* (Vaishya) civilization of the capitalist West. It will succumb to the newcomer ... But the West also brings an antidote to the evils of this cutthroat civilization – the principles of socialism, of cooperation, and service to the community for the common good. This is not so unlike the old Brahmin ideal of service, but it means the brahminization – not in the religious sense, of course – of all classes and groups and the abolition of class distinctions (Nehru 1956:431–2).

A more succinct expression of the ancient Hindu caste prejudice against commerce and merchants would be difficult to find. The British, unfortunately, had in their later years and despite the commercial origins of their rule in India, taken over most of the Indian higher-caste attitudes to commerce. The brown *sahibs*, mostly belonging, like Nehru, to these upper castes, found it congenial to adopt these traditional attitudes. What is more, 'socialism' now provided them with a modern ideological garb in which to clothe these ancient prejudices. Commercial success, as in the past, was to be looked down upon and the ancient Hindu disjunction between commercial power (and, increasingly, political power) and social status was to continue.

This identification of socialism with both a contempt for commerce and businessmen, and, by association, that prime symbol of the mercantile mentality – the market – was to colour economic policymaking in the new independent India; for 'socialism' in India has merely provided the excuse for a vast extension of the essentially feudal and imperial revenue economy, whose foundations were laid in ancient India, and whose parameters successive conquerors of India have failed to alter (see Lal 1986).

Thus Nehru identified socialism with bureaucratic modes of allocation,[10] with all that it implies in terms of the power and patronage afforded to the ancient Hindu literary classes which formed much of the bureaucracy. But, in this, Nehru was merely echoing the views of his Fabian mentors.

Thus, in *The Discovery of India*, he quoted with approbation a

[10] See Lal (1985a) for a fuller discussion of the validity of identifying 'socialism', as it has been in India, with *dirigisme* and bureaucratic modes of allocation.

statement of R. H. Tawney's that, 'the choice is not between competition and monopoly, but between monopoly which is irresponsible and private and a monopoly which is responsible and public' (Nehru 1956:554). He then expressed the belief that public monopolies would eventually replace private monopolies under his preferred economic system which he labelled 'democratically-planned collectivism'. Under such a system, he noted:

An equalization of income will not result from all this, but there will be far more equitable sharing and a progressive tendency towards equalization. In any event, the vast differences that exist today will disappear completely, and class distinctions, which are essentially based on differences in income, will begin to fade away (Nehru 1956:555).

He envisaged this socialist Utopia being established by the supplanting of the price mechanism, whose essential lubricant is private profit and utility maximization. This is evident from the continuation of the above passage:

Such a change would mean an upsetting of the present-day acquisitive society based primarily on the profit motive. The profit motive may still continue to some extent but it will not be the dominating urge, nor will it have the same scope as it has today (Nehru 1956:555).

We need not go into the details of the *dirigiste* system of controls and planning that was progressively set up.[11] The major point that needs to be made is that the control system was based on the predilections of engineers and not economists. This has continued to plague discussions of economic policy in India, not least those concerning various aspects of labour-market performance, such as unemployment. An engineer is trained to think in terms of an essentially fixed-coefficients world. The problem of trade-offs, and the consequent notion of opportunity costs, which is central to an economist's thinking, is alien to the conventional engineer's thought processes.[12] If coefficients are really fixed, then of course

---

[11] These are discussed in Lal (1980a) along with the optimal forms of government intervention, given the well-known limitations of a policy of *laissez-faire*, and the consequent need to deal with various forms of 'market failure'.

[12] It should be said, however, that economists, brought up on various fixed-coefficients planning models, have found it easy and natural to slip into this engineering frame of mind, even when they have explicitly been concerned with various economic trade-offs.

prices do not matter and the system of planning without prices, based on quantitative targets to meet fixed 'needs', becomes rational. Oddly enough, because this happens for historical reasons to be the implicit method underlying the material balance-type planning in the Soviet Union, many socialists, seeking to achieve their Valhalla by imitating the Soviet Union, have just assumed that little can be substituted in production and consumption in the world, and hence the Soviet-type planning methods are economically rational.

By contrast the Gang of Four and in particular the Republic of Korea were luckier to have set up Japan as a model for their development. The famed 'rational picking of industrial winners' by the Koreans was little more than an imitation of the early stages of Japanese development. As this coincided with an efficient development path based on their comparative advantage, this *dirigisme* has not (except in the mid-1970s) proved to be dysfunctional. Moreover, the Japanese model, with its close alliance between commerce and government, does not lead to that contempt of business so characteristic of India's élite.

Lest it be thought that these attitudes were and are confined to those self-serving politicians who have found enormous opportunities for increasing their power and patronage from the rent-seeking entailed by the Indian brand of socialism, I would like to quote from the writings of a distinguished Indian economist, who even his worst enemies would not charge with *raisons des clercs*. He has done as much as most to dispel many of the sillier shibboleths propounded by the 'radical' presses.[13] He rightly discounts the more hysterical reactions about the failures of the so-called Green Revolution and would probably deny most of the assertions made by the 'new orthodox' school, and yet he hankers after the same panaceas. The clue is to be found in his heartfelt objection to the Intensive Agricultural Development Programme (IADP) strategy in its promotion of the profit motive in agriculture. He writes:

the task of developing agriculture is being entrusted to the greed and the acquisitive spirit which motivates capitalists. *In traditional Indian agricul-*

---

[13] Thus there has been a scholastic and in my view futile debate in the pages of the *Economic and Political Weekly*, about whether Indian agrarian relations are capitalist, semi-feudal, feudal or colonial. Rudra has sensibly argued that most of this hair-splitting is not germane to any understanding of the Indian rural scene. See Rudra (1978:398–9).

*ture greed was located and condemned in the professional moneylender, the
speculative trader, etc.* An important discovery of the proponents of the
strategy is that the same greed, the same acquisitive spirit, may also be
found latent in the cultivators; all the components of the strategy are
aimed at further encouraging this spirit ... This clearly stated aim seems
to have been achieved. The 'Holy Grail' which the richer farmers are pursuing is the way of life of the urban middle class; the latter in their turn are
craving the comforts of the consumption society of the West (Rudra
1978:386–7, emphasis added).

This is an obvious echo of Nehru's sentiments quoted earlier.

This then is the crux of the explanation of why so many Indian
intellectuals dislike markets and the price mechanism: that these
depend upon, even if they do not promote, the greed and acquisit-
iveness which, as Rudra explicitly states, were looked down upon
by the literary and politically powerful castes in India. It is this
Brahminical attitude, today imbibed by a large part of the westernized stratum of Indian society, which is at the root of that seeming
raison des clercs which apparently has been taking place in India at
least over the last decade.

This contempt for business, moreover, has been allied with a
breathtaking ignorance of mercantile activity amongst these literary castes. This is the result of the endogenous and occupationally
segregated caste system. In more socially mobile societies there is
always a fair chance that the rulers and their courtiers would have
had some mercantile relatives who would have provided them with
some knowledge of the nature of trade and commerce, and the importance of risk taking and entrepreneurship in the process of development. The caste system has, however, cocooned the Indian
literary castes from any such influences.[14] The danger this rep-

[14] It may be useful to quote the conclusions of the major historian of the Indian
middle classes:
    'Since India's tradition of caste authoritarianism fitted in well with the Imperial
scheme of things, Indian bureaucrats, who usually belonged to higher castes,
were quick to step into the shoes of the British who left India in 1947. Bureaucracy thus continued to retain its hold over business in India and is increasing its
hold with the extension of the state's economic functions. This may be beneficial
to the educated middle classes, since as officers of government they step in as con-
trollers of nationalized industries without any personal stake in them. But it is no
gain to the country as a whole. The system of state control in fact stifles the
growth of entrepreneurial elements which India has in the past badly needed to
speed up production. Traditionally recruited from the literary classes, with no
business acumen, civil servants are most unsuited to accelerate production in
Indian conditions' (Mishra 1960:340).

resented to the prospects of India's economy was masked till fairly recently, when as a result of the administrative revolution which has greatly augmented the means whereby the government can extend the hold of the revenue economy, these literary castes have increasingly intervened in spheres which were traditionally not their province. Their inbred contempt and ignorance of merchants and markets prevents them from recognizing the failures of their past misguided interventions and promotes the evolution of a market economy (albeit controlled through measures which supplement the price mechanism), on which, to a large extent, the future economic prospects of Indians now depend.

There are, however, some hopeful signs that this resulting unworldliness of Indian rulers concerning trade and commerce might be changing. What scribblers cannot achieve, inflation and an excess supply of bureaucrats (see Table 7.17 for the growth of Indian bureaucracy) might at least engender. One of the remarkable features of the changes in the relative wage structure in post-independent India has been the decline in civil service salaries (particularly of those at the top) (see Table 7.18). The corresponding labour market signals have been received by the children of these literary castes who, from casual empiricism, seem to be turning towards non-traditional but more lucrative careers in business and politics. If this means that, in time, the so-called 'policy-makers' in India are less contemptuous and ignorant about trade and commerce, then that substitution of *bania* for Brahmin ideals which Nehru so passionately described, but which is nevertheless essential for India's economic progress, might at last begin to dissolve the intellectual bulwarks of Indian economic stagnation.

Moreover, there also seems to be some hope in the dynamics of what may be termed the political economy of controls. Whereas in the Gang of Four countries the 'environmental' reasons cited earlier probably induced an early shift towards a relatively open market economy which is required for development, in India (and in many other Third World *dirigiste* states) where these 'environmental' circumstances are less favourable, there nevertheless appears to be an inner dynamism which is likely (as currently in India) to lead to attempts to liberalize the economy. Ideas no doubt have some part to play in this conversion, but for an economist the self-interest of the rulers seems to be a more potent source of conversion.

Table 7.17 *Employment in the public sector in India*

	1901	1911	1921	1931	1951	1960	1978
Police (other than village watchmen)	241,892	239,319	222,529	240,532	379,721 (449,344)[a]	..	..
Percentage	10.2	9.6	8.9	8.7	12.6	..	..
Village officers and servants (including village watchmen)	773,397	689,828	531,400	384,177	237,180 (286,935)[a]	..	..
Percentage	32.8	27.6	21.4	13.9	8.0	..	..
Employees of municipalities and district boards	107,976	66,381	82,546	116,487	224,249 (269,560)[a]	..	..
Percentage	4.6	2.7	3.3	4.2	7.6	..	..
Army, navy, air force, employees of state government and union government and non-Indian governments	795,651	717,430	793,890	707,140	1,320,967 (1,823,122)[a]	..	..
Percentage	33.7	28.7	31.9	25.7	51.3	..	..
Total	1,918,916	1,712,958	1,630,365	1,448,336	2,162,117 (2,828,961)	5,498,000	12,943,000

[a] These figures refer only to civilian employees, and are exclusive of public sector employment in railways and manufacturing.
Note: figures are given for years at 10-year intervals. No figures are available for 1941.
Sources: Mukerji (1965:74, Table E). For 1960 and 1978 figures, India, Government of, Central Statistical Office (1982: Table 57).

235

Table 7.18 *Percentage changes in real value of emoluments to Indian central government employees since 1 January 1973* (Rs per month)

					Emoluments as on 1.1.78 after deflation for prices at Index 320		Percentage change	
	Emoluments as on							
	1.1.73		1.1.78				From Col. 2 to Col. 6	From Col. 3 to Col. 7
	Pre-tax	Post-tax	Pre-tax	Post-tax	Pre-tax	Post-tax		
(1)	(2)	(3)	(4)	(5)	(6)	(7)	(8)	(9)
1	196	196	308	308	192	192	−2.0	−2.0
2	1000	954	1363	1281	852	800	−14.8	−16.1
3	1500	1365	1863	1691	1164	1057	−22.4	−22.6
4	2000	1776	2343	2046	1464	1279	−26.8	−28.0
5	2500	2121	2500	2150	1562	1344	−37.5	−36.6
6	3000	2406	3000	2454	1875	1534	−37.5	−36.2
7	3500	2640	3500	2723	2188	1702	−37.5	−35.5
8	4000	3188	4000	2994	2500	1871	−37.5	−41.3

Source: Data compiled by study groups on wages, incomes and prices, May 1978.

The major reason for liberalization from the viewpoint of many Third World states (as judged by the preliminary results of two sets of multicountry comparative studies conducted by the World Bank and the Trade Policy Research Centre) lies in an attempt to regain control over an economy which seems to be less and less amenable to the usual means of government control. The most important symptom of this *malaise* is usually a creeping but chronic fiscal crisis (sometimes but not always reflected in a balance of payments crisis) which has in different forms beset most economies – including industrial ones – in the last decade (for a fuller discussion see Lal and Wolf 1986). Its origins lie in the creation by many states of politically determined 'entitlements' to current and future income streams for various groups in the economy (the deserving poor, industrial labour, regional interests, old age pensioners, and infant, declining or sick industries, to name just a few). These 'entitlements' being implicit or explicit subsidies to some groups have to be paid for by implicit or explicit taxation on other groups in the economy. However justifiable on grounds of social welfare, the gradual expansion of this 'transfer state' leads to some surprisingly dynamic consequences.

The gradual expansion of politically determined entitlements creates specific 'property rights'. The accompanying tax burden to finance them leads at some stage to tax resistance, tax avoidance and evasion and the gradual but inevitable growth of the black or underground economy. This has been the case with both industrial and developing countries in the past decade, and the 'black economy' is now variously estimated to account for 15–50 per cent of Indian GNP. Faced with inelastic revenues but burgeoning expenditure commitments, incipient or actual fiscal deficits become chronic. These can only be financed by three means: domestic borrowing, external borrowing or the levying of the inflation tax. Many countries, particularly those in Latin America, have tried all three – with dire consequences. Domestic borrowing to close the fiscal gap leads to the crowding out of private investment (which is generally the mainspring of growth) and a diminution in the future growth of income – and thus the future tax base. The fiscal deficit may be financed by foreign borrowing for a time, particularly as in the mid-1970s when real interest rates were low and even negative. But this form of financing is inherently unstable. Thus if, as happened in the late 1970s, world interest rates rise and the ability of the economies to generate the requisite export surpluses to service high debt interest costs is limited through policy induced distortions inhibiting exports (for example, the maintenance of overvalued exchange rates and high and differentiated effective protective rates which are an indirect tax on exports), the debt service ratio can become unviable. Foreign lending can therefore cease abruptly, leading to the kind of 'debt crisis' which has plagued Latin America in the 1980s.

The third way of financing the deficit through the inflation tax is also unviable in the medium term as it promotes a further growth of the black economy, and a substitution of some indirect or direct form of foreign currency based money substitute for domestic money as a store of value. The tax base for levying the inflation tax thus shrinks rapidly. With taxes being evaded, domestic and foreign credit virtually at an end, and with private agents having adjusted to inflation to evade the inflation tax, the government of the day finds its fiscal control of the economy near vanishing point. It may not even be able to garner enough resources to pay the functionaries required to perform the classical state functions of providing law and order, defence and essential infrastructure. This dynamic process whereby the expansion of the transfer state leads to the unexpected and very un-Marxist withering away of the state has rarely reached its full *dénouement*, though in some Latin American countries it must be pretty close![15]

However, well before things reach such dire straits, attempts are usually made to regain government control. Two responses by the government are possible – an illiberal and a liberal one. Fortunately the illiberal one is rarely observed. This consists of a further tightening and more stringent enforcement of direct controls. Tanzania provides an example. However, if this tightening is effective and, as a result, if the private use of the net of tax income received from legal productive activity declines to the level where untaxed subsistence activities are preferable, producers may seek to escape the controls by virtually ceasing to produce the 'taxed' commodities altogether. The tightening and enforcement of controls could lead to an implosion of the economy (see Collier *et al.* 1984 for such an interpretation of recent Tanzanian economic policy and its outcomes). The government might then find that as producers return to untaxable subsistence activities, the very *production base* over which it seeks control has shrunk or disappeared!

The other responses to regain government control are more usual. These involve regaining fiscal control through some economic liberalization of the economy. These usually half-hearted liberalization attempts involve some tax reforms, monetary contraction and some measures of export promotion to raise the economy's growth rate as well as the yield from whatever taxes are still being paid, and to improve the debt service ratio in the hope that this will lead to a resumption of voluntary foreign lending. But *unless the underlying fiscal problem which is largely that of unsustainable public expenditure commitments is tackled, these liberalization attempts have usually been aborted.* Without a commitment to rescinding unviable 'entitlements', the liberalization attempts have tended to worsen the fiscal situation; with the lowering of tax rates and lags in supply response, revenues do not rise and may even fall initially. The necessary reductions in money supply to contain inflation lead to a reduction in even the limited seigniorage

---

[15] For example, in Peru it is estimated that over 70 per cent of the labour force in Lima works in 'illegal' activities. The government has no domestic or foreign credit. Inflation is high and rising, and nearly 70 per cent of the money supply is in dollar-denominated deposits.

being previously extracted. The unwillingness to allow 'exit' entails a rise in the deficits of unviable loss-making public enterprises as well as any sick units newly taken over, as the liberalization exerts competitive pressures on unviable firms. Moreover, in those cases where the liberalization attempt has been accompanied by large public or private capital inflows (often to finance the continuing and at times increasing public sector deficit), there has been an appreciation of the real exchange rate which has sometimes been accompanied by inflationary pressures arising from inappropriate nominal exchange rate policies (e.g. Sri Lanka; see Lal 1985a). This has hurt potential export growth, so that when the capital inflows diminish, the incipient fiscal deficit is once again reflected in a chronic balance of payments problem which is then sought to be controlled in the bad old ways, and the liberalization process is reversed.

The above patterns were observed in a large number of countries which attempted to liberalize in the 1970s. The major lesson I would draw from the preliminary results of the two sets of comparative studies referred to above is that liberalization is often undertaken to gain fiscal control, but if nothing is done to rescind unsustainable public expenditure entitlements, a stabilization/ balance of payments crisis eventually emerges which undermines the attempt to liberalize the economy.

The lessons for India are obvious. The vast expansion of the revenue economy in India has generated a fiscal problem for the state. With some Indian states unable to finance even their salary budgets from tax revenues, and the general explosion in euphemistically termed non-Plan expenditures, the worldwide fiscal crisis is now also manifest in India. But, as the Latin American experience in the 1970s has shown, it would be a snare and a delusion to hope to postpone the necessary fiscal adjustments by covering the incipient deficits through foreign borrowing. There is no viable alternative to curtailing public expenditures on non-productive 'entitlements'. Thus stabilization of the economy no less than any prospective liberalization also entails a willingness to overcome the resistance of those in the public sector whose 'entitlements' need to be rescinded.

The new Indian Government's professed aim to liberalize the Indian economy can thus be looked upon as a reaction to the past growth of the underground economy (and its implication for government control) in the country. However, the 'environmentally' determined instinct to concentrate on liberalizing domestic rather than the foreign trade components of commodity markets still rules policy. Thus while necessary tax reforms and the dismantling of various inefficient industrial controls is planned, trade liberalization remains in the shadows. However, despite the rhetoric, India does not provide a large domestic market for industrial goods. The danger of liberalizing the domestic market without a simultaneous recourse to trade controls is that it might fuel the development of a highly protected, concentrated and inefficient domestic capitalism. This would justify all the dire predictions India's literary castes have always made about the likely inequitable and sordid outcome of giving business and commerce its head. Thus, at least for the immediate future, because of the dead weight of both 'ideas' and 'environment' as much as the power of vested interests of its people, it seems unlikely that India will be able to use industrialization as it should to transform living standards in the spectacular manner of the East Asian Gang of Four.

8

JAPAN:
MODEL FOR EAST ASIAN
INDUSTRIALIZATION?

Several arguments have contributed to the popularity of the hypothesis that Asian countries owe their successful growth experience to following a Japanese 'model' of development. One of these is the 'late starter' theme. Japan industrialized after Western Europe and the United States with all the disadvantages – but also the advantages – of such a late start. It may be seen either as the last of the major countries of today to undergo an industrial transformation or as the first (and to date the most successful) of the developing countries to industrialize. It has frequently been argued that the East Asian countries that began to industrialize in the 1950s and 1960s were also late starters (Kazushi and Rossovsky 1968), and that they accordingly followed similar industrialization paths to that followed by Japan. A number of characteristics stemming from Japan's particular economic history have more recently been present in other East Asian countries, thus contributing to the notion of a Japanese or East Asian model of industrial development. They include high savings and investment rates, an emphasis on export performance, active entrepreneurship and high productivity of capital and labour. A common ethnic/cultural outlook based on Confucian ideology is often regarded as the most important ingredient of a Japanese–East Asian model (Kim 1983).

The East Asian countries have a schizophrenic love–hate relationship with Japan typical of the attitudes of former colonies to former imperial powers. Sometimes they seek to learn from the Japanese experience, but sometimes they regard the Japanese experience as being of little importance in their rapid growth.

The construction of 'typical' models of growth goes back to the 1950s and 1960s (Kerr *et al.* 1960). It has been revived recently in the East Asian context. A specifically Japanese model has, however, not been developed. Identifying the principal characteristics of a Japanese model of industrialization thus occupies the first part of this paper. The second section seeks to determine if such a model has been used in East Asia – whether consciously, by conscious imitation or because of the similarity of 'initial conditions' to those of Japan from which the East Asian countries started their industrial development. The final section draws together the analytical conclusions.

THE JAPANESE MODEL OF
INDUSTRIALIZATION

In contrast to most Western countries and the United States, it became clear at an early stage of its industrial development that Japan was so poorly endowed with raw materials for industrialization that it would have to become an exporter of industrial goods from the start to ensure foreign exchange availability for its raw material imports and to meet the cost of imported technology and expertise needed to 'catch up' with industrial countries. But Japan did not opt for a simple outward oriented industrial strategy. Almost from its initial steps towards industrialization it began to introduce a complex of incentives for both import substitution and exports. Tariffs were supported by non-tariff barriers which largely captured the domestic market for domestic producers. Subsidies, mainly through privileged access to credit facilities, also supported domestic production. Restrictions on the import of capital, particularly in the form of direct foreign investment, were an important characteristic of successive Japanese autarkic economic regimes.

Exports, however, had to be won. For this Japan had to marshal the strength of its textile, footwear and other labour-intensive industries from the 1900s. By the 1920s it had gained the benefits of specialization and economies of scale that brought low costs and reasonably low prices to that part of the domestic Japanese market characterized by competition in spite of marginal pricing for export. Typically of late starters, the quality and design of such Japanese goods as clothing, textiles, toys and trinkets were initially low, but these export industries soaked up surplus labour from the countryside and urban areas, helping to create a large domestic market by raising family incomes. It did not matter that initially Japan aimed at the bottom end of world markets. It took some fifty years for Japanese goods, initially with the assistance of key foreign technicians and the adoption and adaptation of new technologies, to become world leaders in industries as complex as motor vehicles and electronics.

Japan's particular course of economic evolution also strongly influenced the relationships between government and private enterprise and between managers and employees. Both sets of relationships are usually seen as important components of the Japanese industrialization model. Superficially such relationships have often been explained in terms of Confucian striving for harmony. Confucian forms of respect for elders and for the family certainly contributed to the successful organization of enterprises, but it is now well established that there are many such opportunities within every ideology. The Confucian ethic parallels the Protestant ethic. How ideologies are interpreted in business behaviour partly depends on historical circumstances but it is mainly a reflection of economic policies. China up to 1949 and the Republic of Korea to the end of the Rhee regime were regarded as hopeless economic cases. Yet the same countries with the same basic ideologies began to grow overnight once appropriate policies were put in place. A similar revolution took place in Taiwan in the 1950s. All three economies thus demonstrated that the Confucian ideology, like others, was suited either to stagnation or to growth: actual outcomes depended on the particular combination of economic circumstances and policies.

The cooperative relationship between government and private enterprise in Japan dates back mainly to the beginnings of industrialization when governments took the initiative to establish 'heavy' industries with (for the times) large-scale investment to provide appropriate economies of scale and imported technology. It was argued that such 'import substitution' was essential to industrialization but that suitable private entrepreneurs were not available to shoulder the risks and large scale of the necessary investment. Between 1905 and 1945 Japan's economy was frequently on a wartime footing, reinforcing relationships between the leading large conglomerates that dominated the economy and governments. Bureaucratic links were established from both sides. While Japan achieved a considerable measure of industrialization up to the Second World War, the withdrawal of the principal industrial countries into heavily protectionist regimes in the 1930s, wartime imperatives and the ensuing structural weaknesses made economic development, particularly in terms of increases in the standard of living, very slow despite close business and government relationships.

After the Second World War the power of the Japanese monopolistic conglomerates was considerably reduced and the economic policy framework began to be liberalized. Governments, mainly through the Ministry of International Trade and Industry (MITI), continued to provide incentives to industrial entrepreneurs through an indicative planning framework reinforced by production subsidies, border protection, infrastructural facilities and credit instruments. Such initiatives were important in securing raw materials and their transportation to Japan, making monopolistic and monopsonistic forays into world markets to avoid damaging surges of supply or demand that would otherwise have played havoc with prices. MITI also played a major role in protecting the domestic market from imports as long as possible, though the natural protection of the Japanese language and the distribution network probably made redundant much of the tariff and quantitative import restriction structure that MITI built. With such policies leading to high economic rents large entrepreneurs were only too happy to live in Confucian amity with each other, their workers and the governments of the day. Small sacrifices in giving up some sales or making less than optimal (from a private point of view) investments were minor sacrifices made to secure a highly favourable economic policy framework that permitted high profits through the marginal pricing of exports at the cost of domestic consumers. In any case, through the growth of liberal lobbying in other ministries, notably the Ministry of Finance, firms which wanted to steer clear of government intervention were able to do so.

MITI had no difficulty in 'picking the winners' when Japan was merely following in the path of older industrial countries although the Ministry was only a moderately competent grave digger for the 'senile' industries that had to give way to competition from newly industrializing countries. Given the rapidity of economic growth in the 1950s and 1960s, the Japanese industrial adjustment process was slow and probably much costlier in social terms than it would have been if it had been left to the operation of markets. When it came to picking the winners in new industries in more recent industrial restructuring, MITI was no more successful than bureaucracies elsewhere. It fostered some 'winners' but hindered others. Overall 'Japan Inc.' grew out of the force of circumstances and play of opposing interest groups rather than from the Confucian ethic.

The apparently unique characteristics of benign industrial relations were also heavily influenced by the circumstances of Japan's industrialization. From the beginning of industrialization in the late nineteenth century there was an ample supply of unskilled and semi-skilled, particularly female, labour, but there was a shortage of skilled workers, technicians and managers. There were similar surpluses and shortages in many East Asian developing countries in the 1950s and 1960s. When Japan began to industrialize, master and apprentice relationships that were associated with the Middle Ages in Western Europe still prevailed. These relationships were adapted to bind skilled workers and staff to the newly emerging industrial (and service) enterprises to conserve skills to the enterprise that created them. Company unions were formed. In the 1950s and 1960s acute labour shortages created by rapid growth strengthened the lifetime employment system. Ample supplies of skilled workers, technicians and managers who emerged from the slowing down of growth in the 1970s immediately led to a move towards more liberal policies and practices and more open-ended employer/employee relationships. Many industrialists began to argue that new times required more adaptable employment conditions.

For the majority of the workforce, particularly for the female workers who dominated industrial employment in the early years of industrialization, there were no lifetime employment opportunities and no employment security. The industrial workforce employed by the firms that were subcontractors to the major assembly firms bore the brunt of short- and long-term business cycles: when orders slackened, they were dismissed. Trade unions (as distinct from company unions) developed eventually, but they were too weak in the face of the division of labour into long-term, potentially long-term and casual workers, and the large volumes of unskilled and semi-skilled workers until the 1950s, to be as effective as workers in older industrial countries in establishing their organizations. Rapid increases in standards of living retarded the growth of trade unions when more liberal political conditions and open labour markets made them possible.

A hundred years ago, as they began to compete with firms from older industrial countries, skilled labour shortages taught Japanese managers the value of non-confrontational labour management for high labour productivity. It was clear that non-monetary incentives as well as monetary rewards could be used to encourage collaboration between managers and workers. The bonus system was developed to reward high productivity. Together with the high cost of housing and relatively slow growth of social security (except for the privileged long-term workers) it encouraged high savings. The Confucian ethic was undoubtedly useful in attaining productivity and national savings goals, but ideology must not be mistaken for the substance of economic policies.

Several characteristics commonly regarded as being part of the Japanese model of industrialization turn out to be common to all successfully industrializing countries. Thus Japan had a long history of primary education inherited from the Tokugawa – pre-Meiji restoration – period. Literacy rates were close to 100 per cent by 1900. From the 1900s modern secondary and post-secondary education was stimulated to modernize administrative machinery, corporate management and technology. Large corporations supplemented state efforts. The feudal ideology that permeated education reinforced group orientation and discipline.

Japan's education system was not, however, unique. High literacy rates in Korea reach back to the twelfth and thirteen centuries, laying a foundation for the post-colonial period after the Second World War. Primary education was common in Taiwan in the 1930s, and technical secondary and post-secondary education grew rapidly in both countries in the 1950s and 1960s. Hong Kong and Singapore rapidly increased their educational infrastructures after the Second World War. Thailand, like Japan, had a long history of literacy based on Buddhist schools, and together with the other Southeast Asian countries it rapidly increased education facilities after the Second World War. High educational achievement turns out not to be merely characteristic of Japan but typical of all rapidly-growing countries.

High rates of household savings, and their effective mobilization, are often regarded as another characteristic of the Japanese model, but similar factors to these already noted in Japan, notably lack of social security and housing, stimulated savings in other East Asian countries. The institutional forms were often quite different. For example in Singapore, where public housing and social security were available, the National Provident Fund played an important role in savings. In most East Asian countries a vigorous banking system transformed savings into investment. High savings and rigorous intermediation are also characteristics of all rapidly industrializing countries though the forms may differ.

The institutional, anti-monopoly reforms of the post-Second World War era markedly increased competitiveness among large Japanese firms. The relatively large domestic market made for competition among the small and medium-sized firms that had to innovate and adjust their technologies and product mix constantly for mere survival, let alone for growth. Subcontracting led to a high rate of entry to – and exit from – manufacturing industries. These characteristics are also common to all rapidly industrializing countries. The competitive pressure of export markets was particularly intense in Hong Kong, Taiwan and Singapore, and more recently it has grown in labour-intensive industries in Thailand. Where the highly competitive model has not been followed because of high levels of incentives to large firms, as in the Republic of Korea, growth and exports of manufactures have faltered from time to time.

A number of features of the Japanese model are peculiar to Japan. They have not been generally applied in East Asian countries. The most important of these is the Japanese restriction on the inflow of private direct foreign investment. With the exception of the Republic of Korea where private direct foreign capital inflows are almost as restricted as in Japan, all the East Asian countries have utilized inflows of private direct foreign capital, and their accompanying technologies, very intensively. For the small economies particularly (Singapore, Hong Kong, Malaysia and Taiwan), private direct foreign investment and technology imports have been essential to the catching up process. In Singapore some 75 per cent of manufacturing output and exports comes from wholly foreign-owned firms or joint ventures. Private direct foreign investment is particularly important for market access to industrial countries, including Japan. Japan has become the largest or second largest foreign investor in most East Asian countries.

Without such measures these countries would not have been able to compress Japan's 100 years of industrialization effort into one generation.

The Japanese balanced management system has not been replicated in other East Asian countries. Company unions are not common. Managers of large corporate firms regard employees as the most critical asset of a corporation. Together with government pressures to maintain employment, corporations have made strenuous efforts to avoid reduction in their permanent workforce during recessions and reorganizations, particularly when skilled labour was scarce.

The management commitment to lifetime employment in large firms in part reflects the fact that most of a corporation's chief executives have come up its management ladder together, sharing the same values. They are able to persuade the workforce that the welfare of all employees and the corporations' competitive success depends on producing. Competition in domestic and export markets is clearly understood.

Cooperation among business corporations in Japan ranges from low to high, depending on the kind of activity and the type of corporations involved. Some firms pool their money and efforts together in industry associations to strengthen the collection, analysis and dissemination of data and other information on production, distribution and marketing of their products and services. Employers join together to engage in similar activities on labour–management issues including wages during the 'spring offensive' of wage negotiation.

Firms also form strong pressure groups to make private-sector views known to the public and make representations to the government (central or local) on major issues such as environmental regulation, tax reforms and public expenditure policies affecting corporations. At the same time, particularly in oligopolistic situations, they compete fiercely to develop and market new products and services as well as new technologies.

Traditionally, business corporations affiliated with Mitsui, Mitsubishi or Sumitomo maintain a relatively high degree of group solidarity by cooperating and/or coordinating their research and development, production, distribution, marketing and servicing of products and services. Parent firms keep a strong tie with their respective subsidiaries in the day-to-day conduct of their business. On the other hand, competition may be quite intense between business firms neither affiliated nor related to each other. Increasing market competition at home and abroad has in recent years led to more rational business relations among group-affiliated corporations to increase intra-group competition and diversify intra- and inter-group cooperation.

Overall, the picture is not very different from most industrial and industrializing countries. As 'Japan Inc.' suggests, there are thick layers of cooperation between government departments and the private sector at the national and local levels to formulate and implement economic and social policies on such major issues as education, environment, employment, industrial adjustment, international trade and investment, and balance of payments.

Effective two-way communication is established by ensuring business representation on various government advisory committees as well as by maintaining joint government–business sessions on specific issues affecting the private sector. Placement of retired high-level bureaucrats in key managerial positions of private-sector corporations has also facilitated government–business cooperation. This technique, too, is common in all industrial and industrializing countries.

Corporations encourage young people to complete higher education so as to meet the requirements for better trained engineers and managerial staff. Pay and promotion systems place those with higher and better educational attainments on a track of faster and larger pay increases, faster promotion and more challenging and satisfying jobs including overseas assignments. On-the-job and other in-service training is emphasized. Qualifying examinations for possible managerial candidates, which look not only at their technical, professional and/or managerial skills and competence, but also at the social outlook and intellectual horizons required by managers in increasingly complex organizations with diversified worker needs, are becoming increasingly popular.

Productivity improvement through gain-sharing policies are geared to improving corporate productivity and enhancing the economic well-being of all, including manual workers. Although exhortation plays a role, the principal tool for increasing productivity consists of fiscal and financial incentives.

Because productivity improvement largely results from economies of scale and changes in technologies, national and local governments have provided tax incentives such as accelerated depreciation allowances and tax credits for fixed investment and for research and development investment outlays. At the time when capital coefficients were increasing across-the-board, those tax benefits were essential to inducing the private sector to invest in new technologies, production processes and product development.

Tax incentives for export promotion were used during the 1950s and 1960s to orient private sector investors towards export industries, expanding their investment beyond domestic needs and requirements, and thus reaping the benefits of the economies of scale as well as strengthening their price and quality competitiveness on international markets. In addition to some direct government subsidies and administrative assistance, a number of government financial institutions were created to provide low-interest loans to strategic industries for productivity improvement and export promotion.

To the extent that productivity improvement also results from changes in work methods, greater efficiency of individual workers and stable labour–management relations, corporations established small group activities such as quality control circles, valuation of engineering methods, group incentive schemes and joint labour–management consultation schemes.

The zero defects movement (the *kanban* system), zero inventory schemes and other improvements in work methods were established in various industries to suit their respective needs and requirements. Larger firms encourage their subcontractors to adopt such improved work methods wherever possible to reduce unit costs of production and thereby remain competitive. National, prefectural and local governments assist small business enterprises in adopting and learning improved work methods.

Anti-inflationary measures to provide a stable economic climate for steady increases in real wages consistent with increases in productivity are an important component of policy. Wage increases are limited to increases in the cost of living and productivity. A majority of corporations have established profit-sharing plans so that employees can participate in share ownership.

Egalitarian wage policies are based upon a consensus of management and unions or employees. It is argued that increases in productivity result from the efforts of all the employees and that the economic and financial health of a corporation rests essentially upon all, managers and non-managers, participating in corporate activity. Wage differentials between top executives and the lowest-paid clerical and factory workers are extremely narrow by either Western or developing country standards.

When corporate profits fall because of recessions, the chief executives suffer the largest salary cuts; low-paid workers' wage cuts are postponed and they are for short periods. In some corporations the lowest-paid workers do not become subject to wage cuts at all although their earnings are likely to be reduced because of shorter working hours. Corporations have also provided a variety of fringe benefits to all employees, regardless of rank and title in the corporate hierarchy. In this way business corporations have been able to obtain support from all employees in constant efforts to improve productivity.

Fiscal and financial measures have been devised to accelerate the process of industrial restructuring to maintain the competitiveness of Japanese industry. Tax incentives for research and development expenditures, accelerated depreciation allowances for actual plant and equipment investment and low-interest loans from government financial institutions are available for new industries.

Declining industries, on the other hand, establish joint industry funds to phase out a certain portion of the plant and equipment in operation each year. The National Employment Stabilization Fund is used to retrain redundant workers and transfer them to jobs in growing industries. Industrial adjustment assistance for declining industries and their workers enables the national economy to benefit from better resource allocation by sharing the burden of adjustment with those adversely affected by industrial restructuring. Declining industries do not receive tariff or non-tariff protection to prolong their survival and revive their international competitiveness. 'Picking the losers', however, has been far more difficult than encouraging new industries. Political intervention to retard the process is common.

Agricultural and other primary industry protection is encouraged for national security reasons. The political strength of this sector has enabled such protection to remain longer and be larger than called for by the ordinary processes of adjustment. The cost of agricultural protection to consumers and the government has been far beyond the level that government would require them to bear. Distortions to the national economy have been extremely serious through such agricultural pricing policies. Japan's argument for maintaining freer trade and open international economy regimes has been marred by the agricultural tariff and non-tariff barriers successfully imposed by a small but politically powerful sector of the economy.

Nevertheless, however distorting Japanese agricultural pricing and protectionist policies have been in terms of resource allocation and international trading relations, their effects on income maintenance of the farm sector have been positive, contributing to a fairer distribution of income at the national level. Also contributing to this have been government subsidies for those working in low-productivity sectors of the national economy and the variety of transfer payments made to the weakest segments of the population including the aged and the handicapped. The monetary and fiscal policy measures that have been successful for some time in restraining consumer price increases in general and those for basic human needs in particular have also been additional policy inputs to maintaining a fair distribution of income in the country.

While industrialization in Japan and developing East Asian countries is often quite similar, the similarities are more apparent than real. Some policy measures adopted by the newly industrializing East Asian countries have been quite similar to measures taken by Japan, but the effects, because of differences in basic characteristics, have not been the same as in Japan.

STRUCTURAL, INSTITUTIONAL AND POLICY CHARACTERISTICS OF EAST ASIAN DEVELOPING COUNTRIES

The labour force of the East Asian countries, while well educated and disciplined, has an individualistic orientation. While workers in several countries compare favourably with their counterparts in Japan, their individualistic characteristics prompt them to respond more quickly to short-term pecuniary incentives. They change their employers readily. They are less susceptible to group discipline and group-oriented incentives. There has been a steady improvement in the technical and professional quality of labour as a result of ever-increasing opportunities for higher education and the strong pressure of market competition.

While the development of human resources has been emphasized, as indicated by educational policies, not enough attention has been paid to the effective mobilization and utilization of the manpower already developed at the corporate and national levels. For example, in Singapore the labour shortage that emerged with high growth in the 1970s was dealt with by importing cheap labour from neighbouring countries. The introduction of labour-saving technologies and methods of production and a more rational use of labour came only as a result of government-induced high wage policies in the early 1980s. The high level of worker mobility from one employer to another, while meeting the objectives and goals of individuals for raising their earnings and job satisfaction, may have high social costs. Efforts by corporations and governments to reduce high worker mobility have not been successful.

The East Asian countries have been able to mobilize high rates of household and corporate savings, as shown by high levels of gross domestic capital formation as a percentage of GDP. This has been particularly significant in the newly industrializing countries with rising capital–output ratios reflecting a shift of the economies to a more capital-intensive structure.

Whereas the thrifty nature of petty and small business entrepreneurs and farmers has contributed to a high savings propensity, high real rates of interest have also contributed. In the Republic of Korea and Taiwan compulsory employee savings schemes were introduced in early years, but they have not been replaced by tax incentive schemes for small savers. In Singapore the Central Provident Fund and Skill Development Fund have in effect compelled paid employees and corporations to save in the form of contributions to the public funds.

Foreign capital inflows, including private direct foreign investment flows, have been fairly substantial, also contributing to high proportions of gross domestic investment to GDP (see Table 8.1). Capital was attracted by the favourable investment climate that included political stability, high growth policies, abundance of a well-educated and well-disciplined workforce, well-developed networks of transportation, communications and other infrastructural and investment incentives including tax holidays, export incentives, and the free remittance overseas of corporate profits, interest and other earnings.

Multinational corporations have not only brought financial resources but, more importantly, technology, management and access to markets as well. They have also contributed to human resource development and utilization through in-service education

Table 8.1 Shares of East Asian country manufactured exports in major country markets, 1970 and 1980

Exporters	Importers									
	USA	Canada	Japan	Near-industrializing countries	ASEAN	China	Western Pacific	EC	OPEC	World
USA (1970)	..	75.3	43.2	17.1	15.6	..	24.6	11.6	12.8	15.9
(1980)	..	74.4	34.5	18.5	19.3	12.1	23.7	9.1	10.4	13.5
Canada (1970)	28.1	..	2.7	0.7	1.2	1.5	12.3	1.9	0.6	5.5
(1980)	20.9	..	2.0	1.4	1.1	1.6	8.1	0.8	0.7	3.2
Japan (1970)	21.9	5.7	..	46.2	35.4	46.9	18.3	2.6	10.5	9.7
(1980)	26.0	6.6	..	40.2	33.2	42.7	21.9	4.1	16.9	11.5
Near-industrializing countries (1970)	6.7	1.4	7.0	4.4	5.9	0.2	4.3	1.0	2.1	2.2
(1980)	13.5	3.2	16.1	7.8	10.5	8.9	9.1	2.4	4.9	4.7
ASEAN (1970)	1.8	0.4	5.1	1.7	9.3	3.6	2.1	0.7	0.4	1.2
(1980)	3.9	0.6	8.7	4.2	9.2	4.2	3.9	1.1	1.1	2.0
China (1970)	..	0.1	1.4	4.7	2.8	..	0.7	0.2	1.0	0.4
(1980)	0.7	0.3	3.7	7.1	2.0	..	1.6	0.6	0.5	0.8
Western Pacific (1970)	62.5	83.2	64.7	76.3	73.3	52.7	66.1	19.9	27.9	37.8
(1980)	67.7	85.9	70.7	80.7	78.0	72.0	72.4	18.9	35.5	37.8
EC (1970)	30.0	13.4	26.4	17.4	22.7	35.8	27.1	65.8	58.9	49.4
(1980)	25.3	10.7	20.4	14.7	17.5	19.6	21.1	64.8	48.9	47.1
OPEC (1970)	0.1	..	0.3	0.1	..	0.1	0.1	0.2	0.6	0.2
(1980)	..	..	0.3	..	0.1	0.3	0.1	0.1	1.6	0.3

Source: United Nations (1982).

and training programs. They have quite often provided a climate of business competition which has pressured indigenous firms, private and public, to become more cost and quality conscious in production, more customer-tailored in marketing and more employee-oriented in management.

All the newly industrializing countries have an abundance of entrepreneurs active in production, distribution and provision of goods and services. Although often criticized as preoccupied with seeking high rates of financial return in the short run, they have spearheaded many small but important innovations through competition. Many have grown to be large, modern enterprises, joining with foreign investors to set up diversified multinational operations in their own countries and elsewhere.

Private sector entrepreneurs have been active in modernizing their production technologies, machinery and equipment as well as in exporting. Supported by high-growth government policies and in pursuit of greater competitiveness in international markets, some corporations have been importing capital goods to reduce unit costs of production and also to diversify their output to meet changing market demands.

While exports of manufactures have been rising faster than for any other groups of countries, imports of capital goods have also been rising faster. As a result, a steady increase in current account deficits has been observed, except in Taiwan which has already joined Japan in maintaining a current account surplus for some time (see Table 8.2). Current account deficits, however, have been rising at a much slower rate for the industrializing than for the near-industrializing East Asian countries, thus allowing them to have greater room for adjustment to continue their high growth policies.

As private sector entrepreneurs become more experienced they can take greater risks. Nevertheless, there has been little investment in research and development for new production technologies in new products or in product adaptation. New technologies and products have been imported instead through licensing arrangements, or in joint equity ownership with foreign firms, or by purchase of foreign patents. It is cheaper and less risky to import proven technologies than to develop new ones.

The East Asian governments, however, have in recent years begun, mainly through tax incentives and low-interest loans, to encourage indigenous and foreign corporations to invest in research

Table 8.2 *International trade, investment and balance of payments for Japan and East Asian countries, 1960–82*

Country and country grouping	Average annual growth rates of exports (%)		Manufactured exports as % of total		Capital goods imports as % of total		Current account deficits (US$ million)		Net direct investment (US$ million)	
	1960–70	1970–82	1960	1982	1960	1982	1970	1982	1970	1982
Hong Kong	12.7	9.4	80.0	97.0	10	23	:	:	:	−77
Korea, Rep. of	34.7	20.2	14.2	90.1	12	23	−623	−2679	66	2093
Singapore	4.2	:	26.0	44.7	7	28	−572	−1279	93	:
Taiwan	:	:	29.3	90.8	:	:	−10	2357	:	:
Indonesia	3.5	4.4	0.8	4.2	17	36	−310	−5458	83	133
Malaysia	6.1	3.8	6.0	27.8	14	37	8	−3445	94	1230
Philippines	2.3	7.9	3.2	23.6	36	23	−48	−3356	−29	253
Thailand	5.2	9.1	1.4	35.3	25	26	−250	−1144	43	185
Japan	17.2	8.5	79.0	97.0	9	7	1980	6977	−260	−4085

Sources: World Development Report, 1984 (World Bank, various years); Asian Development Bank (1984).

and development so that they may become more competitive in international markets.

The near-industrializing countries – Indonesia, Malaysia, Thailand and the Philippines – have somewhat different characteristics to the newly industrialized countries. Partly because of more rigid social structures, the conservative influences of religious traditions and the sheer weight of rural poverty, the spread of modern mass education (higher education in particular) has lagged, creating a shortage of qualified technical, professional and managerial manpower in most of the less industrialized East Asian countries. At the same time, the problem of dealing with the surplus supply of poorly educated and unskilled workers remains to be solved. Wide differentials in wage and salary earnings between the two categories of the workforce are common. Individualism among workers, and in social institutions, has accelerated the substantial disparity in earnings.

In Thailand and the Philippines, surpluses of workers with higher education have emerged in recent years. This results partly from the inadequate attention paid by higher educational institutions to the characteristics of manpower demand and also reflects excessively high returns on investment in college and university education in these countries. There will be a narrowing of earnings differentials between the less and the better educated in the future, as is happening in most of the industrial countries where higher percentages of the population tend to complete college and university education.

As in the industrializing countries, household and corporate savings are high, owing partly to the high savings propensity among high income segments of the population, and partly to various tax incentives given to corporate savings. A well-developed network of banking and financial institutions, together with high rates of interest paid to depositors, has also contributed to high savings in these countries. But savings are less stable than in the newly industrializing countries because of commodity price fluctuations, and the utilization of savings is lower than in the industrializing economies. The extremely low levels of commodity prices of the last few years have reduced domestic savings in the primary commodity exporting countries.

Domestic savings tend to be utilized less effectively because of sharp business fluctuations, structural rigidities and regulatory interventions found in capital markets, and the conservative policies and practices of banking and financial institutions. A large number of indigenous enterprises and transnational corporations have been operating below capacity and the annual inflow of direct investment from overseas declined in the early 1980s. In some of these countries there has been an outflow of domestic savings because of continued uncertainties created by political instability and consequent economic crises.

In most of the less industrialized East Asian countries private-sector entrepreneurship has been restrained by highly protectionist, import-substitution policies whereby tariff and non-tariff barriers have protected domestic manufacturers from import competition, while at the same time making their imports of capital goods less costly under prevailing overvalued exchange rates. Social policies of some governments in the region, that give economic and social preferences to particular racial groups, while desirable from the standpoint of political equity, have reinforced social uncertainties among some of the non-preferred groups, causing them to invest elsewhere in socially more favourable places.

An extensive umbrella of government interventions in private-sector activities has been responsible for a passive attitude on the part of businessmen to innovation and productivity improvement. Governments in Malaysia, Republic of Korea and Singapore have therefore introduced policies to private state-owned corporations and statutory boards which encourage competition and greater efficiency in resource use.

CONCLUSION

The above discussion suggests that there are three growth and industrialization models in East Asia: the Japanese, the newly industrialized country and the near-industrializing country models. While these three models represent three different stages of economic development, each with a different set of structural, institutional and policy factors and characteristics, there are also differences within each model.

The structural, institutional and policy characteristics of these models are interactive, with each affecting the other two, but the interaction does not always produce the same result. When the structural and institutional characteristics of the two models and/or sub-models are not identical, even identical policy measures produce different results. The performance of more advanced countries can therefore not merely be copied.

When Japan pursued modernization in the Meiji period, the structural and institutional dimensions of several contemporary Western societies were studied. However, Japan adopted a set of policies quite different from those of the societies it studied to take advantage of the structural and institutional characteristics of the Japanese economy and society carried over from the pre-Meiji period. Similarly, while a new set of policies, together with radical institutional changes, were effected by the Allied Occupation Forces immediately after the Second World War, only those measures consistent with the basic tenets of Japanese society have survived to contribute to the attainment of national goals of rapid growth and structural transformation.

STEPHAN HAGGARD[*]

9

THE POLITICS OF
INDUSTRIALIZATION IN
THE REPUBLIC OF KOREA AND TAIWAN

Over the 1970s, export-oriented industrialization achieved the status of a new orthodoxy in the development community. Import-substituting industrialization had long been subject to criticism on theoretical grounds, but the sustained economic success of the East Asian NICs – Republic of Korea, Taiwan, Hong Kong and Singapore – provided empirical ammunition for the critics. In addition to reducing the bias against exports through realistic exchange rate policies and selective import liberalization, the 'outward-oriented' strategy has been associated with a broader array of economic reforms: encouragement of foreign investment, financial reforms and, in general, a rationalization of incentives to reduce price and factor market distortions (Balassa 1981a). Though the mechanisms by which increased exports lead to increased growth remain a subject of some uncertainty, these countries are taken to vindicate neo-classical prescriptions, 'taking off' as the result of policies that allowed them to more fully exploit comparative advantage. Despite their heavy reliance on trade, the East Asian NICs continued to do well during the international economic turbulence of the seventies. As the *World Development Report* (1981:26) summarizes, 'the flexibility that an outward orientation provides has outweighed the vulnerability that it risks' (World Bank, various years).

There is an unremarked puzzle in the attention given to the East Asian 'model'. If export-oriented industrialization is superior as a

* This paper has profited from comments by Chung-in Moon, David Steinberg, Robert Wade, Kym Anderson and Clive Hamilton.

strategy, why has policy reform elsewhere proved so infrequent and hesitating? Why do countries persist in pursuing 'irrational' policies? Why, to repeat David Morawetz's question: 'Are the emperor's new clothes not made in Colombia?' (Morawetz 1981).

The answer is to be found at least in part in the interaction between politics – both domestic and international – social structure and policymaking. While numerous studies have noted the correlation between policy reform and improved economic performance, virtually no attention has been given to the political and institutional setting in which economic policy is made and implemented.

Reform attempts are triggered by economic slowdowns, fiscal and foreign exchange crises that are themselves frequently the result of previous policy choices. Even when the failings of previous policy are widely evident, however, reform involves political risk and the shifting of benefits among different groups in society or sectors of the economy. At the extreme, as in the case of land reform, governments seek to change the fundamental social, political and economic relations in society. Yet even when the welfare losses associated with policy change are minimal or short term, political resistance can emerge from previously protected groups or from within the government itself. As Grindle argues:

what is implemented may thus be the result of a political calculus of interests and groups competing for scarce resources, the response of implementing officials, and the actions of political elites, all interacting within given institutional contexts (Grindle 1980:12).

This paper develops three sets of arguments about the political economy of export-led growth in the Republic of Korea and Taiwan, two countries which, despite numerous differences, have exhibited similar capabilities in sustaining growth-oriented policies. The arguments can be extended to Singapore and Hong Kong and it is hoped they are relevant to discussions of policy reform elsewhere.

The first argument concerns the political and policymaking institutions, and is applicable to all four of the East Asian NICs. Reform and the pursuit of consistent policy were in each case facilitated by political systems in which the economic policymaking process was relatively *insulated* from direct political pressures and compromises. In all cases, legislatures are historically weak or non-existent and other channels of political access and representation tightly controlled, even under nominally democratic regimes.

Economic policymaking was in all cases *centralized* in agencies with a strong 'technocratic' cast that could rely on relatively efficient, meritocratic bureaucracies for policy implementation. More importantly, policy decisions were given firm backing by political élites for whom economic performance was a central component of political legitimation, explicitly invoked in some instances to justify authoritarian rule. These political structures have given economic policy uncommon credibility, while permitting flexible responses to changing conditions. Bureaucratic infighting over economic policy has by no means been absent, but political élites have prevented the development of the ideological and institutional cleavages within the government which are common in many developing countries. This institutional configuration should also not be taken to imply the 'stability' of the political system as a whole, though this is frequently invoked as an explanation for rapid growth. While Taiwan has a highly institutionalized one-party system, the military's periodic involvement in the politics of the Republic of Korea has produced periods of popular resistance and political instability.

The second argument concerns the organizational strength and political power of key social groups. Those groups which have in other settings historically opposed market-oriented reforms – or industrialization itself – were organizationally weak and/or integrated into 'top-down', corporatist organizations in which the central government exercised significant authority. The organization of broad opposition coalitions was therefore discouraged. This social backdrop of relatively weak 'rent-seeking groups' or 'distribution coalitions' (Olson 1982) enhanced the ability of policymakers to launch and sustain policy reforms which, while having beneficial *long-term* effects, demanded the political control, or even elimination, of previously privileged groups. This relative political autonomy can be seen in the state's relationship with the rural sector, labour, and even with business.

Taiwan and the Republic of Korea are frequently cited as examples of the economic benefits of land reform. Land reform enhanced agricultural productivity while contributing to a relatively egalitarian distribution of assets and income. These land reforms were only possible, however, because of unique political circumstances, including support from the United States and, more importantly, the existence of political élites with limited or expendable ties to the traditional landholding class.

The political consequences of land reform were no less significant than the economic effects. First, land reforms reduced the influence of potentially anti-industrial rural élites. Second, the reforms secured a support base for both regimes in the countryside, pre-empting the possibility of rural-based revolutionary movements seen in China, the Philippines and Vietnam. Third, the reforms were accompanied by new organizational mechanisms, such as Taiwan's rice-fertilizer barter system, which expanded the state's resources by tapping into the surpluses generated by rising rural productivity and output. The state replaced the landlord, channelling resources into other developmental purposes, including industrialization.

For a variety of reasons specific to the individual cases, labour movements in Taiwan, Republic of Korea, Hong Kong and Singapore have been historically weak and, where periodically active, as in Singapore and the Republic of Korea, either controlled or repressed. Only in Singapore does the evidence suggest that the control of labour was *motivated* by the dictates of an outward-looking economic strategy. None the less, as Fields has argued more cogently, a wage policy that promotes market-clearing rates is an important ingredient for successful manufacturing export-led growth (Fields 1984).

The weakness of labour and the effective co-opting of the peasantry, coupled with periodic repression and economic success itself, contributed to a broader political phenomenon that differentiates the East Asian cases from most other developing countries: a relative vacuum on the left. While military governments and parties of the right have by no means been immune from the temptation to pursue nationalistic and interventionist economic policies, left-wing, 'socialist' and 'Marxist' parties and governments share a consistent ideological animosity towards the private sector, foreign investment and market-oriented policies more generally. It is an important irony that economic development in East Asia has been more egalitarian than in Latin America, South Asia or Africa where leftist and populist parties and labour movements have periodically exerted strong political and ideological influence on government policy.

The state's relative autonomy is not limited to labour, however: the political power of business is also circumscribed in the East Asian cases. It is clear that domestic entrepreneurs have benefited from market-oriented policies and industrial incentives and that all of the governments in the East Asian NICs are strongly supportive of business. It is also true that the functioning of a mixed economy rests on business confidence and an adequate flow of information between the public and private sectors. None the less, there is evidence suggesting that state élites retain significant independence from business in the formulation of economic policy. Government generally controls the channels of business access to decision-making and has played a role in both the Republic of Korea and Taiwan in establishing and financing some of the most important peak business associations. More importantly, the governments of the Republic of Korea, Taiwan and Singapore have retained important instruments for influencing business behaviour, some highly discretionary. Overlooked or downplayed in economists' accounts of the East Asian experience, these instruments were used to exercise *political* control over the private sector.

Political independence from business may in fact be a crucial factor in explaining the ability to shift policy in a more outward-looking direction. With their strategic location in the economy, superior resources and organizational capabilities, the private sector in the developing world is well placed to exploit political power for rent-seeking ends. As Bates has argued in discussing African industrialization efforts, 'government intervention, excess demand and the conferral of privileges are. . .all part of the political process by which public programs create vested interests. . .' (Bates 1981:99). Import-substitution in the Third World usually has deep political roots, while those efficient firms which could be internationally competitive are unaware of the fact, and thus politically 'unavailable' to act as a counterweight to inward-looking policies. Policy reform demands the *political* capability to break the cycle of rent-seeking and speculative economic behaviour by encouraging, easing and in some cases forcing, productive activity. The 'instruments' for achieving this are by no means limited to market incentives, however, and must be traced to the basic political relationship between the public and private sectors.

The third argument concerns a set of *international* political conditions which have had an important bearing on East Asia's development. Japan's defeat in the Second World War made the United States the pre-eminent political power in the region. The outbreak of conflict on the Korean peninsula extended the Cold War to Asia, altering the United States' strategic perception of the region and creating expanded political and economic commitments to the Republic of Korea and Taiwan. The growth of a regional economy in the Pacific Basin cannot be understood without reference to this underlying strategic context. As with the Marshall Plan in Europe, the extension of aid and the encouragement of regional economic interdependence served three interlocking purposes: economic reconstruction; buttressing the position of pro-American political élites; and cementing strategic relations with economic ties. Land reforms in both countries were actively encouraged and assisted by the United States, and import substitution in the fifties was financed largely by American aid.

American advisers played a role in the shift toward export-led growth as well. The conditions under which policy-relevant knowledge is diffused and successfully adopted are poorly understood. It is clear, however, that the political and aid ties between the United States and the Republic of Korea and Taiwan resulted in peculiarly close working relationships between United States officials and their local counterparts. These 'transnational coalitions' worked together in formulating policy, often in tacit collusion against other parts of their own governments. This is not to suggest that the aid relationship was always harmonious, particularly in the Republic of Korea during the fifties. Donors and recipients clashed over aid levels and specific projects, and the United States sought on several occasions to manipulate aid to achieve particular policy goals. Such specific efforts at leverage were probably less important in fostering reform than the recognition that long-term aid commitments would decline. This pushed the Republic of Korea and Taiwan to diversify their international economic relations, establish links with multilateral organizations and find new sources of foreign exchange through expanded exports and foreign investment (Steinberg 1984).

External security threats have also played an important role in the political and economic development of the Republic of Korea and Taiwan, though their importance in explaining policy reform is difficult to assess. Both the Republic of Korea and Taiwan are divided states, and competition with communist counterparts no doubt provides an additional spur to economic development. In Taiwan an outward-looking economic policy has become a self-conscious complement to foreign policy. The cultivation of a diversified set of economic relationships has partly substituted for formal political recognition. More importantly, perhaps, 'security' has been invoked, sometimes controversially, as a justification for the military's presence in the politics of the Republic of Korea and the continued dominance of politics by the Kaomintang (KMT) in Taiwan. The existence of external communist threats has the effect of limiting the range of internal political debate.

In the following section I explore the politics of industrialization in the Republic of Korea and Taiwan in more detail. In the final section I suggest some of the implications of the argument for current debates on policy reform.

INDUSTRIALIZATION IN THE REPUBLIC OF KOREA AND TAIWAN

There are underlying similarities in the growth paths of the Republic of Korea and Taiwan. Both were first integrated into a regional economy as primary product exporters under Japanese auspices. Both faced problems of reconstruction from war (twice in the Republic of Korea), and the severing of traditional export markets. These problems initially dictated an import-substituting course which was to last through the fifties. Both had extensive land reforms, though Taiwan's received more consistent government support. In the wake of slowed economic performance and the prospect of declining aid commitments, both undertook policy reforms that launched export-led growth at roughly the same time: in Taiwan between 1958 and 1962; in the Republic of Korea after the installation of a new government under Park Chung Hee in 1961. Both benefited from the auspicious timing of their reform efforts, entering world markets at a time of unprecedented trade liberalization and growth. Over the seventies and eighties, export-led growth entered a new phase. Both the Republic of Korea and Taiwan sought to diversify and upgrade into new product lines through a new, and contested, role for import-substituting policies.

Two phases of this economic history will be emphasized, since they are most relevant to current debates on export-oriented industrialization. First, what was the political economy of import substitution in the two cases? Second, what political factors help account for the policy reforms of the late fifties and early sixties? Some brief observations will be offered on the political and economic adjustments of the seventies and early eighties.

Republic of Korea

Initially Korea and Taiwan were integrated into the Japanese empire as 'agricultural appendages'.[1] Particularly after the attack on China in 1937, however, the Japanese and colonial governments worked closely with the *zaibatsu* in coordinating large-scale industrial investments in the Republic of Korea. The contribution of colonial industrialization to the latter country's subsequent development was limited by its enclave nature, the dominance of Japanese in management, the location of most heavy industry in the North and the over-use and cannibalization of plant during the war. These disadvantages were partly offset by the development of an indigenous entrepreneurial-managerial class, but the legacy of Japanese colonial administration was dictated by post-war politics – both domestic and international.

Upon the defeat of the Japanese, the left acted quickly to proclaim the aim of a People's Republic. Apprehensive at this development, the American military government sought to assemble a moderate centralist coalition, in part through urging and supporting land reform. The net effect of American policies, however, was to strengthen the right, particularly by bolstering the bureaucracy, police and new military forces (Cumings 1981, 1983). The Americans did nothing to dismantle the Japanese legal and judicial system, which tied the courts closely to the large and unreformed police forces, giving central authorities a flexible weapon in controlling opposition. Peasant uprisings in 1947 were suppressed and leftish unions replaced by unions with close links to the government.

Thus despite the democratic institutions imposed by the Americans, Syngman Rhee was able to maintain a significant degree of executive autonomy, aided by extensive resources in the hands of the bureaucracy. These included Japanese properties and influence over the distribution of American aid. The Korean war gave Rhee a reprieve from growing domestic political opposition, eased tensions with the increasingly sceptical Americans, further weakened

---

[1] On the economic effect of Japanese colonialism, see Pao-San Ho (1984).

the left and thus allowed him to consolidate his political hold.

Import-substitution had a particular political base. After the war, a link developed between the United States aid program, Rhee's Liberal Party and political supporters, and the bureaucracy. Large-scale purchases of *won* at the official rate by resident United States forces constituted a major incentive to maintain an overvalued exchange rate. Aid and control over import licences gave Rhee an instrument in securing the loyalty of the army, bureaucracy and favoured firms. Licences were issued on political grounds, permitting select companies to realize high returns through pure arbitrage. According to one study, the Liberal Party had interests in at least 50 per cent of all private projects receiving United States aid.[2] Under these conditions, there were few incentives to reform despite pressure from the Americans. Preoccupied with domestic political issues, Rhee consistently ignored efforts within his own bureaucracy to give greater coherence to policy, coming to rely increasingly on coercion to control political dissent (Lee 1968). GNP growth declined from a post-war high of 7.7 per cent in 1957 to 5.2 per cent in 1958 and 3.9 per cent in 1959. The decline in primary production was even more precipitous, with a growth rate of—0.9 per cent in 1959.

The visible corruption of the regime finally forced Rhee's resignation. Despite its reformist intentions, the new Chang Myon government could not control the rapid political mobilization and polarization among its own supporters. A politically ill-timed stabilization effort only increased the fragile regime's difficulties. The gradual disintegration of the Second Republic left a vacuum into which the military, with few ties to the existing élite, stepped unopposed.[3]

A number of institutional changes made during the period of military rule from 1961 to 1964 established the particularly statist orientation that has characterized development in the Republic of Korea since. The state was strengthened in two ways. First, a range of new instruments of economic control and planning were devel-

---

[2] See Kim (1975), US Congress (1960) and Jones and Sakong (1980). The best overview of the relationship between politics and economic development remains Cole and Lyman (1971). On the politics of land reform in the Republic of Korea and Taiwan see Hsiao (1981).

[3] The weakness of the Second Republican government and the process of political disintegration are described by Han (1974).

oped, including the creation of an Economic Planning Board that combined planning and budgetary functions with control over aid funds. Economic plans that had languished since the late fifties were pushed forward. The banking sector, later to be a key tool of government policy, was nationalized. Channels of communication and implementation within the bureaucracy were streamlined and a new emphasis placed on performance.

Second, despite the return to democracy in 1964, the government had become more *politically* centralized and insulated as well. Decision-making was centred in the executive and new organs of political control, most notably the Korean Central Intelligence Agency, came into existence. The organization of agricultural co-operatives and labour unions was centralized, with lines of authority running directly to the government. The distinction between the ruling party and the government was frequently blurred.

The consolidation of political authority, the centralization of policymaking and the political commitment to economic development did not of themselves constitute a strategy. All factions of the military saw economic growth as a primary task, particularly given the political problem of high levels of urban unemployment. Park even justified the *coup* on economic grounds. While Rhee could exploit long-standing nationalist credentials, Park was forced to stake his political legitimacy on improved economic performance.

Radical junior officers favoured a 'self-reliant' course emphasizing investment in basic industries. Following early economic failures that included indiscriminate foreign borrowing and an expansionist macroeconomic policy, the junta initiated a stabilization program in late 1963, one which neither the Rhee administration nor its short-lived successor was capable of pursuing. The hands of the economic technocrats were strengthened. The final economic reforms came in 1964, after the elections which returned Park to the presidency as a civilian. Spurred by the prospect of declining aid commitments, the reforms had their origins in the Economic Planning Board, working closely with and drawing intellectual inspiration from AID, the IMF, the World Bank and independent American advisers. Key measures included a sizable devaluation and consistent policies promoting exports, but had a distinctly political foundation.

Initially the junta had vigorously attacked the 'illicitly accumulated wealth' of several of the wealthiest entrepreneurs, but, as Kyung-dong Kim notes, it found itself in a dilemma:

the only viable economic force happened to be the target group of leading entrepreneurial talents with their singular advantage of organization, personnel and capital resources (Kim 1976).

A tacit alliance thus emerged between the Park regime and large domestic business, though one based on a new policy regime. By altering trade and exchange rate policies and manipulating access to credit, zero-sum sources of economic rent were reduced. Through a complicated system of incentives and supports, a free-trade system was simulated for those firms willing to export, while mechanisms such as generous wastage allowances provided additional payoffs.

This incentive structure was supplemented by a new *formal* institutional framework linking business and government, including government-controlled business organizations and monthly export meetings, chaired by Park himself, which allowed representatives of business to meet with government officials at the highest level.[4] More difficult to document were the *informal* networks linking business, government and Park's Democratic Republican Party. Financial scandals and a heated debate over financial disclosure in the early eighties seem to confirm the widely held belief that business has provided large amounts of money to the ruling party's political activities.[5]

The launching of the new strategy did not go unopposed. Opposition came to a head in the Republic of Korea–Japan treaty crisis. During the military interregnum, Park recognized that a successful settlement of the country's property claims would provide crucial economic resources to his regime in the short run while creating the possibility of future aid and investment. In late 1962 the military reached an agreement with the Japanese on a settlement that included a US$300 million grant, US$200 million in government to government credits and US$100 million in commercial financing. These new economic ties gave ammunition to those who saw the settlement as a capitulation to Japanese economic domination. For opponents of normalization, the treaty crisis reflected not only

[4] See Kim (1976:470). For the parallel phenomenon on Taiwan see Cole (1967).
[5] On the kerb market scandals and financial irregularities of the early 1980s and their connection to the political system, see *Far Eastern Economic Review* (21 May 1982, 20 October 1983, 10 November 1983, 26 April 1984).

popular anti-Japanese sentiment, but a battle over the legitimacy of the Park government itself. As J. A. Kim argues:

the primary issue throughout the political crisis in Korea was not opposition to Japan, but opposition to the Korean government, which it was feared would use financial resources from Japan to further consolidate its internal control, and in so doing would create an economic dependence on Japan in order to stay in power (Kim 1975:257; see also K. B. Kim 1971).

The opposition stressed themes that have remained constant among the political opposition in the Republic of Korea until today. These included the relative neglect of agriculture, the urban marginalism associated with extremely rapid growth, regional disparities among the provinces resulting from government favouritism and, perhaps most important, the political disadvantages of a strategy based on a close alliance between an insulated government, big business and foreign capital. Through the rapid growth of the sixties, Park maintained a solid, though not overwhelming, base of support. A referendum allowing him to stand for a third term in 1969 was hotly contested, both within and outside his own party. New signs of opposition appeared during the early seventies, including increased student protests, labour activism and, above all, the strong showing in the 1971 elections of Kim Dae Jung, who threatened to knit these disparate protests into a concerted movement. Invoking threats to national security, Park declared a state of emergency in December 1971 and in October the following year martial law was instituted, the constitution suspended, the National Assembly dissolved, the universities closed and all political parties banned. Over the seventies, amendments to labour legislation further strengthened the hand of the government *vis-à-vis* the trade union movement.

Institutional reform, the change in political leadership and the presence of the Americans were undeniably factors in the change of the economy. Park's interests in securing domestic legitimacy demanded a reversal of the drift of the Rhee period. The military was willing to give a group of incentive-oriented bureaucrats the political 'space' and strong support that had not been available under Rhee and Chang Myon. The ability to manipulate finance and other incentives eased the transition for firms which might not otherwise have realized their competitiveness. Control of labour facilitated the exploitation of comparative advantage. Park's domi-

nation of the political system permitted the economically important opening to the Japanese, while limiting the challenge from an
opposition at least rhetorically committed to a more 'balanced'
strategy. In short, a strong autonomous state appears central in
explaining the choice and implementation of the outward-looking
strategy in the Republic of Korea.

The Yushin Constitution opened a new phase in political life in
the Republic of Korea and was followed by a changed emphasis in
economic strategy, summarized in the ambitious Heavy and Chemical Industry Development Plan of 1973 (Haggard and Moon
1983). The plan was the direct result of executive initiative, with
important input coming from the heads of some of the largest
groups. The plan was prepared by a special committee around
Park, working closely with the industry-oriented Ministry of Commerce and Industry and bypassing more 'liberal' sceptics in the
Economic Planning Board. Changed economic conditions –
increasing protectionism, competition from other NICS and developing countries, the presumed disadvantages of light manufacturing – were cited to justify the Plan, but politics clearly played a role
as well.

A series of international events during the seventies, from the
rapprochement with China, to the American defeat in Vietnam to
Carter's human rights policy, raised uncertainties in Seoul about
the firmness of the United States defence commitment. Heavy industrialization appeared to be a solution for a number of problems.
It would build the basis for a domestic defence industry and lead to
a deepening of the overall industrial structure. As the first economic initiative following Yushin, it would assist Park's efforts to
legitimize the political system.

The numerous economic defects of the Heavy and Chemical
Industry Development Plan have been rehearsed elsewhere,[6] but
political consequences should be noted. While the nature of the
political system was the main target of the opposition in the late
seventies, the negative economic consequences of the heavy industrialization drive included an apparent erosion of equity, an
increase in business concentration and a corresponding neglect of
the small and medium-sized firms that constituted the backbone of
the light manufacturing sector. These economic imbalances contributed to an increase in labour conflicts, particularly over the

[6] For a critical review of the plan, see Korea Exchange Bank, *Monthly Review*,
December 1980.

course of 1979, when the opposition sought to make common cause with disaffected workers in several highly visible and politicized disputes.

The political system under Chun Doo Hwan exhibits a basic continuity with the Yushin period. In some areas, particularly in relations with organized labour, the Chun regime has been more control-oriented than its predecessor. New labour legislation enacted in December 1980 radically reduced the power of the national trade union movement. Labour union membership dropped sharply during the 1981–84 period.

The 'labour question' is tied to a broader set of issues surrounding the transition to democracy that go beyond the scope of this paper (Sung-joo 1985). It is certain, however, that as the transition to democracy proceeds, a new range of political pressures will be placed on economic decision-making that did not operate in the past. The opposition, strengthened by a surprisingly strong showing in elections in February 1985, has sought to exploit various economic issues, such as the country's relatively large foreign indebtedness. This has forced ruling party legislators to seek a greater voice in the making of economic policy.

The effects of renewed political activity are already visible. The consolidation of Chun's power was accompanied by a turn in economic policy back towards a more balanced course, with efforts to liberalize economic management on a number of fronts. These included trade liberalization, liberalization of foreign investment, the restructuring of the heavy and chemical industries and the return of the banking sector to private hands. These actions have elicited strong responses not only from the political opposition, but from private sector interests normally allied with the government and portions of the bureaucracy itself.[7] While there is a trend towards the liberalization of economic management, the actual pace of reform has been shaped by political and bureaucratic conflict, and is likely to be more gradual than policy pronouncements would indicate.

Taiwan

Unlike the Republic of Korea and Singapore, Taiwan exhibits a fundamental political continuity over the entire post-war period.

[7] These debates can be seen in various issues of *Business Korea*. See, for example, 'Who should be blamed?' (2(12), June 1985:20–2).

Initially more 'statist' in economic orientation than any of the other NICs, the KMT underwent a gradual change in economic orientation over the fifties under the combined influence of reform-minded planners, such as K. Y. Yin, and American advisers. Unlike the Republic of Korea, where many Japanese properties fell quickly into private hands, the KMT initially retained control of virtually all assets in the modern sector, creating resentment among the Taiwanese. The support and incentives provided to the private sector beginning in the fifties, however, permitted a unique division of labour to develop between the mainlander-dominated KMT which monopolized the political sphere and the private sector in which Taiwanese came to play a steadily increasing role. Over time, the KMT has successfully recruited Taiwanese into the party and bureaucracy but the country's centralized, one-party political structure has remained intact, and helps explain the ability of the KMT to sustain growth-oriented policies.

Taiwan was to begin its post-war history under highly insulated political leadership. On the mainland the KMT was deeply factionalized, but, as Lloyd Eastman notes, 'tended...to be neither responsive to political groups or institutions outside the government. It became, in effect, its own constituency' (Eastman 1974:286).[8] In the immediate post-war period, corruption, persistent fiscal deficits and irrational monetary policies compounded the economic problems of reconstruction and civil war. Over 1948 and 1949, inflation spiralled out of control, exacerbating the very social cleavages that had contributed to Communist successes.[9]

The more divisive splits within the KMT were attenuated with the move to Taiwan and Chiang Kai Shek's reassertion of control over the party. Taiwan's social and political environment was more tractable than that on the mainland in part because the KMT itself lacked any political connections with local landowning élites. Following an island-wide revolt in February 1947, key Formosan nationalists, Communists and other leftists were either liquidated, driven into exile or silenced, effectively limiting the scope of political debate for a generation.

The aim of recapturing the mainland provided the Nationalists with the rationale for the imposition of martial law which remains

---

[8] See also the study of the KMT's relations with business on the mainland by Coble (1980).
[9] See Chou (1963) on the trauma of hyperinflation.

in effect today. Martial law was used to justify controls on labour unions and student organizations, groups that had been important in undermining the KMT's authority on the mainland. An extensive internal security apparatus developed. A party reform, carried out between 1950 and 1952, strengthened internal party discipline, while also admitting early errors on the island, purging corrupt elements and moving to recruit Taiwanese into the party.

In the second half of 1949, American aid began to arrive, giving the KMT a crucial breathing space within which to consolidate its political power. Aid supported a series of economic reforms that reflected the painful political lessons the KMT had drawn from its experiences on the mainland. In response to the inflation the KMT had imported from the mainland, a successful stabilization program was launched with prices gradually stabilizing by 1954. A series of innovative financial reforms was initiated beginning in 1950, including real interest rates for depositors.[10] Conservative financial and monetary policies have been a distinguishing feature of Taiwan's development since.

The motivations behind the land reform of 1949–53 were political as well as developmental. Though land reform had long been a plank in the KMT platform, the party on the mainland had neither the interest nor the political capacity to carry it out. The land issue had, of course, been a key element in the mobilization strategy of the Chinese Communist Party. With few ties to local rural élites, with a large pool of beneficiaries and with a clear preponderance of force that could be deployed if required, the reform proved relatively smooth.

The regime's early commitment to economic development was also seen in a series of important institutional reforms. In 1953 an Economic Stabilization Board (ESB) was formed, chaired by the Governor and later by the Premier, with committees to deal with different development issues. A National Association of Industry and Commerce provided a channel for communicating government decisions to business.

In contrast to Rhee, the KMT maintained relatively harmonious relations with American aid personnel.[11] American advisers sat in

---

[10] The policy reforms of the early 1950s are described in Tsiang (1980).

[11] The most extensive discussion of United States aid to Taiwan is Jacoby (1966). Jacoby's views are challenged in Griffin's more critical assessment (Griffin 1973). See also Ho (1978).

on ESB meetings, and through the highly influential and autonomous Council on United States Aid (CUSA) worked with
American-oriented counterparts. The Joint (i.e. Chinese-
American) Committee on Rural Reconstruction (JCRR) performed a similar function in promoting land reform and
agricultural development. The influence of American aid on
Taiwan's development strategy should not be oversold, given the
importance in the government of reform-minded Chinese. In addition, there were periodic differences between the Americans and
the government on such issues as the speed of divestment of
publicly-held properties and the size of the military budget. None
the less, members of the American aid team did play a role in pressing for land reform, divestment of state-owned industrial properties, laws and policies providing incentives to private investment
and, perhaps most importantly, a greater autonomy for technocrats in the making of economic policy.

These changes in economic policy did not come without debate
within the party. Over the fifties, the economic strategy that
emerged was based on import substitution, a cautious strengthening of the private sector under state guidance, a gradual reduction
of the role of public enterprises in the economy and extensive land
reforms. The economic ideology of the KMT, based on Sun Yat-
sen's 'Three Principles of the People', combined private ownership
of the productive machinery, government intervention and control
of productive assets in an eclectic mix.[12] According to Sun, government provided a necessary countervailing force to the particu-
larism of private interests, but a wide array of policies could still be
justified by reference to the 'Three Principles'. Over the fifties, significant policy debates centred on the proper extent of the state's
role in the economy, and even on the priority that should be given
to the island's economic development given the government's
stated goal of recapturing the mainland. American advisers sided
with the economic reformers. While divestment of state-owned
enterprises and a loosening of economic controls was resisted by
conservative elements within the party, protectionist instruments
and sector-specific policies in industries such as textiles had the
effect of bolstering a relatively inexperienced private sector. In-

---

[12] For a study of Taiwan's development that emphasizes the role of ideology see
Gregor, Chang and Zimmerman (1982).

itially the main beneficiaries of government policies were mainlanders, but Taiwanese profited as well, including those large landlords who received shares in public companies as compensation for the land reform. Perhaps of even wider political significance was the fact that small Taiwanese entrepreneurs benefited, as owners of family factories and those previously engaged in commerce took advantage of the new incentives to move into manufacturing.

As import-substitution ran into market limitations in the late fifties, the Americans argued strongly for a new round of policy reforms, in part because of new aid priorities that called for 'self-sustaining growth', free enterprise and the gradual reduction of assistance. American aid officials explicitly sought to manipulate aid as a lever for reform, including a simplification of the exchange rate system, the relaxation and rationalization of some import restrictions and new investment incentives. The principle of devaluation coupled with selective trade liberalization was adopted as a conscious policy goal in April 1958, marking a new willingness to follow the counsel of liberal planners within the economic bureaucracy who were promising a greater degree of 'self-reliance' through the new economic program. The wider-ranging 19-Point Program, formally adopted in January 1960, incorporated a number of American and Chinese proposals, committing the government to encourage savings and investment, to remove controls and hidden subsidies, to strengthen tax administration, to improve the budget system, to develop money and capital markets, to establish a unitary exchange rate and to encourage exports.[13]

Despite its pro-business slant, the new strategy diverged from *stated* business interests. Exchange rate policies were strongly opposed, while some business élites had sought a cartelization of the domestic market and increased protection and subsidy. No evidence exists that business was a political force acting on behalf of policy reform, nor were business organizations consulted extensively prior to the shift in policy.

Once again the policy reforms were accompanied by institutional reforms within the government that gave greater leeway to technocrats, including the creation of the Council for International Economic Cooperation and Development which centralized previously

[13] For a detailed analysis of the reforms, see Lin (1972) and Galenson (1979).

dispersed planning activities and an Industrial Development and Investment Centre which, in the words of one government official, acted as a counterweight to the more protectionist Industrial Development Commission of the Ministry of Economic Affairs. As in the Republic of Korea, the move into international markets was aided by both price and non-price incentives to export, including import exchange entitlements, tax remissions, low-cost loans and subsidies by newly-invigorated sectorial industrial-cum-trade associations.

In summary, the KMT was in a strong position both organizationally and politically to concentrate on economic reforms and was powerfully motivated to do so by past political and policy failures. Financial stabilization was achieved early and import substitution was not allowed to develop political roots. The KMT used a combination of direct repression, land reform and economic incentives to consolidate its political hold while co-opting Taiwanese into the economic and political system, including the bureaucracy and party itself. While never developing a full-fledged corporatist political structure, the party did penetrate key social organizations, including labour unions, and acted to control autonomous political activity through a network of political cadres. Most political activity was restricted to the local level, and even encouraged there, where clan politics and factionalism absorbed opposition energies. The scope of effective, organized political opposition at the national level was thus even narrower in Taiwan than in the Republic of Korea, and, until the late seventies, was confined largely to a handful of dissident intellectuals or 'independents' lacking in effective organization.[14]

Only a few abbreviated observations can be made about the seventies and eighties, primarily by way of contrasting the choices made by the Republic of Korea and Taiwan. While it is difficult to generalize across a range of policies, Taiwan's adjustment strategy was more cautious and conservative than the Republic of Korea's. In the late sixties and early seventies, Taiwan also began to face a number of external economic vulnerabilities in connection with export-led growth. Similar arguments were made about the necessity of deepening the industrial structure.[15] While the Republic of

[14] On the political development of Taiwan, see Jacobs (1978) and Bogert (1984).
[15] This line of thinking was influenced by a series of reports commissioned by A. D. Little Inc. (1973a, 1973b).

Korea's push into heavy industry was largely the purview of an increasingly concentrated private sector, a new generation of state-owned enterprises emerged in Taiwan in sectors including petrochemicals, steel and shipbuilding. The government's share in gross domestic capital formation increased accordingly. By the late seventies, however, the cost of proceeding too far in this direction had been acknowledged. Greater attention was given to infrastructural investment in Taiwan than in the Republic of Korea through a succession of widely publicized 'major projects'. The shift to emphasize technology-intensive products also appears to have come earlier, though policy pronouncements must be weighed against actual performance in both countries, since both retained comparative advantage in such industries as textiles, apparel, shoes and electronic components well into the seventies. Differences are also visible in the style of adjustment to the oil shocks. Taiwan pursued a conservative 'gold standard' approach, maintaining a fixed rate for its currency against the dollar and adjusting through domestic deflation and curbing imports. The Republic of Korea did not deflate, but devalued, pushed exports aggressively and increased international borrowing.

The reasons for these alternative choices hinge in large part on economic variables, such as market size, and differences in the orientation of economic planners in the respective bureaucracies. Two broader political speculations may be offered, however. First, Park's concern with the domestic reception of the Yushin constitution might have made a deflationary macroeconomic course a less attractive alternative than it appeared in Taiwan, where inflation was traditionally viewed with alarm and where the political system seemed more solidly institutionalized.

Equally important, however, were the increasing external political pressures Taiwan faced over the seventies. These pressures cannot be overlooked in examining Taiwan's commercial diplomacy and economic policy. The American opening to China, the forced 'withdrawal' from the United Nations and the increased diplomatic rivalry between Taiwan and the People's Republic of China for diplomatic recognition seemed to threaten Taiwan's economic livelihood. In fact foreign investment dropped only briefly in the wake of American de-recognition, but the well-publicized withdrawal of such firms as Pan Am and the First National Bank of Chicago seemed to underscore the vulnerability of Taiwan's economy to outside political events. The effort to expand and diversify export markets and sources of foreign investment, towards Europe, for example, must be seen in part as a political effort to establish ties that would substitute for formal political ones (Simon 1980).

Taiwan's domestic political system also faced new pressures over the seventies. These included the growth of *tang-wai* or non-party politicians and the flowering of a number of literary and critical magazines that offered some loose organization to opposition forces. Several incidents, beginning with an election-related riot in the town of Chung-li in November 1977 and including the Kaohsiung incident in December 1979, raised questions about the political future of the island. As in the Republic of Korea, the legislature's formal powers remain weak, but in both countries a more vocal generation of young legislators have used the power of interpolation to scrutinize government policy, producing a wider public debate over economic issues. This issue of succession has also become the object of intensive speculation.

The KMT seemed better placed to engineer political adjustments than either Park Chung Hee or Chun Doo Hwan, however. The difference lies in the continuity of Taiwan's political order, which in turn must be traced to its highly developed one-party system. In the Republic of Korea, opposition parties and organizations have developed, within some constraints, during democratic interludes in the fifties, from 1964 to 1971 and in the brief opening in the wake of Park's assassination in 1979. This tradition of opposition was never erased during the authoritarian periods and neither Park nor Chun proved wholly successful in their efforts to legitimize authoritarian rule. In Taiwan, opposition figures have been allowed to act individually but opposition organization has been proscribed and potential opposition skilfully co-opted. In contrast to the KMT, neither Park nor Chun built effective party organizations that would link state and society. Unlike Taiwan, there is also virtually no organized political life below the national level that would provide a channel for grievances. These factors have made the political system in the Republic of Korea much more volatile, and call into question common explanations of growth that stress the importance of political 'stability'. None the less, Taiwan will also face political changes, including increased demands for a more democratic system, that are likely to widen the range of political pressures on the government, making the task of economic management more complex.

Comparative historical reconstructions such as those offered here suffer from several methodological weaknesses. The number of cases is small, the number of variables large. Since the different factors are difficult to weigh, there is the risk that favoured explanations are highlighted at the expense of others. One way of managing this problem is by widening the number of cases to include examples of failure as well as success or by attempting broader cross-national comparisons. While such efforts to be more systematic are certainly welcome, the findings are likely to be sobering.

The logic of the argument bears re-stating. It is assumed that policy reforms, including land reform, contributed to the acceleration of growth in both the Republic of Korea and Taiwan. Both the inclination to reform and the capacity to implement and sustain a new policy course were influenced by political factors. Many reforms that are economically rational entail short-run political risks, face entrenched societal and ideological opposition or depend on bureaucratic capabilities and technical expertise that are lacking.

Several policy implications might be drawn from these findings. First, since policymaking is the result of a balance of bureaucratic forces, institutional reform can be a prelude to policy reform. In both cases, policy reform was preceded by institutional changes that gave greater decision-making power to technocrats. Aid donors and international organizations might invest more in institution building and the training of technical personnel who will subsequently act as sympathetic counterparts within the bureaucracy.

Second, the political risk associated with particular policies must be weighed more explicitly. No policy that is seen to weaken the political authority of a particular government is likely to be implemented. In some cases, persuasion of the long-term economic benefits may be enough. Outside donors should play a more active role in explaining the logic of economic policies to citizens and leaders. In other instances, however, resources may be made available to reduce political risk and ease the transition. This 'insurance' function of aid has been given inadequate attention (Krueger 1981; Nelson 1984).

If outside donors must be sensitive to political risk, they must also be alert to political opportunity. Reform efforts are launched at crisis points when the need for economic policy change dovetails with the political interests of state élites. Political failure on the mainland jolted the KMT into a more developmentalist outlook: the debates of the fifties were more over the means of achieving that goal than the goal itself. In the Republic of Korea, the failures of Rhee and the initial efforts of the military government created *political* incentives for policy reform. It is crucial for outside actors to be sensitive to these crisis points when political leaderships are more open to wide-ranging reforms.

A final point emerges from the foregoing story. Accelerated growth was not the result of any one policy, whether import liberalization or exchange rate reform, taken in isolation. In both cases, reforms were extensive, and included not only changes in economic incentives but a more fundamental realignment of the relationship between the public and private sectors. This inclines me to a slightly pessimistic set of conclusions. While there are lessons to be learned from these cases, they might not be easily transferred from one political context to another. A number of historical contingencies, including extensive American interest and assistance and peculiar social and political structures, provided crucial background conditions for reform. Policy is unquestionably an important input to development. Overemphasizing it, however, can lull us into an unwarranted optimism by suggesting that economic development can be accelerated 'if only' the correct policies are put in place. Historical experience suggests the size of that 'if'. Positive theories of public policy and historical analysis of particular cases – in short, investigations of the policy *process* – are needed to supplement the wide literature on the *consequences* of policy reform.

10

ECONOMIC GROWTH IN THE
ASEAN REGION:
THE POLITICAL UNDERPINNINGS

The importance of political factors in influencing the economic performance of various countries (and, more specifically, of the ideological climate prevailing at any particular time) is so obvious and widely recognized as to need little repetition here. In the region we are considering, one has only to mention Indonesia's amazingly rapid turnaround after 1967 from an abysmal record of economic and administrative deterioration under Sukarno in the early 1960s towards the steady growth that has occurred throughout the Suharto era. In the Philippines, conversely, the economic decline of the early 1980s revealed that even an autocrat like President Marcos, backed by competent technocrats, experienced businessmen and lavish loans from foreign bankers, cannot keep economic growth plans on track if the political circumstances adversely affect their implementation.

But how do we proceed to the next step in analysing the political correlates of successful – or unsuccessful – economic performance? It is easy to identify various political factors which are *not* conducive to economic growth, political instability being the most obvious candidate for that dubious honour, although by no means the only one. Corruption, waste, extravagance and overregulation also take their toll. It is not easy, however, to determine what combination of factors *is* favourable to growth. One cannot even conclude that political stability alone is a sufficient condition, although something like it may be a necessary condition. When we start to consider why 'ASEAN's Other Four' (which I will hereafter refer to as the ASEAN Four, when Singapore is excluded from consideration)[1] have had such strikingly better growth rates than most other parts of the world over the last decade, except the NICs (Taiwan, Republic of Korea, Hong Kong and Singapore), as well as an impressive level of real 'development' in its broader sense, we are dealing with so varied a set of political factors in each case that the search for some explanatory hypothesis or model or paradigmatic explanation is peculiarly difficult.[2] None of them, moreover, has been free from political instability in some form or other during the last forty years. This was true even in Singapore before 1963. The search for causes will lead us far beyond simple correlations of that kind.

Previous writings on the political development of these Southeast Asian countries are not of much direct help in this. The major works on the politics of these countries were mostly written in the decades before the era of rapid growth. The political scientists working on them in the early post-war decades were mainly preoccupied with quite the opposite problem of explaining 'underdevelopment' in Southeast Asia, or were interested in the workings of the political systems there, which combined modern institutions like parties and parliaments with beliefs and behaviour patterns which were rooted in age-old traditions.[3] Others concentrated their attention on neo-colonialism and the dependency syndrome – that is not on growth as a success story but as a more dubious consequence of exploitation or repression, the 'development of under-

---

[1] Although Singapore is commonly categorized as one of the East Asian NICs ('the Gang of Four') and has enjoyed a rate of economic growth well in excess of 'ASEAN's Other Four' (the term is taken from Glassburner 1984), it is such an important element within the Southeast Asian world, particularly for the economies of Malaysia and Indonesia, that for some purposes we will need to make reference to it here, although for others it is more usefully categorized with the NICs. As I will not be giving any attention to Brunei, all references to ASEAN have to do with the pre-1984 ASEAN of five states only, not the present six.

[2] In order to avoid arguments about the perennial growth-versus-development issue, I must stress at the outset that I am here talking solely about 'growth' in the narrow sense of rate of increase in GDP, and no more than that. 'Development' in its ideal sense of course entails much more than mere growth of GDP.

[3] The major works on the politics of Southeast Asia relevant to this comment are: Kahin (1952) and Golay *et al.* (1969) on the region in general; Wertheim (1956), Feith (1962), McVey (1963) and Anderson (1972) on Indonesia; Wilson (1962), Riggs (1966), and Siffin (1966) on Thailand; Lande (1965) and Wurfel (1959) on the Philippines; and Pye (1962), Ratnam (1965) and Milne (1967) on Burma and Malaysia–Singapore. It was these works which established the basic parameters within which most subsequent political analysis has been conducted, although in some cases these have been modified by important later works, such as Crouch (1978), Girling (1981a) and Funston (1980).

development'.[4] Even in the Southeast Asian countries where economic growth was proceeding reasonably well in the 1950s and 1960s (e.g. Malaysia and the Philippines), political stability seemed at that time too frail to be taken for granted. Conversely, Thailand has frequently been described as politically unstable because of the frequency of *coups* there and the prominent political role of the military; yet Thailand has had considerable continuity of personnel and policies, as well as the consistently most impressive rate of economic growth of the ASEAN Four since 1960. More important, in my view, is the fact that Thailand's changes of government were merely superficial digressions within a political system which has been characterized by a high degree of institutional and élite continuity. In fact, élite cohesion is such an important underpinning to the various other characteristics of the Thai political system that I am inclined to stress it as one of the key factors, though a complex one, in that country's economic success story.[5]

By comparing the socio-economic character of the élites in the ASEAN countries and their relations with government, with foreign capital and with other classes in their respective societies, we can obtain a much better understanding of the reasons why some countries have performed better and others worse than others in the development stakes. Before I turn to the five case studies in detail, I will give some attention to the fast-growth NICs for the light they throw on this problem, giving particular attention to an analysis by Haggard and Cheng (1983) which I have found quite illuminating on the issue of class relations there and the roles of various élite groups. But it would be foolish to suggest that one can explain everything by reference to this one factor. I claim nothing more than that if we start to look for explanations along these

[4] The neo-Marxist and dependency theory literature on Southeast Asia has not, in my view, produced many works that have had wide acceptance or influence on scholarly rather than partisan grounds; among the best are Robinson (1982) on Indonesia; Hewison (1983), Flood (1976) and Elliott (1978) on Thailand; and Stenson (1976) on Malaysia–Singapore. Various articles in the *Bulletin of Concerned Asian Scholars* have also been useful, although they are often more tendentious than informative.

[5] The best illustration of this point, relative to the Malaysian situation shortly after the May 1969 racial riots, can be found in Wang (1981b) which provides an illuminating account of the complex interrelationships between the English-educated and Malay-educated among the Malay élite, the English-educated and Chinese-educated among the Chinese élite and the Indian community leaders. His discussion of the central issues of ethnic politics in Malaysia is a model of analytical rigour and informative detail.

Table 10.1 *Gross domestic product growth in ASEAN and NICs*

	Per cent per annum		GNP per capita 1960–82 (% per annum)
	1960–70	1970–80	
Thailand	8.4	7.2	4.5
Malaysia	6.5	7.8	4.3
Indonesia	3.9	7.8	4.2
Philippines	5.1	6.2	2.8
Singapore	8.8	8.5	7.4
Hong Kong	10.0	9.3	7.0
Korea, Republic of	8.6	9.1	6.6
Taiwan (GNP)	10.0	9.6	n.a.

Sources: *World Development Report*, 1982, 1984 (World Bank, various years); for Taiwan, adapted from Hsiung (1981: 134, 139).

lines, we will probably find many useful clues. We can push back the frontiers of our ignorance a little; but we are unlikely to discover complete enlightenment about causation. I am not proposing a definitive 'model' or paradigm of explanation, analogous to the abstract models economists use. Political scientists have to work with such a multitude of unquantifiable elements in their equations that to claim the geometrical or arithmetical precision beloved of economists would simply involve them in a wild goose chase. However, we can make a start by identifying the more important factors and taking into account some of the patterns of interaction that have occurred in different situations.

ANALYTICAL APPROACHES

Since so little of an analytical character has yet been written on the political underpinnings of rapid growth in the ASEAN Four countries I will approach this question by way of some attempts to analyse the success of the NICs in terms of policies and politics, some of which offer suggestive parallels and contrasts.

Little (1979a:449) provided one of the first and most comprehensive explanations of the rapid growth of the NICs and Japan in his essay on Taiwan. He considers seven frequently mentioned types of explanation, ranging from the character of their resource endowments to cultural affinities to being simply 'lucky in their circumstances'.[6] None of these, as he shows, provides an adequate basis for an explanation of why four such very different economies have had such uniquely high rates of growth: so 'The main part of any explanation must come from government and economic policies' (Little 1979a:465).

Little then examines four factors relevant to the latter heading, as follows:

Periods of very rapid growth and stable government have been contemporaneous...

Stability and strength go together, but the latter is most important for economic policies and planning... Good policies may not be immediately popular... time is not on the side of a government that faces strong opposition and periodic free elections...

Strong government is not enough. Many countries have strong governments but very poor economic performance. The government must also be determined to advance economic development. All these governments ... have perceived economic development as the primary means of establishing their legitimacy and consolidating their support. Development must embrace the mass of the people ... but it has not needed to be populist...

[Although these are all capitalist economies, with small public sectors]: The philosophy seems to be that a private company should not have a monopoly of intermediates used in further production... Also, there may be some fear of excessive private power (Little 1979a:466, 467).

Planning is flexible and in all four countries the price mechanism is accepted (in general) as an efficient instrument of resource allocation. All of them have very free labour markets (Singapore, however, does not) with the price of labour being determined primarily by supply and demand; there is little or no government interference in labour markets, neither is there labour legislation nor resort to collective bargaining.

Dealing specifically with Taiwan's industrial boom of the 1960s (for which 'it is hard to find any good explanation'), Little con-

[6] The seven factors commonly mentioned as part of the explanation of the NICs' success, most of which Little regards as far more qualified contributions than are generally recognized, are as follows: (a) that they were 'lucky in their circumstances'; (b) that their smallness has been an advantage; (c) that being islands or peninsulas makes for an outward-looking orientation; (d) that they were fortunate in their starting point as moderately developed ex-colonies; (e) that large foreign aid flows made a critical difference; (f) that the Vietnam war stimulated growth (mainly in the Republic of Korea, only indirectly in Taiwan); and (g) that cultural affinities and the influence of neo-Confucian value systems boosted growth.

cludes that it is largely accounted for by Taiwan's taking account of her one cheap resource, labour (Little 1979a:481), and 'there can be no doubt whatever that the main cause of the acceleration was the series of changes in trade and exchange rate policies' (ibid.:474). The new policies created a situation in which 'exports, but only exports, could be manufactured under virtually free trade conditions ... there is probably on balance no discrimination against exports' (ibid.:475–6).

It is this last factor, the lack of discrimination against exported manufactures, that Little tends to stress most, along with a variety of contributory factors, in his explanation of Taiwan's success, as also of the other three NICs. Few would disagree that at the policy level this has been a crucially important consideration, not found in many other developing countries, and in the ASEAN Four only in the form of export processing zones, as in Malaysia and the Philippines. But Little does not have much to say about other factors, including the political and social circumstances which have made it possible to carry through export-oriented policies in the NICs of a kind that would probably have aroused insuperable opposition in Indonesia, Thailand, or even the Philippines. He barely mentions the authoritarian, repressive aspects of the political structures of the NICs, which were particularly important in the early stages of their industrial development. While this aspect of the picture has often been overstressed by radical critics of these regimes, that is no reason for their defenders to ignore it altogether. It has been an integral part of the socio-political background.

That criticism could be made, too, of the analysis proffered by Hofheinz and Calder (1982), who deal with China, North Korea and Japan as well as the NICs, in their chapter on 'The patterns of benign growth'. While they tend to put more emphasis than Little on political and cultural factors, these are overshadowed by their stress on economic virtues of an old-fashioned kind.

Governments are 'leaner' here, with less than 20 per cent of GNP going to them in taxes. Revenues are put to good use in building up infrastructure instead of being wasted in redistributive policies or in 'unproductive desires for consumption'. They are all 'low-inflation, high-growth countries', which run balanced budgets and 'pay their bills annually without borrowing, either domestically or internationally'. They 'tend to run on cash not credit, as they always have traditionally, and this conservatism continues to inform public policy'. All have achieved high rates of employment and have pursued policies which have eliminated mass unemployment. They have devoted relatively small proportions of their budgets to welfare expenditures, yet have managed to avoid grossly regressive patterns of income distribution.

All these governments have achieved a reasonably high level of support from their people, according to Hofheinz and Calder; their populations support and trust government 'without relying on it or demanding too much from it'. The two authors say little about the respective significance of repressive political and judicial institutions or restriction of democratic freedoms, as compared with voluntary consent, in producing this acquiescence, apart from a brief reference in a section on 'Public and Private Power' to the East Asians' 'more positive view of organisation and government' and their belief that 'the state was responsible for the well-being of the people . . . not to dole out welfare but to create it'.

In all these countries there is a basic distrust of 'pure market orientation' and of the pursuit of private profit without due regard for the welfare of the community, also stemming in part from their Confucian heritage of ideas about the relationship of governments to private individuals. Growth has occurred there not because of an absence of 'controls on freewheeling business activity, but because governments have encouraged certain forms of economically profitable activity while discouraging others. The utopians of laissez faire will have to look elsewhere for their models', they conclude (Hofheinz and Calder 1982:37, 68).

That last sentence deserves emphasis, since the NICs are so often cited by advocates of 'small government' and the virtues of private enterprise as if these were the secrets of their success. Patently they were not, except perhaps in Hong Kong. The economic successes of these regimes have derived, on the contrary, from their ability to combine a high degree of government control over economic life – and substantial public sector activity in certain fields – with strong encouragement to the private sector. It has been their success in finding the right mix of public and private sector activities, appropriate to their circumstances and institutions, that has been crucial; and that is a matter of political judgment.

Johnson (1981) mentions four more narrowly political elements in the abstract model he puts forward to explain the East Asian high growth system. These are the importance of 'a heavy and consistent investment in education for all the people', a marked but never openly acknowledged 'separation between reigning and ruling' (in which 'the politicians reign and the state bureaucrats rule'), a strong commitment to 'market-conforming methods of intervention' in economic life, and the existence in all these countries of a pilot planning agency performing think-tank functions for their economies (Johnson 1981:11–14). Again there is little mention of the authoritarian or repressive aspects; the stress is nearly all on the output side of policymaking, not on who makes the inputs. What he means by the distinction between 'reigning and ruling' is essentially that the bureaucrats maintain political stability by 'holding off the demands of pressure groups . . . that would contradict or divert the main developmental effort and, by providing space for an élite, highly educated bureaucracy to operate', leaving the bureaucrats to 'respond to the needs of groups upon which the stability of the system rests (above all, the farmers) or forcing the bureaucrats to alter course slightly when they have gone too far'. I suspect that this is a rather idealized or oversimplified interpretation of these modern variants of an older Mandarin tradition in the four NICs, but that is a matter of secondary importance here. What is most striking about this analysis, however, is the fact that *none* of the four elements in Johnson's explanation could be said to be strongly evident in any of the ASEAN Four countries, except perhaps the last.

An explicitly political analysis of the success of the NICs which I have found more satisfactory in explaining their growth record and potentially more illuminating about the ASEAN Four is contained in Haggard and Cheng (1983). Because their analysis develops out of the tradition of dependency theory (as applied to the very different circumstances of Latin America), it is focused mainly on the respective roles and interrelationships of local, foreign and state capital in the development process. This is not the place to elaborate their argument and conclusions at length; but several points are of particular relevance here.

Their categorization of the NICs as 'insulated developmentalist states' is a useful one, for it highlights one of the key dimensions of difference between them and the ASEAN Four. Haggard and Cheng also show how in all the East Asian NICs 'growth coalitions' have been created which were favourable to the kinds of export-oriented industrial development policies pursued there and which were able to contain, suppress or out-manoeuvre other groups in those societies which were opposed to such policies (Haggard and Cheng 1983:44–5). Something similar has happened in the ASEAN Four since the 1960s, but the differences in this respect turn out to be more significant than the similarities, in my view, mainly because the political structures and class relationships have been so very different. Peasant organizations, the working classes and trade unions have been excluded from effective political action in the ASEAN Four countries over the last twenty-five years, as also in the NICs, although they had been very prominent during the earlier years of turbulent mobilization politics in the immediate post-colonial period. But to tell this story solely in terms of the re-pression of popular forces, as many radical interpretations do, is to overlook several more interesting and significant features of the changes that have occurred among the élite groups which consti-tute those 'growth coalitions'. Processes of class formation and rudimentary class consciousness can be discerned there as both a consequence and cause of these changes; but it is a class formation of a rather different pattern from that usually hypothesized by the more old-fashioned Marxists who have tried to deal with this phenomenon in Eurocentric terminology.[7] Haggard and Cheng have explored the complex and significantly different patterns of relationships that have emerged in the NICs between the newly emerging domestic bourgeoisie, foreign capital (an important ele-ment in each case, but not a dominant one), and the state, with its bureaucrats and technocrats and entrenched interests; all these ele-ments have been striving to manipulate government policies to serve their own purposes and have acquiesced in those policies because of their success in generating a dynamic economic growth process.

Haggard and Cheng go on to show how both the local business classes and 'the state' have managed to avoid being subordinated to the interests of foreign capital and the much overestimated multi-national corporations, having become strong enough to pursue national interests more or less autonomously. They stress that there is no single 'East Asian model' of development, for there are

---

[7] I dealt more fully with this question as it relates to Indonesia in a paper entitled 'Property and power in New Order Indonesia', presented at the Association of Asian Studies conference in San Francisco in March 1983.

striking differences in the growth patterns of the four NICs; nor do they attribute their success to the fact that all four have adopted outward-looking, export-oriented growth strategies. They point up certain similarities between them in respect of the sequences and timing of key transitions in their development trajectories. More-over, relations between the state, the indigenous business classes and the multinational corporations have changed over the course of time, in particular the relationships of dependency and rivalry between the latter. Foreign capital has not been able to exert as much power over the local business classes or the governments of these countries as a crude version of dependency theory might imply. The governments of the NICs have retained a sufficient degree of autonomy to pursue national interests without undue subservience either to the multinational corporations or to the local business classes, and have in due course become strong enough to act as their master, not their servant. In the cases of the Republic of Korea and Taiwan, both former colonies of Japan, but launched along very different growth paths by their experience of orientation towards the Japanese economy before 1945, embryonic groups of local manufacturers were able to become sufficiently well estab-lished during the early import-substitution industrialization phase of development in the 1950s to ensure that they could survive in the face of competition from foreign capital when the switch towards export-oriented industrialization occurred in the 1960s.[8] By the time foreign investors came on to the scene in a big way, the local business class was fairly well established and the governments took care that their interests were not blatantly subordinated. For these countries, the sequence and timing of the transition from import-substitution industrialization to export-oriented industrialization was also fortuitous in that it occurred at a time when world demand for the commodities they were able to export was expanding rapidly. Latecomers were not to find it so easy to penetrate industrial-country markets. The Republic of Korea and Taiwan were fortunate, too, in that their import-substitution industrial-ization phase did not last very long, certainly not long enough for deeply entrenched vested interests to become established and hos-tile to exposure to world markets.

[8] The Japanese colonial period of Taiwan's and Korea's early modernization and in-dustrialization is well summarized in Cumings (1984).

How and why did this come about? The story differs for all four of the East Asian NICs and would take too long to summarize here, but it is noteworthy that all four have had strongly authoritarian governments which are 'insulated' in various ways from pressures from below, from the broad masses of people. In this respect, they are rather different from most of the ASEAN Four, which, although also authoritarian in differing degrees, have had to remain responsive to popular pressures throughout much of the post-war era.[9] Their governments are shielded also against direct pressure from business groups, their policies being determined more by bureaucrats and technocratic specialists than by clamorous politicians or parties representing sectional interests. While the political arrangements have differed substantially amongst the four NICs, their socio-economic patterns have provided ample scope for both domestic capitalists and the multinational corporations to flourish there. Organized labour and left-wing politicians have been excluded from political power. Hence both local capitalists and the multinationals, being beneficiaries within this 'growth co-alition', have been quite willing to acquiesce in whatever policies or political arrangements these four quite authoritarian governments have devised.

Turning now to the ASEAN countries, we have one very useful discussion of the extent to which their governments are 'insulated' from pressures from below or from power groups within the élite in a study by Crouch (1984). His study is about the prospects for regional economic cooperation within ASEAN, and his major concern is thus about the degree to which these governments are able to pursue policies based on 'national economic criteria' and isolate themselves from the 'pressures of particular sectional interests'. In general his conclusions on this are pessimistic, but his analysis of the five governments and social structures, summarized very

---

[9] Indonesia and the Philippines experienced quite substantial periods of turbulent political mobilization after 1945, as did Malaysia to a lesser degree. Singapore had 15 years of mobilization politics and vigorous party competition before the PAP's electoral victory of 1963 paved the way for the elimination of opposition parties and the creation of a virtual one-party state. Thailand experienced varying degrees of quasi-parliamentary government with intense factional competition between 1945 and 1958, most of it dominated by the army-backed Marshal Phibul Songgkhram, but it could hardly be called democratic. Between 1969 and 1971, under Sarit and Thanom, only a brief period of very limited parliamentary politics was permitted.

crudely in Table 10.2, is directly relevant to our interests here. He rightly shows that the Singapore Government is highly insulated from pressures from both above and below, the Malaysian less so, the Indonesian Government impervious to pressures from below but not from above, and Thailand's government (since 1973) the most open to pressures from both below and above. In general I do not disagree with his conclusions on that score, although I diverge in some respects from his analysis of the situation in Thailand. Crouch describes the political system there as having 'a narrow social base' and rather uncertain long-term prospects of maintaining the present semi-parliamentary system of government, which he thinks would again be overthrown by the military, were it not for factional disagreements among the senior officers. The government is 'not able to formulate important policies relatively independently of particular business interests' (Crouch 1984:73). I am more struck by the fact that Thailand's rate of economic growth since 1960 has been the highest in the ASEAN Four, despite less favourable resource endowments than the others, and that its socio-political structure has been changing slowly but significantly from the 'bureaucratic polity' pattern predominating in the 1960s to something a good deal more pluralistic by the 1980s.

Crouch has much that is useful to say about the importance in these countries of the newly emerging urban 'middle class' (which he defines quite specifically) as a buffer against authoritarianism, corruption, unfairness and inefficiency. He sees such a class as much stronger in Singapore and Malaysia (the most highly urbanized countries in Southeast Asia) than in the others. I do not disagree with any of this, but I do not think we can formulate a satisfactory explanation of fast and slow growth in the ASEAN countries since 1945 simply along these lines, in terms, essentially, of broad socio-economic structures and their relationship to the political system. I agree with him about the need to look into the interaction of various classes in relation to the political institutions of each country (and into the processes of class formation which are taking place there in very different ways), but this is a nebulous area. We must take into account also the nature of the economic interests involved, the prevailing ideology and social ethos in each country – they differ quite remarkably from one to another – and the feedback effects of economic growth upon the political and social systems. In the case of Thailand, I believe the development of a commercial 'middle class' or bourgeoisie since the early 1960s

Table 10.2 *Governmental autonomy in ASEAN*

	Pressures from below	Pressures from above	Size and strength of middle class
Singapore	Government effectively insulated – little scope for working-class pressure.	Government insulated from pressure by local businessmen: clear separation between government and business groups.	Larger middle class than other ASEAN states, with stake in the existing order. Large working class seen as a potential threat.
Malaysia	More open to pressures, especially from Malay peasantry, than Singapore – some scope for pressures from below. But government becoming more autonomous.	More open to business pressures than Singapore, but better able to resist them than other ASEAN governments.	Fast-growing middle class, benefiting from government policies, hence generally supporting them.
Philippines	Relatively impervious to pressures from below since 1972 – indirect influence only.	Governments highly susceptible to pressure from élite vested interests, especially under Marcos's 'crony capitalism'.	Prosperous 'middle class' relatively smaller than Malaysia, too weak to resist authoritarianism. 'Oligarchy' (land-based) remains influential.
Thailand	Increasingly open to pressures from below since 1973.	Also highly susceptible to business pressures: close ties between business and government (especially pre-1973). Autonomy of technocrats relatively low.	Middle-class beneficiaries of development still smaller than Malaysia or Philippines – a 'tiny' proportion of total population.
Indonesia	Impervious to pressures from below (except on Islamic issues).	Highly susceptible to pressures from élite. Close ties between military leaders and business interests.	Very small middle class and still relatively powerless on key economic issues, corruption, arbitrary power etc.

Source: Adapted from Crouch (1984).

has changed the general structure of the political system quite significantly, as Crouch himself shows. The main divergence between his approach and mine is that he is inclined to view 'pressures from above' as an inhibition upon the economic 'rationality' of the technocrats, whereas I am less inclined to believe this. My main purpose is to explain the political basis of rapid economic growth, which was not his aim; hence I will be looking at the characteristics of the 'élites' of these countries in a broader, more diffuse sense than Crouch.

GROWTH RATES OF ASEAN AND NEWLY-INDUSTRIALIZED COUNTRIES

There are basically two questions to be answered. Why have the growth rates of the ASEAN Four been generally higher since the 1960s than those of most other developing countries? And why have they not achieved such high rates as the NICs? It is easier to suggest specific answers to the second question, by reference to various handicaps upon them, whereas the first begs all the difficult and basic questions touched on above.

Part of the answer to the first question may be, moreover, an historically specific rather than a general explanation. The ASEAN Four and NICs alike were all lucky in their timing in the 1960–70s. Various circumstances combined to favour them in the crucial early stages of industrialization, helping to get the momentum of growth started, particularly the 'pull' effects of Japan's rapid growth and the great outflow of Japanese capital that followed after 1970. The stimulus given by United States off-shore purchases during the Vietnam war also gave an important boost to Thailand and Singapore at a time when it was crucial. The oil boom gave a major fillip to Indonesia and Malaysia. In addition, access to world markets was not the problem then that it has become in the 1980s. This does not in itself explain why the growth rates of the ASEAN Four have been so much higher than those of Latin American countries which squandered opportunities instead of seizing them, but it does underline the importance of having such opportunities. It also reminds us that the causes of rapid growth may have been, at least in part, contingent and temporary rather than structural and enduring, a thought worth remembering as their growth rates turned down significantly in the hard times of 1985–86.

To explain why the ASEAN Four have not achieved the phenomenally high growth rates of the NICs, it is sufficient to note the following factors which weighed upon them:

(*a*) *Size and degree of urbanization.* The ASEAN Four have all had large rural hinterlands to draw into the orbit of the modern, capital-intensive commercialized economy, whereas the NICs were relatively small and if not already highly urbanized rapidly became so.[10] Growth rates in agriculture have rarely exceeded 4–5 per cent per annum.

(*b*) *The legacies of colonial rule.* The economic structures and policies inherited from the former colonial rulers have had distorting effects, inappropriate to the requirements of rapid growth in the modern world and have had to be changed in the ASEAN Four countries (but much less so in the NICs), sometimes at very high economic or political costs.

(*c*) *The ambivalence towards foreign capital and the economic nationalism associated with those legacies have at times posed difficulties for governments and constraints upon them, varying in intensity from one to another.* The dominance of British capital in Malaysia until the late 1960s and of Dutch in Indonesia until 1957–58 had no parallel in any other ex-colony. In the Philippines, United States capital had a symbolic and psychological significance far in excess of its actual quantity.[11]

(*d*) *The dominant position of Chinese businessmen.* This has been an issue of great sensitivity and sometimes politically explosive potential in all the ASEAN Four countries. None of the NICs has ever had to cope with anything like this problem. The presence of the various Chinese minorities in Southeast Asia has been a mixed blessing.[12] While their entrepreneurial talents have been beneficial in contributing to the opening up of regions and societies where indigenous enterprise and capital were scarce, the social and political problems associated with the Chinese minorities are quite

---

[10] The levels of urbanization in Southeast Asia, except in Malaysia, are low even by Third World standards (Jones 1975).

[11] On United States capital in the Philippines, see Golay (1966); on the other Southeast Asian countries, see Golay *et al.* (1969).

[12] On the Southeast Asian Chinese, see Somers-Heidhues (1974) and papers from a conference of the ANU's China and Southeast Asia Project on 'Changing Identities of the Southeast Asian Chinese', June 1984, by Wang Gungwu and J. A. C. Mackie.

disproportionate to the numbers involved because of their higher socio-economic status. All four governments have at times sacrificed efficiency-maximizing considerations to the imperatives of economic nationalism involving measures disadvantageous to ethnic Chinese. Fortunately, measures of this kind have been less blatantly discriminatory over the last twenty years or so (except in Malaysia) than in the earlier post-war years; in fact, most of the heat has gone out of the problem in Thailand and the Philippines. However, it will take a long time before it ceases to be a constraint upon government policymaking in Indonesia and Malaysia, and it is because of the post-colonial significance of the ethnic Chinese, as well as of foreign capital, that economic nationalism remains a pervasive force in the ASEAN Four.

(*e*) *Domestic capital formation*. Domestic savings rates have been high in NICs, but relatively low in the ASEAN Four – except in so far as the local Chinese businessmen have been able to mobilize capital among their own kinsmen. Hence the local business classes have tended to rely more heavily upon the state for bank credits and subsidies than their counterparts in the NICs. The political and ideological implications of this are significant. Such businessmen are not likely to be attracted towards economic doctrines redolent of *laissez-faire* or more competitive market forces, especially if the main beneficiaries are likely to be foreign investors or the local Chinese.

THE FIVE ASEAN COUNTRIES

In dealing with these countries individually, I have kept in mind the factors I have been discussing over the last few pages. However, I have not attempted a tight schematic analysis in the brief space available, but have tried to bring out the key socio-political factors relevant in each country to the overall questions about why growth has been fast in some places and at various times, and slow in others. I am primarily interested in élite consensus or fragmentation in all this, and their effects upon government policies.

Thailand

Thailand is by no means the richest or best-endowed country in ASEAN, but its overall rate of growth since 1958, when an army-backed government under Marshal Sarit assumed power by *coup d'état*, has been faster and steadier than that of any other ASEAN country except Singapore: 8.4 and 7.2 per cent per annum in the 1960s and 1970s. This has given a 1960–82 per capita rate of increase of 4.5 per cent, slightly better than Malaysia's rate and far better than the Philippines', both of which started from a higher level and have significant advantages in natural and human re-source endowments. Thailand's average per capita income was less than half that of the Philippines in 1960 but had risen above it by 1984/85. This is quite an impressive record for a country whose prospects appeared far from promising in the late 1950s, after a decade of unimpressive economic performance and apparent pol-itical instability.

Four factors must be mentioned in any explanation of this suc-cess story: agricultural diversification; the development of a manu-facturing sector with a strong export orientation; generally cautious, prudent financial management; and a gradual process of change in the socio-economic basis of the political system generally, as a more thoroughly capitalist bourgeoisie begins to emerge there.

Agricultural diversification has been the main source of Thai-land's high growth rate. It was spurred initially by an extensive road-building program, particularly in the poor, dry Northeastern region. The land frontier has been steadily pushed back in many parts of the country, although there are signs that the natural limits (under present technology) are now being reached. But whereas Thailand used to depend on four main products for its export earn-ings (rice, rubber, teak and tin) these have been supplemented since 1960 by corn, kenaf, sugar, cassava, oil-seeds and fruits, and by manufactured goods. Agriculture still accounts for over 50 per cent of Thailand's exports, although as a fraction of GDP it declined from 40 to 28 per cent between 1960 and 1977. Without this increase of output in the agricultural sector and the redistri-bution of resources towards the urban and manufacturing sectors since 1960, Thailand's rate of growth could not have been nearly as rapid (see Chapman 1984).

At the same time, light manufacturing industry developed stead-ily at a rate of over 11 per cent per annum between 1965 and 1983, partly under the stimulus of foreign capital inflows in the Sarit-

Thonom years (1958–73). Although the share of manufactures in GDP increased only from 14 per cent in 1965 to 19 per cent in 1983, exports of manufactured goods increased sharply between 1960 and 1981, from 2 to 27 per cent of all exports. At first the government followed an import-substitution industrialization policy based on high tariff protection, but a gradual change towards an export-oriented strategy occurred during the 1970s.[13] The manufacturing sector has never played anything like the same role as an engine of growth, however, as it did in Taiwan and the Republic of Korea. Many of Thailand's industries are still relatively inefficient and dependent on support or disguised subsidies from the government. There is a heavy reliance on imported equipment, technology and raw materials, while much of Thailand's industry tends to be capital-intensive rather than labour-intensive. Wages in the manufacturing sector have not constituted a major stimulus to growth and new investment; in fact, real wages appear to have declined since the mid-1970s, although they had been rising before that. Despite those shortcomings, however, manufacturing has been an important field of activity for Thailand's newly emerging capitalist class, so its socio-political significance has been very great.

The kind of generally cautious, conservative form of financial management and macroeconomic policy generally practised by the Thai government (until the early 1980s, at least: public-sector borrowing has increased markedly in recent years) has not always proved conducive to economic success in other countries. But in Thailand it has kept the country's currency generally strong, foreign exchange reserves healthy and the inflation rate low, all of which encouraged private sector investment. Funds borrowed from abroad have generally been put to productive use, not to show-piece glamour projects, as in the Philippines. The influence of Thailand's more technocratically-oriented and competent civil servants is said to have increased perceptibly over recent years. Also, the levels of professionalism, rationality and predictability in public administration appear to be much higher than they were in the 1950s, when policymaking was an intensely political battlefield

[13] For more details on the shift from import-substitution industrialization to an export-oriented industrialization strategy in Thailand, see Akrasanee (1980) and Hill and Jayasuriya (1985). The statistics on manufactured exports are from *World Development Report*, 1984:236 (World Bank, various years).

for infighting between rival military-bureaucratic cliques. While the extent of this change should not be exaggerated and some commentators are sceptical about it, the changing character of the political system does appear to have enhanced the influence of Thailand's technocrats and reduced that of the former cliques, as we shall see.

The political change can be characterized as a shift from a thoroughgoing 'bureaucratic polity' dominated by the armed forces and authoritarian generals in the 1950s to a more diversified and pluralistic society in the 1970s, with an emergent but still weak capitalist class and a semi-parliamentary form of government. The latter, although still far from full democracy, is more clearly on the way towards it than the country was before 1973. Under the authoritarian regimes headed by Phibul, Sarit and Thanom, prior to the brief 'democratic experiment' (1973–76), representative institutions and civil liberties were severely curbed. The exercise of political and economic power was earlier held tightly in the hands of a set of interlocking military–bureaucratic cliques and factions which controlled a host of government-owned businesses run by the various ministries. These constituted an important source of patronage, spoils and corruption for the officials involved. Although the military leadership and the civil bureaucracy were formally distinct, they were closely linked both in the exercise of their official powers and in their private business dealings. Many were also connected by family ties, for nearly all came from the small network of old aristocratic–bureaucratic families which had provided the country's senior civil servants and military officers throughout the twentieth century.[14] Outside this élite circle, there was, prior to 1960, virtually no autonomous sphere of political activity, no indigenous 'capitalist class' or group of rich peasants, although there was a substantial group of ethnically distinctive businessmen of Chinese origin, whom I will refer to as the Sino–Thai, who were powerless and vulnerable.[15]

Thailand's political system was categorized as a 'bureaucratic

---

[14] On the structure of Thailand's upper class, see the contribution of Silcock and Evers to Silcock (1967); also Girling (1981a) and Hewison (1981, 1983). Even so ardent a champion of Thailand as Silcock (1967:87) wrote of 'an administrative élite with a rigid class structure and characteristics only moderately favourable to economic development'.

[15] The classic treatment of the Chinese minority in Thailand is in Skinner (1957, 1958); see also Szanton (1983) and Mackie (1985).

polity' by Riggs in 1964 and for many years that term seemed entirely appropriate.[16] There was virtually no independent sphere of representative or participatory political activity outside the ranks of the bureaucracy between 1958 and 1973. The political infighting of the bureaucratic cliques and factions virtually *was* the politics of Thailand. The participants were nearly all members of the traditional aristocratic–bureaucratic élite, which was not significantly opened up to newcomers by the adoption of meritocratic principles and the expansion of higher education until the 1960s. Unlike the situation in more pluralist democratic societies where political forces generally reflected the distribution of social and economic forces in the society at large, Thailand's political system seemed to represent a reversal of that state of affairs. Political power was the source of patronage, licences and economic opportunity. The Sino-Thai capitalists were regarded by Riggs as mere 'pariah entrepreneurs', not true capitalists, because their wealth and property did not constitute an independent source of power. Riggs was utterly pessimistic that in such a society the business community could ever give birth to 'a coherent middle class capable of organizing itself politically'.

Twenty years later, it is clear that Thailand's 'bureaucratic polity' has gradually changed in two significant respects. Something like an independent 'middle class' has begun to emerge in Thailand, and the political system has become more pluralistic, less authoritarian and almost a 'quasi-democracy', while the behind-the-scenes influence of the armed forces, although still considerable, has been much reduced. The political parties which sprang up during the three tempestuous years of the 'democratic experiment' have become too strongly established to be swept away. The two prime ministers since 1978, Generals Kriangsak (1978–80) and Prem (1980–), hold office as much by their ability to manipulate party support in parliament as their predecessors did through their ability to manipulate factional support in the army.

Several elements in the cluster of social changes which have accompanied this political transformation deserve comment. A distinct 'middle class', or capitalist bourgeoisie, in Thailand, has

---

[16] The work of Riggs (1966) was for a long time regarded as the most authoritative treatment of the 'bureaucratic polity' theme, along with the more prosaic but equally valuable work of Siffin (1966); the changes in the system since the 1960s are well summarized in Girling (1981a, 1981b).

begun to emerge, the very phenomenon that Riggs thought imposs-ible.[17] This has occurred partly because of the growth of a dozen or so very large, powerful Sino-Thai business conglomerates and partly because the ethnic distinction between the Sino-Thai and the few Thai indigenous businessmen has become blurred almost to the point of insignificance. The successful integration of the Sino-Thai minority into Thai society has done more to eliminate the signifi-cance of the ethnic boundary in Thailand than anywhere else in Southeast Asia. Simultaneously, the very considerable business interests of this predominantly Sino-Thai capitalist class have strengthened the pluralistic character of the new political system. There are still business and social links between many of these big businessmen and key bureaucrats and politicians, but the bureau-crats and military officers no longer hold the whip hand in the way they used to. Social and educational mobility within Thailand's urban society have also been changing the character of the élite rapidly over the last twenty years. Its aristocratic features have declined in importance and its meritocratic–technocratic aspects have come more prominently to the fore.

The large corporate business empires which now dominate the modern, commercialized sector of the Thai economy are highly diversified in their investments. Some exercise indirect political influence through the particular political parties they support or through personal contact at the élite level. But the political links are of a very different kind from those described by Riggs and Wilson in the 1960s, when a small number of army-based cliques had quasi-monopolistic control over whole industries (rice trading, textiles, sugar, the Bangkok 'pork monopoly', etc.). Economic power at this level is more diffused than it was, despite the exist-ence of these huge structures – or perhaps because of the elements of countervailing power they have created in the socio-economic system. This is not to say that vested interests have disappeared by any means, or lost their political clout. But no one or two clusters of politico-economic power can any longer dominate the entire system, as they did twenty or thirty years ago.

Because of these changes, Thailand's politico-economic system

---

[17] Hewison (1983) has dealt extensively with this topic; a condensation of his data on the financial élite of Thailand can be found in Hewison (1981). Direct foreign investment has been a relatively small fraction of gross investment in Thailand (Hill and Johns 1985: Table 2).

has ceased to be the essentially inefficient and patronage-dominated structure it was in the 1950s; it has become a relatively open, competitive, pluralistic and dynamic one. (There are still many pockets of inefficiency, of course, but the system no longer revolves around them.) This seems to be in large part because the government itself has directed its policies towards opening up wider opportunities for private-sector activity and towards eliminating or minimizing the semi-monopolistic bureaucratic-business field which Riggs saw as the besetting evil of the bureaucratic polity. It has been an extraordinary transformation in a country with such a narrowly circumscribed sphere of party political life.

All this has occurred within a framework of considerable ideological and social cohesion at the élite level, something that has been quite unlike, for example, the highly fragmented Indonesian post-independence élite. Not having been severely disrupted by direct colonial rule and the traumas of war or the decolonization process, Thailand's élite has maintained a high degree of continuity, cohesion and also adaptability. It has been a relatively undifferentiated élite, with blurred lines of distinction and status between the old royal and aristocratic families, and the new bureaucratic, military or educated middle-class families who have achieved upward social mobility in the twentieth century. It has even been able to incorporate wealthy Chinese businessmen into the fold without undue strain. Its ideology is extraordinarily conservative, anti-Communist and yet eclectic, with the trilogy of 'King, Nation and Religion' almost unchallenged at its core (Girling 1981a: 208–13). It is very different from the essentially capitalist, property-owning élite in the Philippines (few élite families in Thailand own property on that scale, apart from the Sino-Thai businessmen), from the essentially bureaucratic élite of Indonesia and from the aristocratic-bureaucratic Malay élite, which has the most in common with it. The essential stability of the Thai political system and social structure, barely ruffled by periodic changes of government and military *coups*, has been largely due, I believe, to this underlying élite cohesiveness.

To that extent, it might be appropriate to apply the Haggard–Cheng term 'growth coalition' in a loose sense to the combination of bureaucrats, businessmen, military officers and technocrats who have been responsible for shaping Thailand's economic strategies over the last twenty years or more. They have been in broad agreement about the goals and methods associated with the government's development strategies, and they are in some respects a loose 'coalition'. However, Thailand could certainly not be categorized as an 'insulated developmentalist state', similar to the NICs, since its government has had to be responsive to extra-bureaucratic and extra-élite pressures (except, perhaps, during the most authoritarian years of Sarit and Thanom) and to vested interests within the élite, especially since the opening up of the political system after 1973.

The Philippines

If Thailand has been an economic success story despite its initial disadvantages, the Philippines has been a failure despite its great initial advantages. It is tempting to lay the blame for this solely on President Marcos – and on his wife and family with their vast wealth and the business interests acquired while in office – or on the system of inefficient 'crony capitalism' he created after 1972 under his authoritarian martial law regime. The ultimate responsibility for what has happened since then must, indeed, be borne by Marcos, but as an explanation of the country's poor economic performance, it is insufficient to point the finger only at him. The Philippines economy had not been performing well in the 1960s, either, and its growth rate increased considerably after 1972, so he or his policies must be entitled to some credit for that. On the other hand, the political turbulence which followed the assassination of Benigno Aquino in August 1983 and precipitated the acute economic crisis of 1984 can be largely blamed upon the President and the despotic one-man rule he established. Some critics would argue that the troubles of the 1980s are a direct and inevitable outcome of mistaken policies pursued earlier, but explanations of this kind tend to be excessively mechanistic or moralistic.

The analytical difficulty in this case is to determine which of many contributory factors should be given priority as the most crucial part of the explanation of the poor economic performance of the Philippines since independence. The problem needs to be tackled at several levels. The 'contingent' elements in the situation, such as the wasteful prestige projects, the extravagances of Imelda Marcos, the excessive foreign borrowing and the unproductive uses to which that money was put have undoubtedly helped to make a weak economy much weaker and more vulnerable. A wiser or stronger autocrat might have averted many of his country's troubles by pursuing more forward-looking policies. But if we look deeper for the more 'basic' structural causes of the poor economic record of the Philippines, it is clear that they stem back to the decade before Marcos became President. He may be criticized for not rectifying more vigorously the inefficient industrial sector established behind protectionist barriers in the 1950s, the chronically overvalued exchange rate, the constant flight of capital to safer lands, and the capital-intensive character of so much investment in nearly all sectors of the economy, but he cannot be held to be solely responsible for them. There is also a third level of analysis which goes beyond the shortcomings of any one man or his policies to some feature of the basic socio-economic structure of this country, the most sharply stratified society in Southeast Asia.[18]

Why is it that this country which seemed in the 1950s to have so many advantages over its neighbours in the development stakes has been less successful than they have in coming to grips with the modern world and the imperatives of change? Why have so many wealthy Filipinos invested their money abroad, or so many well-educated middle-class Filipinos left their country to seek employment elsewhere? There must be something profoundly wrong with a society where these things happen; perhaps it is a loss of confidence in its future. I suspect the answers have something to do with the character of the Filipino élite, the distribution of property there and an unusually bad case of 'urban bias' in the redistributive effects of government policies, to which we will return later in this paper. Paradoxically, although it is the most thoroughly capitalist society of the ASEAN Four, the Philippines has not coped well with either the capitalist mode of development or issues of social justice, welfare or economic adjustment.

The most deep-seated socio-economic problems of the Philippines can be traced back to the ways in which the country's landed élite contrived to maintain their economic and political hegemony

---

[18] Good accounts of the social structure of the Philippines and of the socio-economic basis of the élite are given in Wurfel (1959), Lande (1965) and Hollensteiner (1963); for useful local studies, see Larkin (1972) and McCoy and de Jesus (1982). The largely Sino-Mestizo origins of the Filipino élite as it emerged in the eighteenth and nineteenth centuries are most fully outlined in Wickberg (1965).

during the 1950s. After the defeat of the insurgency led by the Huk-balahaps and the Philippines Communist Party between 1948 and 1953, the Philippines experienced quite impressive rates of economic growth throughout that decade. The manufacturing sector, in particular, developed rapidly in those years behind the protective walls of exchange controls and an over-valued peso. This contributed to a socially important phase of investment diversification by large numbers of the wealthier élite families in the Philippines out of their traditional base in rural property and the professions into industrial and commercial activities (see Golay 1961; Carroll 1965; and Doronila 1985). The deregulation of imports and exchange controls introduced by President Macapagal in early 1962 marked a sharp end to this strongly protectionist phase of industrialization, ushering in a difficult period of economic and social readjustment in the 1960s, during which no sector of the economy or social class prospered particularly well. But this was the period when a new industrial élite began to emerge in the Philippines (and a new set of vested interests), largely as a result of diversification of the old landed élite into urban investments. Disinvestment of United States colonial-era capital almost certainly out-weighed new investment in this period, while there was relatively little inflow of Japanese capital prior to the 1970s.[19] A flurry of student radicalism and increasingly strident economic nationalism marked the years 1969-71, during which a special Constitutional Convention was elected to consider the possibility of revisions to the 1935 constitution. By declaring martial law in September 1972, however, on the basis of alleged (and apparently trumped-up) Communist threats to the security of the country, President Marcos aborted the proceedings of the convention and assumed sweeping autocratic powers. He was subsequently constrained by little more than the cosmetic changes brought about by the creation of a National Assembly (*Batasang Pambansa*) in 1978 and the formal abolition of martial law in 1981.

What went wrong? The answer most commonly given is that the country very early became 'a classic case of the "Import Substitution Syndrome" ... based on expansion of production of consumer goods for the domestic market behind very high effective protection barriers' (Glassburner 1984:19). But the momentum de-

[19] Fuller details on United States investment, most of it in oil refining, are given in Golay (1966:95-124).

veloped by this spurt of activity was soon lost as the limits of the domestic market were reached at the end of the decade; growth of manufacturing output fell by nearly half. Moreover, when import and exchange controls were abolished in 1962, many of these new industries collapsed because of exposure to outside competition and the manufacturing sector was severely depressed, although high tariff rates were maintained. The distorting effects of these policies were well described by Glassburner as:

a concentration of investment to supply the urban market, using imported techniques which were capital-intensive, thereby contributing to regional income disparities, to the low rate of labour absorption, unemployment, and to deteriorating income distribution (Glassburner 1984:19–20).

This gave rise not only to inefficient use of capital (and under-utilization of labour), but also to increasing dependence on imports of capital and raw materials, especially oil, which aggravated balance of payments problems. Government intervention to remedy those problems merely aggravated the vicious circle, resulting in chronic overvaluation of the peso, more controls and more corruption. Nothing President Marcos was able to do could fundamentally reverse that situation. His major attempt to do so in 1979–80 failed because the unpredictably adverse external economic environment (the second oil shock, then world recession) aborted his program of structural reform. Bad luck with deteriorating terms of trade was another element in that situation. (Thailand had suffered an even more severe decline in her terms of trade between 1975 and 1982 and still prospered.[20] She had not over-borrowed as recklessly as the Philippines.) Another was that the agricultural sector in the Philippines has not grown rapidly enough to create any developmental momentum in the economy as a whole. Despite a 5 per cent growth rate in that sector in the early 1970s, after the 'Green Revolution', the subordination of rural and agricultural interests to the requirements of the government's industrialization strategy has had adverse effects, at a time when extension of the country's agricultural frontier into new areas had been reaching its limits. Thus, despite the quite creditable 6.2 per cent GDP growth rate achieved between 1970 and 1981, 'the economy really missed the chance to take off and soar to the front

[20] From 1975 till 1982, the Philippines suffered a fall in her terms of trade index from 100 to 79. Thailand fell from 100 to 45 (Hill and Jayasuriya 1985:70).

ranks'.[21] Any resemblances between the development strategy of the Philippines and the NICs are really illusory because of the utterly different basis of the economic policies of each in these respects.

When we look towards the political reasons for this poor level of economic performance, there is no shortage of partial explanations, but instead a problem of deciding how and why they are all interconnected. The weaknesses of the executive arm of the government were often blamed for the country's mediocre economic performance during the years of fully democratic institutions before 1972. But despite the 'strong man' image that Marcos tried to project after 1972, he did not prove to be a strong leader when confronted with difficult and unpopular decisions. He claimed that one aim of his 'New Society' was to break the power of the 'old oligarchy'; but apart from essentially *ad hominem* assaults on the property (and in Aquino's case, the person) of old political enemies, he did little to weaken the basic power of the oligarchy generally. In fact, he elevated a new bunch of 'cronies' to even greater heights than any of the old oligarchs, by vesting them with sweeping powers of whole industries, notably sugar and coconuts. His attempts to create a more effective machinery of central bureaucratic controls in the provinces did little to weaken the regional dominance of the leading families in each area. The socioeconomic basis of their power has not been radically changed.

The inefficiencies and inequities resulting from Marcos's 'crony capitalism' are commonly cited in explanation of what has gone wrong over the last decade in the Philippines. I suspect the problem lies deeper than this, however. A buoyant economy should be able to withstand some degree of extravagance and misdirection of resources (as in Indonesia), but in the Philippines' case the waste has been enormous and the economy far from buoyant. It is the social and political correlates of the Marcos growth strategy that seem to have been the most badly handled. The benefits of growth were not at all equitably distributed and did not succeed in reducing income inequalities, as they did in the NICs. The growth of agriculture has lagged, unlike Thailand and Indonesia, despite the 'Green Revolution' in rice cultivation, while manufacturing has not grown

---

[21] The quotations are from Hill and Jayasuriya (1985:2), also citing the Director of the Manila-based Centre for Research and Communication, a 1976 World Bank Report and 1974 International Labour Organization (ILO) Report.

rapidly enough to create jobs or raise wage rates or reduce rural underemployment. It is hardly surprising, in these circumstances, that social and political tensions became steadily worse.

It cannot be said that anything like a NIC-style growth coalition nor an 'insulated developmentalist state' has been created in the Philippines. The élite was too divided in its attitude to the Marcos regime for that, the rift between the 'technocrats' and the 'cronies' surrounding Marcos too bitter and deeply politicized. Perhaps it was too ambitious of Marcos ever to imagine that the New Society could give rise to such a coalition. His political style was always more populist and rhetorical than that of the NICs' leaders – and, more seriously, something of a sham, too verbose and never very credible. Moreover, the element of personal aggrandizement was always too blatant. The Marcos strategy could only have worked if the success of his policies had won him a wide degree of popular support, either from the élite or the masses. For a few years it seemed possible that this might happen, but by the 1980s both groups were turning away from him, and in 1986 his regime crumbled completely.

The problem, however, goes deeper than Marcos and the failure of his strategies. The poor economic performance of the Philippines since 1946 is due also to the shortcomings of its élite, which has little incentive to want to change the basic socio-economic structure.[22] Unlike all the other countries of Southeast Asia, the Philippines has a long-established, relatively homogeneous class of élite families with major interests in rural landed property and urban real estate, as well as considerable local power in their home provinces. Many of these families have diversified their interests out of land into urban business or manufacturing since the 1950s. Many, too, have become leading figures on the national political stage, as well as locally. No other president before Marcos could effectively challenge the entrenched power of this class or its control over the congress. (Magsaysay tried and failed.) Marcos claimed to be doing so, but that was mostly rhetoric. The policies and interests he represented were almost wholly identical with those of the élite. If he *had* seriously embarked upon a restructuring of the economy, he would have hurt some members of the élite, but he did not do so. What the élite now wants in the post-Marcos situation is essentially the same fruits of those policies as they have

[22] A comprehensive discussion of the political and economic factors underlying the 1983 crisis is given in Nemenzo and May (1984).

been enjoying, but without too great an increase in the costs thereof.

The foremost task confronting the post-Marcos regime, is to harness the energies and aspirations of the people of the country, particularly at the upper levels, so that the pursuit of private self-interest again becomes conducive to the advancement of the common good. A country which has some of the best-educated, most enterprising and vigorous citizens of any ASEAN nation, but in which they want nothing so much as to migrate to the United States or any other wealthy country, has a major problem of getting its incentive structures right.

Indonesia

The dramatic reversal of political orientation of Indonesia in 1965–66, from the doctrinaire pseudo-Socialist rhetoric of the Sukarno government to the strongly anti-Communist ideology of the 'New Order' under President Suharto, ushered in twenty years of rapid economic growth which would have seemed quite unbelievable only two or three years earlier, when the economy and administrative system were in a shambles. Both political and economic factors were crucial in bringing about that transformation, of which the most important were the following:

(i) The backlash of intense hostility against the Indonesian Communist Party (PKI) and the former pro-Sukarno forces ('the Old Order') spearheaded by a loose 'New Order coalition' in 1966–67, made up of anti-communist students, intellectuals, Muslim organizations and key elements in the army – a coalition which gradually disintegrated in the 1970s.

(ii) A policy of deregulation and greater reliance on the price mechanism that was adopted to reassert control over the economy at a time when inflation had reached 600 per cent per annum during 1966, from which it was gradually checked back to a single digit level by 1969.

(iii) A substantial inflow of external aid from the West, which was accompanied after a lag of several years by a lesser stream of private foreign investment.[23]

[23] Private direct foreign investment in Indonesia had been negligible in the decade prior to 1968 (except for some continuing but low-level oil company investments); but the annual average figures thereafter are given in Hill and Johns (1985:49).

(iv) An increase in oil production and revenues in the 1970s, especially after the OPEC price rises of 1974 and 1979–80, providing the Indonesian Government with both foreign exchange and budgetary resources on a scale the country had never known, thereby enhancing the effectiveness of the governmental machine at all levels.

(v) A great enhancement of the authority of the government, which has grown stronger throughout this period, with no serious challenges from political parties or mass-based opposition groups, as they have been progressively isolated and silenced.

(vi) An unprecedented increase in rice production since 1967 under the impact of the new 'Green Revolution' technology, which has ensured an adequate supply of food and kept prices to urban consumers low.

There is no puzzle about accounting for the political and ideological turnaround between 1965 and 1967. The economic and administrative chaos of the late Sukarno years were so disastrous that his left-wing slogans and doctrines had virtually discredited themselves.[24] The immediate successes of the policies of the technocrats who were advising President Suharto from 1966 onwards were perhaps more surprising and unforeseeable at the time, but they too seem easily explicable twenty years later. The policies adopted hurt initially, but quickly brought results. Suharto and the army provided the political backing to the technocrats, whose policies soon justified themselves. Tensions arose later between the technocrats and the business-oriented generals, however – tensions which have never entirely disappeared.

The political economy of 'New Order' Indonesia is an endlessly tangled subject and it is impossible to do justice to the complexity of the links between power, policies and property in Indonesia in a few paragraphs, nor about the political basis of the 'New Order' and the reasons why it has been able to sustain appropriate conditions for the government's development program to succeed, whereas Sukarno's had failed disastrously (see Mackie 1967:19–72). All his attempts to tackle economic problems were wrecked by

---

[24] The fullest and best account of the fall of Sukarno and rise of Suharto is Crouch (1978): this carries on the story of the political struggle in post-revolutionary Indonesia covered by Feith (1962) on the years of parliamentary democracy, 1950–59.

an inability to control its budget deficits, inflation and chronic balance of payments problems. Suharto has had few difficulties with these problems since 1968. Why? Critics of the regime stress three factors in answer to this question.

First, the imposition of a strong, authoritarian government in place of a weak and ineffective one made possible by the destruction of the PKI [Partai Komunis Indonesia], along with mass-based labour and peasant organizations, have minimized opposition. Second is the 'borrowed power' (Herbert Feith's phrase) of the massive foreign aid increase after 1967–68, followed by substantial private capital inflow in the early 1970s. In the third place there was a fortuitous increase in oil revenues later in the decade.

All these factors were certainly crucial, but we are still left with unresolved questions. Why was the autocratic rule of President Sukarno so weak and ineffective when it came to making hard administrative and economic decisions, whereas President Suharto's government, operating with (formally) the same constitutional powers, is not? Answers to this question in terms of repression, political prisoners, limitations on dissenting opinions and the 'borrowed power' made available from external sources are indeed part of the story, but not necessarily the most important part. The 'New Order' regime is far from conforming to a Latin American model of rule by terror and systematic brutality. It has many characteristically Indonesian qualities of capriciousness, inefficiency and random humaneness, as well. It has been able to rely on the tacit acquiescence of most of the population from a very early stage because it has constantly succeeded in delivering the goods, something that Sukarno never did. Few Indonesians, including Indonesian Chinese, attempt to leave their country permanently as Filipinos do. More puzzling is the question why the economic policies of the technocrats have in general been followed by President Suharto since 1967 (although not always, for there have been other elements in his government pushing towards divergent objectives), even though this has sometimes required him to apply very unpopular policies. It was politically impossible for the group of 'administrators' to exercise similar powers in the Sukarno era (Feith 1962).

Can it be said that the Suharto government is backed by a 'growth coalition' or represents an 'insulated developmentalist state', as Haggard and Cheng (1983) have described the NICs? The question directs attention to a key element in the situation, but the answer must be a qualified 'yes and no' to both questions – and it is the qualifications that are the most informative part of the answer. In the early years of the 'New Order', the Suharto government was actively supported by a broad coalition of anti-Communist activists made up of student groups, urban intellectuals (the central core of whom were the University of Indonesia economists later known as the 'technocrats'), various militant Muslim organizations and the more strongly anti-Sukarno elements in the army. It looks a little like a growth coalition because of the ideology of development and modernization put forward by the Golkar organization, the symbolic standard-bearer of this anti-Communist grouping and because the economic policies of the technocrats were the outward manifestation of this. But it was not really a 'growth' coalition of the same kind as Haggard and Cheng had in mind; above all, the 'business class' as such was not at all prominent in it initially. In any case, this grouping began to crumble as a political coalition soon after Suharto consolidated his power, largely because he disappointed the early hopes of various groups that they would inherit a substantial share of power themselves. The power base of the Suharto regime was steadily narrowed throughout the 1970s. It relies mainly on Golkar, which is a government-backed state party. The Muslim organizations, in particular, have become increasingly alienated from the Suharto government over religious, ideological and educational issues. By the late 1970s, organized Islam represented the major opposition force with any capability to mount a challenge to the Suharto government (though even that possibility is very remote); so if one were to hypothesize the existence of an implicit 'growth coalition' behind the Suharto regime during the 1970s, it would have to be visualized as a very different grouping from the initial 'New Order coalition', which was committed primarily to anti-Communist and anti-Sukarno *political* goals as much as to an explicitly developmentalist philosophy.

A further difficulty is that while the military leadership and the technocrats constitute key elements behind the Suharto government, committed to the kind of developmental strategy it has been pursuing, the indigenous business class has often been opposed to the government's economic policies in detail, but powerless to change them. There has all along been a significant rift between the embryonic class of small indigenous businessmen and the much larger group of Indonesian Chinese businessmen, who have generally been more successful at taking advantage of the opportunities created for them by the New Order's 'economic miracle'. While the interests of the wealthier Chinese have certainly come to depend heavily on the success of the government's development strategy (despite the fact that many were initially very fearful of this regime), the smaller indigenous businessmen have been far more ambivalent about it, for they have regarded its policies as more beneficial to the Chinese or to foreign capital than to them. The politics of this issue and the broader questions of the social position of the Indonesian Chinese are extremely convoluted, so broad generalizations on the subject can be misleading. But the 'Chinese problem' does represent an element in the equation which makes the political aspects of Indonesia's development strategy a much more complex problem than it is in the NICs. The government has to tread very cautiously in dealing with such a potentially explosive issue and can rarely afford to disregard it.[25]

Whether or not the Suharto regime can be categorized as an 'insulated developmentalist state' is also a moot point. Certainly it comes closer to that than either Malaysia or Thailand, in the sense of being insulated from direct political pressures, either from mass political organizations or more conventional pressure groups. The government cannot afford to disregard entirely the reactions of the public to its policies, of course, but that could equally be said of the NICs. There are degrees of 'insulation' and the Suharto government is certainly in a much stronger position than the Sukarno government in its capacity to push through policies with severely deprivational consequences from time to time.

It is on the score of being a strongly 'developmentalist' state, however, that I would be most inclined to distinguish the political conditions in Indonesia from the NICs, as categorized by Haggard and Cheng, on two grounds. First, while the Suharto government puts great rhetorical stress (and real policy priorities also) on development, modernization and technological advancement – as also does virtually every developing country government – it has other

---

[25] An informative account of the various groups making up the Indonesian business class in the early 1970s is given in Robinson (1982). For general accounts of the social and political position of the Chinese minority in Indonesia, see Mackie (1976) and Coppel (1983); their economic roles are discussed in Mackie (1985).

important objectives, too, which constantly cut across this one. 'Nation-building' and 'national integration', which are code-words for policies aimed at the elimination of religious, ethnic and regional divisions as potential political issues, also have very high priority. The underlying social and political divisions of Indonesia which caused such problems in the Sukarno era have not disappeared since 1965. It is merely their political manifestations which are different. The army leaders are intensely sensitive to the dangers that could face them if the government's control mechanisms were to break down severely. Hence considerations of rapid growth, efficiency and productivity constantly have to be balanced against these more political considerations of maintaining order and control. Second, there is still a strongly tributary character to the massive bureaucratic apparatus of control which envelops nearly all aspects of Indonesian economic and social life. The public sector is very large – and relatively inefficient – because most of the Dutch plantations, banks, trading corporations etc. that were nationalized in 1957–58 are still in the government's hands. State corporations and bureaucratic offices are rarely very dynamic or strongly committed to development in the sense of higher productivity, efficiency or even profitability. Their officials can survive providing they do not 'rock the boat' or cause overt scandal. They tend to define 'development' largely in inchoate terms of the 'social function' of their organizations.

At best this state of affairs results in merely keeping the organizations just ticking over without serious disaster and without great progress; at worst it gives rise to extensive corruption, arbitrary exactions from peasants and businessmen and gross waste of resources. It is a system with few built-in drives towards efficiency or higher productivity, and at the heart of the problem is a deep ideological ambivalence towards 'capitalism', profit-making (which is equated with greed) and 'cut-throat competition', one of Sukarno's favourite curse-words which is still very much in currency in the bureaucratic world. Even President Suharto prefers to extol the virtues of *koperasi* (cooperatives) above capitalism, which is a term he tends to avoid, even though he has presided over an era of dramatic capitalist expansion, spearheaded by the private sector. This profound ideological ambivalence represents the most striking difference, in my opinion, between the Suharto regime and the 'developmentalist' states, as represented by the NICs.

In these circumstances, it is remarkable that the Indonesia technocrats have been able to achieve as much as they have by way of freeing the economy and allowing private investment to flourish, including the substantial inflow of foreign investment in the 1970s (which has tended to dry up in the 1980s), thus generating a moderately rapid rate of growth. Greatly increased government expenditures on development projects during the years of lavish oil boom funds were, of course, also a very powerful stimulus to growth.

But the technocrats were able to achieve more, in relative terms, in the early years of the 'New Order' than they have done in later years. Their emphasis then on deregulation, greater reliance on market forces, budgetary stringency and leaner bureaucracy enabled them to cut through the accumulated undergrowth of controls built up in the Sukarno period, at a time when the bureaucracy was demoralized and politically vulnerable. Unfortunately the lush jungle re-established itself in the early 1970s, as the bureaucracy regained confidence and power. Over-regulation of the economy is again an endemic problem. From time to time, the technocrats are able to muster the political and bureaucratic support necessary to push through a sweeping reform, such as the astonishing 1985 abolition of virtually the entire customs service or the 1983–84 deregulation of the banking system. But it is hard for them to hold the line at all points all the time against the insidious growth of bureaucratic controls for their own sake. Indonesia is now as much a 'bureaucratic polity' as Thailand ever was – and the consequences may not be conducive to either efficiency or economic growth.

Malaysia

Malaysia presents a very different picture from that of its neighbours in three respects. Its mixture of races (about 45 per cent Malay, 35 per cent Chinese, 10 per cent Indian) creates special problems of economic structure as well as political and social tensions. On the other hand, its political system remains, paradoxically, the most 'open', competitive and democratic of all the ASEAN countries, with active political parties and genuine elections, despite various restrictions of civil and political rights and various types of legal and administrative discrimination against ethnic Chinese. It also has a far higher level of per capita GDP than the other ASEAN Four.

The rate of growth of the Malaysia economy (about 7 per cent since independence) has been creditable but not particularly outstanding, considering the excellent infrastructure and flourishing plantation sector left by the British, later supplemented by significant oil revenues since the 1960s.[26] Thailand's similar growth rate has been far more impressive, considering her more limited resources. Malaysia's agricultural sector has not achieved the same degree of diversification and expansion as Thailand's, apart from the development of oil palm production. Malaysia has achieved steady economic growth with relatively little structural change away from the former dualistic, colonial economy based on plantation production and exports. A modest manufacturing industry has been developed since the 1960s, initially on a rather moderate import-substitution industrialization basis, later with a strong export orientation based on export processing zones. The Mahathir government has been discussing a 'second round of import substitution' and high technology, capital-intensive industries.

In its socio-political aspect, the basis of Malaysia's prosperity depends on the capacity of the English-educated leaders of the Malay and Chinese communites, first, to maintain control of the key political parties supported by their respective ethnic groups, so that more extremist Malay and Chinese elements can be kept in check; and, second, to maintain a workable harmony or accommodation at the élite level in governing the country.[27] So far they have been able to do so, even during the crisis of May 1969, which destroyed the old Alliance formula for accommodation. Malaysia's multi-racial élite has gradually become, like Thailand's, a form of meritocracy, with the old Malay aristocracy now merging into bureaucratic, political and business roles, apart from the largely ceremonial sultans. There is not yet anything like the same degree of racial mingling through either intermarriage or business partnerships as in Thailand, however, although business links are slowly developing. The 'middle class' generally could not yet be described

---

[26] The literature on Malaysia's economy is copious, although more attention has been given to issues of income distribution as between ethnic groups and the problems of inequality than to the determinants of growth. Industrial output was growing at 11–12 per cent per annum in the mid-1970s (Fisk and Rani 1982:5). Other useful studies of the Malaysian economy and social system are Silcock and Fisk (1963), Lim (1973), Snodgrass (1980), and Tan Tat Wah (1983).

[27] For three informative external views of this problem, see Funston (1980), Wang (1981b), and, for an insider's view, Mahathir (1970), which is still one of the most provocative and illuminating.

as a 'properties bourgeoisie' to anything like the same extent as in the Philippines, although the trend is in that direction.

Can we categorize Malaysia as an 'insulated developmentalist state' in the Haggard and Cheng sense? Definitely not, for two reasons. The government is not at all 'insulated' from popular demands articulated through Members of Parliament and political parties, as in any representative system. Nor has Malaysia ever had an 'ideology of development' as such. On the contrary, the predominant ideological imperatives behind the National Front and the New Economic Policy are primarily directed towards strengthening the political and economic position of the Malays, a very different objective with a redistributive rather than an expansionist or efficiency-maximizing thrust. The Malaysia Government is strongly committed neither to 'lean government' nor to *laissez-faire* or private enterprise. Government expenditure there amounts to roughly 40 per cent of GDP. There is a great deal of governmental intervention in economic life, but it is true that the government has never had such a strong *dirigiste* tradition as Indonesia (nor the same suspicion of capitalism or private enterprise, except where that is synonymous with Chinese dominance).

Curiously, the puzzle about Malaysia has always been (particularly for Indonesia-watchers) that economic nationalism directed against either British or Chinese ownership of corporate property has been astonishingly restrained.[28] This is probably because the post-colonial economy has never come under really serious strain, because the momentum of growth maintained ever since the 1950s has been sufficient to provide government revenues adequate to meet the demands for special measures to help ensure Malay advancement without requiring especially heavy imposts on Chinese business. Malaysia has never been under the same pressures as the Republic of Korea or Taiwan to miximize industrial growth in order to earn foreign exchange, or to mobilize political support for a 'developmentalist' ideology. Her traditional agricultural exports, supplemented by mining and oil in the 1970s, have expanded well

[28] The chapter on Malaysia in Golay *et al.* (1969) summarizes the relations between the Malaysia Government and the British plantations and trading houses in the early years of independence, when few major changes occurred. Since then, a controlling interest in several British plantation companies, most notably Guthries, has been purchased by the government and a brief period of mild hostility towards the British developed, reflecting the attitudes of Prime Minister Mahathir. But apart from that, the structure of corporate enterprise in Malaysia has changed relatively little over the last thirty years.

enough to meet her most urgent needs. Her trading regime has always been, as under the British, an externally-oriented and open-market system, although by no means a *laissez-faire* one. She has been able to coast along as much by good luck as by especially skilful or tightly disciplined economic management.

We cannot really talk about a 'growth coalition' in Malaysia, supporting the government's development strategy out of a strong commitment to, and vested interest in, developmental objectives. Her political dynamics are completely different from those of the NICs; governments rely for their political backing on party and factional support within coalitions, as in any other representative system, although with perhaps a little more arm-twisting in some cases. (But they do not rely much on the military, either.) What we do see there that is reminiscent of the NICs' situation is a fairly high degree of mutual understanding between the more technocratic members of the bureaucracy, some key ministers and the economically more enlightened leaders of the main parties, all of whom realize that it could be self-defeating to adopt or advocate policies that would kill the geese that lay the golden eggs, that is, the network of private enterprise businesses. But this is all expressed as much in terms of ethnic politics as of economic principles or doctrines. The more temperate Malay leaders know it would be counterproductive politically as well as economically to utilize government pressures too blatantly against efficient Chinese businesses. The Chinese know they have to acquiesce in certain policies and public expenditures which subordinate considerations of efficiency to those of political harmony and what the Malays perceive to be equity.

To conclude, the mechanisms of government have worked fairly successfully in Malaysia since independence to ensure that economic growth has proceeded at a moderate pace. This growth has not been quite as fast as in Thailand or the NICs, and arguably not as fast as a country as well endowed with natural and human resources as Malaysia should be growing if all sectors were being operated at maximal efficiency; but, given the explosiveness and complexity of the racial issue, the overall rate of economic progress could have been far worse. Because of the salutary element of 'openness' and political pluralism in the system, Chinese businessmen subjected to excessive pressures from bureaucrats have been able to use political defence mechanisms to some extent and this has worked to limit 'squeeze' and outright corruption, which is such an irremediable problem in more authoritarian societies. Business and economic issues have not become a political football here to the same extent as they have sometimes done elsewhere. There is the same kind of professionalism and technical competence among the bureaucrats, especially those who are ethnic Chinese, as we noted in Thailand. (But it is harder to identify a distinct group of 'technocrats' in Malaysia.) The system of legal procedures and property rights inherited from the colonial regime has been maintained fairly effectively by a judiciary which is proud of its independence.

In all these respects, Malaysia is still far better off than Indonesia and roughly on a par with Thailand. As long as she can continue to keep the socio-political rift between Malays and Chinese within bounds – and preferably reduce the economic gap that has separated the two communities over recent decades – the political circumstances prevailing there should enable her to maintain a rate of growth similar to Thailand's and well ahead of Indonesia's.

Singapore

As a success story in the developmental stakes, does Singapore serve as any sort of object lesson about the political conditions of rapid growth within the ASEAN countries? Its socio-economic structure as a city-state and the socio-cultural implications of its having a predominantly Chinese population make it so different from its neighbours that it certainly cannot be regarded as any sort of a 'model' for them. It much more clearly belongs in the class of 'insulated developmentalist states' than they do, in terms of both its development-oriented economic strategy and the Peoples Action Party (PAP) government's high degree of autonomy and insulation from pressures from below. It has been virtually a one-party state ever since Lee Kuan Yew demolished the opposition *Barisan Sosialis* in the two elections of the 1960s, and its government clamps down heavily on trade unions and political dissent, as hard as any of the other ASEAN states or even the NICs; although it allowed wages to rise substantially after 1979 in order to push investment away from labour-intensive industries. Yet there are some similarities with the ASEAN Four and even some lessons for them too.

Of the other ASEAN states, only the Philippines can be considered as at all as close in character as Singapore to Haggard and Cheng's 'insulated developmentalist state', but in growth performance the Philippines and Singapore have been poles apart. Both have strongly authoritarian governments, but whereas Singapore's economic strategy has been brilliantly successful,[29] the Philippines has failed badly. That is due more to the character of the growth strategies pursued by each country than to the political conditions underpinning those strategies. On the latter question, however, we can say that if one compares the shrewd political judgment of Lee Kuan Yew and the tight party discipline of the PAP with the aimless leadership formerly provided by Marcos and his Kilusan Bagong Lipunan (KBL), Singapore's success is readily explicable.

The political underpinnings of Singapore's turn towards export-led growth and an open-door policy towards foreign investment (a policy which has made foreign capital a much more important factor than local capital in Singapore's recent development) are well summarized by Haggard and Cheng (1983:44–5):

First, the consolidation of single-party rule and the exclusion of the left allowed Lee Kuan Yew and the economic bureaucracy to pursue a 'pragmatic' approach to industrialization, which despite PAP's rhetorical commitment to socialism entailed a primary role for the private sector, strict control of labour and the mobilization of the whole society behind economic goals. The 'situational imperative' created by the break with Malaysia made an export-oriented strategy attractive, but given the weakness of domestic firms in manufacturing ensured a heavy reliance on foreign firms. Incentives were high and controls minimal. The ability of the PAP to control labour and present an image of political stability made the city-state attractive to foreign investors.

It is noteworthy that the level of foreign investment in Singapore in the 1970s per head of population was more than twelve times the level in Indonesia and Thailand in the years 1969–81, so it is hardly surprising that Singapore's economy has prospered. And since there was no strong reason for political opposition to foreign investment from either the working classes, to whom it meant jobs, or the

[29] Singapore's rate of growth of GDP in the first half of 1985, however, was less than 1 per cent and in the second quarter it actually declined with large-scale lay-offs of workers and many small businesses closing (see *Far Eastern Economic Review*, 22 August 1985).

very weak indigenous business class, who were simply in no position to compete in substantial export-oriented industries, the political conditions were highly conducive to foreign capital inflow, to a degree that has occurred in no other Asian country except Hong Kong.

There is a minor puzzle about the relationship between the indigenous capitalist class in Singapore and the PAP government, however, in so far as the former has never exerted a very overt influence upon either the party or the government, as one might have expected. In fact, in the PAP government's earliest years its relationship with the old *towkays* of the colonial era and the Chinese-owned banks was distinctly hostile because of their initial fears about the government's links with the Communists.[30] Lee's later break with the pro-Communist wing of the party in 1961 did not entirely eliminate that suspicion and antagonism on either side, but the fact is that the PAP has subsequently relied primarily on public enterprise and foreign investment as the central pillars of its development strategy. The activities of Singapore's capitalist class have been confined primarily to the financial and commercial sector or professional and salaried occupations rather than manufacturing industry. Few of its leaders have ever had much influence with the government or the Party.

The question of how Lee Kuan Yew was able to eliminate political opposition and bring the initially *Barisan*-dominated trade union movement under PAP control is a more complex one. There was a considerable element of Machiavellian skill and ruthlessness in the way he achieved that goal; it was not something that could initially be taken for granted as being inevitable. In the 1960s, the basic social cleavage underlying the political situation in Singapore was that the *Barisan Sosialis* was able to draw upon the support of the Chinese-speaking lower classes while the PAP relied primarily upon the English-educated middle class and professionals. In order to consolidate the power of the PAP after he had demolished the *Barisan* as an effective opposition force in the National Assembly by political sleight-of-hand in 1968, Lee had to bridge this socio-

[30] Shortly before and after the PAP came to power following its first electoral victory in 1959, a good deal of Singapore capital was ostentatiously shifted to Kuala Lumpur by several large companies which were, in effect, drumming up a 'red scare' on the basis of Lee Kuan Yew's then still very radical anti-colonist rhetoric. See the chapters by Lee Sheng Yi, George Thomson, and E. K. Y. Chen in Chen (1979).

cultural fault-line and render it politically irrelevant, something he has succeeded in doing by means of a complex educational strategy, which has proved highly successful in the 1980s.[31] Any explanation of Lee's political success which fails to take account of this factor in the equation, or attributes it solely to sheer authoritarianism or an alliance with foreign capital, is a gross oversimplification, but in a state of only two million people, his personal dominance over both his party and the government has undoubtedly been a key factor in their success.

CONCLUSION

It is clear that the ASEAN Four do not resemble the NICs in respect of being either 'insulated developmentalist states' or of being backed by cohesive 'growth coalitions' in their upper classes. They come closer to the latter condition than the former in some cases, but in none has there been the same single-minded drive towards maximizing growth, raising productivity all round and eliminating inefficiencies as in the NICs. Economic nationalism and its ideological legacies have constituted far more significant political constraints upon governments in the ASEAN Four than in the NICs, both in so far as the role of foreign capital is concerned and, most strikingly at some times and places, as far as the economic roles of the Southeast Asian Chinese minorities are concerned. It has had a distorting effect on the purely 'developmental' priorities of governments in the ASEAN countries by requiring that they direct resources also towards the socio-political goals associated with 'indigenization'. Fortunately this has been a factor of diminishing importance in Thailand and the Philippines since the 1950s, although anti-Chinese sentiments have by no means vanished entirely even there.

While we can discern from the ASEAN story no obvious political preconditions of rapid growth, it does seem clear that situations in which technocrats or efficient bureaucrats have had a major influence upon economic policymaking have been more conducive to growth than situations where bureaucracies have been highly politicized or where governments have had to take account of par-

---

[31] The contribution of the PAP's educational policies to the bridging of the rift between Chinese-educated and English-educated is summarized in Borthwick (1985) and Wilson (1978).

ticular interests or pressure groups. We can see, too, that for two reasons rapid growth tends to be obstructed in situations where large bureaucracies or public-sector industries exist. They are generally cumbersome, inflexible and incapable of rapid adaptation to changing conditions. Moreover, their political masters are rarely able to call them to account fully in cases of failure, waste or inefficiency. They are inclined to 'run to fat', whereas private businesses are subject to constant market pressures to remain 'lean'.

Worst of all are situations where vested interests dependent upon monopolies, monopsony, protection or other forms of disguised subsidy are strong enough to obstruct efforts to achieve administrative or political reform. Deeply entrenched élites, as in the Philippines, have a particularly stubborn capacity to resist changes to the *status quo*.

A high degree of consensus within the élite on the basic objectives of economic policy seems to be a crucially important condition of successful economic performance. Where the élite is seriously fragmented, as in Indonesia before 1965 (and also initially in Malaysia and Singapore), governments have to be primarily concerned with power-maintenance strategies rather than longer-term economic objectives. In the early post-war years, the political instability of all Southeast Asian countries was due in large part to the fact that various sub-groups within their élites were bidding for power on the basis of diverse ideological and political appeals. Since the 1960s, the consolidation of an urban middle class in all these countries has been a striking feature of their socio-political development – and this class has been the main beneficiary of growth-oriented economic strategies. The urban working classes and peasantry, who had in some circumstances played significant political roles in the turbulent years of the decolonization process, have been progressively excluded from political influence (except in the Philippines, via the New People's Army).

The Philippines has had the most long-established and economically muscular middle class in Southeast Asia, not significantly riven by a 'Chinese problem' like the others. Yet it has been deeply faction-ridden and divided since 1972 in its attitudes to the Marcos regime. In Thailand, a relatively strong urban middle class has been emerging over the last thirty years, converting the Thai aristocracy, bureaucracy, salaried and professional classes and the Sino-Thai commercial and industrial bourgeoisie into a relatively homogeneous whole. This has meant general backing for Thailand's recent governments and a degree of élite cohesion over broad national goals which is unparalleled in Southeast Asia, except perhaps in Singapore, where a similar process has been occurring, but with a very different ethnic mix. Much the same has been happening in Malaysia, although the ethnic line of distinction is much sharper there and its political manifestations far more problematical. In Indonesia something similar is occurring, but the urban middle class is still very new and weak. Élite fragmentation in the early post-war years was a major factor in the political instability of the Sukarno era; it has been diminishing gradually under the Suharto regime, although there is still a long way to go.

There is much more we need to know about the ways in which the strength of governments, the character and direction of national economic strategies and the interests of these newly emerging middle classes interact. But it is along the lines sketched out above, I believe, that we can most fruitfully investigate the political and socio-economic aspects of fast growth in the ASEAN countries.

WILLIAM J. O'MALLEY

11

CULTURE AND
INDUSTRIALIZATION

Culture has not been popular in recent years in explanations and analyses of development. Culture, after all, is a soft concept, neither easily pinned down in its nature nor absolutely distinguishable in its workings. This means, of course, that the influence and effects of culture are difficult to foresee and to quantify. In a world where development is increasingly identified with economic development and where economic development is bound ever more tightly to economic planning (which demands substantial measures both of foresight and of quantification) one of the reasons for the relative insignificance of cultural considerations is clear, and two others are also prominent. First, cultures are almost by definition specific, and their intrusion into discussions forces an uncomfortable compromise between universalities and particulars, between general laws and anecdotes. Second, linked with the notion that cultures are different are the seeds of the notion that the worth of cultures might be different, a notion that can all too readily be twisted into abhorrent denigration or *a priori* condemnation of cultural traits and of peoples who display them. Yet, to ignore culture largely on the grounds that it is awkward to deal with is both intellectually unsatisfying and potentially costly. This paper will attempt to indicate how some important aspects of culture fit, almost organically, the style of institutional arrangements underlying the rapid economic progress in some East Asian countries over the past few decades and will raise some cultural points bearing on the attempts of Southeast Asian countries to emulate the more successful of their northern neighbours. Tracing every cultural factor from its roots through its often subtle mediating effects to the repercussions of its impact is obviously not feasible, but it is not necessary to do that in order to indicate that culture can make a difference and therefore must be borne in mind and somehow be born again in analyses.

CULTURE

Few of the major terms connected with the humanities and the social sciences have absolutely clear definitions, but the boundaries within which culture is somehow to be confined are fuzzier than for most. Culture can be, generally speaking, 'the way of life of a people', 'a people's ordered system of values and symbols', or, combining these two, 'a people's interpretation of the way in which they interact with their environment and each other'.[1] It is not as important here to elucidate the different levels of meaning connected with different definitions as it is to point out the major elements which they have in common: the sharing among a people of values, norms, expectations, and interpretations. Culture, in effect, is the binding element that ties individuals together through their integrated patterns of behaviour, thought and communication, and as such it acts to include some individuals within the group in question and to exclude others from it.[2] Because of the nebulous quality connected with this binding element, culture is often discussed in terms of its major manifestations – religion, social organization, interinstitutional arrangements, even evinced attitudes. But the vagueness associated with the concept of culture, the fact that it is difficult to say precisely how culture operates and where its realm ends, has not been sufficient cause to deny its influence on individual or group actions or to ignore its use as a contributing explanatory mechanism.

[1] There have been a number of serious attempts to summarize and clarify the various ways in which the concept of culture has been used or defined; the most notable among them are Kroeber and Kluckhohn (1952) and Kaplan and Manners (1972). Such works inevitably do a better job of criticizing and categorizing concepts than they do of positing more useful concepts themselves.

[2] Keesing (1974:73–97) has attempted to move out of vaguer notions of culture by positing the idea that culture is basically connected with what someone understands about the guidelines that others in his group follow. Culture is thus essentially the rules of the game, picked up while playing and subject to change as circumstances alter.

CULTURE AND ECONOMISTS

When development economics was still young and potentially respectable, the need to account for, or at least examine, culture and cultural factors was not seen as a superfluous activity by theorists, and it is notable that economists interested in Southeast Asia were among those who helped to generate a major debate on the topic.

Boeke (1966), who worked in the Dutch East Indies for twenty years before assuming the chair of Tropical-Colonial Economics at the University of Leiden, was the one who most emphatically turned the culture card face-up on the table. In a thesis he first advanced as a student, and then elaborated on, modified, and occasionally obfuscated for the rest of his working life,[3] Boeke argued the case for dualism. According to his interpretation, the impact of full-blown capitalism arriving from afar had literally split indigenous societies in Indonesia in two. A small segment could adapt quite easily to the new prevailing system and its demands, but the great bulk of the Indonesian population could not. Instead, they returned into an economic world characterized as rural, immobile, localized, and oriented towards a goods rather than a money economy.[4] These people, in Boeke's view, lived their lives by other economic rules than those required to play the game of economic growth, and they had to be protected and nurtured in their own sheltered environment until they could, in the very long run, be raised to a level of awareness at which they would be able to defend their own interests and thus compete successfully. Though his primary emphasis remained on the Indonesian case, Boeke was willing to make the argument that his theory had wide application elsewhere and that it provided clarification for developments, or the lack of them, in many tropical societies (Boeke 1953).

Boeke's cultural-based explanation – that most colonized people had values and expectations inimical to the requirements of rapid economic advancement – was supported to some extent by Hagen, who had a strong familiarity with Burma. Hagen likewise saw the existence in underdeveloped countries of inherited economic

[3] For discussions on the topic, see the collection of essays gathered together as Boeke (1966).
[4] The most succinct elaboration of the theory was presented by Boeke in his inaugural lecture upon taking up his chair at Leiden, later translated and published as 'Dualistic Economics' in Boeke (1966).

norms and values which would hinder growth, and he looked to, although he was not optimistic about implementing, a rapid push which would change those values as a key element in an accelerated drive towards economic progress. Failing that, development was bound to be a long-term, multi-generational effort, possible only through education away from cultural obstacles (Hagen 1957, 1962, 1968).

The thinking of Boeke and Hagen posed an immediate challenge to the rapidly evolving sub-discipline of development economics: if a particular culture ordained a reluctance or an inability to conform to expected economic behaviour, the application of the laws of economics alone might be insufficient to suggest the proper path towards optimal development.

This challenge was most firmly met by Higgins, a professional economist who had also had experience working in Indonesia. Addressing Boeke, Higgins noted that the dualism which fascinated the Dutch scholar was not confined to tropical or to colonial areas but existed as well in Europe and North America, where it was capable of being addressed and analysed through the application of standard economic principles (Higgins 1955). What was needed was not a new economic framework, but the disaggregation of the elements which collectively were viewed as dualism, the analysis of those separate elements using existing social science ideas, and the formulation of informed policies for addressing specific difficulties. Instead of the existence of the almost unaddressable social or sociological dualism which Boeke discerned, Higgins substituted smaller constituent components which lent themselves to individual diagnosis and treatment by economists. Higgins's answer to Hagen was a more pragmatic one: if Hagen was right, and cultural obstacles could thwart economic development plans, there was nothing to be gained but little to be lost in trying to implement those plans anyway; if Hagen was wrong, there was nothing to be gained but much to be lost in refraining from urging a development push based on economic principles (Higgins 1959:309–13).

Generally content with these answers, and with the directions towards which they pointed, the profession has not been overly concerned about cultural questions since. But two notable features connected with that early economics/culture debate deserve to be brought out also. First was the admirable refusal of those involved in it to settle for any simple answer than that 'they are different in essence', an answer that could easily have led to racist categorization and to condescension. Second was the assumption on the part of all involved that if culture had any role to play in the development process, it was likely to be a negative one, thwarting or impeding the hoped-for progress rather than facilitating it.

In the years since the early debate on culture and economics ended, the most noteworthy feature in the world economy has been the startling progress of East Asian countries. The dimensions of that progress do not need any great elaboration here, for even general figures are impressive enough on their own. Throughout the 1960s and the 1970s, Japan, Republic of Korea and Taiwan, which will be the countries considered in this section as East Asian growth centres, averaged some 7–9 per cent growth in GNP per capita each year.[5] In that same period, they greatly reduced the percentage of GDP coming from agriculture (from around 13 per cent to 5 per cent for Japan, 37 per cent to 20 per cent for the Republic of Korea, and 33 per cent to 11 per cent for Taiwan). In the 1970s the average annual growth rate for exports was 9.1 per cent for Japan, and an incredible 25.7 per cent for the Republic of Korea and 28 per cent for Taiwan. Of those exports, manufactured goods took the lion's share, growing from 85 per cent of total exports from Japan in 1965 to over 96 per cent in 1980; the equivalent figures for the Republic of Korea show a leap from 60 to 95 per cent and for Taiwan from 42 to 91 per cent. Though the picture varies somewhat for Japan, which has a much larger population base than the other two, which started from a higher economic plateau (some US$500 per capita income in 1960, as opposed to only US$150 for Taiwan and the Republic of Korea), and which thus has been able to service a far stronger domestic market, the importance of manufacturing and of

[5] There are any number of ways to group together the countries involved in the East Asian growth phenomenon: Little Dragons, Gangs of Four, NICs, East Asia, and so on. I have treated only these three countries simply because they cluster together easily and because their combination of a rural hinterland and a widening industrial base makes them seem a model for Southeast Asian countries.

   For my purposes here, I am interested in figures only for trends and orders of magnitude. Those cited here and elsewhere are taken from the appropriate Far Eastern Economic Review's *Asia Yearbook*.

exports of manufactured goods in providing much of the drive for economic growth is clear. The chief reason for the East Asian miracle appears to be that the countries assiduously followed the proper export-oriented scheme at a time when world markets for their chief products (automobiles, electronics, appliances, footwear, textiles and shipping) were strengthening (see for example Little 1981). There are a number of other factors, however, intimately connected with this basic reason, and here a number of those factors (the role of government, the nature of the private firm, and the relationship between those two) will be examined briefly in the light of the region's cultural background.

POST-CONFUCIAN CULTURE

Though they were for a few decades earlier in the century temporarily united under a single empire, Japan, the Republic of Korea and Taiwan have had separate histories, and their traditions vary widely. Within Japan, within the Republic of Korea and within Taiwan, there are also different groups of people with various social and religious orientations. Nevertheless, there is a background culture binding these peoples and these countries together, a culture steeped in Confucianism which they share with China, with Hong Kong, and with Chinese overseas.[6] Confucianism has gone through any number of metamorphoses over the course of two and a half millennia, but key elements of it have endured from its first formal consolidation of still earlier traditions and values to the present, when its influences are spoken of as post-Confucian to distinguish it from an earlier state ideology. Confucianism is not a religion stressing an afterlife; it is a code of ethics and conduct, meant to guide the relationships between human beings. The important relationships in Confucianism are hierarchical, between generations, within families, between ruler and ruled. The duty of the subordinate in these relationships is to show respect, loyalty and deference; the duty of the superior is to give the proper moral example, to act in the way that his status requires. Within these relationships, a common understanding of what is mutually expected obviates the need for much forthright communication.

[6] Specialists will rightly insist that the differences among these countries are deep and crucial, and that lumping Japan and the Republic of Korea together with Taiwan as Confucian states begs important questions which the intellectual histories of those countries raise.

In the Confucian ideal, government was only indirectly for the people, and it was neither of nor by them. The purpose of government was correct administration of correct policies, the standards of correctness being determined by the applied wisdom and experience of educated and experienced higher officials. The government best suited for this task was a centralized bureaucracy, authoritarian in nature. It was responsible for running the country, and not directly for the welfare of the people; if the country were run well, the welfare of the people would almost necessarily be heightened. Those in charge of administration were expected to maintain high standards, and their education was intended to enable them to be aware of those standards and to strive in the correct way to achieve them. Recruitment into the administrative corps was based on rigorous examination, an examination based not on specific skills or on detailed knowledge of work-related tasks but rather on a strong familiarity with the classics and their lessons. This examination system served, at least theoretically, to keep bureaucratic, and thus social, advancement open to members of all backgrounds and occupational groups (though there was among the bureaucrats, predictably, a high concentration of those from *literati* families). But the examination material itself acted to place stress on the goal of Confucian education: to learn from the past the proper relationships between people and the proper measure of things.

Even more important in Confucian considerations than the government was the prime institution in society, the family, for within the way in which a family was properly organized was the model on which the government should run. Respect and support were the chief currents in the family, and those currents flowed from younger to older, and from female to male. Sons were to honour fathers, wives were to honour husbands, younger brothers were to honour older brothers, and the living were to honour the generations which had gone before and which had left behind an endowment of traditions and a material heritage. Again, within the family the ideal was not to discuss in detail the way in which personal interactions ought to occur, but to have learned that way from the abundant examples around it and to move comfortably within the bounds of an established relationship.

Within the family, then, as within the government, a system based on respect and on common acknowledgment of mutual obligations lay at the heart of Confucian values. What was of crucial importance was not a person himself but the stylized links which bound him to others.

INSTITUTIONS

Against this background sketch of the Confucian tradition, we come now to a brief consideration of governments, companies, and relations between these two in the three East Asian countries of Japan, Taiwan and the Republic of Korea.

The chief characteristic of the three governments is that they represent strong states, that is they, in Cumings's words, 'can formulate policy goals independently of particular groups, they can change group or class behaviour, and they can change the structure of society' (Cumings 1984:7). The state in these countries, then, is not a *res publica* and is only indirectly responsible for and to the people. In the Republic of Korea and Taiwan, which have lived under militarily threatening situations for three and a half decades and where the military and a strong central party predominate, this situation is clear. Japan, however, has had a democratic form of government since the Occupation, and its capacity to 'formulate policy goals independently of particular groups' depends on the split in roles between the elected politicians and ministry on one hand and the professional bureaucracy on the other. The former take public positions, mobilize popular support, and deal directly with interest and pressure groups; the latter is busy with the task of formulating and implementing policy, free from the interference of lobbyists or short-term problems.[7] (Perhaps the essential difference between the two is illustrated by the case of Takeo Fukuda, the administrative head of an important ministry; as a bureaucrat accused of taking money from private interests, he 'had no honorable course but to resign and turn politician, later becoming prime minister' (Sayle 1985:40).) While these governments feature powerful and remote bureaucratic structures, many of the key positions in them are filled not by narrow specialists but by generalists, usually men of good and broad education, with a commitment to the management of broad tasks rather than a need to labour away on the particular.

---

[7] This has been characterized for Japan as the difference between 'reigning' and 'ruling' (Johnson 1982).

Companies in the three countries, though Japan has carried this furthest, are important social as well as economic institutions. Ideally, they are organized in community-like, almost family-like ways, with a strong emphasis on team spirit and mutual respect. In the larger and more successful firms, employees, both managers and labourers, are almost guaranteed life-long employment and predictable advances in rank and in salary (advances in responsibility, however, do not come automatically; demonstrated capacity is an important criterion here). The result, reinforced by the comparatively small difference between the salaries of those at the top and the wages of those at the bottom, is a highly-developed sense of loyalty, a willingness on the part of each to put oneself out and make personal sacrifices, of time, of money, of emotion, for the good of the collective effort which is the company.

The links between government and industry in Japan, Republic of Korea and Taiwan have been the crucial element in the economic success those countries have enjoyed. The reputations as 'Japan, Incorporated', 'South Korea, Incorporated', and 'Taiwan, Incorporated' which those places have come to earn in the West are well-deserved, for government and industry front up as one body in world markets. Behind that appearance of unity, however, is a complex cooperative effort. Because the state is strong in these countries, the appropriate administrative bodies can make policy decisions that will do damage to important firms and even undermine entire industries; through its research funds, its credit facilities, and its marketing-strategy capacity, the state can likewise boost the prospects of still others. But experience has demonstrated to industry executives that such strategic decisions are generally based on profound expertise and a reading of long-range trends, and that the state is interested in a mutual effort directing the entire economy along the most promising lines. Competitiveness can still be retained by corporations doing what they do best, while the government provides guidance or assistance based on a longer and wider view. The result has been the evolution of a common effort between government and corporate interests, based on the realization, according to Johnson writing about Japan, that 'the state needs the market and private enterprise needs the state; once both sides recognized this, cooperation was possible and high-speed growth occurred' (Johnson 1982:318). This cooperation is undoubtedly eased by the fact that top businessmen and officials in each of the three countries share a common educational experience, often at the same prestigious universities, and that bureaucrats can and do retire into private business or even into senior positions in the political parties.

Seeing the highlighted aspects of government, private enterprise, and the relationship between them in these three East Asian countries in juxtaposition with the ideals and values embodied in important Confucian institutions, one cannot help but be struck by the fit. The concepts of service, of respect, of mutual cooperation permeate both. Obedience towards authority and deference towards superiors are fostered by Confucianism and are intrinsic to the workings of the major institutions lying beneath the economic success in Japan, Republic of Korea and Taiwan. A willingness to subordinate the interests of the person to those of the group, a trait inculcated by Confucian teachings, has been at the heart of the co-operative social effort that has supported this East Asian style of growth. A strong temptation therefore exists to correlate the two somehow and even to attempt to see a causative factor directly at work. The attempt would be easily thwarted: if Confucianism is responsible for the comparative ease with which this speedy growth has ensued, why do we have a case where Confucian ideals and values have been around in their highly formulated fashion for twenty-five centuries while this kind of dynamic, cooperative effort has taken place in only the last twenty-five years? What about China itself, where there are over a billion inheritors of the Confucian tradition but a marked ambivalence towards its values and its value among leaders there who are highly desirous of rapid growth? And why are there still large groups of people in these three East Asian countries – people presumably equally imbued with Confucianist sensibilities – who have either dropped out from or who have not been included in this development drive? Still, it is difficult to ignore the fact that it is precisely these societies, in this part of the world and with this shared heritage, which have been outstandingly successful in recent decades in swiftly adapting their economic systems in keeping with the changing demands of the world market. If direct causation running from culture to this export-oriented, government-guided, corporation-led economic effort is ruled out, the possibility of some other exercise of cultural influence still exists. The experience of the Southeast Asian neighbours of these three countries, however, does not make the tracing of cultural influence any easier.

Although Southeast Asia, in a scholarly tradition that stretches back only four decades, is considered a single region, variety rather than uniformity is its chief characteristic in almost every field. Certainly this is the case in economic performance over the past fifteen years. While it is possible to generalize about the accomplishments of the East Asian growth states, such an effort comes to grief in Southeast Asia. Burma, despite a fortunate resource endowment (it was for years the only country exporting both food and fuel), stagnated economically for two decades after 1960 and has begun to make progress only in the last few years. The Indochinese states, plagued by decades of military conflicts, returned to something like economic normalcy as late as 1980, and though satisfactory economic progress has been reported since then, those countries have started a late economic drive from a base that is one of the lowest in the world. Singapore's pattern of rapid growth based on export-oriented industrialization closely resembles that of Hong Kong, Republic of Korea and Taiwan, and the Southeast Asian city-state is often listed with those places when growth is being discussed. Tiny Brunei, with a population of only 200,000 and vast revenues from oil exports, has an average per capita income of over US$20,000 a year. Grouping these countries together obviously entails difficulties. But there are fewer difficulties connected with generalizing about the economic performance of the other four ASEAN states – Indonesia, Malaysia, Thailand and the Philippines. In the 1970s the economies of these countries grew at the highly encouraging rate of some 6–8 per cent per year. Their significant agricultural sectors all increased production in that period, but because of rapid growth in other sectors of the economy, the relative importance of agriculture fell, to the point where it now accounts for only 20–25 per cent of GNP in all four countries. Encouraged by the comparatively low wages of domestic labour, and mindful of the example being set by the Republic of Korea, Singapore, Taiwan and Hong Kong, each of the four has taken steps to develop a manufacturing sector oriented towards production for the world market. The course of this success story changes in more recent years, however, as the Filipino economy has been staggered by a multiplicity of problems and the growth of Indonesian and Thai economies has slowed somewhat in the face of world recession.

CULTURE IN SOUTHEAST ASIA

If the economic scene in Southeast Asia is difficult to describe in general terms, culture in that region is murkier still. Population groups run the gamut from Stone Age peoples to Javanese and Vietnamese, who are inheritors of rich traditions spanning thousands of years. The major religions include Theravada Buddhism in Burma, Thailand and Cambodia; Islam in Malaysia, Indonesia and Brunei; Christianity in the Philippines; and Mahayana Buddhism in Vietnam, where it joins with a strong Confucian element. Since all of these religions entered the regions from their places of origin elsewhere, all have had to make concessions to, or accept accretions from, the belief systems which preceded them. This means that the major religions are practised in a local variant, and the situation is complicated still further by the presence of large religious minority groups in each country. What is more, there are throughout the region important ethnic minorities with their own cultures, both autochthonous minorities and those who have arrived more recently from outside the area – chiefly Chinese, Arabs and Indians. As is to be expected, there are significant splits even within these imported minorities. With these great variations between countries, and great variations even inside countries, it is naturally difficult to generalize about culture in Southeast Asia. But a number of points can be made, especially in comparison with the situation in East Asia.

First, the major belief systems in Southeast Asia are definitely religions. They stress the importance of an afterlife, where a good place depends on one's individual performance in this life. In Christianity and Islam, the key relationship is not between superior person and subordinate person, but between person and God; actions between people are important, but the correct handling of interpersonal relationships is in essence a means to heaven and not an end in itself. In Buddhism, again, relationships between people are meant to be smooth, not simply because they ought to be smooth but because smooth relations do not distract one from attaining merit.

Second, family in Southeast Asia is not quite as important as it is in East Asia. The reach of the extended family is not as far nor its tug as strong. (The relative scarcity until recently of family or clan names is a clue to this; royal families are something of an exception to this rule.) The conditions for veneration of preceding generations were different also; the leading historian of early Southeast Asia reminds us that 'no special respect was paid to mere forebears ... Ancestor status had to be earned' (Wolters 1982:6).

Third, the position of women in Southeast Asia has differed markedly from that assigned them in Confucian cultures. In the Confucian ideal, women were viewed as house-bound, self-effacing, and submissively supportive (though, of course, many women in East Asia led lives which were far from conforming to that ideal). In most Southeast Asian societies, however, women have had active and public roles to play in society and in the economy. East Asia's recent economic success owes much to the rapid deepening and widening involvement of women in the paid labour force, but the same kind of contribution cannot be expected in Southeast Asia. There, women have long been major economic actors, and their diversion into new sectors of employment will necessarily come at the expense of their contributions in the old.

Fourth, where the brief Japanese imperial interlude in the East Asian countries touched on above had, if anything, a unifying cultural effect among them, the impact of Western colonialism in Southeast Asia divided it. British, French, Spanish, Dutch, American and Portuguese colonial influences were felt; the periods of consecutive colonial presence ranged from more than four and a half centuries in Portuguese Timor to fewer than four and a half decades in parts of Sumatra and Malaya; and Thailand was not colonized at all, merely forced to act like a colonized area. This chequerboard pattern left behind a mixed legacy of institutions – administrative, economic and social – which have demanded cultural adaptations.

Finally, whereas in East Asia the dominant cultural motif, Confucianism, is a set of values idealizing (and ideal for) administrators, in Southeast Asia the major religions do not necessarily work that way. Both Buddhism and Christianity have their own hierarchies running parallel to state bureaucracies; the potential exists (and has always existed) for those religious networks to act either in tandem with or in opposition to the secular administrative structure, and they have done both at different periods of time. Because it has no intermediaries between God and mankind, the form of Islam practised in Southeast Asia has no hierarchical structure, but religious community leaders and important religious teachers have rarely been incorporated into the state with any success. Religion thus does not provide the same kind of automatic support for government in Southeast Asia that Confucian values are able to do in East Asia.

INSTITUTIONS IN SOUTHEAST ASIA

Many of the Southeast Asian governments in the period immediately following independence were weak states, in the sense that they were either submissive to the control of small groups within the population (in Cambodia, Laos, Malaysia and the Philippines) or were incapable of agreeing upon or implementing policy (Burma and Indonesia). Over the course of time, however, as single-party dominance has emerged as an established phenomenon, as the military has gained greater power, and as state bureaucracies have grown in size and in expertise, governments in the region have become markedly stronger. Despite earlier ideals and present-day subterfuges, only in Malaysia does one find the combination of a representative body with policymaking capabilities and a loyal opposition which could conceivably come to power legally and initiate new policies.

There are a number of different types of major business concerns in Southeast Asia, and their structures and orientations can differ widely. First, there are private firms left over from the colonial period, usually concentrated in commerce, in extraction, or in production of bulk goods for domestic markets; their managerial staff might now have a higher percentage of local than of expatriate personnel, but the pattern of a relatively high labourer-to-manager ratio still persists. Second, there are government firms, either taken over from (public or private) colonial companies or established recently as capital-intensive industries; their labourer-to-manager ratio is likely to be much lower as the influence of bureaucratization makes itself felt. Third, there are international firms with expatriates in the key management positions, indigenous personnel in the other management positions, and a well-checked labour component; these firms are concentrated in banking and commerce, in assembly or licensed production for local consumption, and, more recently, in special-export-zone production for markets overseas. Fourth, there are government-protected firms, strong in the processing and servicing fields; these operate under a blanket of licences and other forms of assistance. And fifth, there are local firms operating on a competitive basis; a disproportionate number of these are owned and run by local Chinese businessmen.

The connection between government and industry in Southeast Asia is not as harmonious or as fruitful as in East Asia. Because governments in the region control some firms and protect still others, and because the interests of those special firms have to be guarded, it is difficult for governments to be seen as even-handed or balanced in their treatment of industry as a whole; forceful economic decisions emanating from a government, then, are likely to arouse suspicions of favouritism rather than received as considerations based on a wider perspective. Governments in Southeast Asia do not as a rule (Singapore is something of an exception) have the capacity to offer detailed and considered long-range analyses, nor can they provide much in the way of marketing assistance overseas. There is personnel movement between government and business in Southeast Asia, but the form it takes is not always propitious: in too many instances, it simply means the retirement of an unpromotable public servant or military officer into either a government-controlled firm or into a firm seeking to deepen its government protection. The relationship between government and industry in Southeast Asia is made still less comfortable by the fact that not only do officials and business leaders seldom share common educational experiences but they are often also members of different ethnic or regional groups, separated by their walls of stereotypes.

THE FIT IN SOUTHEAST ASIA

Since it is difficult to generalize about economic progress in Southeast Asia and impossible to generalize about culture there, it is no mean task to attempt to explore the fit between important values and the pace and form of industrialization in the region. However, one fact is obvious. In all of Southeast Asia, only two governments – those of Singapore and Indonesia – have made unequivocal commitments to development. In the others, concerns about ethnic balance or regional instability or regime maintenance have frequently taken priority over development, but in Indonesia and Singapore, over the last twenty years, development has inevitably come first – along different paths and with different results so far, according to their different natural endowments. However, it is precisely those two governments which are consciously engaged in a process of trying to shape a national culture, and each of the two countries is bound together more by what their people have in common in the future than by what they had in common in the past. Elsewhere in the region, perhaps, governments, as the ultimate arbiters of values, have to be more concerned about losing traditions than about establishing new ones, for it is thus far a moot point as to whether and how culture affects development, but there is no doubt that development affects culture.

CONCLUSION

Just over twenty years ago, three important works appeared treating the relationship between culture and economic change in Southeast Asia: Geertz (1956, 1963), Ayal (1963), and Maung (1964). All three said (with proper and eloquent academic reservations in the case of Geertz) something at least guardedly optimistic about the possibilities of establishing a link between culture and economic orientation. On the basis of their sensitive understanding, they provided guidelines for prognostications about future developments. Those guidelines have not proved particularly useful. According to Ayal, the Thais, because they were too individualistic and insufficiently socially oriented, were ill-prepared for economic progress; Thailand's economy grew at the rate of some 8 per cent per year for the following twenty years. The Burmese, Mya Maung noted, had a culture and traditions which thwarted the government's economic development plans; after fifteen years of being thwarted by the government, Burma's economy has been moving along at a 6 per cent annual growth rate since the late 1970s. Geertz saw pious Muslim traders as an important formative element in an emergent Indonesian middle class; an Indonesian middle class has emerged, there are still pious Muslim traders, and the two are not related. Despite these setbacks, and numerous other ones like them, it is important not to throw out the baby with the bathwater. The difficulty in establishing in a useful way any connection between culture and development does not necessarily mean that there is no connection, that such a connection would not be useful, or that the difficulty cannot be overcome. In distinct efforts, separated by distance and time, there is guidance along a research path that appears to be the most promising for an exploration of the culture/industrialization nexus. Castles (1967), in work done twenty years ago on the cigarette industry in a Javanese town, found more convincing (and better, as things turned out) reasons for worrying about pious Muslim traders than Geertz had for seeing the future in them, and George Hicks and Gordon Redding, at the start of a long-term project (Hicks and Redding 1983, 1984a, 1984b), are looking at management techniques within Chinese firms. Important in both of these is a willingness, after seeing the problem, to focus on particulars in the first instance; that is, to attempt to handle only specific cultural elements in relation to specific economic actions and decisions, instead of, perforce, talking vaguely about culture and development as whole concepts. This might lack the initial glamour of grand theorizing, but it cannot help but be more effective in enabling scholars to grapple with more concrete elements in manageable units. This approach, however, would require that, instead of letting anthropologists or sociologists do the dirty work for them, people with economics training would have to spend large amounts of time looking at the connection between people and ideas instead of that between statistics and ideas. Such a development would be laudable, but it seems unlikely, given the culture of economists.

BIBLIOGRAPHY

Adelman, I. and Robinson, S., 1978. *Income Distribution Policy in Developing Countries: A Case Study of Korea*, Oxford, Oxford University Press.

Aghazadeh, E. and Evans, D., 1985. Price distortions, efficiency and growth. Institute of Development Studies, University of Sussex (mimeo).

Ahluwalia, J., 1985. *Industrial Growth in India – Stagnation Since the Mid-Sixties*, Delhi, Oxford University Press.

Ahluwalia, M. S., 1978. 'Rural poverty in India: 1956–57 to 1973–74', *Journal of Development Studies*, 14(3): 298–323.

Akrasanee, N., 1980. 'Economic development in Thailand and ASEAN economic cooperation with special reference to commodity problems' in R. Garnaut (ed.), *ASEAN in a Changing Pacific and World Economy*, Canberra, ANU Press: 315–38.

1981. 'Trade strategies for employment growth in developing countries' in A. O. Krueger and others (eds), *Trade and Employment in Developing Countries, 1. Individual Studies*, Chicago, University of Chicago Press: 393–432.

Amsden, A. H., 1984a. The state and Taiwan's economic development. Graduate School of Business Administration, Harvard University (mimeo).

1984b. 'Taiwan' in S. Lall (ed.), *Exports of Technology by Newly-Industrializing Countries*, in *World Development*, Special Issue, 12(516): 491–504.

Anderson, B., 1972. 'The idea of power in Indonesian culture' in C. M. Holt (ed.), *Culture and Politics in Indonesia*, Ithaca, Cornell University Press: 1–70.

1982. 'Perspective and method in American research in Indonesia' in B. Anderson and A. Rahin (eds), *Interpreting Indonesian Politics: Thir-*

344

teen Contributions to the Debate, Ithaca, Cornell Modern Indonesia Project, Interim Reports Series No. 62: 69–83.

Anwar, M. A., 1980. 'Trade strategies and industrial development in Indonesia' in R. Garnaut (ed.), *ASEAN in a Changing Pacific and World Economy*, Canberra, ANU Press: 207–31.

Ariff, M. and Hill, H., 1985a. *Export Orientated Industrialization: The ASEAN Experience*, Sydney, George Allen and Unwin.

1985b. Industrial policies and performance in ASEAN's 'Other Four'. Paper for 15th Pacific Trade and Development Conference, 26–29 August, Tokyo.

forthcoming. 'Protection for manufactures in ASEAN', *Asian Economic Journal*.

Arndt, H. W., 1983. 'Financial development in Asia', *Asian Development*, 1(1): 86–100.

1984. *The Indonesian Economy: Collected Papers*, Singapore, Chopmen Publishers.

Asian Development Bank, 1977, 1983, 1984, 1985. *Key Indicators of Developing Member Countries of ADB*, Manila, Asian Development Bank.

Ayal, E., 1963. 'Value systems and economic development in Japan and Thailand', *Journal of Social Issues*, 19: 35–51.

Baechler, J., 1975. *The Origins of Capitalism*, Oxford, Blackwell.

Bagchi, A., 1976. 'Long term constraints on India's industrial growth, 1951–1968' in E. A. G. Robinson and M. Kidron (eds), *Economic Development in South Asia*, London, Macmillan: 170–92.

Balassa, B., 1977. *Policy Reform in Developing Countries*, Oxford, Pergamon Press.

1981a. 'The process of industrial development and alternative development strategies' in B. Balassa (ed.), *The Newly Industrializing Countries in the World Economy*, New York, Pergamon Press: 1–24.

1981b. *The Newly Industrializing Countries in the World Economy*, New York, Pergamon Press.

1982a. 'Development strategies and economic performance: a comparative analysis of eleven semi-industrial economies' in B. Balassa and Associates (eds), *Development Strategies in Semi-Industrial Economies*, Baltimore, Johns Hopkins University Press: 38–62.

1982b. 'The structure of incentives in six semi-industrial economies' in B. Balassa and Associates (eds), *Development Strategies in Semi-Industrial Economies*, Baltimore, Johns Hopkins University Press: 22–37.

and Associates, 1971. *The Structure of Protection in Developing Countries*, Baltimore, Johns Hopkins University Press.

and Associates, 1982. *Development Strategies in Semi-Industrial Econ-*

omies, Baltimore, Johns Hopkins University Press.

Balasubramanyam, V. N., 1980. *Multinational Enterprises and the Third World*, Thames Essay 26, London, Trade Policy Research Centre.

Balogh, T., 1963. *Unequal Partners*, 2 vols, Oxford, Blackwell.

Bardhan, P., 1970. 'On the minimum level of living and the rural poor', *Indian Economic Review*, 5(1): 129–36.

Bates, R., 1981. *States and Markets in Tropical Africa*, Berkeley, University of California Press.

Baum, R., 1982. 'Science and culture in contemporary China: the roots of retarded modernization', *Asian Survey*, 1(12): 1166–86.

Bautista, R. M., 1980. 'Trade strategies and industrial development: with special reference to regional trade preferences' in R. Garnaut (ed.), *ASEAN in a Changing Pacific and World Economy*, Canberra, ANU Press: 175–201.

1981. 'The 1981–85 tariff changes and effective protection of manufacturing industries', *Journal of Philippine Development*, 8(102): 1–20.

1983. *Industrial Policy and Development in the ASEAN Countries*, Manila, Philippine Institute for Development Studies, Monograph Series No. 2.

1984. 'Recent shifts in industrialization strategies and trade patterns of ASEAN countries', *ASEAN Economic Bulletin*, 1(1): 7–25.

Power, J. and Associates, 1979. *Industrial Promotion Policies in the Philippines*, Manila, Philippine Institute for Development Economics.

Bhagwati, J., 1978. *Anatomy and Consequences of Exchange Control Regimes*, Cambridge, Ballinger Publishing Co.

and Srinivasan, T. N., 1978. *Foreign Trade Regimes and Economic Development: India*, Columbia, National Bureau of Economic Research.

Bhattacharya, D., 1979. *A Concise History of the Indian Economy, 1750–1950*, 2nd edition, New Delhi, Prentice Hall of India.

Billerbeck, K. and Yasugi, Y., 1979. 'Private direct foreign investment in developing countries', *World Bank Staff Working Paper*, No. 348, Washington DC, World Bank.

Boeke, J. H., 1953. *Economics and Economic Policies of Dual Societies – As Exemplified by Indonesia*, New York, Institute of Pacific Relations.

1966. *Indonesian Economics: The Concept of Dualism in Theory and Practice*, The Hague, van Hoeve.

Bogert, C., 1984. The politics of unorganization: the Kaomintang on Taiwan. Ph.D. dissertation, Harvard Business College.

Bohn-Young Koo, 1982. Role of foreign direct investment in recent Korean economic growth. Seoul, Korean Development Institute,

Working Paper 8104.

Boltho, A., 1981. 'Italian and Japanese postwar growth: some similarities and some diferences', *Rivista Internazionale di Scienze Economiche e Commerciali*, 28: 626–41.

—— 1984. Was Japan's industrial policy successful? Magdalen College, Cambridge (mimeo).

Booth, A. and McCawley P. (eds), 1981. *The Indonesian Economy During the Suharto Era*, Kuala Lumpur, Oxford University Press.

Borthwick S., 1985. Education and Chinese identity in Indonesia. Symposium paper for Changing Identities of the Southeast Asian Chinese since World War II, ANU, Canberra.

Bradford, C., 1984. 'The Nic's: confronting US "autonomy"'' in R. Feinberg and V. Kallab (eds), *Adjustment Crisis in the Third World*, New Brunswick, Overseas Development Council, Transaction Books: 119–38.

Carroll, J. J., 1965. *The Filipino Manufacturing Entrepreneur*, Ithaca, Cornell University Press.

Castles, L., 1967. *Religion, Politics and Economic Behaviour in Java: The Kudus Cigarette Industry*, New Haven, Yale University Southeast Asia Studies.

Chakravarty, S., 1977. 'Reflections on the growth process in the Indian economy' in C. D. Wadhwa (ed.), *Some Problems of Indian Economic Policy*, 2nd edition, Delhi, Tata McGraw Hill: 113–36.

Chapman, E. C., 1984. 'Thailand's recent economic growth' in M. G. Adams (ed.), *Economic Development in East and Southeast Asia: Implications for Australian Agriculture in the 1980's*, Canberra, Australian Government Publishing Service: 205–17.

Chatterjee, G. S. and Bhattacharya, M., 1971. 'On rural-urban differentials in consumer prices and per capita household consumption in India, by levels of living', *Sankhya*, The Indian Journal of Statistics Series B, 33(1–2): 355–70.

Chen, E. K. Y., 1979. *Hyper-Growth in Asian Economies: a Comparative Study of Hong Kong, Japan, Korea, Singapore and Taiwan*, London, Macmillan.

—— 1983. *Multinational Corporations, Technology and Employment*, London, Macmillan.

—— 1984. 'Hong Kong' in S. Lall (ed.), *Exports of Technology by Newly Industrializing Countries*, in *World Development*, Special Issue, 12(5–6): 481–90.

—— 1985. The newly industrializing countries in Asia: growth, experience and prospects. Hong Kong University, Department of Economics, Discussion Paper 55.

Chen, P. S. and Evers, H., 1978. *Studies in ASEAN Sociology, Urban*

Society and Social Change, Singapore, Chopmen Publishers.

Chenery, H. B., 1979. *Structural Change and Development Policy*, London, Oxford University Press.

and Bruno, M., 1962. 'Development alternatives in an open economy: the case of Israel', *Economic Journal*, 72(285): 79–103.

and Syrquin, M., 1975. *Patterns of Development, 1950–1970*, London, Oxford University Press.

and Syrquin, M., in press. 'The semi-industrial countries' in H. B. Chenery, S. Robinson, and M. Syrquin (eds), *Industrialization and Growth: A Comparative Study*, London, Oxford University Press.

Robinson, S. and Syrquin, M., (eds), in press. *Industrialization and Growth : A Comparative Study*, London, Oxford University Press.

Chia, S. Y., 1980. 'Singapore's trade and development strategy and ASEAN economic co-operation, with special reference to the ASEAN common approach to foreign economic relations' in R. Garnaut (ed.), *ASEAN in a Changing Pacific and World Economy*, Canberra, ANU Press: 241–72.

China, Republic of, Central Bank, various years. *Financial Statistics, Taiwan District*, Taipei.

Statistical Department, 1982. *The Trade of China (Taiwan District) 1981*, Taipei, Inspectorate General of Customs.

Choo, H., 1980. 'Economic growth and income distribution' in C. R. Park (ed.), *Human Resources and Social Development in Korea*, Seoul, Korean Development Institute: 277–335.

Chou, S., 1963. *The Chinese Inflation*, New York, Columbia University Press.

Chow, S.C. and Papanek, G. F., 1981. 'Laissez-faire, growth and equity – Hong Kong', *Economic Journal*, 91(362): 466–85.

Christensen, L. R., Cummings, D. and Jorgensen, D. W., 1980. 'Economic growth 1947–73, an international comparison' in J. W. Kendrick and B. N. Vaccara (eds), *New Developments in Productivity Measurement and Analysis*, National Bureau of Economic Research Studies in Income and Wealth, 44, Chicago, University of Chicago Press: 595–691.

Clark, C., 1940. *The Conditions of Economic Progress*, London, Macmillan.

Coble, P., 1980. *The Shanghai Capitalists and the Nationalist Government, 1927–1937*, Cambridge, Harvard University Press.

Cole, A., 1967. 'The political roles of Taiwanese entrepreneurs', *Asian Survey*, 7(9): 645–54.

Cole, D. C. and Lyman, P., 1971. *Korean Development: the Interplay of Politics and Economics*, Cambridge, Harvard University Press.

and Park, Y. C., 1983. *Financial Developments in Korea: 1945–78*, Cambridge, Harvard University Press.

and Patrick, H., 1984. Financial development in the Pacific Basin market economies. Paper for the 14th Pacific Trade and Development Conference, Singapore.

Collier, P. *et al.*, 1984. The Macroeconomics of liberalisation – with an application to East Africa. London, Trade Policy Research Centre (mimeo).

Coppel, C. A., 1983. *Indonesian Chinese in Crisis*, Kuala Lumpur, Oxford University Press.

Corden, W. M., 1984. 'Booming sector and Dutch Disease economics: a survey', *Oxford Economic Papers*, 36(3): 359–80.

and Neary, J. P., 1982. 'Booming sector and de-industrialization in a small open economy', *Economic Journal*, 92: 825–48.

Council for Economic Planning and Development, 1984. *Taiwan Statistical Data Book 1984*, Republic of China.

Crouch, H., 1978. *The Army and Politics in Indonesia*, Ithaca, Cornell University Press.

1984. *Domestic Political Structures and Regional Economic Cooperation*, Singapore, Institute of Southeast Asian Studies.

Cumings, B., 1981. *The Origins of the Korean War: Liberation and the Emergence of Separate Regimes 1945–1947*, Princeton, Princeton University Press.

(ed.), 1983. *Child of Conflict: The Korean American Relationship, 1943–1953*, Seattle, University of Washington Press.

1984. 'The origins and development of the Northeast Asian political economy: industrial sectors, product cycles and political consequences', *International Organization*, 38(1): 1–40.

Dandekar, V. M. and Rath, N., 1971. *Poverty in India*, Poona, Indian School of Political Economy.

Datta, U. and Chowdhry, R., 1983. 'Behaviour of capital labour ratios in the Indian economy 1950–1971' in E. A. G. Robinson and P. R. Brahmanande (eds), *A Case Study of India*, Vol. 1, London, Macmillan: 163–87.

Datta-Chaudhuri, M. K., 1981. 'Industrialization and foreign trade: the development experiences of South Korea and the Philippines' in E. Lee (ed.), *Export-Led Industrialization and Development*, Singapore, ILO Asian Employment Programme: 47–79.

Dawling, J. M. and Soo, D., 1983. Income distribution and economic growth in developing Asian countries. Manila, Asian Development Bank, Staff Paper No. 15.

Desai, A., 1981. 'Factors underlying the slow growth of Indian industry', *Economic & Political Weekly*, Annual Number.

Donges, J. B. and Riedel, J., 1977. 'Expansion of manufactured exports in developing countries: an assessment of supply and demand issues', *Weltwirtschaftliches Archiv*, 113(1): 58–87.

Dore, R., 1985. 'Financial structures and the long-term view', *Policy Studies*, 6(1): 10–29.

Doronila, A., 1985. 'The transformation of patron–client relations and its political consequences in the postwar Philippines', *Journal of Southeast Asian Studies*, 16(1): 99–116.

Drake, P. J., 1984. The development of equity and bond markets in the Pacific region. Paper for the 14th Pacific Trade and Development Conference, Singapore.

Dutta, B., 1980. 'Intersectoral disparities and income distribution in India, 1960–61 to 1973–74', *Indian Economic Review*, 10(2): 119–38.

Eastman, L., 1974. *The Abortive Revolution: China Under Nationalist Rule, 1927–1937*, Cambridge, Harvard University Press.

Economic Commission for Europe/UN Centre on Transnational Corporations, 1983. Industrialization and trade of developing countries: some reflections on the participation of transnational corporations. ECE/UNCTC, Geneva (mimeo).

Elias, V. J., 1978. 'Sources of economic growth in Latin American countries', *Review of Economics and Statistics*, 60: 363–70.

Elliott, D., 1978. *Thailand: Origins of Military Rule*, London, Zed Press.

Enos, J., 1984. 'Government intervention in the transfer of technology: the case of South Korea', *IDS Bulletin*, 15(2): 26–31.

Economic and Social Commission for Asia and the Pacific, 1981. *Statistical Yearbook for Asia and the Pacific 1980*, Bangkok, ESCAP.

Fei, J. C. H., Ranis, G. and Kuo, S. W. Y., 1979. *Growth with Equity: The Taiwan Case*, New York, Oxford University Press.

Feith, H., 1962. *The Decline of Constitutional Democracy in Indonesia*, Ithaca, Cornell University Press.

Fields, G. S., 1980. *Poverty, Inequality and Development*, Cambridge, Cambridge University Press.

1984. 'Employment income distribution, and economic growth in seven small open economies', *Economic Journal*, 94(373): 74–83.

Fisk, E. K. and Rani, O. (eds), 1982. *The Political Economy of Malaysia*, Kuala Lumpur, Oxford University Press.

Flood, E. T., 1976. *The U.S. and the Military Coup in Thailand: A Background Study*, Washington, Indochina Resource Center.

Fransman, M., 1985. Conceptualizing technical change in the third world in the 1980s: an interpretative survey. Department of Economics, University of Edinburgh (mimeo).

Funston, J., 1980. *Malay Politics in Malaysia: A Study of UMNO and PAS*, Singapore, Heinemann Educational Books.

Galenson, W. (ed.), 1979. *Economic Growth and Structural Change in*

Taiwan: The Postwar Experience of the Republic of China, Ithaca, Cornell University Press.

Garnaut, R. (ed.), 1980. *ASEAN in a Changing Pacific and World Economy*, Canberra, ANU Press.

Gastil, R., 1973. 'The new criteria of freedom', *Freedom at Issue*, 17: 3–23.

    1984. 'The comparative survey of freedom 1984', *Freedom at Issue*, 76: 3–15.

Geertz, C., 1956. 'Religious belief and economic behaviour in a central Javanese town: some preliminary considerations', *Economic Development and Cultural Change*, 4(2): 134–58.

    1963. *Peddlers and Princes: Social Development and Economic Change in Two Indonesian Towns*, Chicago, University of Chicago Press.

Gillis, M., 1984. 'Episodes in Indonesian economic growth' in A. Harberger (ed.), *World Economic Growth: Case Studies of Developed and Developing Countries*, San Francisco, Institute for Continuing Studies: 231–64.

Girling, J. L. S., 1981a. *Thailand: Society and Politics*, Ithaca, Cornell University Press.

    1981b. *The Bureaucratic Polity in Modernizing Societies*, Singapore, Institute of Southeast Asian Studies.

Glassburner, B. (ed.), 1971. *The Economy of Indonesia: Selected Readings*, Ithaca, Cornell University Press.

    1984. *ASEAN's 'Other Four': Economic Policy and Performance Since 1970*, Kuala Lumpur and Canberra, ASEAN–Australia Joint Research Project, Economic Papers No. 10.

Golay, F., 1961. *The Philippines. Public Policy and National Economic Development*, Ithaca, Cornell University Press.

    1966. 'Economic collaboration: the role of American investment' in F. Golay (ed.), *Philippine American Relations*, Manila, Solidaridad.

    1983. Social and economic problems facing the Philippines 1983–2000. Paper for Committee for Industrial Development of Australia, August.

    et al., 1969. *Underdevelopment and Economic Nationalism in Southeast Asia*, Ithaca, Cornell University Press.

Gregor, A. J., Chang, M. and Zimmerman, A., 1982. *Ideology and Development: Sun-yat Sen and the Economic History of Taiwan*, Berkeley, University of California Press.

Griffin, K., 1973. 'An assessment of development in Taiwan', *World Development*, 1(6): 31–42.

Grindle, M. S., 1980. 'Policy content and context in implementation' in M. S. Grindle (ed.), *Politics and Policy Implementation in the Third World*, Princeton, Princeton University Press: 3–39.

Hadley, E., 1970. *Antitrust in Japan*, Princeton, Princeton University Press.

Hagen, E. E., 1957. 'The process of economic development', *Economic Development and Cultural Change*, 5(3): 193–215.

1962. *On the Theory of Social Change: How Economic Growth Begins*, Homewood, Dorsey.

1968. *The Economics of Development*, Homewood, Irwin.

Haggard, S. and Cheng, T., 1983. State strategies, local and foreign capital in the Gang of Four. Paper for American Political Science Association Conference, Chicago, September.

and Moon, C., 1983. 'The South Korean state in the international system: liberal, dependent or mercantile?' in J. Ruggie (ed.), *The Antinomies of Interdependence*, New York, Columbia University Press: 131–91.

Hamilton, C., 1983. 'Capitalist industrialization in East Asia's four little tigers', *Journal of Contemporary Asia*, 18(1): 35–73.

Han, S. S., 1974. *The Failure of Democracy in South Korea*, Berkeley, University of California Press.

1984. 'Of economic success and Confucianism', *Far Eastern Economic Review*, 126(51): 104–6.

Harberger, A. C., 1983. 'Dutch Disease: how much sickness, how much boom?' *Resources and Energy*, 5(1): 1–20.

1985. 'Observations in the Chilean economy, 1973–83', *Economic Development and Cultural Change*, 33(3): 451–62.

Havrylyshyn, O. and Aiikhani, I., 1982. 'Is there a cause for export pessimism', *Weltwirtschaftliches Archiv*, 118(4): 651–63.

Healey, J. M., 1965. *The Development of Social Overhead Capital in India, 1950–60*, Oxford, Blackwell.

Helleiner, G. K., 1973. 'Manufactured exports from less developed countries and multinational firms', *Economic Journal*, 83(329): 21–47.

Heston, A., 1983. 'National income' in D. Kumar (ed.), *The Cambridge Economic History of India*, vol. 2, Cambridge, Cambridge University Press.

Hewison, K. J., 1981. 'The financial bourgeoisie in Thailand', *Journal of Contemporary Asia*, 11(4): 395–412.

1983. The development of capital, public policy and the role of the state in Thailand. Ph.D. dissertation, Murdoch University, Perth.

Hicks, G. L. and Redding, S. G., 1983. Culture, causation and Chinese management. University of Hong Kong, February (mimeo).

1984a. 'The story of the East Asian "economic miracle"; Part One: economic theory be damned', *Euro-Asia Business Review*, 2(3): 24–32.

1984b. 'The story of the East Asian "economic miracle"; Part Two: The culture connection', *Euro-Asia Business Review*, 2(4): 18–22.

Hicks, J. R., 1969. *A Theory of Economic History*, Oxford, Clarendon Press.

Higgins, B., 1955. 'The "Dualistic Theory" of underdeveloped areas', *Ekonomi dan Keuangan Indonesia*, 3(2): 58–78.

—— 1959. *Economic Development: Principles, Problems and Policies*, New York, Norton.

Hill, H., 1985. Foreign investment and industrialization in Indonesia. Canberra, ANU, May (mimeo).

—— and Jayasuriya, S., 1985. *The Philippines: Growth, Debt and Crisis. Economic Performance During the Marcos Era*, Canberra, ANU, Development Studies Centre Working Paper No. 85/3.

—— and Johns, B., 1985. The role of direct foreign investment in developing East Asian countries. Canberra, ANU (mimeo).

Hirschman, A. O., 1981. *Essays in Trespassing: Economics to Politics and Beyond*, Cambridge, Cambridge University Press.

Hirschman, C. R., 1975. *Ethnic and Social Stratification in Peninsular Malaysia*, Washington, American Sociological Association.

Ho, S., 1978. *Economic Development of Taiwan, 1860–1970*, New Haven, Yale University Press.

Hoffmann, L. and Tan Siew Ee, 1980. *Industrial Growth, Employment and Foreign Investment in Peninsular Malaysia*, Kuala Lumpur, Oxford University Press.

Hofheinz, R. and Calder, K. E., 1982. *The Eastasia Edge*, New York, Basic Books.

Hollensteiner, M. A., 1963. *The Dynamics of Power in a Philippine Municipality*, Manila, University of the Philippines, Community Development Research Council.

Hong, W., 1981. 'Export promotion and employment growth in South Korea' in A. O. Krueger (ed.), *Trade and Employment in Developing Countries, 1. Individual Studies*, Chicago, University of Chicago Press: 341–92.

Hosomi, Takashi and Okumura, Ariyoshi, 1982. 'Japanese industrial policy' in J. Pinder (ed.), *National Industrial Strategies and the World Economy*, London, Croom Helm: 123–57.

Hsiao, H.-H., M., 1981. *Government Agricultural Strategies in Taiwan and Korea*, Taipei, Institute of Ethnology, Academia Sinica.

Hsing, M., 1971. *Taiwan: Industrialization and Trade Policies*, London, Oxford University Press.

Hsiung, J. C. (ed.), 1981. *The Taiwan Experience 1950–1980*, New York, Praeger Publishers.

Hughes, H., 1985. *Policy Lessons of the Development Experience*, New York, Group of Thirty, Occasional Paper No. 16.

—— 1986. 'Changing needs of the developing countries in the eighties' in S.

Borner and A. Taylor (eds), *Structural Change, Economic Interdependence and World Development*, Proceedings of the International Economic Association, Seventh World Congress, Madrid, 5–9 September 1983, Vol. 2, London, Macmillan.

and Dorrance, G., 1984. Economic policies and direct foreign investment with particular reference to the developing countries of East Asia. Paper prepared for Commonwealth Secretariat, January.

and Seng, Y. P. (eds), 1969. *Foreign Investment and Industrialization in Singapore*, Canberra, ANU Press.

Ikonicoff, M., 1985. 'Making the most of multinational capital', *Manchester Guardian Weekly*, 4: 13.

International Labour Organisation, 1980. *Export Led Industrialisation and Employment*, Bangkok, ILO.

International Monetary Fund (IMF), various years. *International Financial Statistics*, Washington DC, IMF.

1977a. *Balance of Payments Statistics, Yearbook*, 27(1), Washington DC, IMF.

1977b. *Direction of Trade Statistics Yearbook*, Washington DC, IMF.

1984a. *Balance of Payments Statistics, Yearbook*, 35(1), Washington DC, IMF.

1984b. *Direction of Trade Statistics Yearbook*, Washington DC, IMF.

1984c. *International Financial Statistics Yearbook 1983*, Washington DC, IMF.

1985a. 'Foreign private investment in developing countries', *Occasional Paper* No. 33, January, Washington DC, IMF.

1985b. International Financial Statistics, Tape, Washington DC, IMF.

1985c. *International Financial Statistics Yearbook 1984*, Washington DC, IMF.

India, Government of, Central Statistical Office, 1961. *Estimates of National Income, 1948–9 to 1959–60*, New Delhi.

Central Statistical Office, 1982. *Basic Statistics Relating to the Indian Economy, 1950–51 to 1980–81*, New Delhi.

Central Statistical Office, various years. *Statistical Abstract of India*, New Delhi.

Ministry of Railways, various years. *Reports of the Railway Board*, New Delhi.

National Planning Office, 1978. *Draft Five Year Plan 1978–83*, Planning Commission, New Delhi.

Reserve Bank of, 1977. 'Index numbers of industrial production – revised series', *RBI Bulletin*, February, Bombay.

Inkster, I., 1983. 'Modelling Japan for the Third World' in *East Asia: International Review of Economic, Political and Social Development*. Frankfurt, Cary Campus Verlag, Part I: 155–87.

Jacobs, B. J., 1978. 'Paradoxes in the politics of Taiwan: lessons for comparative politics', *Politics*, 13(2): 239–47.

Jacoby, N., 1966. *US Aid to Taiwan: A Study of Foreign Aid, Self-Help and Development*, New York, Praeger Publishers.

Jha, P. S., 1985. The public sector in India: an appraisal. China Division, World Bank, June (mimeo).

Johnson, C., 1981. 'Introduction – The Taiwan model' in J. C. Hsiung (ed.), *The Taiwan Experience 1950–1980*, New York, Praeger Publishers: 9–18.

1982. *MITI and the Japanese Miracle; The Growth of Industrial Policy 1925–1975*, Stanford, Stanford University Press.

1983. Political institutions and economic performance: a comparative analysis of the government–business relationship in Japan, South Korea, and Taiwan. Department of Political Science, University of California, Berkeley (mimeo).

1985. The Japanese economy: a different kind of capitalism, Department of Political Science, University of California, Berkeley (mimeo).

Jones, E. L., 1981. *The European Miracle: Environment, Economics and Geopolitics in the History of Europe and Asia*, Cambridge, Cambridge University Press.

Jones, G. W., 1975. 'Implications of prospective urbanization for development planning in Southeast Asia' in J. F. Kantner and L. McCaffrey (eds), *Population and Development in Southeast Asia*, Lexington, Lexington Books: 99–118.

Jones, L. P. and Sakong, I., 1980. *Government, Business and Entrepreneurship in Economic Development: the Korean Case*, Cambridge, Harvard University Press.

Jung, W. S. and Marshall, P. J., 1985. 'Exports, growth and causality in developing countries', *Journal of Development Economics*, 18(1): 1–2.

Jung Soo Lee, 1983. 'The external debt-servicing capacity of Asian developing countries', *Asian Development Review*, 1(2): 66–82.

Kahin, G. McT., 1952. *Nationalism and Revolution in Indonesia*, Ithaca, Cornell University Press.

(ed.), 1959. *Government and Politics in Southeast Asia*, Ithaca, Cornell University Press.

Kahn, H., 1979. *World Economic Development*, Boulder, Westview Press.

Kaplan, D. and Manners, R., 1972. *Culture Theory*, Englewood Cliffs, Prentice-Hall.

Karnik, V. B., 1978. *Indian Trade Unions – A Survey*, 3rd edition, Bombay, Popular Prakashan.

Kasper, W., 1974. *Malaysia: A Study in Successful Economic Development*, Washington DC, American Enterprise Institute.

Kazushi, O. and Rossovsky, H., 1968. 'Postwar Japanese growth in historical perspective: a second look' in L. R. Klein and K. Ohkawa (eds), *Economic Growth – The Japanese Experience Since the Meiji Era*, Homewood, R. D. Irwin: 3–34.

Keesing, D. B., 1979. 'Trade policy for developing countries', *World Bank Staff Working Paper* No. 353, Washington DC, World Bank.

Keesing, R., 1974. 'Theories of culture', *Annual Review of Anthropology*, Palo Alto, Annual Reviews Inc.

Kerr, C., Dunlop, J. T., Harbison, F. and Myers, C. A., 1960. *Industrialism and Industrial Man: The Problems of Labor and Management in Economic Growth*, Cambridge, Harvard University Press.

Keynes, J. M., 1926. *The End of Laissez-Faire*, London, Hogarth Press.

Kim, Il Shin, 1983. *Jukyo Bunkaken No Chitsujo to Keizai* [*The Order and Economy under the Influence of Confucian-Based Culture*], Nagoya, Nagoya University Press.

Kim, J. A., 1975. *Divided Korea: The Politics of Development 1945–1972*, Cambridge, Harvard University Press.

Kim, K., 1976. 'Political factors in the formation of the entrepreneurial elite in South Korea', *Asian Survey*, 16(5): 465–77.

Kim, K. B., 1971. *The Korean-Japan Treaty Crisis and the Instability of the Korean Political System*, New York, Praeger Publishers.

Kim, K. S. and Roemer, M., 1979. *Growth and Structural Transformation*, Cambridge, Harvard University Press.

Kim, K. W., 1981. 'South Korea' in C. Saunders (ed.), *The Political Economy of New and Old Industrial Countries*, London, Butterworth: 159–82.

Kirkpatrick, C., 1985. Export oriented industrialization and labour market regulation in Singapore. Seminar paper, Department of Economics, Research School of Pacific Studies, Canberra, ANU.

Kojima, K., 1979. *Japanese Direct Foreign Investment*, Tokyo, Charles Tuttle.

Koo Bohn Young, 1984. The role of government in Korea's industrial development. Seoul, Korea Development Institute Working Paper 8407.

Korea, Republic of, 1985. *Major Statistics of the Korean Economy*, Seoul.

Krirkiat, P. and Kunio, Y., 1983. Business groups in Thailand. Singapore, ISEAS Research Notes and Discussions.

Kroeber, A. L. and Kluckhohn, C., 1952. 'Culture: a critical review of concepts and definitions', *Peabody Museum Papers*, 47(1).

Krueger, A. O., 1978. *Liberalization Attempts and Consequences*, New York, National Bureau of Economic Research.

1979. *The Development Role of the Foreign Sector and Aid*, Cambridge, Harvard University Press.

1981. 'Loans to assist the transition to outward-looking policies', *The World Economy*, 4(3): 271–82.

1983. *Trade and Employment in Developing Countries*, Vol. 3: *Synthesis and Conclusions*, Chicago, Chicago University Press.

1984. 'Comparative advantage and development policy: 20 years later' in M. Syrquin, M. Taylor and L. E. Westphal (eds), *Economic Structure and Performance*, Orlando, Academic Press: 135–55.

Kumar, D. (ed.), 1983. *The Cambridge Economic History of India*, Vol II, C1757–C1980, Cambridge, Cambridge University Press.

Kuo, S. W. T., 1983. *The Taiwan Economy in Transition*, Boulder, Westview Press.

Kuznets, S., 1957. 'Quantitative aspects of economic growth of nations: II Industrial distribution of national product and labour force', *Economic Development and Cultural Change*, 9:1–124.

1966. *Modern Economic Growth*, New Haven, Yale University Press.

Lal, D., 1972. *Wells and Welfare*, Paris, OECD Development Centre.

1973. *New Economic Policies for India*, London, Fabian Research Series 311.

1975. *Appraising Foreign Investment in Developing Countries*, London, Heinemann Educational Books.

1976. 'Agricultural growth, real wages and the rural poor in India', *Economic and Political Weekly*, Review of Agriculture, 26 June: A47–A61.

1978. 'On the multinationals', *ODI Review*, 2:79–98.

1979a. 'Indian export incentives', *Journal of Development Economics*, 6:103–17.

1979b. 'Theories of industrial use structures', *World Bank Staff Working Paper* No. 142, Washington DC, World Bank.

1979c. The continuing hangover. Seminar no. 244, World Bank, December.

1980a. *Prices for Planning. Towards the Reform of Indian Planning*, London, Heinemann Educational Books.

1980b. Field notes on industrial wages in India. Studies in Employment and Rural Development no. 65, World Bank, Washington DC (mimeo).

1983. 'Real wages and exchange rates in the Philippines, 1956–78: an application of the Stolper–Samuelson–Rybczynski model of trade', *World Bank Staff Working Paper* No. 604, Washington DC, World Bank.

1984. *The Poverty of Development Economics*, London, IEA, Hobart Paperback 16.

1985a. 'Nationalism, socialism and planning – influential ideas in the South', *World Development*, 13(6): 749–59.

1985b. 'The real exchange rate, capital inflows and inflation: Sri Lanka 1970–1982', *Weltwirtschaftliches Archiv*, December.

1986. *The Hindu Equilibrium*, Vol I: *Cultural Stability and Economic Stagnation – India* c.1500BC–AD1980; Vol II: *Aspects of Indian Labour*, Oxford, Clarendon Press.

and Wolf, M., 1986. *Stagflation Savings and the State – Perspectives on the Global Economy*, New York, Oxford University Press.

in press. 'Trends in real wages in rural India: 1880–1980' in P. Bardhan and T. N. Srinivasan (eds), *Poverty in India*, New York, Columbia University Press.

Lande, C., 1965. *Leaders, Factions and Parties. The Structure of Philippines Politics*, New Haven, Yale Southeast Asia Studies, Monograph Series No. 6.

Larkin, J. S., 1972. *The Pampangans: Colonial Society in a Philippine Province*, Berkeley, University of California Press.

Lee, E., 1981. *Export-led Industrialization and Development*, Singapore, ILO Asian Employment Programme.

Lee, H. B., 1968. *Korea: Time, Change, and Administration*, Honolulu, East-West Center Press.

Lee, T. H. and Liang, K. S., 1982. 'Taiwan' in B. Balassa and Associates (eds), *Development Strategies in Semi-Industrial Economies*, Baltimore, Johns Hopkins University Press: 310–50.

Lee, Y–S., 1983. The influence of monetary policy on the industrialization of Taiwan. Conference on Industrial Development in Taiwan, Academia Sinica, March [Chinese only].

Leibenstein, H., 1954. *A Theory of Economic-Demographic Development*, Princeton, Princeton University Press.

Leung Chi-Keung, Cushman, J. W. and Wang Gungwu (eds), 1980. *Hong Kong. Dilemmas of Growth*, Canberra, Research School of Pacific Studies, Australian National University.

Liang Kuo Shu, 1984. Comments on Paper by P. J. Drake, for the 14th Pacific Trade and Development Conference, Singapore.

Lidman, R. and Domerese, R. J., 1970. 'India' in W. A. Lewis (ed.), *Tropical Development, 1880–1913*, Studies in Economic Progress, London, Allen and Unwin.

Lim Chong Yah, 1984. *Economic Restructuring in Singapore*, Kuala Lumpur, Federal Publications.

Lim, D., 1973. *Economic Growth and Development in West Malaysia 1947–1970*, Kuala Lumpur, Oxford University Press.

Lim, L. and Gosling, W. A. P., 1983. *The Chinese in Southeast Asia*, Singapore, Maruzen.

Lin, B., 1985. Growth, equity and income distribution policies in Hong Kong. Chinese University of Hong Kong (mimeo).

Lin, C., 1972. *Industrialization in Taiwan 1946–1972*, New York, Praeger Publishers.

Lin, T. B. and Ho, Y. P., 1981. 'Export-oriented growth and industrial diversification in Hong Kong' in W. Hong and L. B. Krause (eds), *Trade and Growth of the Advanced Developing Countries in the Pacific Basin*, Seoul, Korea Development Institute.

Lindsey, C. W., 1981. *Foreign Direct Investment in the Philippines: a Review of the Literature*. Philippines Institute for Development Studies, Working Paper 81(11), October.

Little, A. D., Inc., 1973a. *A National Industrial Development Overview: Guidelines and Strategy for Taiwan*. Taipei, Republic of China. Industrial Development and Investment Centre.

1973b. *Perspectives on Industrial Incentives in Taiwan*, No. 5, Taipei, Republic of China, Industrial Development and Investment Centre.

Little, I. M. D., 1979a. 'An economic reconnaissance' in W. Galenson (ed.), *Economic Growth and Structural Change in Taiwan*, Ithaca, Cornell University Press: 448–508.

1979b. *True Experience and Causes of Rapid Labour Intensive Development in Korea, Taiwan, Hong Kong and Singapore: and the Possibilities of Emulation*. Bangkok, ILO Working Paper WPII-1, Asian Employment Paper (ARTEP).

1981. 'The experience and causes of rapid labour intensive development in Korea, Taiwan Province, Hong Kong and Singapore; and the possibilities of emulation' in E. Lee (ed.), *Export-led Industrialization and Development*, Singapore, ILO Asian Employment Programme: 23–47.

1982. *Economic Development: Theory, Policy and International Relations*, New York, Basic Books.

Scitovsky, T. and Scott, M. F., 1970. *Industry and Trade in Some Developing Countries*, London, Oxford University Press.

Lluch, C., Powell, A. A. and Williams, R. A., 1977. *Patterns and Household Demand and Savings*, New York, Oxford University Press.

Luedde-Neurath, R., in press. 'State intervention and export-oriented development in South Korea' in G. White and R. Wade (eds), *Development States in East Asia*, London, Macmillan.

Lutkenhorst, W., 1984. 'Import restrictions and export promotion measures in Southeast Asian countries: recent developments and future prospects', *ASEAN Economic Bulletin*, 1(1): 43–69.

McCawley, P., 1983. 'Survey of recent developments', *Bulletin of Indonesian Economic Studies*, 19(1): 1–31.

McCoy, A. W. and de Jesus, E. C. (eds), 1982. *Philippine Social History –*

Global Trade and Local Transformations, Manila, Manila University Press and Sydney, George Allen and Unwin.

McKinnon, R. I., 1964. 'Foreign exchange constraints in economic development and efficient aid allocation', *Economic Journal*, 74(291): 388–409.

1973. *Money and Capital in Economic Development*, Washington DC, The Brookings Institution.

1984. Pacific growth and financial interdependence. Paper for the 14th Pacific Trade and Development Conference, Singapore.

McVey, R. (ed.), 1963. *Indonesia*, New Haven, Human Relations Area Files Press.

Mackie, J. A. C., 1967. *Problems of the Indonesian Inflation*, Ithaca, Cornell Modern Indonesia Project, Monograph Series.

(ed.), 1976. *The Chinese in Indonesia: Five Essays*, Melbourne, Thomas Nelson.

1985. Changing economic roles and ethnic identities of the Southeast Asian Chinese – with special reference to Indonesia. Paper for ANU Symposium, Changing Identities of the Southeast Asian Chinese since World War II, Canberra.

Madan, B. K., 1977. *The Real Wages of Industrial Labour in India*, New Delhi, Management Development Institute.

Maddison, A., 1971. *Class Structure and Economic Growth – India and Pakistan Since the Moghuls*, London, Allen and Unwin.

Magaziner, I. and Hout, T., 1980. *Japanese Industrial Policy*, Monograph 585, London, Policy Studies Institute.

Mahathir bin Mohamad, 1970. *The Malay Dilemma*, Singapore, Donald Moore for Asia Pacific Press.

Mason, E., 1984. 'The Chenery analysis and some other considerations' in M. Syrquin, L. Taylor and L. Westphal (eds), *Economic Structure and Performance; Essays in Honor of Hollis B. Chenery*, New York, Academic Press: 3–22.

et al., 1980. *The Economic and Social Modernization of the Republic of Korea*, Cambridge, Harvard University Press.

Matthews, R., 1959. *The Trade Cycle*, Cambridge, Cambridge University Press.

Maung, M., 1964. 'Cultural value and economic change in Burma', *Asian Survey*, 4: 757–64.

Michell, T., 1984. 'Administrative traditions and economic decision-making in South Korea', *IDS Bulletin*, 15(2): 32–7.

Milne, S., 1967. *Government and Politics in Malaysia*, Boston, Houghton, Mifflin.

Minhas, B., 1970. 'Rural poverty, land redistribution and development', *Indian Economic Review*, 5(1): 97–128.

Mishra, B. B., 1960. *The Indian Middle Classes*, London, Oxford University Press.

Mitra, A., 1977. *Terms of Trade and Class Relations*, London, F. Cass.

Mody, A., 1985. Recent evolution in microelectronics in Korea and Taiwan: an institutional approach to comparative advantage. Boston University (mimeo).

Morawetz, D., 1977. *Twenty-five Years of Economic Development: 1950–1975*, Baltimore, Johns Hopkins University Press.

1981. *Why the Emperor's New Clothes are Not Made in Colombia*, Baltimore, Johns Hopkins University Press.

Morishima, M., 1982. *Why Has Japan Succeeded? Western Technology and the Japanese Ethos*, Cambridge, Cambridge University Press.

Morris, M. D., 1974. 'Private investment on the Indian subcontinent, 1900–1939, some methodological considerations', *Modern Asian Studies*, October: 535–55.

1979. *Measuring the Condition of the World's Poor: The Physical Quality of Life Index*, Oxford, Oxford University Press.

Mukerji, K., 1965. *Levels of Economic Activity and Public Expenditure in India*, Poona, Grokhale Institute.

Murty, G. V. S. and Murty, R. N., 1977. 'On differential effects of price movements', *Indian Economic Review*, 12(2): 169–80.

Nam, C. H., 1981. 'Trade, industrial policies, and the structure of protection in Korea' in W. Hong and L. Krause (eds), *Trade and Growth of the Advanced Developing Countries in the Pacific Basin*, Seoul, Korea Development Institute: 187–217.

Naya, S., 1985. *Resources, Trade, Technology and Investment – Southeast Asia in the Pacific Co-operative System*, Honolulu, East-West Center, Resource Systems Institute, Working Paper 85, January.

Nayyar, D., 1978. 'Transnational corporations and manufactured exports from poor countries', *Economic Journal*, 88(349): 59–84.

Needham, J., 1954. *Science and Civilization in China*, Cambridge, Cambridge University Press.

Nehru, J., 1956. *The Discovery of India*, 6th edition, Calcutta, Signet Press.

1962. *An Autobiography*, New Delhi, Allied.

Nelson, J., 1984. 'The politics of stabilization' in R. Feinberg and V. Kallab (eds), *Adjustment Crisis in the Third World*, New Brunswick, Transaction Books: 99–118.

Nelson, R. N., 1956. 'The low level equilibrium trap', *American Economic Review*, 46(5): 894–908.

Nemenzo, F. and May, R. J. (eds), 1984. *The Philippines after Marcos*, London, Croom Helm.

Nishimizu, M. and Robinson, S., 1983. *Sectoral Growth in Semi-industrial*

Countries: a Comparative Analysis, Washington DC, Division Working Paper no. 82–6, World Bank, December.

North, D. C., 1981. *Structure and Change in Economic History*, New York, Norton.

Nozick, R., 1974. *Anarchy, State and Utopia*, Oxford, Basil Blackwell.

Organisation for Economic Co-operation and Development, 1975. *Geographical Distribution of Financial Flows to Developing Countries 1971/74*, Paris, OECD.

1979. *The Impact of the Newly Industrializing Countries on Production and Trade in Manufactures*, Paris, OECD.

1980. *Geographical Distribution of Financial Flows to Developing Countries, 1976/79*, Paris, OECD.

1981. *Geographical Distribution of Financial Flows to Developing Countries, 1977/80*, Paris, OECD.

1984. *Geographical Distribution of Financial Flows to Developing Countries, 1980/83*, Paris, OECD.

and Bank for International Settlements, 1985. Statistics on external indebtedness: bank and trade-related non-bank external claims on individual borrowing countries and territories, at end December 1984. Paris and Basle, BIS/OECD.

Olson, M., 1982. *The Rise and Decline of Nations*, New Haven, Yale University Press.

Oshima, H. T., 1980. 'Manpower quality in the differential economic growth between East and Southeast Asia', *The Philippine Economic Journal*, 19(3): 380–406.

Ozawa, T., 1980. *The Role of TNCs in the Economic Development of the ESCAP Region: Some Available Evidence from Recent Experience*, Bangkok, CTC-ESCAP.

Pang Eng-Fong, 1983. *Education, Manpower and Economic Development in Singapore*, Singapore, Singapore University Press.

1983. Foreign direct investment in Singapore. Paper prepared for OECD Development Centre, Paris.

Pao-San Ho, S., 1984. 'Colonialism and development: Korea, Taiwan and Kwantung' in R. H. Myers and M. R. Peattie (eds), *The Japanese Colonial Empire: 1895–1945*, Princeton, Princeton University Press: 347–98.

Park, H. and Westphal, L., 1986. 'Industrial strategy and technological change: theory versus reality', *Journal of Development Economics*, 20(1): 1–42.

Parry, T. G., 1980. *The Multinational Enterprise: International Investment and Host-Country Impacts*, Greenwich, Connecticut, JAI Press.

1984. 'International technology transfer: emerging corporate strategies', *Prometheus*, 2(2): 220–32.

Pempel, T., 1978. 'Japanese foreign economic policy: the domestic bases for international behaviour' in P. Katzenstein (ed.), *Between Power and Plenty*, Madison, University of Wisconsin: 139–90.

Pitt, M. M., 1981. 'Alternative trade strategies and employment in Indonesia' in A. O. Krueger and others (eds), *Trade and Employment in Developing Countries 1. Individual Studies*, Chicago, Chicago University Press: 181–238.

Post, T. and Richman, L., 1982. 'The largest industrial companies in the world', *Fortune 500*, 23 August: 183–201.

Power, J. H. and Sicat, G. P., 1971. *The Philippines: Industrialization and Trade Policies*, London, Oxford University Press.

Pye, L. W., 1962. *Politics, Personality and Nation Building, Burma's Search for Identity*, New Haven, Yale University Press.

and Pye M., 1985. *Asian Power and Politics: the Cultural Dimensions of Authority*, Cambridge, Harvard University Press.

Rana, P., 1983. 'The impact of the current exchange rate system on trade and inflation of selected developing member countries', *Asian Development Bank Economics Staff Paper* No. 18, Manila, ADB, Economics Office.

Ranis, G., 1979. 'Industrial development' in W. Galenson (ed.), *Economic Growth and Structural Change in Taiwan*, Ithaca, Cornell University Press: 206–62.

1980. 'Prospective Southeast Asian development strategies in a changing international environment' in Economic Growth Department (ed.), *New Directions of Asia's Development Strategies*, Tokyo, Institute of Developing Economies: 1–28.

1984. 'The dual economy framework: its relevance to Asian development', *Asian Development Review*, 2(1): 39–51.

Ratnam, K. J., 1965. *Communalism and the Political Process in Malaya*, Kuala Lumpur, University of Malaya Press.

Ray, R. K., 1979. *Industrialisation in India – Growth and Conflict in the Private Sector 1914–47*, Delhi, Oxford University Press.

Reuber, G. L., *et al.*, 1973. *Private Foreign Investment in Development*, Oxford, Clarendon Press.

Reynolds, L. G., 1983. 'The spread of economic growth to the Third World: 1850–1980', *Journal of Economic Literature*, 21(3): 941–80.

Rhee, Y. W., Ross-Larson, B., and Pursell, G., 1984. *Korea's Competitive Edge, Managing the Entry into World Market*, Baltimore, Johns Hopkins University Press for the World Bank.

Riaz, H. (ed.), 1976. *Singapore: Society in Transition*, Kuala Lumpur, Oxford University Press.

Riedel, J. R., 1974. *The Industrialization of Hong Kong*, Tubingen, J. C. B. Mohr–Paul Siebeck.

Bibliography

1979. 'Economic dependence and entrepreneurial opportunities in the host country – MNC relationship' in R. G. Hawkins (ed.), *The Economic Effects of Multinational Corporations*, Greenwich, Connecticut, JAI Press: 235–53.

1984a. The external constraint to long-term growth in developing countries. Monograph prepared for Trade Policy Research Centre meeting on 'Participation of developing countries in the international trading system', Wiston House, West Sussex, October.

1984b. 'Trade as the engine of growth in developing countries, revisited', *Economic Journal*, 94(373): 56–73.

Riggs, F. W., 1966. *Thailand: the Modernization of a Bureaucratic Polity*, Honolulu, East-West Center Press.

Robinson, R., 1982. 'Culture, politics and economy in the political history of the New Order', *Indonesia*, 31: 1–30.

Rosenberg, D. A. (ed.), 1979. *Marcos and Martial Law in the Philippines*, Ithaca, Cornell University Press.

Rosenstein-Rodan, P. N., 1961. 'International aid for underdeveloped countries', *Review of Economics and Statistics*, 43(2): 107–38.

Rudra, A., 1974. 'Semi-feudalism, usury, capitalism, etc.', *Economic and Political Weekly*, 9(48): 1996–7.

1978. 'Organisation of agriculture for rural development in India', *Cambridge Journal of Economics*, 2: 381–406.

Rueff, J., 1963. *Report on the Economic Aspects of Malaysia: by a mission of the International Bank for Reconstruction and Development*, Washington, DC, World Bank.

Satyanarayana, Y., 1981. Wage trends in India – 1830–1976: A compilation of data, studies in employment and rural development. August, World Bank, Washington DC (mimeo).

Sau, R., 1981. *India's Economic Development*, Delhi, Longmans.

Saxonhouse, G., 1983. 'What is all this about "industrial targetting" in Japan?', *The World Economy*, 6(3): 253–73.

Sayle, M., 1985. 'Japan victorious', *New York Review of Books*, 32(5): 33–40.

Scitovsky, T., 1985. 'Economic development in Taiwan and South Korea: 1965–80', *Food Research Institute Studies*, 19(3).

Scott, B., 1985. 'National strategies: key to international competition' in B. Scott and G. Lodge (eds), *U.S. Competitiveness in the World Economy*, Boston, Harvard Business School Press: 71–143.

Scott, M. F., 1976. 'Investment and growth', *Oxford Economic Papers*, 28(3): 317–63.

1979. 'Foreign trade' in W. Galenson (ed.), *Economic Growth and Structural Change in Taiwan*, Ithaca, Cornell University Press: 308–83.

1981. 'The contribution of investment to growth', *Scottish Journal of Political Economy*, 28(3): 221–6.

Sen, A. K., 1973. *On Economic Inequality*, Oxford, Clarendon Press.

1976. 'Poverty: an ordinal approach to measurement', *Econometrica*, 44(2): 219–31.

1981. 'Public action and the quality of life in developing countries', *Oxford Bulletin of Economics and Statistics*, 43(4): 287–319.

1983. 'Development: which way now?', *Economic Journal*, 93(372): 745–62.

Shaw, E. S., 1973. *Financial Deepening in Economic Development*, New York, Oxford University Press.

Short, P., 1983. The role of public enterprises: an international statistical comparison. DM83/84, Washington DC, IMF.

Siffin, W., 1966. *The Thai Bureaucracy. Institutional Change and Development*, Honolulu, East-West Center Press.

Silcock, T. H., 1967. *Thailand: Social and Economic Studies in Development*, Canberra, ANU Press.

and Fisk, E. K. (eds), 1963. *The Political Economy of Independent Malaya*, Canberra, ANU Press.

Simon, D., 1980. Taiwan, technology transfer and transnationalism: the political management of dependency. Ph.D. dissertation, Berkeley, University of California.

Sivasubramanian, S., 1977. 'Income from the secondary sector in India, 1900–47', *The Indian Economic and Social History Review*, 14(4): 427–92.

Skinner, G. W., 1957. *Chinese Society in Thailand: an Analytical History*, Ithaca, Cornell University Press.

1958. *Chinese Leadership and Power in a Chinese Community in Thailand*, Ithaca, Cornell University Press.

Snodgrass, D. R., 1980. *Inequality and Economic Development in Malaysia*, Kuala Lumpur, Oxford University Press.

Solow, R. M., 1957. 'Technical change and the aggregate production function', *Review of Economics and Statistics*, 39: 312–20.

Somers-Heidhues, M., 1974. *Southeast Asia's Chinese Minorities*, Hawthorn, Longmans Southeast Asia Series.

Steinberg, D., 1984. *On Foreign Aid and the Development of the Republic of Korea: the Effectiveness of Foreign Assistance*, Washington DC, Agency for International Development.

Stenson, M., 1976. 'Class and race in West Malaysia', *Bulletin of Concerned Asian Scholars*, 8(2): 45–54.

Streeten, P., 1977. 'Changing perceptions of development', *Finance and Development*, 14(3): 14–16.

Sung, Y., 1984. Development strategies and productivity issues in Asia –

the case of Hong Kong, Chinese University of Hong Kong, December (mimeo).

Sung-joo, H., 1985. The politics of democratization in Korea: problems and opportunities. Paper presented at the XIVth International Political Science Association World Congress, Paris, July.

Szanton, C., 1983. 'Thai and Sino-Thai in small town Thailand: changing patterns of interethnic relations' in L. A. Gosling and L. Y. C. Lim (eds), *The Chinese in Southeast Asia*, Vol. 2, Singapore, Maruzen Asia for the Economic Research Centre, National University of Singapore: 99–125.

Taizo, Yakushiji, 1984. 'Government in spiral dilemma: dynamic policy interventions vis-à-vis Japanese auto firms, c. 1900–1960' in Akoi Masahiko (ed.), *An Economic Analysis of Japanese Firms*, Amsterdam, North Holland: 265–310.

Tan, A. H. H. and Hock, O. C., 1982. 'Incentive policies and economic development: Singapore' in B. Balassa and Associates (eds), *Development Strategies in Semi-Industrial Economies*, Baltimore, Johns Hopkins University Press: 280–309.

Tan Tat Wah, 1983. *Income Distribution and Determination in Malaysia*, Kuala Lumpur, Oxford University Press.

Thavaraj, J. K., 1960. 'Capital formation in the public sector, 1898–1938' in Indian Conference on Research in National Income, *Papers on National Income and Allied Topics*, Vol. 1, London: 215–30.

Tilman, R. (ed.), 1969. *Man, State and Society in Contemporary Southeast Asia*, New York, Praeger Publishers.

Timmer, C. P., 1973. 'Choice of technique in rice milling in Java', *Bulletin of Indonesian Economic Studies*, 9(2): 57–76.

Trezise, P., 1983. 'Industrial policy is not the major reason for Japan's success', *The Brookings Review*, 1: 13–18.

Tsao, Y., 1982. Growth and productivity in Singapore: a supply side analysis. Ph.D. dissertation, Cambridge University.

Tsiang, S. C., 1980. 'Exchange rate interest rate and economic development: the experience of Taiwan' in N. Neilov, L. Klein and S. C. Tsiang (eds), *Quantitative Economics and Development*, New York, Academic Press: 309–46.

1984. 'Taiwan's economic miracle: lessons in economic development' in A. C. Harberger (ed.), *World Economic Growth: Case Studies of Developed and Developing Countries*, San Francisco, Institute for Continuing Studies: 301–27.

Turner, H. A., 1981. *Last Colony: But Whose? A Study of the Labour Movement, Labour Market and Labour Relations in Hong Kong*, Cambridge, Cambridge University Press.

United Nations, 1956. *Yearbook of International Trade Statistics*, New

York, United Nations.

1958. *Yearbook of International Trade Statistics*, New York, United Nations.

1962. *Yearbook of International Trade Statistics*, New York, United Nations.

1970–81. *Commodity Trade Statistics, Statistical Papers Series D*, New York, United Nations.

1981. *Yearbook of International Trade Statistics*, New York, United Nations.

1982. *Yearbook of International Trade Statistics*, New York, United Nations.

United Nations Centre on Transnational Corporations, 1978. *Multinational Corporations in World Development: A Re-examination*, New York, United Nations.

United Nations Conference on Trade and Development, 1978. *TNCs and Expansion of Trade in Manufactures and Semi Manufactures*, Geneva, UNCTAD, TD/B/C.2/197.

various years. *Handbook of International Trade and Development Statistics*, New York, United Nations.

United States Congress, House Committee on Foreign Affairs, 1960. *Report on Economic Assistance to Korea, Thailand and Iran*, Washington DC, US Government Printing Office.

Vaidyanathan, A., 1977. 'Constraints on growth and policy options', *Economic and Political Weekly*, 12(38): 1643–50.

van Agtmael, A., 1984. *Emerging Securities Markets*, London, Euromoney Publications.

Viksnins, C. J., 1980. *Financial Deepening in ASEAN Countries*, Hawaii, Pacific Forum.

Wade, R., 1979. 'Fast growth and slow development in South Italy' in D. Seers, B. Schaffee and M. Kiljunen (eds), *Underdeveloped Europe: Studies in Core-Periphery Relations*, Brighton, Harvester Press: 198–221.

1982a. *Irrigation and Agricultural Politics in South Korea*, Boulder, Westview Press.

1982b. 'Regional policy in a severe international environment: politics and markets in South Italy', *Pacific Viewpoint*, 23(2): 99–126.

1982c. 'The system of administrative and political corruption: canal irrigation in South India', *Journal of Development Studies*, 18(3): 287–328.

1983. 'South Korea's agricultural development: the myth of the passive state', *Pacific Viewpoint*, 24(1): 11–28.

1984a. 'Dirigisme Taiwan-style', *IDS Bulletin*, 15(2): 65–70.

1984b. 'Review of public expenditure and India's development policy

1960–1970', *Economic Development and Cultural Change*, 32(2): 437–44.

1985a. 'Eastasian financial systems as a challenge to economics: lessons from Taiwan', *California Management Review*, 27(4): 106–27.

1985b. 'Taiwan', *Some Pacific Economies*, Economic and Social Research Council Newsletter, 54: 12–15.

in press. 'State intervention in "out-ward looking" development: neoclassical theory and Taiwanese practice' in G. White and R. Wade (eds), *Developmental States in East Asia*, London, Macmillan: chapter 2.

Wang Gungwu, 1981a. *Community and Nation: Essays on Southeast Asia and the Chinese*, Sydney and Singapore, Allen and Unwin with Heinemann Educational Books, for the Asian Studies Association of Australia.

1981b. 'Malaysia: contending elites' in Wang Gungwu, *Community and Nation: Essays on Southeast Asia and the Chinese*, Sydney and Singapore, Allen and Unwin with Heinemann Educational Books, for the Asian Studies Association of Australia: 232–48.

1985. The study of Southeast Asian Chinese identities. Symposium paper, Changing identities of the Southeast Asian Chinese since World War II, ANU, Canberra.

Warr, P., 1986. *Export Promotion via Industrial Enclaves: the Philippines Bataan Export Processing Zone*. Canberra, Working Paper in Trade and Development No. 86/9, ANU.

Wertheim, W. F., 1956. *Indonesian Society in Transition*, The Hague, W. van Hoeve Ltd.

Westphal, L. E., 1978a. Industrial incentives in the Republic of China (Taiwan). Washington DC, World Bank (mimeo).

1978b. 'The Republic of Korea's experience with export-led industrial development', *World Development*, 6(3): 347–82.

1982. 'Fostering technology mastery by means of selective infant industry protection' in M. Syrquin and S. Teitel (eds), *Trade, Stability, Technology and Equity in Latin America*, New York, Academic Press: 255–80.

et al., 1981. 'Korean industrial competence: where it came from', *World Bank Staff Working Paper* No. 469, Washington DC, World Bank.

et al., 1984. 'Republic of Korea' in S. Lall (ed.), *Exports of Technology by Newly-Industrializing Countries*, in *World Development*, Special Issue, 12(5/6): 505–34.

and Kim, K. S., 1982. 'Incentive policies and economic development: Korea' in B. Balassa and Associates (eds), *Development Strategies in Semi-Industrial Economies*, Baltimore, Johns Hopkins University Press: 212–79.

Kim, L. and Dahlman, C., 1984. Reflections on Korea's acquisition of technological capability. Washington DC, Development Research Dept, World Bank (mimeo).

White, G., and Wade, R. (eds), in press. *Development States in East Asia*, London, Macmillan.

Wickberg, E., 1965. *The Chinese in Philippine Life*, New Haven, Yale University Press.

Wilson, D., 1962. *Politics in Thailand*, Ithaca, Cornell University Press.

Wilson, H. E., 1978. *Social Engineering in Singapore: Educational Policies and Social Change, 1819–1972*, Singapore, Singapore University Press.

Wolf, C., 1979. 'A theory of nonmarket failure; framework for implementation analysis', *Journal of Law and Economics*, 22(1): 107–39.

Wolf, M., 1981. *Indian Exports*, Baltimore, Johns Hopkins University Press.

Wolters, O. W., 1982. *History, Culture and Religion in Southeast Asian Perspective*, Singapore, ISEAS.

World Bank, 1976. *The Philippines. Priorities and Prospects for Development*, Washington DC, World Bank.

1984. *World Tables*, Washington DC, World Bank.

1985. *World Debt Tables, 1984–5*, Washington DC, World Bank.

various years. *World Development Report*, New York, Oxford University Press.

Wu, Y. and Wu, C-H., 1980. *Economic Development in Southeast Asia: The Chinese Dimension*, Stanford, Hoover Institution Press.

Wurfel, D., 1959. 'The Philippines' in G. McT. Kahin (ed.), *Government and Politics in Southeast Asia*, Ithaca, Cornell University Press: 421–502.

Yoshiro, K. (ed.), 1982. *Changing Value Patterns and Their Impact on Economic Structure*, Tokyo, University of Tokyo Press.

Young, S., 1984. *Problems of Trade Liberalization in Korea*, London, Trade Policy Research Centre.

Yusuf, S. and Peters, R. K., 1984. *Is Capital Accumulation the Key to Growth? Neoclassical Models and Development Economics in Korea's Investment Policies*, Washington DC, World Bank.

Zymelman, M., 1980. *Occupational Structure of Industries*, Washington DC, World Bank.

Zysman, J., 1983. *Governments, Markets and Growth: Financial Systems and the Politics of Industrial Change*, Ithaca, Cornell University Press.

INDEX

Africa, 12, 16, 26, 144
agriculture, 6, 23, 24, 56, 184, 188;
    India, 219; Korea, Republic of, 32,
    83, 103; Malaysia, 318; NICs, 72;
    Philippines, 103, 309; Taiwan, 27,
    83, 103; Thailand, 299, 318
aid, 11, 24, 25, 95, 98–107, 111, 124,
    265, 276, 311, 313; agencies, 104;
    bilateral to multilateral, 105; budget,
    103, 104; conditions for growth, 24,
    25; effectiveness, 105; Europe and
    Japan, 105; import substitution, 104;
    military, 98, 103; United States, 11;
    without policy, 105; see also
    Indonesia; Korea, Republic of;
    Malaysia; Philippines; Singapore;
    Taiwan
Andean Group, 166; see also Latin
    America
Argentina, 166, 176, 184
Association of Southeast Asian
    Nations (ASEAN), 283–324;
    exports, 68, 80, 81; GDP, 286;
    government autonomy, 295;
    industrial growth, 94; resource-rich
    countries, 67, 93
Asia, 64, 68; see also Southeast Asia
Asian Development Bank, 25, 106
authoritarianism, 2, 38, 290, 293

balance of payments, 51, 71, 84, 88,
    89, 108, 109, 126, 256
banks, 132, 133, 136–8; bank credit,
    132, 133, 176–8; bank flows, 95, 97;
    banking system, 12, 133, 173
Bataan export processing zone, 108;
    see also Philippines

bonds, as international capital, 97
Borda score, 19
borrowing, 59–63, 106–9, 136, 176,
    186, 237, 239; Hong Kong, 25;
    Korea, Republic of, 25, 97, 124, 126;
    multilateral, 24; Philippines, 124;
    Singapore, 25; Taiwan, 25, 126
Brazil, 41, 132, 166, 171, 176; see also
    Latin America
British financial system, 131
Brunei, 337
budget aid, see aid
budget support, 104
Burma, 166, 337, 338, 342

Cambridge equation, 188
Capital: accumulation, 40, 41;
    commercial, 97; 'crowding out', 110;
    debt crises, 123; external trade, 61;
    flight, 306; flows, 61, 97, 123–7, 253;
    formation, 107, 164; goods (exports)
    97, (industries) 6; growth, 45;
    human, 116; imported, 88, 97;
    inflow, 56, 57, 62, 99–102, 107, 108,
    127; intermediate goods, 7;
    international, 97; labour, 59, 62, 97;
    market, 12, 59, 86, 131, 133; output
    ratio, 62; physical, 88; private and
    social costs, 97; supply, 124; volume,
    97; see also foreign capital
capital-intensive activities, 6, 72, 143
capital-intensive investment, 306
capital–labour ratio, 97, 203
capital–output ratio, 62
caste system, industrial, 205; see also
    India
Central America, 166, 167

370

centralized decision making, 38, 157, 262

Chang Myon, 268, 271; *see also* Korea, Republic of

chemicals industry, 33, 84, 114

Chile, 15, 165, 166; adjustment problems, 165; copper, 187, 194; debt crisis, 194; export-led growth, 171; external shock, 190; inflation, 172; tradables, 187–9; *see also* Latin America

China, People's Republic of, 2; autarkic growth, 39; competitive threat to NICs and Southeast Asia, 92; cultural revolution, 26; domestic savings, 63; science, 26

Chinese minorities, 324

Chun Doo Hwan, 273, 280; *see also* Korea, Republic of

cigarette industry, *see* Indonesia

class structure, *see* Malaysia; Thailand

clothing industries, 71, 72, 78, 79, 113, 114, 120

Colombia, 53, 58, 166, 171; *see also* Latin America

colonial past, 27, 297

comparative advantage, 40, 41, 56, 58, 59, 120, 153

competition, 2, 72, 84, 153, 249

computable general equilibrium model, 59

concessional loans, 98

Confucianism, 26, 38, 223, 241, 243, 332–4, 336, 337

cooperation, public and private, 158, 161, 243, 249, 335

copper production, 76, 112, 187, 194

cork production, 72, 78

corporate financing, 136

Costa Rica, 167, 171

cotton, 199; and jute, 200

Council for Economic Planning and Development, *see* Taiwan

credit: bank, 149, 173; markets, 185; preferences, 83; preferential access, 88; subsidies, 123; suppliers, 97, 136

credit-based financial system, 132–4, 157

crony capitalism, *see* Philippines

cultural revolution, *see* China, People's Republic of

culture, 26, 38, 327–30; and development, 343; and economics, 342; and economists, 329–31; atavistic traits, 26; factor for success, 2, 3, 26; post-Confucian, 332–4

currencies, overvalued, 87, 89, 104

current account deficits, 255

customs reforms, 90

debt, 61, 89, 90, 95, 106, 108, 125–7, 132, 134, 165; accumulation, 61; crisis, 12, 123, 191, 192, 194, 237; debt–equity ratios, 132, 136

democracy, 2, 38

deregulation, 311

devaluation, 30, 62, 89, 90; *see also* currencies

developing countries, 1, 2, 4, 6, 19, 28, 38, 40, 45, 53, 64, 226; growth, 44, 47; labour, 47; protection, 72; transformation, 41

development, 1, 12, 40, 49, 56–8, 67; agricultural, 103; banks, 106, 149; bottle-necks, 111; capital-intensive, 88; egalitarian, 263; export-oriented, 36; human resource, 41, 93; index of, 4; indicators, 14; new industries, 130; post-war, 39; potential, 58; strategies, 56; theories, 39; *see also* direct foreign investment

direct foreign investment, 11, 95, 97, 98, 107–24, 127, 144, 150; and domestic investment, 110; borrowing, 108, 124; development, 109–11, 122; employment opportunities, 116; government policy, 123; human capital formation, 116, 117; know-how transfer, 111–19; private, 96, 221, 247, 317; skills formation, 116; tax revenues, 122; technology, 109, 110, 116, 118; textiles, 115; trade, 111, 114

dirigisme, 33, 37, 199, 204, 208, 210, 211, 214, 231

disposable income, 9

domestic policies: capital, 298; credit, 176; demand, 40, 49–51, 53, 55, 58, 83; investment, 107, 110; market, 7, 14, 59, 83, 92; prices, 180; products, 59, 62; saving, 9–12, 63, 127, 146, 257

Dominican Republic, 167, 171

drawbacks on duties, 88

'Dutch Disease', 24, 93

Economic Planning Board, *see* Korea, Republic of
economies of scale, 63, 154
economy: agrarian to industrialized, 81; agricultural, *see* agriculture; black, 237; closed, 44; crisis in, 71, 308; growth of, 3, 6, 12, 15, 40, 83; labour-abundant, 88; market, 59; model of, 51; open, 62, 146; outward-oriented, 51; protected, 59; regulation, 87
Ecuador, 166, 170, 171; *see also* Latin America
education, 21, 26, 27, 249, 257, 290
electrical machinery, 76, 79
electrical products, 113–15
electronic components, 79
élitism, 285, 304, 310, 325; *see also* India; Malaysia; Thailand
employment, 4, 8, 15, 41, 72, 93, 159; and employee loyalty, 251, 335; and employee savings schemes, 253; and wages, 15–18; Hong Kong, 116; India, 199, 201; Japan, 245; Korea, Republic of, 7, 63; Malaysia, 26, 116; manufacturing, 16, 88, 90; NICs, 83; Taiwan, 7, 63
Engel functions, 50, 55
engineering products, 114
entrepreneurship, 27, 37
equilibrium: growth, 44–8; models, 40, 56, 57, 59
Europe: businesses, 147; markets, 113
European Community, 73, 78, 79, 81
exchange controls, 83, 87; and exchange rate, 15, 30, 35, 58, 62, 83, 89, 97, 105, 148, 165, 173, 180–2, 186, 194, 239, 288, 306; *see also* foreign exchange
export growth, 7, 35, 50, 51, 53, 56, 62, 66–9, 71, 83, 88, 91, 92, 171
export-led growth, 170, 171, 265, 266, 322
export orientation, 36, 66, 83, 84, 105, 260, 300, 318
export processing zones, 108, 114, 117, 288, 341
export promotion, 33, 34, 52, 62, 67, 88, 225
exports, 71, 73, 86, 331; of ASEAN countries, 77, 81; machinery, 76, 79; manufactures, 7, 56, 57, 71, 72, 76, 78, 81, 91, 288; of NICs, 68, 70, 73, 74; primary, 7, 53, 55,76; processed materials, 78; raw materials, 75; resource-based, 40, 57; *see also* Indonesia; Korea, Republic of; Malaysia; Philippines; Singapore; Taiwan
external shock, response to, 66, 137, 190

fabrics manufacture, 75
fertilizers, 34
First World War, 201
fishing industry, 78, 112
food processing, 72, 105, 113
footwear manufacture, 91, 113, 242
foreign capital, 14, 95, 97, 98, 108, 110, 111, 127, 221, 292, 323
foreign exchange, 7, 11, 12, 33, 40, 41, 59, 84, 89, 109, 137, 181
free trade, 30, 33, 114, 142, 151, 198, 210, 213

'Gang of Four', 2, 195; *dirigisme*, 204, 208; forced industrialization, 198; free industrial labour markets, 206; import substitution, 204; Japanese model for development, 232; neutral trade regime, 198; protection, 198
Gang of Three, 169
Generalized System of Preferences, 91
Germany, 200; banks, 132, 136
government: control of direct foreign investment, 144–5; financial instruments, 131–9; incentives, 36, 153; intervention, 35, 81, 84, 87, 93, 130, 132, 136, 141, 151, 152, 162, 223, 238
Greece, trade liberalization, 58
Green Revolution, 312
gross domestic product, 5, 11, 12, 14, 35, 83, 105
gross national product, 2, 4, 5, 11, 50, 109, 127; average export ratios, 64; growth, 5, 53

heavy industries, 33, 34, 50, 51, 72, 84, 86, 90, 155, 214, 243
Hinduism, 222, 230
Honduras, 167
Hong Kong, 1, 4–6, 12, 14, 16, 18, 24, 35, 37, 39, 57, 67, 167; absence of central bank, 34; aid, 25, 98, 103; British subsidies, 103; direct foreign

investment, 97, 114, 116, 119, 120; economic performance, 152; entrepreneurship, 27; entrepôt past, 27, 36; infrastructure, 30; international capital market, 126; investment by Cantonese, 27; literacy, 246; non-interventionism, 29; outward-oriented manufacturing, 48; technology transfer, 129; trade-free economy, 81; trade unions and workers, 34
human resources, 25–7, 252

imports, 51, 56, 57, 59, 62, 78, 81, 89; import control, 32, 140; import growth, 71; import liberalization, 30, 56; import rationing, 89; import substitution, 6, 36, 50–1, 53, 58, 63, 84, 86–8, 90, 169, 260, (Gang of Four) 204, (India) 225, (Japan) 242, (Korea, Republic of) 32, 83, 103, 151, 213–14, 266, 292, (Malaysia) 33, 318, (Philippines) 103, 307, (Singapore) 30, 81, 204, (Taiwan) 83, 103, 104, 151, 266, 292, (Thailand) 33, 300; industrialization, forced, 224; inefficiency, 61
income, 6, 9, 19, 20, 49, 55, 66, 91; agricultural, 24; disposable household, 19; distribution, 4, 6, 15, 18–21, 36, 93, 215, 219, 252; elasticity, 50; levels of, 5, 50, 51, 55
India: Annual Survey of, 219; capital-labour ratio, 202, 203; caste system, 205, 230, 233, 234; Census of Manufacturing, 219; chronic fiscal crisis, 236; contempt for business, 229, 233, 234; cotton and jute, 199, 200; *dirigisme*, 214, 231; domestic savings, 63; economic growth, 195; employment, 199, 201; export growth, 200; export promotion, 225; history, 198–210; import substitution, 224, 225; income distribution, 215, 219; industrial disputes, 207, 208; industries, 200; infrastructure, 29, 211; Intensive Agricultural Development Programme, 232; investment, 9, 63, 201, 203, (foreign) 221; labour, 210, (and trade unions) 206, 208, (laws) 211, (legislation) 206, (market) 205; mercantile class, 228; multinational

exports, 112; National Planning Office, 222; poverty, 215–17; price ratios, 220; productivity, 203; protection, 201, 203, 208; public sector, 212, 222, 223, 235; stagnation 210–24; state intervention, 156; steel, 200; sugar, 201; textiles, 199; threat to NICs, 92; trade liberalization, 240; unemployment, 231; wages, 218, 219
Indochina, 166, 337, 340; *see also* Vietnam
Indonesia, 4–6, 12, 14, 15, 17, 21, 35, 67, 167, 311–17; aid, 103, 311, 313; bureaucracy, 317; business class, 314, 315; Chinese in, 315; cigarette industry, 343; Communist Party, 311; devaluation, 89, 90; *dirigisme*, 33; domestic economy, 89; economic performance, 283; exports, 33, 40, 69, 76, 78, (clothing) 79; government authority, 312; Guided Democracy, Guided Economy, 33; import substitution, 33; inflation, 311; inward orientation, 87; justice, 29; life expectancy, 21; macroeconomic reforms, 33; middle class, 342; oil, 35, 69, 71, 312, 313, 317; Pertamina, 124; population density, 25; private foreign investment, 311, 317; protection, 33; public sector, 316; rice production, 312; traditional strategies, 39
Industrial Development Board, *see* Taiwan
industrial strategy, 84, 134, 147–54, 162
industry, 50, 84, 86, 87, 90, 169; *see also* heavy industries
inflation, 12, 14, 15, 64, 84, 89, 97, 164, 171, 250, 311; and investment, 172
input–output coefficients, 49–51
input–output model, 55, 56, 59
interest rates, 11, 12, 84, 124, 133, 135
international finance, 14, 24, 185
International Fund for Agricultural Development, 106
International Monetary Fund, 104–6, 108, 110, 117, 164
intervention, successful, 154–63
investment, 9, 11, 12, 47, 61, 89, 92, 98, 110, 149, 153, 201; and inflation,

172; capital inflows, 107; domestic, 107, 108; intra-regional, 119; private, 84; public, 104; ratios, 171; *see also* direct foreign investment
inward orientation, 1, 51, 61–3, 87, 88, 151
iron and steel industry, 71, 72, 112
Israel, 51, 53, 56
Italy, 160
Ivory Coast, 58

Japan, 41, 51, 56, 79, 103; banks, 133, 136–8; central bank, 133; competition, 247, 249; debt–equity ratios, 132; democratic government, 334; Development Bank, 149; development strategy, 47; distribution of income, 252; export growth, 53, 79, 200; export ratios and GNP, 64; footwear manufacture, 242; foreign investment, 114, 115, 247; heavy industry, 243; higher education, 249; import substitution, 242; industrial policy, 148; industrial relations, 243, 245, 246, 248, 250, 251; Japan Inc., 162, 245, 249, 335; literacy and education, 246; manufactures, 51; MITI, 137, 244; model of development, 232, 241; multinationals, 144; pre-war experience, 56; productivity, 203, 249, 250; protection, 155, 251; public–private cooperation, 158, 248, 249; research and development, 145; stagnation, 26; tax incentives, 250; textiles, 78, 205, 242; trade unions, 245
Joint Commission for Rural Construction, 105

Kaomintang, 266, 274, 275–8, 282; *see also* Taiwan
Kim Dae Jung, 271; *see also* Korea, Republic of
Korea, Republic of, 1, 4–7, 11, 14–16, 18, 24, 41, 67, 166, 167; agriculture, 32, 83; aid, 24, 25, 103; and Taiwan, 63, 266, 269, 279, 281, 292; banks, 133, 136–8; borrowing, 61, 124, 127; colonial experience, 27; debt, 127; debt–equity ratios, 132; direct foreign investment, 111, 247;

dirigisme, 214; domestic savings, 127; Economic Planning Board, 137; exports, 39, 50, 51, 53, 122, 169, 170, 214, 224; government intervention, 130, 213, 214; heavy and chemical industries, 33, 72, 84, 155, 214; import substitution, 33, 213; international finance, 125, 165; investment, 47, 61, 149; iron and steel, 72; Korean War, 27; land reform, 18, 262, 263; light manufactures, 50, 51; literacy, 246; multinationals, 112, 113, 144; outward orientation, 48, 51, 53; political history, 267–70, 272, 273; protection, 32, 33, 36; public–private cooperation, 145, 158; state-owned companies, 84; technology, 117, 118, 120; trade, 41, 81, 135, 187–9; unemployment, 16

labour, 15, 17, 45, 47, 59, 63, 66, 67, 72, 83, 93, 97, 153, 288; absorption, 88; costs, 120; efficiency, 206; laws, 206, 208, 211; management, 246; markets, 16, 17, 20, 34, 63, 86, 205, 206, 287; migration, 83; movements, 34, 159, 263; quality, 26, 47, 86; structure, 85
labour-intensive activities, 6, 7, 72, 105; exports, 35; manufactures, 67, 72, 73
laissez-faire policies, 18, 28, 148, 162, 198–200, 210, 211, 213
land reform, 18, 262, 263, 266, 275, 281
Latin America, 12, 16, 28, 58, 156, 164, 166, 167, 169, 170, 171, 179; borrowing, 186, 239; debt, 127, 237; multinationals, 144; Southern Cone, 166, 173
leather industry, 72, 78, 113
Lee Kuan Yew, 321–4; *see also* Singapore
liberalization of economy, 104, 151, 238, 239
licensing, 118, 120
lifetime employment, *see* Japan
light manufacturing industries, 50, 51, 56

machinery, manufacture for export, 72, 73, 76, 84, 86; *see also* electrical machinery

Malaysia, 4–6, 11, 27, 30, 67, 167, 317, 321; agriculture, 318; aid, 103, 105; class structure, 318; clothing exports, 79; direct foreign investment, 115, 116, 120, 122; economic growth, 285, 318, 319, 321; élites, 318; export processing zones, 288; female education and employment, 26; government intervention, 19, 319; import substitution, 33, 87, 318; manufactures, 33, 58, 318; middle class, 294, 318; multinationals, 113, 114; oil, 71; race relations, 317, 319, 321; technology, 318

manufacturing industries, *see* Hong Kong; India; Indonesia; Japan; Korea, Republic of; Malaysia; Philippines; Singapore; Southeast Asia; Taiwan; Thailand

Marcos, F., 283, 305, 306–3, 310–11, 322, 325; *see also* Philippines

metal processing, *see* Taiwan

Mexico, 51, 132, 167, 170, 171, 177

microelectronics, 150

middle class, 294, 302, 318, 325, 342

mineral resources, 23, 41, 56, 72, 93, 184, 188

Ministry of International Trade and Industry (MITI), *see* Japan

money supply, definition, 176, 185, 186, 188

Multi-fibre Agreements, 91

multinational organizations, 109, 111, 112–15, 117, 144, 253, 255, 292

National Wages Council, *see* Singapore

natural resources, 6, 23, 24, 76, 93, 111, 160, 228, 299

Nehru, J., 229, 230–1, 233, 234

neo-classical theory of economics, 2, 28, 37–9, 41, 44, 59, 141, 142, 150–2, 260; development, 1, 37, 38, 130, 131, 147; model, 29, 39, 40, 44, 45, 47, 48, 62, 149

newly industrialized countries (NICs): and ASEAN, 92; and Asia, 67; and East Asia, 4, 6, 7, 21, 33, 76, 78, 81, 91; and Japan, 286; and Southeast Asia, 79; economic intervention, 290; exports, 67, 68, 70, 71, 72, 75; government control, 289, 292; imports, 68; labour and left-wing power, 293; multinationals, 292;

near-NICs, 4, 6, 7, 21; trade–income ratios, 68, 75

oil, 6, 34, 35, 71, 73, 76, 86, 89, 93, 279, 312, 313, 317; boom, 12, 171, 296; crisis, 15, 69, 78; OPEC, 69, 106, 312; prices, 68, 71, 84, 89, 124

outward orientation, 39, 48, 51, 53, 56, 58, 61–4, 151, 260, 292

paper and paperboard manufacture, 72

Paraguay, 166, 171; *see also* Latin America

Park Choong Hee, 32, 33, 266, 270, 271, 272, 280; *see also* Korea, Republic of

People's Republic of China, *see* China, People's Republic of

Peru, 166, 176; *see also* Latin America

petrochemicals, 34, 115, 150

Philippines, 4–6, 11, 14–17, 24, 67, 167, 169, 305–11; agriculture, 309; aid, 103; borrowing, 106, 124; clothing exports, 79; crony capitalism, 309, *see also* Marcos, F.; debt, 127; direct foreign investment, 120; economic crisis, 71, 283, 305, 308; economic growth, 19, 21, 285; education, 257; export processing zones, 288; exports, 34, 69, 76; import substitution, 34, 87, 307; income distribution, 20; manufactures, 17, 69, 76, 89; multinationals, 114; oil, 89; social inequality, 304, 306; trade liberalization, 58; unemployment, 16

plastics industry, 114

plywood industry, 78

poverty, 11, 15, 20, 21, 27, 215–17, 219

primary products, 7, 50, 53, 56, 57, 58, 71, 72, 76, 81, 87

production: and labour structure, 85; domestic, 50, 56, 87; labour costs, 120; marketing, 37; primary, *see* primary products; technology, 115, 118

productivity, 23, 41, 45, 47, 58, 63

protection, 32–4, 58, 61, 72–3, 86–8, 90–2, 97; India, 151, 198, 201, 203, 208; Japan, 155–6, 251, 258; Korea, Republic of, 36, 83, 143, 151, 155–6; Latin America, 151; NICs, 84;

Philippines, 306; Taiwan, 30, 83, 143, 151, 155–6; Thailand, 300
public sector, 104, 129, 146, 161, 176, 222, 316

racial tension, 258, 317, 319, 321
raw materials, 71–3, 75, 79, 84, 87, 89
religion, role of, 338–40
Rhee, Syngman, 267–8, 269, 271, 275; *see also* Korea, Republic of
rice production, 312
rubber production, 72, 76, 78
Rueff Report (World Bank), 105

Sarit, Marshal, 299, 301; *see also* Thailand
savings and investment, 9, 11–13, 61–3, 98, 109, 110, 246, 247, 253
school enrolment, 21, 22; *see also* education
Second World War, 5, 27, 95
securities, 12, 131, 133
semi-industrial countries, 40, 41, 45, 47
Singapore, 1, 4–6, 11, 12, 14, 16, 24, 67, 167, 321–4; aid, 25, 98, 103, 105; capital, 126; domestic bank credit, 178; entrepôt past, 27; exports 39, 79, 322, 337; foreign investment, 27, 111, 117, 120, 247, 322, 323; government invervention, 30, 321; guest workers, 18; import substitution, 30, 81; imported labour, 18, 253; manufactures, 30, 81, 247; middle class, 294; multinationals, 112, 113, 115; National Provident Fund, 247; National Wages Council, 18; protection, 30; Second World War, 27; technology transfer, 117; wages, 18
social inequality, 306
social security, 247
Solow's equation, 39, 44, 45, 47
South Asia, 16, 26
Southeast Asia, 76, 86, 257; agriculture, 337; bureaucracies, 325, 340; Chinese, 297, 324; colonialism, 297, 339; culture, 338–42; domestic capital formation, 298; domestic savings, 257; economic growth, 170, 285, 296, 297, 324, 337, 338; education, 257; élites, 285, 298, 325; ethnic minorities, 298, 325, 338;

exports, 71; export processing zones, 288, 341; Gang of Three, 167, 169, 171; government intervention, 258; investment/GDP ratios, 171; manufacturing, 67, 79, 338; middle class, 294, 325; military power, 340; nationalism, 324; politics, 284, 285, 325, 340; protection, 258; public–private cooperation, 341; religion, 338, 340; surplus labour, 257; underdevelopment, 284; urbanization, 297; women and family, 339
Southern Cone, *see* Latin America
Sri Lanka, 2, 15, 20, 239
steel industry, 34, 200
sugar industry, 201
Suharto, 311, 312–16, 326; *see also* Indonesia
Sukarno, 33, 87, 311, 312–16, 326; *see also* Indonesia
supply and demand, 9, 17, 44, 59, 97, 131

Taiwan, 1, 4–7, 11, 15, 16, 24, 67, 157, 278; agriculture, 27, 83; aid, 24, 25, 98, 103, 276, 277; banks, 133, 137, 138; colonial experience, 27; Council for Economic Planning and Development, 137; debt–equity ratios, 132; direct foreign investment, 97, 120; domestic market, 92; exchange rate, 30, 288; exports, 39, 51, 53, (duty) 142; foreign exchange, 41; free trade, 142; government intervention, 130; import substitution, 30; income distribution, 20; Industrial Development Board, 140; industrial park, 86; industry, 27, 83, 84, 155; labour and employment, 63, 83, 288; land reform, 18, 262, 263, 275; literacy, 246; manufactures, 17, 41, 51, 142; metal processing, 120; multinationals, 112, 113, 144; outward orientation, 48, 51; political history, 273–7; politics, 262, 266, 279, 280; protection, 30, 83, 139, 140, 143, 204; public–private cooperation, 145; technology, 83, 120; trade, 30, 81, 135, 139, 141, 255
tariffs, 61, 62, 83, 84, 86, 87, 91, 139
taxation, 83, 88, 90, 122, 148, 228, 236;

incentives, 250
technological change, 49, 50, 152
technology, 6, 9, 83, 86, 88, 89, 93,
113–20, 154; transfer, 98, 110,
117–20, 129
textiles, manufacture, 72, 75, 78,
113–15, 120, 199, 205, 242
Thailand, 4–6, 11, 17, 67, 167, 298–
305, 318; agriculture, 299;
bureaucracy, 302; class structure,
318; direct foreign investment, 120;
élites, 285, 304; export orientation,
300; financial management, 299; free
trade, 33; import-substitution, 300;
manufactures, 58, 69, 76, 287, 288,
299, 300; middle class, 294, 302, 303;
military power, 301; multinationals,
114; natural resources, 39, 40, 299;
political history, 300–1; politics, 285,
288, 294, 301–2, 304; protection, 71,
87, 300; timber industry, 71, 72, 76,
78, 112
tradables, 50, 165, 166, 180, 182–4,
187–9
trade: changing pattern of NICs, 71–6;
changing pattern of Southeast Asia,
76–81; liberalization, 53, 58, 81, 91,
92, 141, 171, 240; patterns, 17, 49,
55, 71, 81; policies, 30, 40, 56, 64,
67, 81–90, 91, 92, 105
Trade Policy Research Centre, 236

trade unions, 34, 206, 245, 321
transport equipment, 32, 72, 86, 114
Turkey, 41, 51, 58, 203

underemployment, 16, 88
unemployment, 15, 16, 231
United States of America: aid, 24, 98,
103, 104, 265; Council of Economic
Advisers, 148; debt–equity ratios,
132; direct foreign investment, 108,
114; economic expansion, 68; export
ratios, 64; financial systems, 131;
imports, 78, 79, 154; multinationals,
112; trade restrictions, 91; wholesale
price index, 180, 181
Uruguay, 166, 171, 172, 176; *see also*
Latin America

Venezuela, 41, 166, 171; *see also* Latin
America
Vietnam, 98, 263, 272, 338; *see also*
Indochina

wages, 41, 50, 84, 219; and
employment, 15–18
World Bank, 4, 19, 25, 90, 104, 105,
106, 164, 236, 260; *World
Development Report*, 19, 164, 166,
168, 260

Yugoslavia, 51, 53, 203